The
Literary Life
and Other Curiosities

ROBERT HENDRICKSON

The
Literary Life
and Other Curiosities

REVISED AND EXPANDED EDITION

A Harvest Book

Harcourt Brace & Company

San Diego   New York   London

First published in hardcover by The Viking Press, 1981,
and published in paperback by Penguin Books, 1982.

"To a Thesaurus" from *The Column Book of
Franklin Pierce Adams* by Franklin P. Adams.
Copyright 1928 by Doubleday.
Used by permission of Doubleday, division of
Bantam Doubleday Dell Publishing Group, Inc.

Library of Congress Cataloging-in-Publication Data
Hendrickson, Robert, 1933–
The literary life and other curiosities/Robert
Hendrickson. — Rev. ed., 1st Harvest ed.
        p.   cm. — (A Harvest book)
Includes index.
ISBN 0-15-652787-1
1. Authorship — Miscellanea. I. Title.
PN165.H4   1994
808.88′2 — dc20   94-6208

Designed by Camilla Filancia
Illustrations edited by Barbara Knight

Printed in the United States of America
First Harvest edition 1994
A B C D E

TO THEIR GRACE,

THE EXXON CORPORATION

Sɪɴᴄᴇ ᴅᴇᴅɪᴄᴀᴛɪᴏɴ ᴘᴀɢᴇs are usually blank and a waste of space, and since *The Literary Life* has been planned to treat everything about books and writers from colophons to afterwords, what better place for a few words about the art of book dedication. Authors still dedicate books to friends and lovers, strangers and relatives, animals (Aretino dedicated one to his monkey), even to ideas, but rarely if ever to flatter someone in a brazen appeal for patronage. But (Exxon please note!) ancient authors knew better. Almost all of them, including Horace, Virgil, and Cicero, expected something in return for their dedications, and by the seventeenth century, book dedications had become positively slavish as authors vied for patrons. Writers got up to fifty guineas for a dedication at the time, and some included more than one dedication in a book—Edward Young's *Night Thoughts*, for example, had a dedication for each of the seven nights of the week. One author, a Thomas Jordan, "prefixed high-flown dedications to his books with blanks for the name, the blanks being separately and surreptitiously filled in by a hand-press, so that there was a special dedicatee for every copy."

This dedication by an English author in 1815 is about as abject, servile, and groveling as a dedication can get:

> To the Right Honorable the Earl of Breadalbane. May it please your lordship, with overpowering sentiments of the most profound humility, I prostrate myself at your noble feet, while I offer to your lordship's

high consideration these very feeble attempts to describe the indescribable and ineffable beauties of your lordship's delicious estate of Edinample. With tumid emotions of heart-distending price, and with fervescent feelings of gratitude, I beg leave to acknowledge the honor I have to serve so noble a master, and the many advantages which I, in common with your lordship's other menials, enjoy from the exuberance of your princely liberality. That your lordship may long shine with refulgent brilliancy in the exalted station to which Providence has raised you, and that your noble family, like a bright constellation, may diffuse a splendor and glory through the high sphere of their attraction, is the fervent prayer of your lordship's most humble and most devoted servant.

Laurence Sterne parodied literary dedications in *Tristram Shandy*, inscribing the dedication page with the words: "To be let or sold for fifty guineas."

Author James Ronald dedicated his book *This Way Out* (1940) "To My Creditors, whose increasing impatience has made this book necessary."

In his anthology *Parodies* (1960) Dwight Macdonald parodies dedications with the following dedication:

To my dear sons
Michael and Nicholas
without whose school bills
this anthology would not have been made.

British humorist Jerome K. Jerome dedicated his *Idle Thoughts of an Idle Fellow* (1886) to his best pipe.

When someone told English author Douglas William Jerrold that a hack writer planned to dedicate his next book to him, Jerrold replied sadly: "Ah, that's an awful weapon he has in his hands!"

CONTENTS

PREFACE TO THE REVISED EDITION

The Literary Life has found readers all over the world in the last ten years, inspiring letters from correspondents as far off as Saudi Arabia, Japan, China, India, and even Tonga, as well as from readers in America and Europe. All but a few kindly provided the additions, corrections, and suggestions I solicited in the original Preface (following), which inspired me in turn to expand the book. Besides adding a sorely needed index and much more on non-English-speaking writers, I have included a new chapter ("Of Editors and Agents"); added new material throughout equivalent to another one–two chapters, or some 25 percent of the work; and made corrections wherever they were needed and known. I'd like to say again that I hope the reader has as much fun with this new updated book as I have had working on it and enjoying the company of the thousands of literary figures in its pages. My thanks this time go out to my agent Frank Freudberg and editor John Radziewicz, whose faith in this project made it possible, and as always to my wife, Marilyn, who makes me possible. On a lighter but important note, I should add that the Exxon Corporation, to which I dedicated *The Literary Life*, did not, as requested, give any evidence of becoming my patron. Well, maybe this time. And I hereby extend the offer to Mobil Oil as well.

—R. H.
Peconic, N.Y.
March 4, 1993

I HOPE YOU have as much fun with this book as I have had. After some five years spent working on it, I'm happy to say that I'm still not quite sure how to classify it. It is, for example, the only book I know that begins (on the dedication page) even before the preface. What it certainly is is a hybrid, and since hybrids are usually hardy if anything, perhaps it will live a long life. Dealing with every aspect of the literary life from, say, "The Ode on a Fake Grecian Urn" to the writing on or in crossword puzzles and fortune cookies, this is a book for those who love books and language, ranging over many centuries and civilizations. Its ancestors might be D'Israeli's *Curiosities of Literature*, Brewer's *Dictionary of Phrase and Fable*, or Walsh's *Handybook*, among other books impossible to pigeonhole. Leafing through its pages at random, one encounters entries on writing habits, writing without habits (in the nude), sex and writing, murdered writers, critics who were quite literally murderers, the longest list of the longest words in the language, the best and worst words in the language, the highest-paid authors, starving writers, parsimonious publishers, literary lovers, unhappily married authors, athletic authors, alcoholic authors, gluttonous authors, computer literature, poems composed in dreams, poetic blackmail, mad poets, the poet who posed as a woman, the most prolific writers, the fastest- and slowest-working writers, the life spans of authors, unusual endings of authors, and the last words of authors. There must be tens of thousands of facts here, but I have tried to link these together by category in essay form to make the book more than the reasonably complete compendium of literary curiosities that it certainly is. Literary hors d'oeuvres these are, mostly, to be sure, but they are tidbits that we all enjoy, no matter how much the puritan in us protests that they are "trivial details," and many a good meal can be made of these morsels, even if one just dines out on them. For better or worse there is no book quite like it, and I hope *The Literary Life* will grow in size over the years with additions (and corrections) from readers, whose contributions are invited on all of the subjects covered or any of those I'm sure I've missed.

In closing, let me thank the many writers past and present who may have made it possible that this book will see the worms eat me before the bookworms (or shredders) gnaw through its pages. There is no space to acknowledge all these, for often one entry alone here is the fruit of a score or more books noted in the long research for this work or during a lifetime of jotting down anecdotes, information, and lines I found enlightening or entertaining. I must, however, gratefully thank my editor, Barbara Burn, who suggested and did so much to help shape this social history of the literary life, and my wife, Marilyn, who worked so hard on the book that it is only through her own modesty (or infinite wisdom) that her name does not share the title page with mine.

Far Rockaway, N.Y.
November 11, 1980

The
Literary Life
and Other Curiosities

CHAPTER ONE

Writing: The Act & the Art

WRITERS ON WRITING

THE FASCINATION of the silent midnight, the veiled lamp, the smouldering fire, the white paper asking to be covered with elusive words; the thoughts grouping themselves into architectural forms, and slowly rising into dreamy structures, constantly changing, shifting, beautifying their outlines,—this is the subtlest of solitary temptations, and the loftiest of the intoxications of genius.
—from *The Letters of Henry Adams*

I love being a writer. What I can't stand is the paperwork.
—Peter De Vries

WRITING FOR POSTERITY, OR ANYTHING FOR ART

THE TRUE ARTIST will let his wife starve, his children go barefoot, his mother drudge for his living at seventy, sooner than work at anything but his art.

—George Bernard Shaw

If a writer has to rob his mother, he will not hesitate; the "Ode on a Grecian Urn" is worth any number of old ladies.

—William Faulkner

WHY BOOKS ARE WRITTEN

THE APPEARANCE of a new book is an indication that another man has found a mission, has entered upon the performance of a hefty duty, activated by the noblest impulses that can spur the soul of man to action. It is the proudest boast of the profession of literature, that no man ever published a book for selfish purposes or with ignoble aim. Books have been published for the consolation of the distressed; for the guidance of the wandering; for the relief of the destitute; for the hope of the penitent; for uplifting the burdened soul above its sorrows and fears; for the general amelioration of the condition of all mankind; for the right against wrong; for the good against bad; for the truth. This book is published for two dollars per volume.

—Robert J. Burdette, preface to
The Rise and Fall of the Moustache (1877)

CRIMINAL ADVICE

INNUMERABLE are the men and women now writing for bread, who have not the least chance of finding in such work a permanent livelihood. They took to writing because they knew not what else to do, or because the literary calling tempted them by its independence and its dazzling prizes. They will hang on to the squalid profession, their earnings eked out by begging and borrowing, until it is too late for them to do anything else—and what then. With a lifetime of dread experience behind me, I say that he who encourages any young man or woman to look for his living to "literature," commits no less than a crime.

—George Gissing,
The Private Papers of Henry Ryecroft (1903)

PLAY THE SEDULOUS APE

Robert Louis Stevenson originated this phrase in a charming essay in which he wrote: "I have played the sedulous ape to Hazlitt, to Lamb, to Wordsworth, to Sir Thomas Browne, to Defoe, to Hawthorne, to Montaigne, to Baudelaire, and to Obermann. . . . That, like it or not, is the way to learn to write." *Sedulous*, from the Latin *sedulus*, "careful," means diligent and persevering in application or attention, so the phrase describes anyone who slavishly imitates somebody.

WARMING UP

Whilst writing the *Chartreuse*," Stendhal said, "in order to acquire the correct tone I read every morning two or three pages of the Civil Code." Willa Cather had to read a passage from the Bible before she got started. Bennett Cerf got his best ideas while sitting on the toilet, and Hemingway had to sharpen a score of pencils before he stood up to write (he wrote standing up after he injured his back in an airplane crash, and he typed only dialogue). Lewis Carroll and Virginia Woolf also worked standing up. Poe often perched his Siamese cat on his shoulder before writing a poem, Thomas Wolfe took long walks before beginning, Balzac had to have his black coffee, and many authors had (and have) to start the day with an eye-opener of a stronger sort (see *Alcoholic Authors*). Kipling couldn't begin unless he had dark ink to work with. "For my ink I demand the blackest," he wrote, "and had I been in my father's house, as once I was, would have kept an ink-boy to grind me Indian ink. All 'blue-blacks' were an abomination to my Daemon. My writing blocks were built for me to an unchanged pattern of large off-white, blue sheets, of which I was most wasteful." Hervey Allen said he had only to lie down and the voices of his ancestors dictated to him. Truman Capote, who called himself a "completely horizontal writer," and who couldn't think or write unless he was lying down (the favorite writing position of Mark Twain and Robert Louis Stevenson, as well), was another writer who needed paper of a special color—yellow—but he *could not* have yellow roses in the room. Jacqueline Susann typed drafts on yellow, blue, pink, and finally white paper. Alexandre Dumas *père* thought it unspeakable not to write his nonfiction on rose-colored paper, his novels on blue paper, and his poetry on yellow paper. He invariably followed this color scheme, whether writing by himself or with the ghosts he often hired to help him. The son of a mulatto general of the French Empire, Dumas *père* was an insomniac whose doctor ordered him to eat an apple a day at seven A.M. under the Arc de Triomphe in the hope that this would help him form regular rising and sleeping habits.

Disraeli dressed in evening clothes while writing his novels, but George M. Cohan had the most expensive habit for warming up. He would often rent an entire Pullman car drawing room and keep traveling until he finished what he was working on. Cohan could turn out 140 pages a night this way.

Henrik Ibsen had one of the strangest working habits of all. He was inspired by a picture of August Strindberg that hung over his desk. Said Ibsen: "He is my mortal enemy and shall hang there and watch while I write."

Even stranger was the practice of Dame Edith Sitwell, who, like the divine Sarah Bernhardt, liked to lie in an open coffin for a while before beginning her day's work. English poet John Donne did the same thing periodically, to prepare himself for death.

STIMULATING HABITS

Sack, or sherry, was apparently Shakespeare's favorite drink, for he mentions it in his plays more than all other wines combined.

As for Alexander Pope, he enjoyed strong coffee, but not so much as Balzac, who drank at least *fifty* cups of it a day—so much that caffeine poisoning was one cause of his death. Dr. Johnson seemed to suffer no ill effects from the twenty-five cups of tea he could drink at one sitting.

Disraeli liked champagne jelly, and Byron gin and water, while Thomas Hobbes had no use for anything stronger than cold water.

The German poet Schiller was turned on by the smell of apples kept in his desk drawer, though he also "stimulated his brain with coffee mixed with champagne."

The American poet Amy Lowell was probably the only woman poet in history to enjoy cigars. In 1915, fearing a wartime shortage, she bought *10,000* of her favorite Manila brand. Another female writer who liked a good cigar was George Sand.

WORKING WITHOUT HABITS

APPLYING the seat of the pants to the seat of a chair was Ernest Hemingway's first rule for writers. But not all authors find this easy. William Blake and his wife once sat nude in their garden reciting passages from *Paradise Lost* as if they were in the Garden of Eden. When a visitor called, Blake cried out: "Come in! It's only Adam and Eve, you know!" Another English poet, Samuel Boyse (1708–1749), was so poor that he pawned all his clothes for food and had to write in bed for six weeks until friends finally assisted him. For some strange reason D. H. Lawrence liked to climb mulberry trees in the nude, but he never wrote while up there. Victor Hugo probably went to the most extreme length to get down to work: he gave all his clothes to his servant with orders that they be returned only after several hours, when he had finished his day's work. Casanova didn't do much writing (or bathing) in his bathtub built for two, but three other men who frequently wrote in the nude were Ben Franklin, who owned the first bathtub in America and liked to write while soaking in it; French playwright Edmond Rostand, author of *Cyrano de Bergerac*, who worked in the bathtub so he wouldn't be interrupted by his many friends; and James Whitcomb Riley, who had himself locked in hotel rooms nude so that he could write without being tempted to drink. Robin Moore, author of *The Green Berets*, says he writes naked, standing up. Hans Christian Andersen would never have worked in the altogether; he was so ashamed of his body that he padded his shirt with newspapers to make himself look more muscular.

WRITING *ALMOST* IN THE NUDE

JOHN CHEEVER told a *Newsweek* reporter that in his early years as a writer he could afford only one suit. "In the morning," he reminisced, "I dressed in this and took the elevator to a windowless room in the basement where I worked. I hung my suit on a hanger, wrote until nightfall, when I dressed and returned to our apartment. I wrote many of my stories in boxer shorts."

SEX BEFORE WRITING

CHARLIE CHAPLIN wrote in his autobiography: "Like Balzac, who believed that a night of sex meant the loss of a good page of his novel, so I believed that it meant the loss of a good day's work at the studio." Chaplin was right about Balzac, though Balzac may not have been right about sex and writing. Balzac did believe that the two acts of love were incompatible and that his writing prowess depended on how much sperm he retained in his body while writing. He once "suffered" an uncontrollable nocturnal emission and claimed that it cost him a masterpiece the following day.

HONORÉ
DE BALZAC

WRITING AFTER SEX

THE PICTURE of George Sand that most people remember best is the one that became celebrated after the Musset/Sand love affair ended in great bitterness on his side. Late at night, when he awoke after an exhausting *nuit d'amour*, Alfred de Musset would see George Sand—heartless bitch!—sitting up in her wrapper in their bedroom, scratching, scratching away at the pages with her pen by candlelight.
—Ellen Moers,
Literary Women (1977)

Musset was so angered when George Sand left him for another man that he wrote the pornographic novel *Gamiani* about her.

SHOULD ANYONE WANT
TO INVOKE A MUSE

O for a Muse of fire that would ascend
The brightest heaven of invention.
—Shakespeare, Prologue to *Henry V*

THE NINE MUSES were the children of Zeus and Mnemosyne (a personification of memory who was one of the six Titans, a daughter of Heaven and Earth). Originally they were goddesses of memory, but Pindar writes that the celestials implored Zeus to create the Muses to sing the great deeds of the gods. It was traditional for authors, especially epic poets, to invoke a particular Muse to help in the act of creation, the appeal for inspiration usually coming near the beginning of a work (as in the *Iliad*, the *Odyssey*, and *Paradise Lost*). While relatively few writers today believe in external forces inspiring them, or the "storm of association," as Wordsworth called it, most depend on inspiration from within rather than the divine afflatus (as Faulkner said of the Muses and inspiration: "No one ever told me where to find it"). Nevertheless, if one's inner inspiration fails, here are the Nine Muses all ready for invoking:

Calliope (her name, pronounced Ka-lie'o-pee, does not rhyme with *rope*, although the musical instrument named after her can; the name means beautiful voice). The chief Muse, usually associated with epic poetry, poetic inspiration, and eloquence, she has as her emblems a pen and a scroll of parchment.

Clio (Klie'o; means to tell of). Muse of history and heroic exploits, who is often represented like Calliope. The British author Joseph Addison used the name Clio as a pseudonym.

Euterpe (Yoo-ter'-pee; means to delight well). Muse of music and lyric poetry, patron of flute players, joy, and pleasure, her symbol is the double flute, which she invented.

Thalia (Tha-lie′uh; means blooming). Muse of gaiety, comedy, and pastoral life, depicted wearing a comic mask and garland of ivy while holding a shepherd's crook and a tambourine.

Melpomene (Mel-pom′i-nee; means to sing). Muse of tragedy, song, and harmony, "the mournfullest Muse" is shown wearing a tragic mask, sword, and garland of grape leaves.

Terpsichore (Terp-sik′o-ree; means dance-liking). Muse of dancing, choral song, and lyric poetry, usually depicted seated and holding a lyre.

Erato (Er′a-toe; from the Greek *eros*, love). Muse of erotic and love poetry, miming, and geometry, shown holding a stringed instrument such as a lyre.

Polyhymnia (Pol′ee-hym′nee-uh; means many hymns). Muse of the chant and inspired hymn and said to be the inventor of the lyre, she is depicted as grave in countenance and wrapped in long, flowing robes.

Urania (Yoo-ray′nee-uh; from *uranus*, sky). Muse of astronomy and celestial phenomena, whose name means "the heavenly one" and whom Milton made the spirit of the loftiest poetry, she is often shown pointing with a wand or staff at a celestial globe she holds in her hand.

Mnemosyne, the mother of the Muses, gave her name to *mnemonics*, the art or science of memory training. Calliope gave hers to an organ composed of steam whistles. *Terpsichorean* means anything pertaining to dance, and *euterpean* is anything having to do with music. The Muses collectively are responsible for *museum*, which literally means the home of the Muses. The first museum was actually a literary academy founded by Ptolemy at Alexandria about 300 B.C. A wit of the time called it a "bird coop of the Muses."

SYNTHETIC INSPIRATION

IN HIS BOOK *Mood Control* (1980), Gene Bylinsky reports that an anonymous biochemist has developed a "creativity pill." According to the scientist, controlled tests demonstrated that those who took the pills wrote better, or at least more creatively, than those who didn't.

SOLITUDE AND WRITING

MY POINT to young writers is to socialize. Don't just go up to a pine cabin all alone and brood. You reach that stage soon enough anyway.

—Truman Capote

A PENCIL is a pencil is a pencil, but pens can be worth a lot of money today. A Parker Black Giant fountain pen that cost $10 in 1916, for instance, would cost $600 presently, while collectors have paid $350 for a $10 1920 Waterman #20 and $300 for a 1920s $20 Swen 14-carat solid gold fountain pen. Cliff Lawrence's *History, Repair, Current Values—Fountain Pens* (Collector Books, P.O. Box 3009, Paducah, Ky. 42001) tells all about collecting fountain pens and there are at least three fountain-pen repair shops in New York City which carry valuable old pens. Probably the most expensive *new* pen one can buy is the German-made Mont Blanc Diplomat, available in platinum for $6,750.

Today a number of well-heeled authors, but no poets, own personal computer "workstations" with full-size dual page color monitor, color laser printer, modem, scanner, CD-ROM, and other state-of-the-art peripheral equipment that cost in excess of $20,000.

The word *typewriter* was coined by American Christopher Latham Sholes, who patented the first practical commercial typewriter in 1868 (slow, difficult machines, intended primarily for the blind, had been invented as early as 1714). Sholes's "type-writer" had only capital letters. Manufactured by Remington, it was owned by Henry James, Mark Twain, and Sigmund Freud, among other famous early experimenters. Mark Twain, in fact, typed *The Adventures of Tom Sawyer* on Sholes's machine in 1875, this being the first typewritten book manuscript (a fact that Twain kept secret in his lifetime because he didn't want to write testimonials or show the uninitiated how to use the machine). Henry Miller was among the fastest of author-typists. Probably the most difficult typewriter in the world to use today, including the new computer models that have memory banks and produce any number of copies, is the Chinese typewriter, which has 5,850 characters and which even an expert can operate at a rate of only about eleven words a minute.

Though some writers—the late Truman Capote among them—have phenomenal memories and don't have to take notes, most use some recording device, usually a pad and pencil or a tape recorder. This is nothing new. Thomas Hobbes—and you can hardly get more conservative than that—invariably walked about with a pen and inkhorn in the head of his staff and a notebook in his pocket.

To those who wish to write stylishly, a desk made by Thomas Chippendale (c.1718–1779) that sold for $195,000 in London several years ago would be a great help; it is the most expensive writing desk ever sold. Failing that, an imposing desk made by Scottish architect Charles Rennie Mackintosh in 1902 might suffice; it went for $177,456 at auction. Mackintosh made two such desks, one for himself and one for a client. According to a description: "Both versions were made of dark stained wood, with the writing cabinet supported on a semi-open base enlivened with stylized mauve glass flowers. Both also have twin doors covering the upper section, which open to reveal vertical dividers, a glittering panel of leaded green, white and mirror glass set in zinc, and mother-of-pearl squares inset in the doors and under the arched framing." The desk sold for $42.10 in 1933, five years after Mackintosh died in poverty.

Voltaire is said to have written some of his love poems in bed, using his naked mistress's back for a desk.

Dante Alighieri, author of *The Divine Comedy*, taught his pet cat to sit on a table and hold a lighted candle between its paws while he did his writing at night.

"BURNING THE MIDNIGHT OIL"

Wee spend our mid-day sweat, our mid-night oyle;
Wee tyre the night in thought; the day in toyle.

I'VE READ that this expression is of American origin, but it obviously isn't, judging only by the above poem. Francis Quarles, English author and later "chronologer to the City of London," wrote about midnight oil in his *Emblems* (1635), and the expressions "consumed the midnight oil" (1744) and "burn midnight oil" (1882) are also first recorded in England. Oils of many types were of course widely used for lamps long before American petroleum made low-priced lamplight available in the mid-nineteenth century. The words mean to sit up late at night working, especially in the pursuit of learning. "It smells of the lamp" (Latin, *olet lucernam*) is an equally old saying, referring to literary work that is overworked and tired from too much burning of the midnight oil. Of authors who consistently burned the midnight oil, Honoré de Balzac is the best example. Like Pliny the Elder before him, Balzac liked to begin work at midnight and write for eighteen hours at a stretch. He did this for weeks on end and was so meticulous a craftsman that he often completely rewrote his novels in proof.

HANDWRITING OF WRITERS

What do you think of my becoming an author and relying for support on my pen? Indeed, I think the illegibility of my handwriting is very authorlike.
—Nathaniel Hawthorne,
in a letter written while a student at Bowdoin College

MODERN EDITORS can be glad that, thanks to the typewriter and the word processor, they don't have to cope with the likes of these authors, the worst of the worst in penmanship:

Victor Hugo—his manuscripts were "a sort of battlefield on paper, in which the killed words were well stamped out and the new recruits pushed forth in anything but good order."

Lord Byron—in his almost illegible "scrawl" he usually made additions to the proofs of his work which were longer than the original text.

Charlotte Brontë—her handwriting "appeared to have been traced by a needle."

Thackeray—he wrote so small that his neat handwriting could hardly be read; he once said he would take to writing the Lord's Prayer on his thumbnail if he failed at literature.

Cervantes—he lost his left hand at the Battle of Lepanto against the Turks and had trouble writing with his right hand, according to one traditional tale.

Charles Dickens—his handwriting was as small as Thackeray's but very sloppy and was usually in blue ink on blue paper.

Frederick Marryat—copyreaders had to leave pins in his manuscript when they stopped in order to pick up their place later.

Horace Greeley—he wrote so illegibly that a fired employee used his letter of discharge as a recommendation letter for another job; his instructions to a sign painter to paint "Entrance on Spruce Street" over a door were interpreted and painted as "Editor on a Spree."

Sydney Smith—"I must decline reading my own handwriting twenty-four hours after I have written it; my writing is as if a swarm of ants, escaping from an ink-bottle, had walked over a sheet of paper without wiping their legs."

Jules Janin—he once rewrote a manuscript rather than try to decipher it for the printer.

Thomas Carlyle—he was left-handed, as were Michelangelo, Cole Porter, and Jack the Ripper; a printer who had recently come to England for employment said on being handed one of Carlyle's manuscripts: "What have you got that man here! I fled from Scotland to get away from him!"

Balzac—printers who handled his manuscripts refused to work more than an hour at a time on them.

Montaigne—his handwriting was so bad that he hired a secretary, but the secretary's handwriting was worse than his and as a result parts of his Italian journal remain unintelligible today.

Edgar Allan Poe probably had the best handwriting of any noted author. When he won a prize for his "Ms. Found in a Bottle" he was helped "by the beauty of his handwriting."

WRITING BY SIGNING

WHEN ILL in the South Pacific and unable to hold his pen or even speak, Tusitala, or "The Tale Teller," as the natives called Robert Louis Stevenson, dictated his stories with his fingers by the signing alphabet.

NOSE WRITING

ALDOUS HUXLEY often wrote with his nose, though he produced none of his masterpieces this way. "A little nose writing," he notes in *The Art of Seeing*, "will result in a perceptible temporary improvement of defective vision." Huxley's eyesight was so bad that he learned Braille to relieve his eyes; he often read at night in bed, hands and book under the covers. A follower of Dr. William Bates, the author practiced the ophthalmologist's exercises for improving eyesight. Any myopic writer or reader who wants to try need not dip his nose in ink. Simply fix your eyes on the end of your nose and move your head as if you were writing a word, sentence, or anecdote.

ACCIDENTALLY DESTROYED MANUSCRIPTS

*T*HERE IS a legend that Sir Isaac Newton's little dog Diamond knocked over a candle on his master's desk and started a fire that destroyed records of many years of research and experiments. On seeing the disaster, Newton is said to have exclaimed, "Oh, Diamond, Diamond, thou little knowest the damage thou hast done!"

Antiquarian John Warburton (1682–1759) collected fifty or sixty rare Elizabethan and Jacobean plays, three of which now survive as the priceless Lansdowne manuscripts at the British Museum. Most of the often unique plays were destroyed when Warburton left them in the care of his cook, Betsy Baker, who burned them for fuel or used them to put under pie bottoms.

When his servant used pages from his translations of Lucretius to dress his wig, an enraged Molière threw the rest of the manuscript into the fire.

Thomas Carlyle had to rewrite the entire first volume of his *History of the French Revolution* when John Stuart Mill borrowed the manuscript to read and his maid burned it, mistaking it for wastepaper. This happened at a time when Carlyle "had not only forgotten the structure of it, but the spirit it was written with was past. . . ." He wrote to his brother that he felt like a man who had "nearly killed himself accomplishing zero."

"To the pure all things are pure," Sir Richard Burton wrote in the introduction of his translation of the *Arabian Nights*, but his wife thought that the papers the translator of the *Kama Sutra* left behind when he died in 1890 were obscene. She burned them all, including at least one completed book in manuscript.

In a fit of anger, scholar William Ainsworth's wife threw the manuscript of his almost completed Latin dictionary into the fire; it took him three years to write it over again.

A long poem included in Edwin Arlington Robinson's *Captain Craig* (1902) was lost and finally recovered in a brothel, where his editor had left it.

So illegible was the Circe episode of James Joyce's *Ulysses* that the husband of the third typist trying to decipher it mistook the manuscript for scrap paper and threw it in the fire. Luckily, New York collector John Quinn had a "fair copy" of the section and agreed to supply a photographic copy of this to Sylvia Beach, who first published *Ulysses*.

In his expatriate days Ernest Hemingway lost a whole trunkful of early manuscripts when it was left aboard a train in France. John Steinbeck, like Newton before him, saw the only draft of a book destroyed by a dog. Steinbeck's setter pup Toby chewed into confetti half of the first draft of *Of Mice and Men*. "Two months' work to do over again," the author wrote at the time. "I was pretty mad, but the poor little fellow may have been acting critically. I didn't want to ruin a good dog for a manuscript I'm not sure is good at all. He got only an ordinary spanking." Later, when *Mice* was panned in some quarters, Steinbeck felt even more strongly that the dog was a good critic. "I'm not sure Toby didn't know what he was doing when he ate that first draft," he wrote in another letter. "I have promoted Toby-dog to be lieutenant-colonel in charge of literature. But as for the unpredictable literary enthusiasms of this country, I have little faith in them."

Another "helping hound" is contemporary author Jeffrey Konitz's dog. "To Rufus, who edited Chapter 27," reads the dedication in Konitz's novel *The Guardian*. The 180-pound Great Pyrenees rated this praise because he chewed Chapter 27 to pieces. Konitz had no copy of the chapter and claims he wrote a better one "the second time around."

"LET'S GO TO THE DEVIL" AND OTHER OLD LITERARY TAVERNS

SHAKESPEARE, Donne, Ben Jonson, Sir Walter Raleigh, Beaumont and Fletcher, and many other greats frequented The Mermaid Tavern on Bread Street in London, and Francis Beaumont wrote the following verse about it:

> *What things have we seen*
> *Down at the Mermaid! heard words that have been*
> *So nimble, and so full of subtle flame,*
> *As if that every one from whence they came*
> *Had meant to put his whole wit in a jest,*
> *And had resolved to live a fool the rest*
> *Of his dull life.*

The Devil Tavern, Temple Bar, in London, was another favorite haunt of literary men in Shakespeare's time and Ben Jonson often watered there. It isn't the origin of the expression "go to the devil," but its habitués often made a play on the old words.

The Mitre Tavern, standing in Mitre Court south of Cheapside in London, was popular in the days of Shakespeare and Jonson. East of it on Fleet Street stood a second Mitre Tavern, this one a favorite of Dr. Johnson and his Literary Club.

The Cheshire Cheese, off Fleet Street in London, was also frequented by Dr. Johnson, Boswell, Goldsmith, Sheridan, and other members of their group.

The White Hart Inn in Southwark was another famous literary tavern, which Shakespeare mentioned in *2 Henry VI* as the headquarters of Jack Cade, the Irish adventurer who marched on London with a mob. Later Dickens made the inn, which survived until 1889, the meeting place for Mr. Pickwick and Sam Weller.

The George and Vulture, too, was used by Dickens as a meeting place for his characters in *Pickwick Papers*. It still stands in London, not far from the Bank of England, and is the meeting place for the present-day Pickwick Club.

The Boar's Head Inn, which used to stand in Eastcheap on the site of the statue of William IV, was made famous by Shakespeare or rather by his Falstaff. Oliver Goldsmith and Washington Irving wrote charming essays about the inn, which stood until 1831.

La Belle Sauvage (the beautiful savage woman), which lasted until 1941, was famous in the sixteenth century for the plays put on in its courtyard. It later became the site of the Cassell publishing house.

The Man with a Load of Mischief was a pub on Oxford Street that had a sign painted by Hogarth "showing a man carrying a woman and a lot of other *impedimenta* on his back."

Many present-day English pubs are named after authors and their creations, among them Shakespeare, Jonson, Milton, Macaulay, Steele, Scott, Falstaff, and Robinson Crusoe. Very few are so named in America. Most recent American literary watering holes have been located in New York City, Manhattan's most famous including The Algonquin, Costello's, The White Horse Tavern, Cholmondolys, and Elaine's.

THE MERMAID TAVERN

Souls of Poets dead and gone,
What Elysium have ye known,
Happy field or mossy cavern,
Choicer than the Mermaid Tavern?
Have ye tippled drink more fine
Than mine host's Canary wine?
Or are fruits of Paradise
Sweeter than those dainty pies
Of venison? O generous food!
Dressed as though bold Robin Hood
Would, with his Maid Marian,
Sup and bowse from horn and can.

I have heard that on a day
Mine host's signboard flew away
Nobody knew whither, till
An astrologer's old quill
To a sheepskin gave the story,
Said he saw you in your glory,
Underneath a new-old sign
Sipping beverage divine,
And pleding with contented smack
The Mermaid in the Zodiac.

Souls of Poets dead and gone,
What Elysium have ye known,
Happy field or mossy cavern,
Choicer than the Mermaid Tavern?
—John Keats

LITERARY COCKTAIL PARTIES

COCKTAIL PARTIES have been traced back as far as ancient Athens, where you could drop by a neighbor's early in the evening with your own goatskin of wine and be treated to a variety of "provocatives to drinking" that included caviar, oysters, shrimp, cheese, and even marinated octopus and roasted grasshoppers. The literary cocktail party is a creature of recent times, possibly evolving from the literary dinner parties so popular in the nineteenth century. Sherwood Anderson died of peritonitis and complications after swallowing a toothpick with an hors d'oeuvre at a cocktail party.

"TAKING TO JOURNALISM AND STRONG DRINK"

*I*T IS SAID of English author John Mitford (1782–1859) that he "took to journalism and strong drink." Mitford was paid a shilling a day by his Grub Street publisher, "of which he expended tenpence on gin and twopence on bread, cheese and an onion." Rent he had not, as he "lived in a gravel pit, with pen, ink and paper" for the last forty-three days of his life.

THE PEN IS MIGHTIER THAN THE SWORD

A JOURNALIST," Napoleon said, "is a grumbler, a censurer, a giver of advice, a regent of sovereigns, a tutor of nations. Four hostile newspapers are more formidable than a thousand bayonets."

It was, however, Edward Bulwer-Lytton who invented "the pen is mightier than the sword," in his play *Richelieu* (1839):

> *Beneath the rule of men entirely great,*
> *The pen is mightier than the sword.*

Long before, in his *Anatomy of Melancholy* (1621), Robert Burton had written: "The pen is worse than the sword." Cervantes, in *Don Quixote* (1605), expressed an entirely different point of view: "Let none presume to tell me that the pen is preferable to the sword." Curiously enough, two great writers, Sophocles and Demosthenes, were the sons of swordmakers, the equivalent of munitions makers in our time.

FLEET STREET

*F*LEET STREET in London has been synonymous with journalism since the end of the eighteenth century, when the first newspaper was published there. The street takes its name not from fleet reporters writing stories while type is being set but for the Fleet River that ran alongside it.

GRUB STREET HACKS

Here lies poor Ned Purdom, from misery freed,
Who long was a bookseller's hack;
He led such a damnable life in this world,
I don't think he'd wish to come back.
                                        —Oliver Goldsmith

GRUB STREET in London was known a century before Dr. Johnson's lifetime as the stamping ground of (depending on your perspective) needy writers or literary "hacks" (from *hackney*, a horse or carriage anyone could hire). When compiling his famous *Dictionary of the English Language* (1755) the Great Cham defined Grub Street as "much inhabited by writers of small histories, dictionaries and temporary poems; whence any mean production is called grub-street." The term lasted even after the street name disappeared, probably because it suggests writers *grubbing* (from the Middle English *grobben*, "to dig") for money for *grub* (as Johnson himself was forced to do) and often producing cheap works in the process—though Balzac and a hundred others have proved that money-grubbing and great literature are not necessarily incompatible.

Grub Street cannot be found in London today. It has been called Milton Street since 1830, which, ironically, suggests the great poet John Milton. But it was not for the blind, impoverished Milton, who lived in the neighborhood for many years and is buried in St. Giles in the ward, that Milton Street was renamed. It remembers a builder and landlord named Milton who owned most of the houses on Grub Street at the time.

Said Sir Walter Scott when he was close to death from literary labors: "If there is a mental drudgery which lowers the spirits and lacerates the nerves, like the toil of a slave, it is that which is exacted by literary composition, when the heart is not in unison with the work upon which the head is employed. Add to the unhappy author's task sickness, sorrow or the pressure of unfavorable circumstances and the labor of the bondsman becomes light in comparison."

POTBOILER

ALL MEN who have to live by their labour have their potboilers," Hazlitt wrote, and an obscure English poet lamented: "No far-vring patrons have I got, /But just enough to boil the pot." A *potboiler* is, of course, a literary work written to make a living, a task performed to keep the pot boiling. Financial gain is the only object in writing one, but sometimes genius transcends the immediate object and the result is a work of art. Dr. Johnson's "philosophical romance" *Rasselas* (1759), for example, was written "over the nights of one week" to meet the cost of his mother's funeral and to pay off her debts. Coleridge's *Ancient Mariner* has been called "the most sublime of potboilers to be found in all literature."

WILLIAM FAULKNER ON POTBOILERS

IN TELLING of the birth of *Sanctuary* (1931), William Faulkner observed that he was hungry. "[I began] to think of books in terms of possible money," he recollected. "I took a little time out, and speculated what a person in Mississippi would believe to be current trends, chose what I thought was the right answer and invented the most horrific tale I could imagine and wrote it in about three weeks." One imagines Shakespeare doing the same with that blood-and-horrors *Titus Andronicus*, if, indeed, he wrote it.

THE GREAT AMERICAN NOVEL

FRANK NORRIS wrote, "The Great American Novel is not extinct like the Dodo, but mythical like the Hippogriff . . . the thing to be looked for is not the Great American Novelist, but the Great Novelist who shall also be American."

Observed Jack London a little later, "I'd rather win a water-fight in a swimming pool, or remain astride a horse that is trying to get out from under me, than write the great American novel."

GREAT RECEPTIONS FOR NOVELS, OR, "DID LITTLE NELL DIE?"

THE FIRST MODERN English novel of character, *Pamela, or Virtue Rewarded* (1740–1741), by Samuel Richardson, was a great success with the public and went into two editions even before it was reviewed. Part One had been published in November 1740 and as with Dickens's novels in a later age, extracts appeared in newspapers, readers eagerly awaiting the novel's outcome. Readers throughout England were ecstatic to learn that the heroine triumphed at the end, that virtue had been rewarded, and it is said that at Slough "the enraptured villagers rang the churchbells for joy." The same thing happened at Preston in Lancashire, where a maid explained to a woman who asked why the bells were ringing: "Why madam, poor Pamela's married at last; the news came down to us in the morning's paper."

Richardson, whose *Pamela* became the model for epistolary novels, had, when he was a boy of thirteen, regularly written love letters for three young women who didn't know what to write to their lovers.

Dickens's *The Old Curiosity Shop* commanded even greater interest among the reading public than *Pamela*. In New York City 6,000 people crowded the wharf where the ship carrying the magazine with the last installment of the novel was to dock. Finally, the ship approached, but the crowd could not wait. Spying the captain on deck, all cried out as one the burning question: "Did little Nell die?"

NOVEL LONGEST IN PROGRESS

*T*HE PRIZE in contemporary letters apparently belongs to Harold Brodkey's *Runaway Soul*, which has been described as a long Proustian novel. This, Brodkey's first novel, was contracted for in 1960 and still wasn't finished eighteen years later when Farrar, Straus & Giroux decided it couldn't wait any longer. So Mr. Brodkey went over to Alfred A. Knopf. According to the original publisher, "The book had been completed in one Websterian sense," but the author would "change his mind . . . cut one chapter out . . . add three or four more" and the novel "became sort of a life in progress." Mr. Brodkey finally switched back to Farrar, Straus & Giroux and *Runaway Soul* was published in 1991, after thirty-one years.

OTHER LONG LITERARY GESTATIONS

*W*ROTE Thomas Wolfe in a letter to Maxwell Perkins about *Look Homeward, Angel*: "Although I am able to criticize wordiness and overabundance in others, I am not able practically to criticize it in myself. The business of selection and revision is simply hell for me—my efforts to cut out 50,000 words may sometimes result in my adding 75,000."

Wolfe was a "putter-inner," to use F. Scott Fitzgerald's phrase, and had trouble finishing his books, a problem he shared with many authors. Plato is said to have rewritten the first sentence of *The Republic* fifty times; Hemingway rewrote the last page of *A Farewell to Arms* thirty-nine times; Sinclair Lewis took seventeen years to finish *Main Street*; and Katherine Anne Porter worked on *Ship of Fools* over twenty years.

Virgil took ten years to write the *Aeneid* and believed it still needed about three years' work when he died.

The Roman poet Horace said that all purple patches (*purpureus pannus*) should be deleted from literary work and it should be put away for eight years before being reedited and published—for it could never again be recalled except by time.

EUGENE O'NEILL ON CUTTING

*R*USSEL CROUSE asked Eugene O'Neill if he would shorten the script of *Ah, Wilderness!* so that the curtain could fall earlier. Finally, O'Neill, always adamant about cutting a word from his plays, reluctantly agreed. The next day he called Crouse and told him, "You'll be happy to learn I cut fifteen minutes."

"How?" Crouse replied ecstatically. "Where did you do it? I'll be right over to get the changes!" "Oh, there aren't any changes in the text," O'Neill explained, "but you know we've been playing this thing in four acts. I've decided to cut out the third intermission."

THE SHORT STORY

*T*HE FIVE REQUISITES to a good short story are brevity, a religious reference, a sexual reference, some association with society and an illustration of modesty," the doctrinaire English teacher instructed his charges.

The next day a student handed in a story that read in full:

" 'My God!' said the duchess. 'Take your hand off my knee!' "

LITERARY LETTERS

Lives of great men all remind us
As we o'er their pages turn,
That we too may leave behind us
Letters that we ought to burn.
—Anonymous

THE LONG AND THE SHORT OF IT

WHEN Victor Hugo wanted to know how his publishers liked *Les Misérables*, he wrote them simply: "?" His publishers shortly responded with a brief: "!," completing the briefest correspondence in history. The longest letter anyone knows about is the 1,113,747-word missive written over an eight-month period ending in May 1976 by Texan Jacqueline Jones to her sister Mrs. Jean Steward in Maine. The longest "letter to the editor" ever published was a 25,513-word epistle that Pennsylvania's *Upper Dauphin Sentinel* ran in 1979 over eight issues. Jack Kerouac claimed that his friend Neal Cassady wrote (and poet Allen Ginsberg lost) a 40,000-word letter to him that was so great a piece of writing it would have made "Melville, Twain, Dreiser, Wolfe, I dunno who, spin in their graves."

DIARY WRITING

Monday. Got up, washed, went to bed.
Tuesday. Got up, washed, went to bed.
Wednesday. Got up, washed, went to bed.
Thursday. Got up, washed, went to bed.
Friday. Got up, washed, went to bed.
Next Friday. Got up, washed, went to bed.
Friday fortnight. Got up, washed, went to bed.
Following month. Got up, washed, went to bed.

Mark Twain recalls this boyhood journal in *The Innocents Abroad*, noting that he opened it one New Year's Day and stopped, discouraged: "Startling events appeared to be too rare in my career to render a diary necessary."

THE ART OF INTERVIEWING

Q. Who invented the interview?
A. The first one probably appeared in the *New York Herald* as recently as 1859, at about the time of John Brown's raid at Harpers Ferry, though some claim that journalist Anne Royall invented the form in an 1825 story about President John Quincy Adams.

Q. Who interviewed whom?

A. Abolitionist Gerrit Smith gave an interview to a *Herald* reporter who remained anonymous.

Q. Didn't the historian James Redpath claim to have started the practice of interviewing?

A. Redpath did many interviews for the *Boston Advertiser* beginning in about 1868, when the interview was fast becoming an American institution.

Q. Name the best American interviews.

A. That's a tough one in this age of the tape recorder, but for consistently interesting interviews I'd have to pick the *Paris Review* series of interviews with writers (collected in book form in five volumes as *Writers at Work,* published by Viking Penguin).

INTERVIEWING BEYOND
THE CALL OF DUTY

Gᴇᴏʀɢᴇ Mᴏᴏʀᴇ (1852–1933) once interviewed his cook, paying her by the hour, to gain the insight into "the psychology of the working class" that enabled the Irish landowner to write *Esther Waters*. Nothing wrong with that, but some writers have gone much further. The most tasteless author who ever pursued verisimilitude was British journalist William Thomas Stead (1849–1912), who went down with the *Titanic*. To research an article on the evils of prostitution, Stead paid a thirteen-year-old girl £10 to work as a prostitute in a London brothel and report the conditions to him. Stead, who was sent to jail for his efforts, is in a class by himself, not quite up to de Sade or von Sacher-Masoch, but a bit worse than English novelist Arnold Bennett (1867–1931). Bennett once bragged that Darius Clayhanger's lingering death scene in the Clayhanger trilogy couldn't be bettered, "because I took infinite pains over it. All the time my father was dying, I was at the bedside making copious notes."

HEADLINE WRITING

Newspaper headlines are an American invention that came into frequent use during the Civil War, but the earliest known example blared forth from the front page of the Tory *New York Gazette* and the *Weekly Mercury* on October 20, 1777. Fortunately for the United States the headline was all wrong:

Glorious News from the Southward. Washington Knocked up—The Bloodiest Battle in America—6,000 of his Men Gone—100 Wagons to Carry the Wounded—General Howe is at present in Germantown—Washington 30 Miles Back in a Shattered Condition—Their Stoutest Frigate Taken and One Deserted—They are Tired—And talk of Finishing the Campaigne.

MAN BITES DOG

If a dog bites a man," editors used to instruct cub reporters, "that's an ordinary occurrence. But when a man bites a dog, that's *news*." The advice and the saying "man bites dog" can be traced back to Oliver

Goldsmith's poem "Elegy on the Death of a Mad Dog," about a dog that "went mad and bit a man," which concludes with the lines:

> *The man recover'd of the bite,*
> *The dog it was that died.*

According to Eric Partridge, this touching poem passed into folklore in a number of versions, possibly including a funny one where a man *did* bite a dog, and finally became the journalistic advice.

THE WRITING ON THE WALL

GRAFFITI has been with us even before Figulus, Ida, or some joker scribbled FIGULUS LOVES IDA on a wall that still stands among the ruins of Pompeii. But the words KILROY WAS HERE reign supreme as graffiti, still more prevalent around the world than phrases like FRANZ KAFKA IS A KVETCH, or the myriad schizophrenic urgings to SUPPORT MENTAL HEALTH. No catch phrase has ever rivaled it, certainly not substitutes like CLEM or J. B. KING, the last said to be inscribed in chalk on thousands of boxcars by a J. B. King who owned them. KILROY WAS HERE first appeared on walls and every surface capable of absorbing it during World War II. From Boston to Beirut, from Malaya to Munich, from outhouses in France to castles on the Rhine it made its appearance and it is still seen today in the remotest corners of the sphere, either freshly inscribed or as a relic of older, if not better, days. At first it was presumed that Kilroy was fictional; one graffitologist even insisted that *Kilroy* represented an Oedipal fantasy, combining *kill* with *roi* (the French word for *king*). But it soon developed that James J. Kilroy, a politician and an inspector in a Quincy, Massachusetts, shipyard coined the slogan. Mr. Kilroy chalked the words on ships and crates of equipment to indicate that he had inspected them and to keep his crews on their toes. From Quincy the phrase traveled on ships and crates all over the world, and Kilroy, who died in Boston in 1962, aged sixty, became the most quoted man since Shakespeare.

EROTIC WRITING

Pornography is Greek for "writing of harlots," the term probably deriving from the signs hung outside ancient brothels. Such writing can be divided into *erotica*, which generally centers on heterosexual love, describing it in detail, and *exotica*, centering on so-called abnormal sex, including sadism, masochism, and fetishism. Pornography can be found in passages of the Old Testament and the plays of Aristophanes and probably goes back far beyond them. Boccaccio's

Decameron (1353) is the first work of modern pornography, and the first masterpiece of English pornography is probably John Cleland's *Memoirs of the Life of Fanny Hill* (1749).

The title of an early "Joy of Sex" was *Sonnetti Lussuriosi* (1524). Written by Pietro Aretino (1492–1556), the book was a collection of verses and erotic drawings showing positions of sexual intercourse and it was an underground favorite in Europe for centuries. The engravings were actually made by Marcantonio Raimondi from drawings by Giulio Romano. Critics were astute in England—John Donne, for one—observing that some "postures" were left out.

At least six courtesans were so proud to have slept with Aretino that they called themselves "Aretines." But many hated the satirist, one critic writing this mock epitaph on him:

> *Here lies the Tuscan poet Aretino*
> *Who evil spoke of everyone but God,*
> *Giving as his excuse, "I never knew him."*

Pornography has thrived only since the late eighteenth century, the English word itself first recorded in 1860, and authors of it since have been as varied as de Sade, Swinburne, and Mark Twain. An excellent reference giving details and titles is R. S. Read's *Register Librorum Eroticorum* (1936).

Porneius was a character in Greek legend who has been called "fornication personified," a good description, as his name comes from the Greek *porneia* ("fornication"). He was the son of Anagnus ("inchastity"), two of his brothers being Maechus ("adultery") and Aselges ("lasciviousness"). Porneius tried to rape Parthenia ("maidenly chastity"), but "the martial maid" killed him with his own spear.

EROTIC AD WRITING

PROSTITUTES in ancient Greece sometimes wore sandals with the Greek for "follow me" tooled in mirror-image on the sole, so that as they walked along the dirt streets they left a trail prospective clients could follow to their rooms.

MAKING IT

*I*N *Tropic of Cancer* Henry Miller notes that while trying to make a living in Paris during the 1920s he "wrote pamphlets introducing the big new whorehouse . . . on the Boulevard Edgar-Quinet." For this "pseudonymous writing," he got a bottle of champagne and some free love (he put it differently) "in one of the Egyptian rooms."

Said Ezra Pound of *Tropic of Cancer*: "At last, an unprintable book that is fit to read."

INSEX

*I*N THE *Winners & Sinners* bulletin he distributed to *The New York Times* staff the late Theodore Bernstein criticized a *Times* headline that read, ELM BEETLE INFESTATION RAVISHING THOUSANDS OF TREES IN GREENWICH. "Keep your mind on your work, buster," he wrote. "The word you want is 'ravaging.' " He titled the piece "Insex."

NARRATIVE HOOKER

*I*SAAC ASIMOV would tell the story of the author whose agent told him his books weren't selling because there wasn't enough sex in them. "Not sexy enough?" the writer shouted. "What are you talking about? Look, right here on the first page the courtesan dashes out of the room stark naked and runs out into the street with the hero following her just as naked and in an explicitly described state of sexual arousal."

"Yes, yes," said the agent, "but look how *far down* the first page!"

EPITAPH WRITING—THE LAST WORD

*T*HE EARLIEST *epitaphs*—the word is from the Greek term for "writing on a tomb"—are found on Egyptian sarcophagi. One of the best-known of early valedictions is that of the Assyrian king Ashurbanipal, a poem said to have been left beside his burial mound at Nineveh in the seventh century B.C.:

I was the king, and while I lived on earth,
And saw the light rays of the genial sun,
I ate, and drank, and loved, and knew full well
The time that men do live on earth was brief
And liable to many sudden changes,
Recesses and calamities. Now others
Will have the enjoyment of luxuries
Which I do leave behind me. For these reasons
I have never ceased one single day from pleasure.

Ashurbanipal, possibly the prototype of the semilegendary Sardanapalus of Greek fable, reputedly leaped into a funeral pyre with his wives and concubines rather than be captured by the enemy, leaving behind a second epitaph: "Eat, drink and love, the rest's not worth this!" At any rate, Greek epitaphs are numerous, a major collection of them to be found in the *Greek Anthology*, including the famous epitaph by Simonides of Ceos on the Three Hundred who fell at Thermopylae:

Go, tell the Lacedaimonians, passer-by,
That here obedient to their laws we lie.

Great English epitaph makers included Thomas Gray, Jonson, Milton, Pope, and Dr. Johnson. Gray appended his own epitaph to his "Elegy Written in a Country Churchyard":

Here rests his head upon the lap of Earth
A youth to Fortune and to Fame unknown.
Fair Science frown'd not on his humble birth,
And Melancholy mark'd him for her own.

Large was his bounty, and his soul sincere,
Heav'n did a recompense as largely send:
He gave to Mis'ry all he had, a tear,
He gained from Heav'n ('twas all he wish'd) a friend.

No farther seek his merits to disclose,
Or draw his frailties from their dread abode,
(There they alike in trembling hope repose),
The bosom of his Father and his God.

Melancholy, too, was the epitaph composed by American author William Gilmore Simms (1806–1870):

Here lies one who after a reasonably long life, distinguished chiefly
by unceasing labors, left all his better works undone.

Poet John Gay's grim self-epitaph on his tomb in Westminster Abbey reads:

> *Life is a jest and all things show it*
> *I thought so once, and now I know it.*

The epitaph on Shakespeare's tomb is doggerel and may be unworthy of the Bard, but he could well have written it:

> *Good friend, for Jesus' sake forbear*
> *To dig the dust enclosed here,*
> *Blest be the man that spares these stones,*
> *And curst be he that moves my bones.*

Edgar Allan Poe's epitaph is

> *Quoth the Raven nevermore.*

Among the most beautiful epitaphs is Joseph Conrad's, taken from *The Faerie Queen*:

> *Sleep after toyle, port after stormie seas,*
> *Ease after warre, death after life, does greatly please.*

And these lines from a poem of his carved on the stone of Paul Laurence Dunbar:

> *Lay me down beneaf de willers in de grass,*
> *Where de branch'll go a-singin' as it pass.*
> *An' w'en I's a-layin' low*
> *I kin heah it as I go*
> *Sayin' "Sleep, ma honey, tek yo' res' at las'."*

Lines from his work are carved on the grave of Thomas Wolfe:

> *The last voyage, the longest, the best.*
> *—Look Homeward, Angel*

Legend has it that the famous epitaph *O rare Ben Jonson* over the grave of the great Elizabethan dramatist is actually the mistake of a stonecutter who didn't know Latin and carved the words instead of *Orare Ben Jonson* (Pray for Ben Jonson). But the carving was actually commissioned by Sir John Young, who wrote it.

Dr. Johnson wrote an epitaph for his good friend Goldsmith:

> *To Oliver Goldsmith, Poet, Naturalist and Historian, who left scarcely any style of writing untouched, and touched nothing that he did not adorn.*

And a printer with a penchant for puns wrote one for himself:

> *Here lies a form—place no imposing stone*
> *To mark the head, where weary it is lain;*
> *'Tis matter dead!—its mission being done,*
> *To be distributed to dust again.*
> *The body's but the type, at best, of man,*
> *Whose impress is the spirit's deathless page,*
> *Worn out, the type is thrown to pi again,*
> *The impression lives through an eternal age.*

There have been many bitter epitaphs by and about wives and husbands, as witness poet John Donne's mock epitaph on his wife. According to the story, which is often distorted, Donne's father-in-law, Sir George More, was so enraged when his daughter married without his consent that he turned the couple out of his house and caused Donne to lose his position as secretary to the lord keeper of the great seal. While considering all that had happened when he moved into his new house, Donne scratched on a pane of glass:

John Donne.
Ann Donne.
Undone.

The following jubilant epitaph, erroneously attributed to English writer John Dryden, actually comes from an Edinburgh, Scotland, graveyard:

> *Here snug in grave my wife doth lie!*
> *Now she's at peace and so am I.*

Cynical mock epitaphs are not always for married folk. Wrote Ambrose Bierce of editor Frank Pixley:

Here lies Frank Pixley, as usual.

Other famous mock epitaphs that were never carved on their authors' headstones include:

The final condensation.
　　　　　—Suggested for his own epitaph
　　　　　by DeWitt Wallace,
　　　　　founder of *The Reader's Digest*

Here lies the Christian, judge and poet Peter,
Who broke the laws of God, and man, and metre.
　　　　　—Lord Peter Robertson

This is on me.
and
Pardon my dust.
　　　　　—Dorothy Parker

Pardon me for not getting up.
　　　　　—Ernest Hemingway

This is all over my head.
　　　　　—Robert Benchley

I knew if I stayed around long enough, something like this would happen.　　　　　—George Bernard Shaw

If, after I depart this vale, you ever remember me and have thought to please my ghost, forgive some sinner and wink your eye at some homely girl.　　　　　—H. L. Mencken

There are many more, but I'll stop here with the excuse that the ancients believed you would lose your memory if you read epitaphs.

"MAY THE EARTH ON HIM LIE LIGHTER . . ."

THOMAS MOORE wrote this mock epitaph for the prolific poet laureate Robert Southey (he wrote one play in three days), who died of overwork, which caused "a softening of the brain."

Beneath these poppies buried deep,
The bones of Bob the bard lie hid;
Peace to his manes; and may he sleep
As soundly as his readers did!

Death, weary of so dull a writer,
Put to his books a finis *thus.*
Oh! May the earth on him lie lighter
Than did his quartos upon us!

KEATS'S GRAVESTONE

This Grave
Contains all that was Mortal
of a
YOUNG ENGLISH POET
Who
on his Death Bed
in the Bitterness of his Heart
at the Malicious Power of his Enemies
Desired
these words to be engraven on his Tomb Stone

HERE LIES ONE

WHOSE NAME WAS WRIT IN WATER

Feb. 24th 1821

*I*N THE WORDS of Francis Thompson, John Keats "was first half-chewed in London" by the critics "and finally spit dying into Italy." His grave is at the Protestant Cemetery, Rome, Italy. Keats died on February 23, 1821, but "since he died after midnight and in papal Rome the day ended with the ringing of the

Angelus," his death was recorded with the next day's date. Keats wanted only the final line on the stone, but his friend Joseph Severn, later buried next to him, prefaced it with the rest. Shelley, who visited Keats's grave, wrote in the preface to his elegiac "Adonais": "The cemetery is an open space among the ruins, covered in winter with violets and daisies. It might make one in love with death to think that one should be buried in so sweet a place."

AN AUTHOR'S HUMAN GRAVESTONES

JEREMY BENTHAM, that same philosopher-author whose clothed skeleton is on display at University College, London, thought that dead people should all be embalmed and used as their own monuments. He called these *auto-icons*. "If a country gentleman have rows of trees leading to his dwelling," he wrote, "the auto-icons of his family might alternate with the trees; copal varnish would protect the face from the effects of rain—caoutchouc the habiliments." But then Bentham also had an unusual pet—a teapot.

BEN FRANKLIN'S EPITAPH

WHEN Benjamin Franklin was twenty-three and a journeyman printer, he composed the following epitaph for himself.

The Body
of
Benjamin Franklin, Printer
(Like the cover of an old book,
Its contents torn out,
And stript of its lettering and gilding,)
Lies food for worms:
Yet the work itself shall not be lost,
for it will (as he believed) appear once more,
In a new
And more beautiful edition,
Corrected and amended
by
The Author.

Franklin got the idea from similar early epitaphs. He never used it, however; his grave in Philadelphia is marked only with the names of himself and his wife. Another mock epitaph was written for Franklin by a contemporary printer:

Benjamin Franklin, a * in his profession; the type of honesty; and ! of all; and although the ☞ of death put a . to his existence, each § of his life is without a ‖ .

THE SUPREME COMPLIMENT
FOR AN EPITAPH WRITER

D R. SAMUEL PARR'S style seems verbose and mannered today, but in the early nineteenth century he was highly regarded as a stylist and especially as a writer of Latin epigraphs. Once he said to a friend, "My lord, should you die first, I mean to write your epitaph." "Dr. Parr," his friend replied, "it is a temptation to commit suicide."

CHAPTER TWO

The Literary Life: Writers & Authors

LITERARY PRODIGIES

THE ROMAN WORD *prodigium* was used to denote an incident of an extraordinary nature to be taken as a prophetic sign bad or good by the entire nation. When adapted to English as *prodigy*, the term at first meant the same, but later became applied to an extraordinary person or animal, one with great mentality or talent, and then to a child possessing these qualities. Since the early sixteenth century, society has known thousands of child prodigies. The most famous authors among them would be:

Aldus Manutius II (1547–1597)—Italian author and printer whose writings were published when he was only nine.

James Crichton (1560–1582)—English scholar and adventurer who mastered a dozen languages and all the sciences, and was an accomplished poet by the time he was thirteen; known as "The Admirable Crichton."

Lope Félix de Vega Carpio (1562–1635)—Spanish dramatist who completed a four-act play (*El verdadero amante*) at age twelve.

Blaise Pascal (1623–1662)—French scientist and philosopher who invented a geometry of his own at age eleven.

Alexander Pope (1688–1744)—English poet celebrated as a prodigy by London wits while in his early teens.

Colen Maclaurin (1698–1746)—Scottish mathematician and author who was made a full university professor—the youngest in history—at age nineteen.

Johann Wolfgang von Goethe (1749–1832)—The greatest of German *Wunderkinder* wrote a novel before he was thirteen, entered college at age sixteen.

Thomas Chatterton (1752–1770)—English poet who published poems written before he was twelve, poems so good that he passed them off as the work of an early poet.

William Holmes McGuffey (1800–1873)—American author of the famed McGuffey's readers, who possessed a phenomenal memory, which enabled him to become a teacher at thirteen.

Alfred, Lord Tennyson (1809–1892)—English poet, composed blank verse at age eight and by fourteen had written two plays and many poems.

Marjorie Fleming (1803–1811)—Before she died of complications from measles or from meningitis, in Kirkeaddy, Scotland, at the age of eight, Pet Marjorie wrote some 10,000 words of diary entries and poems. A favorite of Sir Walter Scott, who called her "my bonnie wee croodlin' doo [cooing dove]" and "the most extraordinary creature I ever met with," Pet Marjorie became the youngest world-famous author in history a half-century after her death, when her diary was finally published and proved a best-seller around the world.

John Stuart Mill (1806–1873)—English philosopher, learned Greek by the age of three, taught his brothers Latin, Euclid, and algebra by eight.

John Ruskin (1819–1900)—English author who taught himself to read at an early age by listening to his parents read the Bible and Shakespeare to him.

Lord Kelvin (William Thomson, 1824–1907)—English scientist and author, was the youngest university student ever at age ten; at seventy-five, he formally matriculated again at Glasgow, in order to maintain his connection with the university, and became the oldest genius ever to return to school.

Jean Arthur Rimbaud (1854–1891)—French poet who wrote some of the poems in his collected works before he was fifteen; his poem "Le Bateau Ivre," which is now hailed as the pioneer of the French symbolist movement, was written when he was sixteen.

Norbert Wiener (1894–1964)—American author and founder of cybernetics, read extensively in science by the time he was five and entered college at eleven.

Daisy Ashford (1881–1972)—An English girl, who was a favorite of James Barrie, wrote a humorous novel in 1890 at the age of nine. *The Young Visiters*, published in 1919, sold over 200,000 copies and critics said that the book deftly portrayed Victorian society, offering penetrating commentary on its shortcomings, and that her characters compared favorably with those of Dickens. Although Daisy was renowned in her time, she never wrote another book, publishing only a few stories that had been written before her novel.

Opal Whiteley (b. 1897)—America's youngest world-famous author, had her childhood diary published in the *Atlantic Monthly* when she was twenty-two, convincing *Atlantic Monthly* editor Ellery Sedgwick that it was the work of a child. Readers throughout the world were enchanted by the work, the London *Times* proclaiming it "the most complete picture of a child's inner life that can be imagined," though some critics have charged it was a hoax. Since her time there have been at least a dozen authors who have published books before they were ten, the youngest of them only four years old.

"YET I AM LEARNING": OLD AGE AND NEW STUDIES

THE FOLLOWING is an extract from Isaac D'Israeli's *Curiosities of Literature* (1791–1793):

Of the pleasures derivable from the cultivation of the arts, sciences, and literature, time will not abate the growing passion; for old men still cherish an affection and feel a youthful enthusiasm in those pursuits, when all others have ceased to interest. . . . In advanced life we may resume our former studies with a new pleasure, and in old age we may enjoy them with the same relish with which more youthful students commence. *Adam Smith* observed to Dugald Stewart that "of all the amusements of old age, the most grateful and soothing is a renewal of acquaintance with the favorite studies and favorite authors of youth"—a remark, adds Stewart, which, in his own case, seemed to be more particularly exemplified while he was re-perusing, with the enthusiasm of a student, the tragic poets of ancient Greece.

Socrates learned to play on musical instruments in his old age; Cato, at eighty, thought proper to learn Greek; and Plutarch, almost as late in his life, Latin.

Theophrastus began his admirable work on the characters of men at the extreme age of ninety. He only terminated his literary labors by his death.

Ronsard, one of the fathers of French poetry, applied himself late to study. His acute genius, and ardent application, rivaled those poetic models which he admired; and Boccaccio was thirty-five years of age when he commenced his studies in polite literature.

Dr. Johnson applied himself to the Dutch language but a few years before his death. The Marquis de Saint Aulaire, at the age of seventy, began to court the Muses, and they crowned him with their freshest flowers. The verses of this French Anacreon are full of fire, delicacy, and sweetness.

Chaucer's *Canterbury Tales* were the composition of his latest years; they were begun in his fifty-fourth year, and finished in his sixty-first.

Ludovico Monaldesco, at the extraordinary age of one hundred and fifteen, wrote the memoirs of his times. A singular exertion, noticed by Voltaire, who himself is one of the most remarkable instances of the progress of age in new studies.

The most delightful of autobiographies for artists is that of Benvenuto Cellini; a work of great originality, which was not begun till "the clock of his age had struck fifty-eight."

Koornhert began at forty to learn the Latin and Greek languages, of which he became a master; several students, who afterward distinguished themselves, have commenced as late in life their literary pursuits. Ogilby, the translator of Homer and Virgil, knew little of Latin or Greek till he was past fifty.

Dryden's complete works form the largest body of poetry from the pen of a single writer in the English language, yet he gave no public testimony of poetic abilities till his twenty-seventh year. In his sixty-eighth year he proposed to translate the whole *Iliad*, and his most pleasing productions were written in his old age.

Michelangelo preserved his creative genius even in extreme old age: there is a device said to be invented by him, of an old man represented in a go-cart, with an hourglass upon it: the inscription *Ancora imparo*:—YET I AM LEARNING!

JUDGED BY THEIR WORK, NOT THEIR YEARS

SOPHOCLES'S SONS are said to have summoned him to court in his old age (he lived to be ninety) so that a jury might find him incompetent to manage his estate on the ground of senility. After he read them the play he had just finished, *Oedipus at Colonus*, the jury sided with him, reasoning that no man in his dotage could write such a work. They even escorted him home as an honor.

A similar story is told of the great diva Luisa Tetrazzini, whose children tried to have her declared incompetent in her late years. The judge dismissed the case after she sang an aria for him in court. (See also *Ages of Authors*.)

RIPENESS AND FLAVOR

LONGFELLOW was asked when an old man how he could write so many happy childlike things, full of joy and wonder. He replied that Governor Endicott's pear tree, 200 years old, "still bears fruit not to be distinguished from a young tree in flavor."

IQs OF AUTHORS

PSYCHOLOGIST Catharine Morris Cox studied the lives of 301 famous historical figures and ranked them according to approximate intelligence in her *Genetic Studies of Genius* (1926). Following are the top seven writers among them and their estimated IQs:

John Stuart Mill—190
Johann Wolfgang von Goethe—185
Thomas Chatterton—170
Voltaire—170
George Sand—150
Lord Byron—150
Charles Dickens—145

JOHANN WOLFGANG VON GOETHE

Surprisingly, Charles Darwin had a projected IQ of only 135, Balzac one of just 130; Cervantes was near the middle of the normal intelligence-quotient group (85–115), with an IQ of 105. Since Dr. Cox's book was published, other studies have given Mill and Goethe IQs estimated at over 200. Emanuel Swedenborg, who rated only a 115 in the Cox book, also rates over 200 today. An IQ of 210 is the highest ever recorded on the Terman Intelligence Quotient index.

INSPIRED IDIOTS

WHEN Horace Walpole dubbed Oliver Goldsmith "The Inspired Idiot," he wasn't aware that the ancient Greeks had often termed prose writers idiots. The word *idiot* first meant an uneducated, ignorant person, which the Greeks considered prose writers (but not poets) to be. This can be seen in the Greek expression "A poet or an idiot" (prose writer). In more recent times Georges Simenon said that Count Keyserling once called him an *"imbécile de génie."*

PROLIFIC AUTHORS

SPANISH AUTHOR Lope de Vega (1562–1635), a prodigy whom Cervantes called "the monster of nature," allegedly wrote some 2,200 plays in his effortless flowing style, although only about 500 survive. Alexandre Dumas *père*, whose total lifetime writings would

LOPE FÉLIX DE VEGA CARPIO

fill more than 1,500 volumes, produced sixty books in one year. In modern times the most prolific author of books is South African Kathleen Lindsay (Mrs. Mary Faulkner, 1903–1973), who wrote 904 novels under six pen names. However, Charles Hamilton (1875–1961), the Englishman who created Billy Bunter and wrote under the pseudonym Frank Richards, often turned out 80,000 words a week writing weekly comics, and his lifetime word production is estimated at about 100 million words, far more than that of Mrs. Faulkner. British author John Creasey and French author Georges Simenon each wrote well over 500 books. Australian Michael Hervey (b. 1920) has published the most short stories—3,500.

MOST PROLIFIC AUTHOR: ANONYMOUS

SINCE Willard Espy has published an excellent book on anonymous literature, there's no need to dwell on the subject in detail here. Certainly tens of thousands of books and pamphlets have been published anonymously since the invention of the printing press, folktales, ballads, nursery rhymes, proverbs, political tracts, poems, novels, and plays among them. Famous anonymous works include Poe's first poems; Richardson's *Pamela*, the first genuine novel in English; Fielding's *Joseph Andrews*; almost all of Jonathan Swift's work; Smollett's *Roderick Random*; all Jane Austen's early works; Gray's "Elegy"; Byron's "Don Juan"; Dryden's "Absalom and Achitophel"; Pope's "Essay on Criticism"; and Tennyson's "In Memoriam."

FASTEST-WORKING AUTHORS

HAVE YOU read my books?" a writer once asked author James Burnett, Lord Monboddo (1714–1799).

"I have not," Burnett replied. "You write a great deal faster than I am able to read."

Shakespeare was known as a very rapid writer. "His mind and hand went together," his publishers Heminges and Condell reported, "and what he thought, he uttered with that easiness that we have scarce received from him a blot in his papers." But even if he should have blotted out a thousand lines, as Ben Jonson quipped, Shakespeare could hardly have matched the speed of several other authors. Lope de Vega, it's said, wrote several of his 2,200 plays overnight and claimed that over one hundred of them had been written in a day each. Sir Walter Scott dictated his novels so fast that his secretaries could barely keep up with him and he finished two of the Waverley novels in three weeks. In 1845 Dumas *père* won a bet by completing the first volume of *Le Chevalier de Maison-Rouge* in seventy-two hours. None of the authors of the goose-quill era, however, could match the speed of many of today's authors. *The Guinness Book of World Records* lists mystery writer Erle Stanley Gardner (1889–1970) as the world's fastest writer, putting British novelist John Creasey in second place. Gardner, who wrote 140 books in his lifetime, dictated 10,000 words a day and once worked on seven novels simultaneously, while Creasey, who produced 564 books, once wrote two books in a single week. Philip Wylie is supposed to have written a full-length Crunch and Des novel for the *Saturday Evening Post* in less than twenty-four hours, which must be the real record. Georges Simenon, whose hundreds of books consistently ranged from good to excellent, used to allot himself six days to write a "Maigret," one of his psychological mysteries.

He would have a complete medical examination and then lock himself in a room until he finished the book. Isaac Asimov said he wrote most nonfiction books in seventy hours. As for modern playwrights, British mystery author Edgar Wallace (1875–1932) wrote his play *On the Spot* in just two and a half days and not a word of it was changed in production. (Wallace wrote his novel *The Three Dates Mystery* in three days.) Nor is good poetry always the result of long reworking. Tennyson, for example, wrote "Crossing the Bar" in a moment while crossing over to Yarmouth from Lymington, jotting down the sixteen lines (almost unchanged in the final version) on an old envelope.

WASTE NOT, WRITE ON

*F*RENCH CHANCELLOR D'Aguesseau noticed that his wife usually came down to dinner ten minutes or so late every evening. Over the period of little more than a year, he completed a book of three volumes while waiting for her and his work became a best-seller when it was published in 1668.

WRITERS' INCOMES

A SURVEY by Philippe Perebinossoff of hundreds of members of P.E.N., the international writers organization, found that the median income from writing in 1978 was $4,700, with 68 percent making under $10,000 and 9 percent earning nothing. A 1990 study raised this median income to a fabulous $5,000, while a 1993 *Time* magazine article reported that "only a dozen or so U.S. poets earn as much as $2,000 from selling their poems."

POORLY PAID AUTHORS

When I first came to Paris, I had 53 francs. Now . . . I have only 40. So long as I haven't made up the missing 13 francs, I shall have to go on writing.
—Alexandre Dumas *père*,
shortly before his death

As of 1978, fifty-four-year-old English author William Gold had devoted twenty years to writing fifteen books and other work totaling over three million words. In this time, he earned just 50 cents, for a short article in an Australian newspaper. I can find no word of his gallant efforts since.

Gold ranks as the least successful author of all time, according to *The Guinness Book of World Records*, but a number of writers have actually *lost* money writing books. The biggest loser was one Thomas Wirgman, who spent more than $200,000 publishing a number of books in which each page was printed on paper of a different color. The books, including his *Grammar of Six Senses*, were all "complete gibberish," according to one critic, but then Wirgman cared only about the sequence of colors. Six copies of his many books were all that ever sold.

Great writers were often poorly paid. John Milton received the "wastepaper price" of £10 in all for *Paradise Lost.* "I never got a farthing by anything I writ except one [*Gulliver's Travels*] about eight years ago," wrote Jonathan Swift. Sigmund Freud was paid $209 for *The Interpretation of Dreams* in 1899. Samuel Boyse (1708–1749), one of the most impoverished of British authors, was so poor that he had to pawn all his clothes and worked while "he sat up in bed with the blanket wrapped about him, through which he had cut a hole large enough to admit his arm, and placing the paper upon his knee, scribbled in the best manner he could." Later in his life Boyse took to going out in the streets even though he had pawned his clothes. In place of a shirt "he cut some white paper in slips, which he tied around his wrists, and in the same manner supplied his neck." Often he would go out wearing just this shirt—no pants or shoes.

It is often forgotten that the greatest writer of all time could not make a living from writing. Shakespeare was paid no more than £8 apiece for his plays (which was the highest price any playwright got at the time), and since he wrote fewer than forty plays, his income from writing during his twenty years in the theater was less than £20 a year. He was not unusual in this regard—Ben Jonson estimated that he made less than £200 from writing plays—but the Swan of Avon had to support himself as a working actor all his life. His income *from all sources* may have been about $50,000 a year after 1599, according to one biographer.

Lord Byron frequently *refused* payment for his poems, preferring to write for "glory."

Edgar Allan Poe looked so bad when he personally submitted the manuscript of "The Raven" to *Graham's Magazine* that although the editors rejected the poem they took up a collection of $15 to give him; he eventually got $10 for "The Raven" but had to wait a year and a half before he pried the money loose from the *New York Mirror*. Balzac was so poor that he had to lock himself up in a secret room to hide from his creditors while writing the *Comédie Humaine*. Herman Melville never got more than $200 for a story and "Benito Cereno" brought him only $85. Longfellow was paid only $15 for "The Village Blacksmith" and $25 for "The Wreck of the Hesperus." Julia Ward Howe received a mere $4 from the *Atlantic Monthly* for her "Battle Hymn of the Republic." Vachel Lindsay swapped rhymes for bread. Erich Maria Remarque sold tombstones. Tennessee Williams wrote $35 pieces for the old magazine *Weird Tales*. Henry Miller couldn't sell anything and dug graves for a living, William Burroughs was an exterminator, Carl Sandburg was a janitor, Faulkner had to run rum, and so on, ad nauseam.

JULIA WARD HOWE

The poverty program in American literature is usually associated with and justified by Henry David Thoreau, who could certainly have penned no panegyric on penury—not when he could budget only 27½ cents a week for food at Walden. Perhaps it is best to conclude with the words of Edwin Arlington Robinson, who wrote to a friend: "You cannot conceive how cutting it is for a man of twenty-four to depend on his mother for every cent he has and every mouthful he swallows. The world frightens me."

QUIZ

AT LEAST three great American writers worked as United States customhouse officials, political sinecures in their day. Name them.

ANSWERS: Hawthorne, Melville, Edwin Arlington Robinson.

FIRST WOMAN TO MAKE A LIVING WRITING

T HE FIRST WOMAN to earn her living as an author seems to have been Mrs. Aphra Behn (1640–1689), who wrote a number of popular plays, poems, and novels, including such tales of love and adventure as *The Fair Jilt*, *The Rover*, and *The Amours of Philander and Sylvia*. Mrs. Behn's *Oroonoko* may have suggested the "noble savage" philosophy to Rousseau. Also a spy for England's Charles II, she is buried in the east cloister of Westminster Abbey.

WELL-PAID AUTHORS

T HE HIGHEST word rate ever paid to a professional author is the $15,000 Darryl Zanuck gave the late James Jones for correcting a line of dialogue in the film *The Longest Day*. Jones and his wife, Gloria, were sitting on the beach when they changed the line "I can't eat that bloody old box of tunny fish" to "I can't stand this damned old tuna fish." The chore of deleting two words and changing four words came to $2,500 a word, far higher than the record amount *The Guinness Book of World Records* credits to Ernest Hemingway. Hemingway received $15 a word for a 2,000-word article on bullfighting that he wrote for *Sports Illustrated* in 1960. His payment came to $30,000, thirty times the going rate at that time for an article of that length.

Hemingway's "The Snows of Kilimanjaro" has probably earned more money than any short story in history. Since its publication in 1936 it has made, including movie rights, close to half a million dollars.

Thomas Dixon's novel *The Clansman*, used by D. W. Griffith as the basis for *The Birth of a Nation*, earned several million dollars when Dixon accepted a 25 percent interest in the film instead of the $7,500 that Griffith owed him for the story and was unable to pay.

To name the highest-paid author of all time is another matter. One would have to consider writers like João de Barvios (1496–1570), given 130,000 acres in Brazil by the king of Portugal for writing his history of Asia. Recent fantastic sales (up to $60 million) for multibook deals also make such calculations difficult, but good choices are Belgian mystery writer Georges Simenon and British mystery author Agatha Christie, whose books have sold over 300 million copies. Other authors have made more money on individual books, but probably no one else has earned so much over the years. Agatha Christie's eighty mysteries have been translated into 103 languages, more than those of any author of adult books except Shakespeare.

Among writers of antiquity the richest was probably the Roman dramatist Seneca, who had a fortune estimated at $30 million. When Seneca died, however, his body was emaciated from undernourishment. He had been living on a diet of wild apples and water "for fear of poison in his food."

Aristotle is said to have had a precious robe that sold for $720,000 after his death, and Plato was once given a present of $480,000 by Dionysus II.

The poet Snorri Sturluson (1178–1241) was the richest man in Iceland.

GENEROUS AUTHORS

AGATHA CHRISTIE's *The Mousetrap*, which has had the longest run of any play in history, with over 10,000 performances when it closed, has brought millions to the author's nephew, to whom she gave the royalties as a gift. Less remunerative but much odder was the royalty playwright Sir James Barrie gave to the child of one of his friends. The boy had been told he would be sick the next day if he ate any more chocolates. "I shall be sick tonight," he replied laconically and helped himself to another piece. Delighted with the epigram, Barrie decided to use it as the basis for lines spoken in *Peter Pan* (1904) and gave his friend's son a royalty of a halfpenny a performance for the copyright. Even more generous was Rudyard Kipling, who gave the manuscript of *The Jungle Book* to the nurse of his first child; in later years she sold it and was able to retire on the proceeds.

AUTHOR-LECTURERS

*I*N A DAY when lecture fees of up to $100,000 are paid celebrity authors, it is interesting to note that in the 1880s Ralph Waldo Emerson, America's first lecturer known to receive a fee, got $5 for himself and oats for his horse as payment. After finishing the lecture, he had to argue over whether the oats were part of the bargain.

VOLTAIRE'S GOVERNMENT GRANT

*V*OLTAIRE, a brilliant mathematician, made a fortune, which allowed him ample time to write as he pleased, by winning a government lottery. Noticing a miscalculation in the government issuance of the lottery, he formed a syndicate, bought up every ticket, and became rich enough on his share to be independent. Years later, in 1891, the artist Claude Monet won 100,000 francs in the French national lottery and was able to devote himself entirely to his work.

SCHOLARLY WRITERS

ACCORDING to legend, the Athenian hero Academus helped Castor and Pollux rescue their little sister Helen when she was kidnapped by the Athenian prince Theseus. Academus revealed Helen's hiding place and she was spared marriage with Theseus, growing up to become the famous "face that launched a thousand ships," and causing the Trojan War. As a reward for his help the Spartans gave Academus an olive grove on the outskirts of Athens, the place later becoming a public park called the Grove of Academus in his honor. Much later, in about 387 B.C., the philosopher Plato had a house and garden adjoining the park and opened a school of philosophy there. He walked and talked with his students in the peaceful olive grove for the rest of his life, was buried near the grove, and his peripatetic successors taught there as well, so his school of philosophy became known as the Academia after the olive grove honoring the eponymous hero Academus. Renaissance scholars later adopted the name *academe* or *academy* for any institution devoted to learning, from the learning of philosophy to the learning of war, and it is from the word *academy* that our word *academic* derives. Possibly the most famous of academies is the Académie Française, founded in 1635, but this literary school has its detractors, too, having been called the *hôtel des invalides de la littérature*. In fact, the exclusiveness or specialization of many academies, along with anti-intellectual bias in modern times, probably accounts for the pejorative literary use of the word *academic*. The poet John Milton seems to be responsible for the wide use of the poetic fancy "groves of Academe" for institutions of higher learning; at least the words occur in his *Paradise Regained*, among other places:

> *the olive groves of Academe,*
> *Plato's retirement, where the Attic bird*
> *Trills her thick-warbl'd notes the summer long.*

Of all the numerous literary references to Helen, the most beautiful of women, the most famous is probably in Marlowe's *Dr. Faustus*:

> *Was this the face that launched a thousand ships*
> *And burnt the topless towers of Ilium?*
> *Sweet Helen, make me immortal with a kiss.*

Academic authors are popularly called highbrow authors, a term that has its roots in phrenology. Dr. Franz Joseph Gall (1758–1828), founder of the "science" of phrenology, gave support to the old folk notion that people with big foreheads have more brains. Gall's lifelong studies showed that the bigger a person's forehead was, the higher his brow, the smarter he would be. This theory was widely accepted through the nineteenth century, until phrenology was discredited by scientists, and led to the word *highbrow* for an intellectual, which is first recorded in 1875. The term is usually used disparagingly and is the source of the similar terms *lowbrow* and *middlebrow*. *Highbrow* writers can be disdainful, supercilious—a word that has a connection with the brow, too. Supercilious is from the Latin *supercilium*, "eyebrow," and the Latin suffix *osus*, "full of." Thus a supercilious person is literally one "full of eyebrow," an etymology that goes well with the image of someone slightly lifting the eyebrow in disdain.

Still common today for scholarly writers is the term *egghead*. Usually a term of mild contempt or derision applied to intellectuals, *egghead* was first used in its present sense to describe Adlai Stevenson and his advisers during the 1952 presidential campaign. Though the physical description better fit Stevenson's opponent, General Eisenhower, the term echoed the popular misconception that all intellectuals have high brows and heads shaped like eggs, the same kind of heads cartoonists give to "superior beings" from outer space. The continued popularity of the expression seems to suggest, sadly enough, that though these heads be admittedly full of brains, they are alien to the "common person." But *egghead* is also used humorously, even endearingly, and may yet become a word with no stigma attached to it.

Many an academic, scholarly, highbrow, supercilious, or egghead author has his *ivory tower*. In the "Song of Solomon" the poet sings that his beloved's neck is "as a tower of ivory," but the phrase in its modern sense has nothing else to do with Biblical poetry. French literary critic Charles Augustin Sainte-Beuve used *un tour d'ivoire* in 1837 to charge that romantic poet Alfred de Vigny evaded the responsibilities of life by retiring to an ivory tower. Whether the charge was justified or not, the image did evoke someone sitting cool and elegant, detached, above it all, and looking down on life. The phrase has become a cliché, especially when applied to scholars or intellectuals. It is seldom used anymore in a kind sense, to indicate a place of refuge from the world's strivings and posturings.

DROPOUTS WHO BECAME GREAT WRITERS

WRITERS who never finished grade school include Charles Dickens, Mark Twain, Maxim Gorky, Alberto Moravia, and Sean O'Casey.

Jack London, Will Rogers, and William Saroyan are among those who never completed high school.

Writers one would expect to have gone to college but who in fact never did include Virginia Woolf and George Bernard Shaw. There are many tales about authors failing writing and literature courses in school. Zola, for example, is said to have gotten zero in French literature while attending the Lycée St. Louis.

LITTLE GIANT AUTHORS

POPE was only four feet, six inches tall (or small); Keats a mere three-fourths of an inch over five feet; Balzac five feet, two inches; the Marquis de Sade the same, with eyes of blue; and Voltaire barely five feet, three inches. Colley Cibber, feuding with Pope, published a letter describing how a young nobleman had some fun with the little poet, a letter which Pope never denied:

> " . . . his lordship's frolic proposed was, to slip his little Homer, as he
> called him, at a girl of the game . . . in which he so far succeeded, that
> the smirking damsel, who served us with tea, happened to have charms
> sufficient to tempt the little-tiny manhood of Mr. Pope into the next
> room with her; at which, you may imagine, his lordship was in as much
> joy, at what might happen within, as our small friend could probably
> be in possession of it: but I . . . observing he had staid as long as without
> hazard of his health he might . . . threw open the door upon him, where

I found this little hasty hero, like a terrible Tom-Tit, pertly perching upon the mount of love! But such was my surprize that I fairly laid hold of his heels, and actually drew him down safe from his danger."

NOBEL PRIZE–WINNING AUTHORS

THE NOBEL PRIZE for Literature has been awarded since 1901, when it was given to French poet René F. A. Sully Prudhomme in preference to Tolstoy. It has since been won by many great writers, including Kipling, Tagore, Hamsun, Yeats, Shaw, Mann, O'Neill, Gide, Eliot, Faulkner, Hemingway, and Camus, but has denied more genius than it has honored. The likes of Tolstoy, Chekhov, Mark Twain, Ibsen, Conrad, Hardy, Rilke, James, Strindberg, Swinburne, Gorky, Brecht, Proust, Valéry, Dreiser, and O'Casey have been ignored or have lost in Nobel balloting to writers whom practically no one remembers, such as Björnson, Laxness, Karlfeldt, Eucken, Heidenstam, Reymont, Sillanpää, and Carducci, to list but a few.

ALFRED BERNHARD NOBEL

The only laureate to refuse the Nobel Prize voluntarily was Jean-Paul Sartre, who, in declining in 1964, wrote, "It is not the same thing if I sign Jean-Paul Sartre or if I sign Jean-Paul Sartre, Nobel Prize winner. A writer must refuse to allow himself to be transformed into an institution, even if it takes place in the most honorable form." In 1958 Russian author Boris Pasternak was forced to decline the award for his novel *Dr. Zhivago* by the Soviet Union, which considered the Nobel "a reactionary bourgeois award."

The Nobel Prize was, of course, established in the will of Swedish millionaire Alfred Nobel. "The day when two army corps will be able to destroy each other in one second," Nobel once predicted, "all civilized nations will recoil away from war in horror and disband their armies." The Swedish inventor of dynamite proved to be wrong in his prophecy, which may have been a rationalization for his invention, but the $9.2 million he left in his will to set up the Nobel Prize Foundation has greatly aided the cause of peace. Nobel Prizes are awarded to persons, irrespective of nationality, who have done outstanding work in the five fields Nobel considered most important to the benefit of humanity: physics, chemistry, medicine and physiology, literature, and peace. (In 1968 a sixth prize was established in economics.) The prizes, given in Stockholm and Oslo on December 10 of each year in which awards are made, consist of about $1.2 million, a diploma, and a gold medal. The judges are all Scandinavians.

PULITZER PRIZE WINNERS

HUNGARIAN-BORN Joseph Pulitzer was persuaded to emigrate to America by an agent who recruited him for the Union Army in 1864. After serving until his discharge a year later, he settled in St. Louis, where he founded the *St. Louis Post-Dispatch* in 1878. But when his chief editorial aide, Col. John A. Cockerell, shot and killed lawyer Col. Alonzo Slayback during a bitter political quarrel, Pulitzer left his paper and moved to New York, where he founded the *New York World* in 1883. He went on to become a congressman and made his paper among the best in the world, despite the fact that he went blind at age forty. A liberal, crusading newspaper, the *World* did much to raise the standards of American journalism, employing many of the greatest reporters and columnists of the day. Absorbed by the Scripps-Howard chain in 1931, it was eventually "merged" out of existence. When Pulitzer died in 1911, aged sixty-four, his will provided a fund to Columbia University, where he had established and endowed the school of journalism, which has been used since 1917 to give annual monetary awards for writing. Prizes in journalism are $3,000 each for local, national, and international reporting; editorial writing; news photography; cartooning; and meritorious public service performed by an individual newspaper. There are also six prizes of $500 for music, first awarded in 1943, and four traveling scholarships. The Pulitzer Prize and the National Book Award are America's best-known literary awards, but Sinclair Lewis and William Saroyan declined the Pulitzer Prize, believing it did not serve literature well.

THE TEN MOST POPULAR WRITERS OF ALL TIME

MORE BOOKS have been published about Shakespeare, Dante, Goethe, Cervantes, and Dickens (in that order) than any other writers. Books about Pushkin, Burns, Schiller, Tolstoy, and Whitman follow.

P.E.N.

P.E.N. is the acronym for the International Association of Poets, Playwrights, Editors, Essayists, and Novelists, founded in 1921 by Catherine Dawson Scott and John Galsworthy, who set up a trust fund for the organization in 1932 with his Nobel Prize money. The organization was named P.E.N. when someone pointed out at the first meeting that the initial letters of *poet*, *essayist*, and *novelist* were the same in most European languages and could serve as a title. P.E.N., with several American branches, has been more active than any literary organization in crusading for the civil rights of authors throughout the world.

THE EDGAR

THE EDGAR is a small bust of Edgar Allan Poe, presented annually to the best writers of detective stories by the Mystery Writers of America. Edgars are awarded in several categories, such as best novel and best short story. Poe himself once won a prize for his "The Gold Bug" (1843), the code in the story developing from his interest in cryptography. Although he did invent the detective story in his "The Murders in the Rue Morgue," "The Purloined Letter," and "The Mystery of Marie Rogêt," the writer is best remembered for his poetry and horror tales.

EDGAR ALLAN POE

Poe published his first book of poems, *Tamerlane and Other Poems*, anonymously and at his own expense. Among his greatest stories are "The Fall of the House of Usher," "The Black Cat," "The Pit and the Pendulum," and "The Tell-Tale Heart"; his best poems include "To Helen," "Israfel," "Ulalume," and

"Annabel Lee." But Poe's genius was never tangibly rewarded in his lifetime. "To coin one's brain into silver," he once wrote, "is to my thinking, the hardest job in the world." He had his best year when he edited the *Southern Literary Messenger*, for $800. His "The Raven" was one of the few poems recognized as a work of genius when it appeared. After his wife's death, Poe claimed that he lived with only "intervals of horrible sanity." He died at age forty, perhaps addicted to drugs, and may have spent his last days stumbling into Baltimore polling places and casting ballots for drinks. "Three-fifths genius and two-fifths sheer fudge," was James Russell Lowell's facile opinion of Poe, but Yeats declared him "always and for all lands a great lyric poet."

POE PARADES PLAINLY

A LITERARY and military tradition has it that Edgar Allan Poe was expelled from West Point in 1831 for "gross neglect of duty" because he appeared at a public parade naked. Parade dress instructions called for "white belts and gloves, under arms" and Poe took them literally. He appeared on the parade ground, rifle balanced on his bare shoulder, wearing nothing but white belt and gloves.

THE FOOTBALL POES

PRINCETON UNIVERSITY'S 1899 football team has to have more literary associations than any eleven in history. Fully six members of the team were named Poe, each of them a great-nephew of Edgar Allan Poe. The team's mascot was not a raven. (See *Athletic Authors*.)

THE LOST GENERATION

U*ne génération perdue,*" remarked Monsieur Pernollet, owner of the Hôtel de Pernollet in Belley. He was speaking to Gertrude Stein and pointing at a young mechanic repairing Stein's car. Young men like the mechanic, Monsieur

Pernollet said, had gone to war, had not been educated properly in their formative years, and were thus a lost generation. Stein remembered Monsieur Pernollet's phrase and applied it to Hemingway and his friends. Hemingway quoted her in *The Sun Also Rises* (1926) and the words became the label for an entire literary generation.

RIBALD WRITERS

*T*HERE IS no lack of stories about the sexual escapades of authors, which since earliest times have generally far surpassed the amorous activities of their most colorful characters. These are some of the lesser known tales.

• The son of the prefect of Cordova Said ibn Judi (d. 897) was as great a poet as he was a warrior—and a greater lover than both. "I traverse the circle of pleasures as a frenzied war horse that has taken the bit in its teeth," he once wrote. "I leave no desire unsatisfied!" Unfortunately, the circle of his pleasures included the wives of fellow officers. One caught him *in medias res* with his wife and skewered them on the same sword.

• The great Italian artist Raphael (Raffaello Sanzio, 1483–1520) is known to have written love sonnets on the backs of his drawings for his *Disputa*, frescoes in the Vatican. Raphael's amorous exploits were legendary in his own time. He had dozens of mistresses in his short lifetime, and the woman he had promised to marry reputedly died of a broken heart while he dallied with the others. Raphael himself is said to have died after indulging in what Vasari called "an unusually wild debauch."

• In his *Utopia* Sir Thomas More (1477?–1535) decrees that young people must see each other stark naked before they are married. He apparently practiced this law in his private life. According to John Aubrey, Sir William Roper came to More's house early one morning with a proposal to marry one of his daughters. More's daughters were both asleep in the same bed, and More led Roper into their room and suddenly whipped off the sheet covering them: "They lay on their backs, and their smocks up as high as their arme-pitts. This awakened them, and immediately they turned on their bellies. Quoth Roper, 'I have seen both sides,' and so giving a patt on the buttock, he made choice, saying, 'Thou art mine.'"

• The old story about Sir Walter Raleigh (1552–1618) throwing his plush coat over a puddle for Queen Elizabeth is probably not true. The poet and adventurer did marry Elizabeth Throckmorton, one of the Queen's maids of honor. According to John Aubrey's *Brief Lives*, he first made love to this maid against a tree in the forest: ". . . fearful of her honor, and modest, she cried, 'Sweet Sir Walter, what do you me ask? Will you undo me? Nay, sweet Walter! Sweet Sir Walter! Sir Walter! Sir Walter!' At last, as the danger and the pleasure at the same time grew higher, she cried in the ecstasy, 'Swisser Swatter! Swisser Swatter!'"

• Molière and other great French literary figures were regulars at French courtesan Ninon de Lenclos's famous salon. Literary legends abound about this apostle of free love and her myriad affairs, including the true story that in her will she left a thousand francs to her attorney M. Arouet's young son—that is, Voltaire. Legend has it that when Louis XIV's mother had her confined in a monastery for her indiscretions, she seduced all 439 monks there. Another tale claims that in her later years her own son, separated from her since infancy, fell in love with her and killed himself on learning that she was his mother. She died in 1705, age eighty-five.

• It is said that English playwright William Wycherley (1641–1716) continued "chasing women beyond his capacity into a bad old age." His last amorous adventure may have been undertaken out of spite, in order to thwart his nephew, the next in line to his family property. In any case, at the age of seventy-five he married a twenty-year-old girl. All the excitement proved too much for him, and he died ten days later.

• When he was approaching his 100th birthday, in 1757, French poet Bernard Le Bovier, Sieur de Fontenelle, abruptly entered the dressing room of Countess Anne Catherine de Ligniville d'Autricourt, a famous beauty of thirty-two, and found her almost completely naked. Very politely he backed out of the room, bowing and saying, "Ah, Madame, if only I were eighty years old again."

• William Byrd's library of 4,000 books was the largest in early eighteenth-century America. The Virginia tobacco planter, author, and colonial official kept a secret diary in shorthand as an avocation, never intending for it to be published. In numerous entries he explores his sexual nature, condemning his lust for "another man's wife" and his attempt (successful) "to pick up a woman." He had no inhibitions about married love, judging by his entry for July 30, 1710: "In the afternoon my wife and I had a little quarrel which I reconciled with a flourish. Then she read a sermon in Dr. Tillitson to me. It is to be observed that the flourish was performed on the billiard table."

• The brilliant Marquise du Châtelet (Emilie de Breteuil, 1706–1749), a scientist, musician, and author, and the first to translate Newton's *Principia Mathematica* into French, became Voltaire's mistress in 1734. For the next fifteen years they lived together at her husband's château in Champagne, which became Voltaire's refuge from the Paris police so often on his trail. But in 1749 Madame met the younger, handsome Jean-François de Saint-Lambert, a vain, vastly overrated poet, who had nonetheless been elected to the French Academy and had a reputation as a great lover, having stolen the Marquise de Boufflers from the Duke of Lorraine. Madame du Châtelet became pregnant and later that year died in childbirth. When she died, Voltaire and her husband took the locket she always wore and anxiously opened it, each hoping that it would contain a memento of himself. All they found was Saint-Lambert's portrait. "This story reflects no credit on either of us," Voltaire said to Monsieur du Châtelet when he recovered his wit. As for Saint-Lambert, he immediately left for Paris, where his reputation preceded him and he became the lover of still another famous literary figure, Madame d'Houdetot—the "Sophie" about whom Rousseau describes his unreciprocated passion in his *Confessions*. Madame d'Houdetot remained Saint-Lambert's mistress for over fifty years, until he died in 1803 at eighty-seven, a poet who had beaten both Voltaire and Rousseau at love, if not literature.

• The brilliant French scientist and encyclopedist Jean d'Alembert (1717–1783) was the illegitimate child of Claudine Alexandrine de Tencin, a former nun, and an artillery officer, the Chevalier Destouches. Having escaped from the nunnery in which her father had enrolled her sixteen years before, Claudine hid in the bed of the chevalier, where the two of them soon produced Jean. When he was born, however, his mother abandoned him on the steps of the Church of St.-Jean-le-Rond, where he was found and eventually adopted. His enterprising mother went from the bed of the chevalier to the beds of Matthew Prior and Lord Bolingbroke. Improving herself all the time, she added Richelieu,

Fontenelle, and the head of the Paris police to her long list of lovers. This interesting woman influenced history with her famous salon as well as her choice of beds, but she is best remembered for her romantic escapades. It is said that she became the regent's mistress by posing as a nude statue in his palace and coming to life when he touched her.

• Though Johann Wolfgang von Goethe (1749–1832) is often painted as wise and austere, "the Wisest of Our Time," as Carlyle put it in *Sartor Resartus*, this consummate artist was a great lyric poet and all his early *Sturm und Drang* works were based on personal experience. Goethe did turn to classicism, but not in his personal life. His wife, Christine, for example, was a lusty woman whose pet name for his penis was *Herr-Schonfuss*, or "Mr. Nice-foot." At a dinner both men attended, the Reverend J. C. Hasenkampf called Goethe's *Werther* a "wicked piece of writing." Looking the author in the eye, he said, "May God improve your perverse heart!"

Goethe simply replied, softly, "Remember me in your prayers."

• Jean Frédéric, Count de Waldeck, who published his second book when he was 100, dropped dead on a Paris street nine years later in 1875, just after turning to eye a pretty woman.

• The great romantic poet Lord Byron (George Gordon Byron, Sixth Baron Byron; 1788–1824) had ancestors who more than rivaled him in adventures and amorous escapades. Byron's great uncle, the handsome William, was called the "Wicked Lord" because of his wild life, rakish ways, and reckless spending. The poet's grandfather, John Byron, who circumnavigated the globe, earned the nickname the "Nautical Lover," for having a wife or mistress in every port. As for Byron's father, Captain John Byron, his devilish ways inspired people to call him Mad Jack Byron. A very handsome man, Lord Byron himself was the devil incarnate to some proper English ladies. One woman, traveling in Geneva, fainted of fear when Byron unexpectedly came into Madame de Stael's salon. His mistress, Lady Caroline Lamb, remarked of him in her diary, "Mad, bad, and dangerous to know." While living in his own Venetian palace, complete with its fourteen servants, a mistress, and assorted pets, including two monkeys, Byron wrote to a friend that "in the evenings I go out sometimes, and indulge in coition always." He proudly claimed he had different women on 200 consecutive evenings.

• While traveling in the Orient, Gustave Flaubert (1821–1880) contracted a venereal disease in the brothels he visited. Despite picking up the malady that killed Maupassant and Baudelaire, among other French writers, he admired fallen women. "I like prostitution," he wrote to Louise Colet. "My heart has never failed to pound at the sight of one of those provocatively dressed women walking in the rain under the gas lamps."

• Count Leo Tolstoy (1828–1910) based Fyodor Ivanovich Dolokhov in *War and Peace* on his uncle Fyodor Ivanovich Tolstoy, a character who could hardly be exaggerated. A duelist who killed eleven men, Fyodor Ivanovich was covered ankle to neck with tattoos. In his adventurous lifetime this libertine and gambler even commanded a round-the-world naval expedition on which the crew mutinied and put him ashore in the Aleutians. One wild story has it that, abandoned there, he made love to a female ape, which he then ate. Tolstoy himself considered sex "degrading," but despite his ascetic beliefs, his prodigious sexual drive lasted at least until he turned eighty, as his wife records in her diary.

• Edmond de Goncourt, the famous diarist, recorded in his journal how the French poet Comte Robert de Montesquiou-Fezensac (1855–1921) had his first love affair with a female ventriloquist, "who while he was straining to achieve his climax would imitate the drunken voice of a pimp." The poet, a bisexual who had Sarah Bernhardt as a mistress for a time, was an odd character who wore thick makeup and frequently took his gold tortoise with him on his walks. It is said that Proust patterned Baron Charlus on the rich count, who spent his entire fortune pampering his male lovers, and that Montesquiou-Fezensac's death was caused by the shock of recognizing himself as the baron's prototype.

• The great economist Thorstein Veblen (1857–1929) had a reputation as a womanizer. "Professor Veblen, we can't have any of that at Harvard," the head of his department told him when he came to Cambridge. Veblen replied that he need not fear: he had seen the women of Cambridge and they offered no temptation.

• The waspish Professor Charles Townsend Copeland (1860–1952) taught English at Harvard for many years beginning in 1893, influencing numerous authors (including John Reed and John Dos Passos). Copeland was noted for his beautiful reading voice and brilliant wit. Observed lean little "Copey" of copulation, "The sensation is momentary and the position ridiculous."

• Cora Stewart, Stephen Crane's (1871–1900) common-law wife, was the madam of a combination bordello and nightclub in Jacksonville, Florida, when he met her. Crane was enchanted by the name of her establishment: the Hotel de Dream.

• In 1909 a former friend of James Joyce's (1882–1941) lied that he had been sexually intimate with the author's wife, Nora, even while Joyce was courting her. Joyce decided to use this story, which he briefly believed, for the main theme of *Ulysses*. He no longer believed it, however, when he began writing the novel five years later and wanted to again feel the jealousy that had inspired him. His wife complained to a mutual friend at the time: "Jim wants me to go with other men so that he will have something to write about." She refused to do so, but did help him by using the salutation "Dear Cuckhold" in at least one letter she wrote to him.

• The bizarre artist's model Baroness Elsa von Freytag-Loringhoven, who painted her shaved head purple, pasted postage stamps on her cheeks, and wore a cake with lit candles for a hat, among myriad eccentricities, took a kind remark American poet William Carlos Williams (1883–1963) made to her as a declaration of love and offered to give him syphilis, which she said had been bequeathed to her by her father and would clear Williams's mind for his poetry. When Williams demurred, she trailed him home to Rutherford, New Jersey, and rang his bell, opening her fur coat to reveal herself naked when he answered the door. "Villiam Carlos Villiams, I vant you!" she cried, and when Williams responded "No! No!" she proceeded to assault him. The baroness, her real name Elsa Ploetz, died a suicide in Paris in 1927.

• Enid Bagnold (1889–1981), the author of *National Velvet* (1935) and *The Chalk Garden* (1956), wrote in her *Autobiography* (1969) that she lost her virginity to the legendary lecher Frank Harris (of whom Oscar Wilde said, "He has no feelings. It is the secret of his success.") when they were colleagues on an English magazine. Wrote Miss Bagnold: " 'Sex,' said Frank Harris, 'is the gateway to life.' So I went through the gateway in an upper room of the Cafe-Royal."

• One of the many artists and writers the generous Ezra Pound (1885–1972) helped over the years was French sculptor Henri Gaudier-Brzeska. Among several benefactions, Pound bought Gaudier a piece of marble from which the sculptor carved a portrait of the poet meant only to represent Pound's emotions. At least one other artist, Horace Brodsky, said that Gaudier had as a joke made a giant phallus of Pound, apparently relating his emotions to a poem entitled "Coitus," which Pound had just published, and the poet's unflagging interest in women. At any rate, Pound liked the work, called *Hieratic Head of Ezra Pound*, and later displayed it in his garden, often scrubbing it clean with soap and water.

• A friend came up in back of Marc Connelly (1890–1980) while the author and wit was lunching at the famed Algonquin Round Table and playfully rubbed his bald head. "Ah, that feels as smooth and soft as my wife's ass," he said.

Connelly quickly ran his own hand over the same area. "So it does," he said, "so it does."

• Undoubtedly in retaliation for the puritanism of her Aunt Cat, who raised her and thought it sinful for even children to be naked at any time, Katherine Anne Porter (1890–1980) in her middle years had her husbands and lovers take nude photographs of her that she promptly sent home to her family.

• In his biography of the avant-garde author Djuna Barnes (1892–1982) Andrew Field writes of her sexual attractiveness in her early years: "A tall and handsome young European from Harvard named Putzi Hanfstaengl (later a Hitler confidant) courted her most intensely. A subsequent lover told me that Putzi once suffered an extremely painful burst blood vessel in his penis while dancing with Djuna."

• According to screenwriter Nunnally Johnson, who told the story to Groucho Marx, "Some drunk dame told James Thurber at a party that she would like to have a baby by him. Jim said, 'Surely you don't mean by unartificial insemination!'"

• e. e. cummings once asked John Dos Passos (1896–1970) if he ever dreamed about sex. When he replied in the negative, the poet explained that sex often enters dreams in many disguises. "Tell me what did you dream last night, for example?" cummings insisted. Dos Passos, by now bored with the entire conversation, finally told him, "Why, I dweamed I had a bunch of as-pawagus and was twying to give it to you."

• Emulating the unrepressed pair in D. H. Lawrence's *Lady Chatterley's Lover* (originally entitled *John Thomas*), William Faulkner (1897–1962) and one of his lovers gave names to their sexual parts—hers Mrs. Bowen and his Mr. Bowen. Faulkner even went so far as to register as Mr. and Mrs. Bowen when they stayed at a Santa Monica hotel.

• Maurice C. Bowra (1898–1971), the classical scholar and wit, was swimming with a group of dons in a section of the Thames at Oxford marked "Men

Only" when a boatload of women appeared. The naked dons scurried from the water, hastily covering their genitals with towels and clothing, but Bowra draped his towel over his head. "I believe, gentlemen, that I am recognized by my face," he later explained.

• After publication of *The Sun Also Rises* (1926), Ernest Hemingway (1898–1961) could, in his own words, "no more make love than Jake Barnes," the novel's emasculated hero. His second wife, Pauline, finally suggested that he pray. "There was a small church two blocks from us and I went there and said a short prayer," he later told a friend. "Then I went back to our room. Pauline was in bed waiting; I undressed and got in bed and we made love like we invented it. We never had any trouble again. That's when I became a Catholic." Hemingway admitted long after publishing *The Sun Also Rises* that his heroine, Brett, was based on Lady Duff Twysden, who died at forty-three of tuberculosis. "Her pallbearers had all been her lovers," he recalled. "On leaving the church, where she had had a proper service, one of the grieving pallbearers slipped on the church steps and the casket dropped and split open."

• Peggy Guggenheim (1898–1979), a patron of the arts in many ways, told the story of the time she was traveling back to Paris with Irish playwright Samuel Beckett and they had to stop in Dijon for a night. Beckett asked for a double room and a delighted Peggy assumed he wanted to sleep with her. But when she climbed naked into his bed that night he said no, he certainly didn't want to make love. "Then why did you take the double room?" she demanded. "It was cheaper," Beckett said.

• American poet Hart Crane (1899–1932) frequently prowled the waterfront nights trying to pick up sailors or, failing that, any man available. While staying with Harry and Caresse Crosby in Paris he outdid himself. One morning, after he and his lover had left, Mrs. Crosby found "on the wallpaper and across the pale pink spread, up and down the curtains and over the white chenille rug . . . the blackest footprints and handprints I have ever seen, hundreds of them." He had picked up a chimney sweep.

• Chilean poet Pablo Neruda (1904–1973) once recalled the joy, excitement, and fear of his first sexual experience, with a woman he did not know and never saw. After threshing wheat with a gang of farm laborers he slept with them that night on a "mountain of straw." In the dark night, he remembered,

> Suddenly a hand slid over me . . . then an avid mouth clung to mine and I felt a woman's body pressing against mine, all the way down to my feet. . . . Little by little my fear turned into intense pleasure. . . . How difficult to make love, without making noise, in a mountain of

straw burrowed by the bodies of seven or eight other men, sleeping men who must not be awakened for anything in the world (for any one might be the husband). And yet we can do anything, though it may require infinite care. A little while later, the stranger suddenly fell asleep next to me, and worked into a fever by the situation, I started to get panicky. It would soon be daybreak, I thought, and the first workers would discover the naked woman stretched out beside me. . . . But I also fell asleep. When I woke up, I put out a startled hand and found only a warm hollow, a warm absence. Soon a bird began to sing and the whole forest filled with warbling. . . .

• In his acceptance speech for the gold drama medal of the National Institute of Arts and Letters, Tennessee Williams (1911–1983) told the following story:

One time, Maureen Stapleton received a phone call from a friend who said that so-and-so was getting married, and the caller said, "Why is she marrying that man? You know he is a homosexual," and Maureen said, "Well, what about the bride?" And the caller said, "Well, of course we know she's a lesbian. And you know they're not even getting married by a real minister, but by one who's been defrocked!" And Maureen said, "Will you do me one favor? Will you please invite Tennessee Williams? Because he'll say, 'Oh, they're just plain folks!' "

• One of Truman Capote's (1924–1984) earliest sexual encounters occurred when he was only six and a half and involved a family of passing gypsies. After giving a gypsy woman a bucketful of water, Capote was asked if he wanted to see the gold at the end of the rainbow. He skeptically handed over a few coins to pay for this miraculous exhibition. The woman promptly pulled up her skirts beyond her waist. She was stark naked and her pubic hair had been dyed a stunning gold. After displaying herself for several moments, she finally instructed him that he should not complain, because he had truly seen the real thing.

LITERARY LOVERS

*T*HE BROWNINGS are familiar to all readers, as are Dante and Beatrice, and Petrarch and Laura, and Swift and Stella. But we never seem to hear much about other great literary love affairs, celebrated in the authors' work and often culminating in marriage. Below are some of the greatest:

Abelard and Héloïse
Aristotle and Herpyllis
Boccaccio and Maria Fiammetta
Burns and "Highland Mary" (Mary Campbell)
Byron and Teresa Guiccioli

Catullus and "Lesbia" (Lady Clodia)
Coleridge and Mary Evans
Dante and Beatrice
Scott Fitzgerald and Zelda Sayre
Fitzgerald and Sheilah Graham
Goethe and Frau von Stein
Hazlitt and Sarah Stoddart
   (though later divorced)
Horace and Lesbia
Dr. Johnson and Mrs. Thrale
Keats and Fanny Brawne
Lovelace and "Althea"
   or "Lucasta" (Lucy Sacheverell)
Montaigne and Mlle. de Gournay
Petrarch and Laura
Plato and Archianassa
Poe and Jane Stith Stanard, the "Helen" of his famous poem
Poe and Virginia Clemm
Poe and Sarah Whitman
Poe and Annie Richmond
Poe and Mrs. Shelton
Pope and Martha Blount
Propertius and "Cynthia" (Hostia)
Rossetti and Elizabeth Siddal
Rousseau and Julie (Comtesse d'Houdetot)
Scott and Charlotte Mary Charpentier
Shakespeare and Anne Hathaway
Sidney and Stella (Penelope Devereux)
Spenser and Rosalind (Rose Lynde)
Swift and Stella (Esther Johnson)
Swift and Vanessa (Esther Vanhomrigh)
Voltaire and Émilie (Mme. Châtelet)
Wordsworth and "Julia" (Annette Vallon)
Wordsworth and Mary Hutchinson
Wyatt and Anna (Anne Boleyn)

ALEXANDRE DUMAS *père*

Not all literary lovers were content to confine their adoration to one or two objects of their affection. Alexandre Dumas, well-named *père*, author of *The Three Musketeers* and *The Count of Monte Cristo*, claimed to have fathered 500 illegitimate children, one of whom is generally known as Alexandre Dumas *fils*, author of *La Dame aux Camélias*. (Dumas *fils*, incidentally, is only one of a number of authors who were illegitimate; others include Boccaccio, Erasmus, Alexander Hamilton, August Strindberg, Guillaume Apollinaire, Henry Stanley, Jack London, and T. E. Lawrence.)

In his later years Dumas was reproached for holding a young actress on his lap while two others rumpled his hair. "Sixty is twenty times three," he replied, "which makes me twenty years old for each of these three young ladies."

Other literary lovers seem to have been as busy as Alexandre Dumas. James Boswell told anyone who would listen that he once made love five times in a row, and he contracted gonorrhea seventeen times over a period of thirty years. Casanova was so busy that he loved two women at a time and his memoirs boast that he seduced thousands, although only 116 of his lovers are named in records of the day.

The Italian poet D'Annunzio bragged that more than a thousand husbands hated him, and that his pillows were filled with the soft locks of his ladies. The novelist Frank Harris had Lloyd's of London insure his card file of the 2,000 women he claimed he seduced in his lifetime. (Author of that by-now-tame piece of pornography *My Life and Loves*, Harris also invented a pornographic card game called "Dirty Banshee," complete with playing cards depicting satyrs and goddesses engaged in sexual acts.)

Héloïse wrote to Abelard that she would rather be "thy strumpet" than the empress of Augustus, but her relatives attacked him and cut off his genitals ("those parts of my body whereby I had done that which was the cause of their sorrow") when they discovered he had made her pregnant.

Robert Burns "seduced women without compunction," according to a biographer. "He is known to have sired, in all, not fewer than fourteen children, nine of them out of wedlock. His daughter Elizabeth, by Anna Park, and his legitimate daughter of the same name were born within a month of each other, and Jean Armour, his wife, suckled them both as uncomplainingly as though they were her own third set of twins."

Benjamin Franklin, who was among the most sexually active of early American authors, often visited London's infamous Hellfire Club (see *The Wit of John Wilkes*) and wrote the following in his poem "Advice to a Young Man on Selecting a Mistress":

> *Fair Venus calls, her voice obey,*
> *In beauty's arms spend night and day*
> *The joys of love all joys excel*
> *And loving's certainly doing well.*

Women writers seem to have been more reluctant to brag or lie about their love affairs and have left fewer records of them. George Sand didn't do badly. Mae West recounted many conquests in her memoirs and claimed that she once made love for fifteen consecutive hours. Sarah Bernhardt had more than a thousand lovers, many of them famous artists and writers, including Edmond Rostand. But a French actress-author, Mademoiselle Dubois, seems to be the champion of both sexes; in her memoirs she claimed her affairs totaled 16,527 over a twenty-year period, or about three a day. That puts even the real Don Juan (Spanish nobleman Don Juan Tenorio) to shame. According to tradition, he had a mere 2,594 mistresses.

Odd literary lovers include the German poet Ulrich von Lichtenstein (c. 1200–c.1276), who cut off his finger and sent it to his lady after she complained that he hadn't been wounded in her honor at a tournament in which he fought.

Lack of space makes it impossible to even summarize literary sexual peculiarities. Cato, for some reason, never made love to his wife when it was thundering. English publisher Leonard Smithers (1861–1907), for another example, devoted himself to deflowering virgins. "Smithers loves first editions," Oscar Wilde said.

A LOVING LAVING AUTHOR

Nathaniel Hawthorne invariably washed his hands before he opened and read any letter from his wife, Sophie, not wanting to contaminate anything touched by her.

WRITERS WHO NEVER GOT MARRIED, WERE UNHAPPILY MARRIED, OR FOOLED AROUND

Legend has made Socrates's wife, Xanthippe, the classic shrew and her name has become proverbial for a quarrelsome, nagging, shrewish wife or woman. In *The Taming of the Shrew* Shakespeare writes:

> *Be she as foul as was Florentius' love,*
> *As old as Sibyl, and as curst and shrewd*
> *As Socrates' Xanthippe, or a worse,*
> *She moves me not.*

The gossips in Athens talked much of Xanthippe's terrible temper and she may have literally driven Socrates out into the open and into his marketplace discussions. But then Socrates may have been a difficult husband, and by some accounts is said to have been unusually ugly and dirty in appearance. Xenophon writes that Xanthippe's sterling qualities were recognized by the philosopher, and various historians, including Zeller in his *Vorträge und Abhandlungen* (1875), argue that she has been much maligned, that Socrates was so unconventional as to tax the patience of any woman, as indeed would any man convinced that he has a religious mission on earth.

Shakespeare's supposed troubles with Anne Hathaway, eight years his senior, have often been the subject of speculation, but the "Poet Laureate of the Court of the Faery" deserves a rest from all charges of cuckoldry and his being trapped into marriage. Other male authors unhappier in matrimony than he include:

Addison	Dickens	Milton
Aristophanes	Donne	Molière
Aristotle	Dryden	Racine
Bacon	Euripides	Shelley
Boccaccio	Hazlitt	Steele
Byron	Jonson	Sterne
Dante	Bulwer-Lytton	Wycherley

GIOVANNI BOCCACCIO

A similar list of female authors unhappy with their husbands could certainly be made. One of the unhappiest was Katherine Mansfield, who in 1910 married a singing teacher eleven years older than she and abandoned him the morning after her wedding night.

Writers who solved the problem by not getting married at all include:

Jane Austen
Emily Dickinson
Henry James
Charles Lamb
Alexander Pope
Adam Smith
Henry Thoreau
Voltaire

John Ruskin's marriage to Euphemia ("Effie") Gray was unconsummated because "Ruskin was so appalled at the sight of her pubic hair that he was unable to bring himself to have relations with her."

Writers who strayed from the marriage bed are legion. A letter written by Benjamin Franklin to Mme. Brillon in 1779, when he was over seventy and she was about thirty, might best summarize their philosophy:

What a difference, my dear friend, between you and me! You find innumerable faults in me, whereas I see only one fault in you (but perhaps it is the fault of my glasses). I mean this avarice which leads you to seek a monopoly on all my affections, and not to allow me any for the agreeable ladies of your country. Do you imagine that it is impossible for my affection to be divided without being diminished? The sounds brought forth from the pianoforte by your clever hands can be enjoyed by 20 people simultaneously without diminishing at all the pleasure for me, and I could, with as little reason, demand that no other ears but mine be allowed to be charmed by those sweet sounds.

RABELAISIAN

*B*ROAD, coarse exuberant humor and sharp satire mark the *Rabelaisian* spirit or style. The word honors the prodigious French humanist and humorist François Rabelais (c.1490–1553), who "drank deep as any man," of life as well as of wine. Rabelais, whose voracious appetites would have sufficed for any two ordinary men, started out as a Benedictine monk, later turning physician, but his immortality rests on his ribald writing, a paean to the good life—love, drink, food—a satire on the bigotry and blindness of Church, state, and pedant. Gross and noble at the same time, marked by vast scholarship, his masterpieces are *Pantagruel* (1533) and *Gargantua* (1535). The last book, though Gargantua had been a figure in French folklore, gives us the word *gargantuan*—enormous, gigantic—from the giant prince of prodigious appetite who was eleven months in the womb, as an infant needed the milk of 17,913 cows, combed his hair

with a 900-foot-long comb, once ate six pilgrims in a salad, and lived several centuries. Pantagruel, Gargantua's son, is just as famous and classic a character. Rabelais, incomparably virile and vivacious, knows no counterpart in any contemporary literature, ranking with Aristophanes. He rejoiced in it all, from copulation to corruption. "Ring down the curtain, the farce is over . . . I go to seek the great perhaps," are said to be his last words. "Let her rip!" (*Vogue la galère*), "The appetite grows by eating," and "Do what thou wilt" were his bywords.

ATHLETIC AUTHORS

On a flat road runs the well-train'd runner,
He is lean and sinewy with muscular legs,
He is thinly clothed, he leans forward as he runs,
With lightly closed fists and arms partially rais'd.
　　　　　　　—Walt Whitman, "The Runner"

EDGAR ALLAN POE, who would hardly suggest an athlete to anyone today, long-jumped twenty-one feet while at West Point (and later horsewhipped a scurrilous critic). The infinitely more robust Walt Whitman not only liked to run, but, like Shakespeare, gloried in all sports, celebrating throughout *Leaves of Grass* the joys of archery, baseball, boxing, horse racing, hunting, riding, riflery, sailing, and swimming. He writes in one poem of swimming in the nude and in another of running naked on the sands in Rockaway. Even sweat was holy to him: "The scent of these armpits aroma finer than prayer."

Melville and Crane were athletic in nature, often alluding to sports, and Hemingway was a good wrestler, arm-wrestler, boxer, and shot, although it is literary legend by now that Max Eastman claimed to have wrestled him down in a publisher's office and that Morley Callaghan knocked him out in the ring.

• Sophocles was a great wrestler and ballplayer.

• Ezra Pound mastered jiujitsu and once threw Robert Frost over his shoulder in a restaurant.

• William Butler Yeats took fencing lessons at forty-five.

• Rudyard Kipling was a devoted golfer and invented winter golf, painting his golf balls red so that he could play in the snow.

• Benjamin Franklin was America's first great swimmer, taught swimming, and invented swim fins.

• Lord Byron, who took boxing lessons from an English champion, was a champion swimmer who swam the Hellespont in the breaststroke fashion of his day. Byron wanted to emulate Leander, the legendary Greek, who fell in love with Hero, the priestess of Venus, and swam the Hellespont every night to visit her; Leander drowned one evening, and Hero, mourning him, drowned herself in the same waters. Byron, who made the swim with a Lieutenant Ekenhead of the Royal Navy, did the four miles (allowing for drifting) in one hour and ten minutes, a good time for the modern freestyle, as anyone who has done four miles will attest. Byron alludes to his swim in *Don Juan*:

> *A better swimmer you could scarce see ever,*
> *He could, perhaps, have pass'd the Hellespont*
> *As once (a feat on which ourselves we prided)*
> *Leander, Mr. Ekenhead, and I did.*

• Swinburne, as powerful a swimmer as Byron, frequently dipped in the English Channel during the winter.

• Edgar Allan Poe once swam seven and a half miles from Richmond to Warwick, Virginia, "against a tide . . . running 2–3 miles an hour."

• Eugene O'Neill was a great swimmer, too, one who looked as if he belonged in the water, and when he lived in Rockaway Beach, New York, he swam every day throughout the winter, when the local waters often turn partially to ice.

• Some famous runners in literature are Alexander the Great's courier Ladas, who ran so fast that he never left a footprint; the legendary Queen Camilla of the Volsci, who could run over water without getting her feet wet, according to Virgil in the *Aeneid*; and the Greek Iphicles, who, Hesiod says, could run over standing corn without bending the ears.

Legend has it that the Greek soldier Pheidippides, a champion of the old Olympic Games and the best runner in Greece, was dispatched from Athens to Sparta to announce the arrival of the invading Persians at Marathon and seek a promise of help. Pheidippides covered the distance of 150 miles over mountain trails in two days, only to find that the Spartans were unwilling to send help until after a religious festival they were celebrating. He then ran back to join his forces in the defense of Athens. Though the bronze-clad Greeks were outnumbered two-to-one, their commander, Miltiades, employed revolutionary tactics and they defeated the Persians on the marshy plain near Marathon village. The invaders retreated across the five-mile-long plain to their ships, leaving 6,400 dead behind them, compared to only 192 Greeks killed in the battle. At this time, Plutarch writes, another runner was dispatched to Athens to herald the great Greek victory and when he completed the 22-mile, 1,470-yard distance, he collapsed and died as he gasped, "Rejoice, we conquer!" However, centuries later Robert Browning, mining legend for his poem "Pheidippides," credited Pheidippides with this last heroic run, too, and his name has been associated with it ever since.

LITERARY POLITICIANS AND SPIES

AUTHORS don't usually make very good politicians and it is hard to name one who succeeded in gaining public office. Jack London, H. G. Wells, Henry George, and Upton Sinclair were all soundly defeated in their election bids, as were Norman Mailer, Jimmy Breslin, James Michener, and Hunter Thompson in recent times. The only elected writers I can find are Dante, who served as one of the six governors of Florence; Sir Thomas Malory, who served in Parliament; Montaigne, mayor of Bordeaux; Victor Hugo, who served briefly in the French National Assembly; Snorri Sturluson, twice president of Iceland; Ignatius Donnelly, a United States congressman; John Greenleaf Whittier, a member of the Massachusetts state legislature; Yeats, who held office in Ireland; and the English authors Richard Sheridan and Hilaire Belloc. Belloc, who was elected to the House of Commons in 1906, had to overcome religious prejudice and made his first campaign speech with a rosary in his hands. "Gentlemen," he announced, "I am a Catholic. As far as possible, I go to mass every day. . . . As far as possible, I kneel down and tell these beads every day. If you reject me on account of my religion, I shall thank God that He has spared me the indignity of being your representative." Another British author elected to Parliament was Robert Bontine Graham, but he was suspended for uttering the word *damn* in a speech. In 1989 playwright Václav Havel was elected president of Czechoslovakia.

Authors who were government spies full-time or part-time include Dante, Christopher Marlowe, John Milton, Daniel Defoe, Andrew Marvell, Aphra Behn, Lord Byron, Rudyard Kipling, Somerset Maugham, John Buchan, and Graham Greene.

CARROT TOPS

*A*s Rosalind says of Orlando in *As You Like It*, "his very hair is of the dissembling color." Rosalind corrects herself about Orlando's hair color (calling it chestnut brown), but villains have frequently been depicted in fiction as red-heads, perhaps due to the tradition that Judas Iscariot had red hair. Redheads were once thought to be so deceitful that the fat of dead red-haired men was used as an ingredient in poisons and fish bait. Actually, it's hard to think of many murderous, lying, or unreliable redheads in history aside from Judas, unless you include Lizzie Borden, Nero, Napoleon, Henry VIII, Cromwell, and General Custer. Red-headed authors in history include Shakespeare, Thomas Jefferson, Emily Dickinson, Mark Twain, George Bernard Shaw, Winston Churchill, Sinclair Lewis, and sportswriters "Red" Smith and "Red" Barber. Baudelaire, I'm fairly certain, was the only writer with green hair.

THE WORLD'S GREATEST
LITERARY GLUTTON

*F*ew literary characters, even Gargantua or Trimalchio, ate more within books than Honoré de Balzac did in real life. A typical meal for the French novelist consisted of a hundred oysters for starters; twelve lamb cutlets; a duckling with turnips; two roast partridges; sole à la Normande; various fruits; and wines, coffee, and liqueurs to wash it all down. Thackeray, who died of overeating, never consumed as much at one sitting.

James Russell Lowell once ate "with knife and fork a bouquet of flowers from the centerpiece of a literary supper," but then Lowell another time perched atop a Boston lamppost and crowed like a rooster for hours. Odder still were the ancient Tatars, who devoured books to "consume the knowledge therein."

Talking about all this literary gluttony brings to mind the expression "aesthete's foot," a synonym for gout coined by drama critic John Chapman, which makes reference to the fact that highly educated people are more often afflicted by this malady associated with rich foods.

ALCOHOLIC AUTHORS

Some of these writers died of acute alcoholism. Others were alcoholics whose drinking hastened their deaths—Stephen Foster, for example, died as the result of a fall he suffered while drunk, Robert Greene after a drinking bout when he combined too much wine and pickled herring. Still others, like O'Neill and Fitzgerald, were reformed alcoholics, though their health had been ruined by drink; and Crane, London, Sterling, and Seabrook were alcoholic suicides. One writer, British poet Lionel Johnson, is repeatedly said to have died after he fell off a barstool, though this tale may not be true.

The following long list is far from complete:

Robert Greene, English dramatist (1558–1592)
Charles Lamb, English author (1775–1834)
Christopher Smart, English author (1722–1771)
Charles Churchill, English poet (1731–1764)
Edgar Allan Poe, American author (1809–1849)
Stephen Foster, American songwriter (1826–1864)
Joaquin Miller, American poet (1841–1913)
Ambrose Bierce, American author (1842–1914)
Paul Verlaine, French poet (1844–1896)
Finley Peter Dunne, American humorist (1869–1936)
George Sterling, American poet (1869–1926)
Stephen Crane, American author (1871–1900)
Theodore Dreiser, American author (1871–1945)
Jack London, American author (1876–1916)
Sherwood Anderson, American author (1876–1941)
Sinclair Lewis, American author (1885–1951)
William Seabrook, American author (1886–1945)
Eugene O'Neill, American dramatist (1888–1953)
Edna St. Vincent Millay, American poet (1892–1950)

Maxwell Bodenheim, American author (1893–1954)
F. Scott Fitzgerald, American author (1896–1940)
Hart Crane, American poet (1899–1932)
Klaus Mann, American author (1906–1949)
Dylan Thomas, Welsh poet (1914–1953)

It has been pointed out that such greats as William Faulkner, Ernest Hemingway, Thomas Wolfe, John Steinbeck, Dorothy Parker, Ring Lardner, John O'Hara, Delmore Schwartz, Theodore Roethke, James Agee, Malcolm Lowry, Dashiell Hammett, and Raymond Chandler were at least for a time serious heavy drinkers, if not alcoholics. Even such unlikely writers as O. Henry, Booth Tarkington, and James Whitcomb Riley were probably alcoholics. O. Henry, who had hypoglycemia, once quipped that he always felt "one drink below par," and it's said that Riley, when locked in hotel rooms by his friends to keep him sober, would bribe bellboys to hold a glass of whiskey up to the keyhole so that he could sip it through a straw. I won't name any living writers who have or had drinking problems. Gore Vidal has been quoted in the *New York Times* as saying that "almost all American writers are alcoholic." Purely as personal opinion I'd say that booze does help some writers write well, but that most great literature is written in spite of the addiction, not because of it. Fitzgerald, for example, wrote *Gatsby* while he was on the wagon. The question of why writers drink heavily (or why anyone does) isn't going to be answered here or anywhere else for a while, but following are several works that offer insight into the problem:

Cup of Fury—an antidrinking tract by Upton Sinclair, the nondrinking son of an alcoholic father.

John Barleycorn—an autobiographical work by Jack London, who tells how he started drinking at age five when carrying pail-loads of beer to his stepfather in the fields.

Under the Volcano—a brilliant autobiographical novel by Malcolm Lowry.

The Lonely Passion of Judith Hearne—a novel by Brian Moore.

"Babylon Revisited"—a story by F. Scott Fitzgerald, which his biographer Matthew J. Bruccoli considers "the greatest alcoholism story in American fiction."

THE GIFT OF TONGUES: GREAT LINGUISTS

*E*LIHU BURRITT, "the learned blacksmith" who "forged metal and Greek verbs with equal ease," is often cited as the world's greatest linguist. Burritt (1810–1879), a self-educated man, worked at the anvil all day and taught himself more than forty tongues at night, translating Longfellow's poems into Sanskrit.

He also gave lectures frequently and often walked 100 miles to fill an engagement. But busy and fluent as he was, Burritt is put to the pale by several of the learned linguists below:

• Mithridates (132–63 B.C.)—The king of Pontus, an area in Asia Minor along the Black Sea, was the Caesar of culture as well as warfare in his kingdom, and was a Cesare Borgia of intrigue as well. A renowned collector of artworks and scientific curiosities, his remarkable memory enabled him to master twenty-two languages—more than anyone known in ancient times.

• James Crichton (1560–1582)—This sixteenth-century prodigy in all fields of human endeavor was called "The Admirable Crichton." He mastered twenty-two foreign languages by the time he was fifteen, including Hebrew, Arabic, Syriac, Greek, Latin, and Slavonian, and doubtless learned more before he died. Crichton could repeat verbatim everything that he had ever read. He often gave exhibitions of his linguistic prowess.

• Sir Thomas Urquhart (1611–1660)—The famous English translator of Rabelais was a polyglot who invented a universal language in which every word could be read backward or forward.

• Sequoyah (c.1770–1843)—This Cherokee Indian is one of the few persons in history known to have invented an alphabet for a living language. It took Sequoyah twelve years to invent his eighty-six-character alphabet or syllabary, all of the characters representing the sounds of spoken Cherokee. The alphabet was so logical and simple that it could be learned in a few days and it made an entire illiterate population literate within a few months.

• Cardinal Giuseppe Caspar Mezzofanti (1774–1849)—Lord Byron called the chief keeper of the Vatican library "a walking polyglot; a monster of languages; a Briareus of parts of speech." (Briareus was a mythical giant with 50 heads and 100 hands.) The cardinal could speak 60 languages and 72 dialects fluently and could translate 114 languages, such exotics as Geez and Chippewa among them. Only Bowring (see below) better deserves the title of "a Briareus of languages." It was Mezzofanti who taught Byron to speak Cockney, of all things!

• Jacob Grimm (1785–1863)—One of the pioneer philologists; Grimm's Law gave the principles of relationships in Indo-European languages. Besides his work in comparative philology and the many languages he mastered, Grimm collected with his brother Wilhelm the world-famous *Grimm's Fairy Tales* (1812) and planned and inaugurated the great *German Dictionary* (1852). The dictionary was finally completed by other scholars in 1971, supposedly the world's longest literary gestation.

• Rasmus Rask (1787–1832)—Born in a peasant's hut in Denmark, Rask mastered several languages, including Icelandic (Old Norse) before finishing grade school. He traveled widely and knew firsthand the thirty or more languages he spoke fluently. One of the three seminal thinkers in the science of linguistics (along with Grimm and Bopp), Rask wrote a great number of grammars of single languages.

• Jean-François Champollion (1790–1832)—Champollion, primarily an archaeologist, mastered many languages, and had an expert knowledge of Hebrew before he was ten. He deserves mention here if only because by his use of the Rosetta Stone (a slab inscribed by the priests of Ptolemy V in hieroglyphic, demotic, and Greek found in Rosetta, Egypt, by Napoleon's troops) he established the principles for deciphering Egyptian hieroglyphics and founded the science of Egyptology.

• Franz Bopp (1791–1867)—The German-born Bopp is considered by many to be the founder of modern linguistics. His enormous researches, which resulted in the establishment of the science of comparative grammar, enabled him to master well over thirty languages.

• Sir John Bowring (1792–1872)—This British statesman was a linguist and translator who could read 200 languages and speak 100 fluently, probably the most accomplished linguist in history. As British governor to Hong Kong, however, Bowring wasn't as proficient; he precipitated a war with China by ordering the bombardment of Canton during a dispute.

• Ivar Andreas Aasen (1813–1896)—A Norwegian philologist and lexicographer, Aasen is the only person known to have created a national language. The author had collected all of his country's difficult regional speech for the books he had written on Norwegian dialects. Out of these he fashioned a popular language, or *folk-maal*, which replaced the Dano-Norwegian his countrymen had previously used, to enable all the nation's different dialect users to understand each other. Aasen has been hailed as having "an isolated place in history as the one man who has invented or at least selected and constructed a [national] language." In order to do this, he not only constructed the new composite language, but also wrote poems and plays in the *folk-maal* to help popularize it.

• Lazarus Ludwig Zamenhof (1859–1917)—The Polish inventor of the famous universal language Esperanto learned at least twelve languages in order to create his artificial one, which probably a million people speak fluently today. (See *Pig Latin and Other Invented Languages*.)

• Dr. Harold Williams (1876–1928)—Williams, a New Zealand scholar, spoke twenty-eight languages.

• Leonard Bloomfield (1887–1949)—Chicago-born Bloomfield wrote a book, *Language*, which "almost alone determined the course of linguistic science in the U.S.," according to one authority. Bloomfield believed a student should be able to speak a language before writing it. By practicing what he preached, he mastered a great number of the world's 2,796 languages.

• Mario Pei (1901–1978)—An Italian-born American long recognized as one of the most prominent authorities and authors on language, Pei created the thirty-seven-language course now called "The World's Chief Languages" at Columbia University. Pei spoke many of the world's languages and it was said that with the possible exception of Schmidt (below), he spoke, read, or understood more tongues than any of his contemporaries.

• Charles F. Berlitz (b. 1913)—The American-born head of the famous Berlitz language schools says he "gets by" in some thirty tongues; he has written books teaching people how to speak over twenty-five languages.

• Georges Schmidt (1915–1990)—A French employee of the United Nations Translation Service, Schmidt was able to translate sixty-six languages and speak thirty of them fluently.

• George Campbell (b. 1912)—A former British Broadcasting Corporation Overseas Service employee, Campbell is said to be the world's greatest living linguist, with a working knowledge of fifty-four languages.

May they all end up in the Mohammedan Seventh Heaven, where every inhabitant speaks *70,000* languages.

A BARREN OF WRITERS, ETC.: COLLECTIVE NOUNS FOR LITERARY PEOPLE

*A*CTORS and actresses come in *companies*, *casts*, *troupes*, and even *entrances* (in the Middle Ages a troupe was called a *cry*). Musicians are collected in *bands* and angels in *hosts*. But what are assemblages of writers called? I've heard of *schools*, *staffs*, *tribes*, *teams*, *strings*, *stables*, and *slates* of writers, but these aren't very good terms of venery. A *brood* or *concentration* of philosophic writers, a *column* of journalists, a *frown* of critics, a *fraid* of ghostwriters? Applying collective nouns designed for other animals might help. An *exaltation* (larks) of poets? A *murder* (crows) of mystery writers? A *stud* (horses) or pornographers? A *tidings* (magpies) of greeting-card writers? A *charm* (finches) of stylists? A *shrewdness* (apes) of publishers? A *watch* (nightingales) of editors? A *wickedness* (ravens) or *clowder* (cats) of critics? A *culture* (bacteria) or *brood* (hens) of bibliophiles? A *pitying* (turtledoves) of lonely hearts columnists? A *barren* (mules) or *mute* (hounds) of blocked writers?

LITERARY COLLABORATORS

APART FROM authors of musical comedies like Gilbert and Sullivan or Rodgers and Hammerstein, there seem to be few of this species who have existed and thrived on a permanent basis. English dramatists Beaumont and Fletcher (Francis Beaumont and John Fletcher) collaborated on about fifteen plays from 1606 to 1616. Good friends, these two, of whose partnership John Aubrey said: "There was a wonderful consimility of fancy. They lived together not far from the playhouse, had one wench in the house between them, the same clothes and cloak, & C." John Dryden wrote that Beaumont was "so accurate a judge of plays that Ben Jonson, while he lived, submitted all his writings to his censure, and 'tis thought used his judgement in correcting, if not contriving all his plots." Fletcher is thought to have collaborated with Shakespeare on *Henry VIII*, among other plays.

The French brothers Goncourt (Edmond and Jules) are still remembered for their gossipy histories, art criticism, realistic novels and plays, as well as for the esteemed Prix Goncourt literary prize that Edmond founded in 1896. Another noted French team was Emile Erckmann and Alexandre Chatrian, who wrote plays and novels under the pen name Erckmann Chatrian in the mid- to late nineteenth century. Charles Bernard Nordhoff and James Norman Hall were a famous American pair who wrote nine highly popular books together, beginning with *Mutiny on the Bounty* (1932) and ending with *High Barbaree* (1945). Today's best-known collaborators are Frederic Dannay and Manfred B. Lee, who worked together on hundreds of mystery novels and stories as "Ellery Queen" before Lee died in 1971. Dannay died eleven years later.

Two well-known contemporary collaborators were Maj Sjöwall and Per Wahlöö, Finnish mystery writers of the Martin Beck books. Several years ago seven reporters on Long Island's *Newsday* wrote a well-received parody of a sex novel, but the record number of collaborators on a novel is probably held by the thirteen writers of the critically successful book *The Floating Admiral* (1930). Among the authors of this mystery were such immortals as G. K. Chesterton, Dorothy Sayers, and Agatha Christie, each writer reading previous chapters passed on by the preceding writer and adding a chapter of his or her own.

Some authors find it hard to collaborate with anybody. Jonathan Swift, for example, once went an entire year without speaking to another person. Dr. Johnson, usually a gregarious man, had periods when he climbed trees in order to avoid visitors. Emily Dickinson grew so reclusive that she would speak with visitors only from the next room. Centuries before, Juvenal thought it was a good idea to live in the country to escape the poets who infested Rome.

LITERARY GHOSTS

"Your plots came in last night," Jack London wrote to Sinclair Lewis late in 1910, "and I have promptly taken nine (9) of them, for which same, according to invoice, I am remitting you herewith check for $52.50."

LITERARY GHOSTS range from authors like Sinclair Lewis, who supplied Jack London with short-story plots, to authors who write complete stories, speeches, company biographies, "autobiographies," and other books for a straight fee or for a percentage, with the understanding that they will receive no credit for the work. Often the work is done for celebrities who can't write well, or haven't the time to write well, and these celebrities have recently included everything from former presidents and first ladies to animals, such as Morris the Cat II. (When Morris the Cat I, who had his own best-selling "autobiography," died, the pet food company he represented groomed another cat for his job, commissioning a talented New York author to write up his method of cat care.)

Authors have sometimes hired other writers to do work that they published under their more famous names. Alexandre Dumas *père*, for example, kept a stable of ghostwriters to churn out formula novels, paying them with little more than food and wine, while Colette got her start ghosting stories for her author-husband, who would lock her in a room until she finished each assignment. Charles de Gaulle was a full-time salaried ghostwriter for Marshal Pétain and wrote his book *The Soldier*; even the eloquent Winston Churchill, according to one biographer, hired university students as ghostwriters to do the first draft of *A History of the English-speaking Peoples*. Of the many famous rulers and politicians who had ghosts write their speeches I need only mention Caesar (his secretary may have coined the immortal words *Veni, vidi, vici*), Emperor Nero (Seneca may have written his speeches), George Washington (Hamilton probably did part of his Farewell Address), Ulysses S. Grant (Mark Twain probably wrote his memoirs), Franklin Roosevelt (Archibald MacLeish and Robert Sherwood, among others, wrote his speeches), and Adlai Stevenson (for whom John Steinbeck wrote). Warren Harding *didn't* use ghostwriters on his speeches, prompting H. L. Mencken to comment: "He writes the worst English that I have ever encountered. It is so bad that a kind of grandeur creeps into it."

Ghosts who work for a straight fee have received as much as $200,000, while at least two ghosts have commanded $20,000 a month. A few ghostwriters working for a share in royalties have made up to 50 percent all the way down the line, realizing half a million dollars and more for their efforts.

Rarely, a famous author will be so kind as to lend his name to a work written by a needy unknown colleague. Dumas *père* did this for Paul Meurice in 1845, signing his name to a novel he wrote not a word of so that Meurice could get a 30,000-franc advance from a publisher—enough for him to "bring off a superb marriage." Meurice got married and the world got *Les Deux Dianes*. It was said at the time that "Everybody has read Dumas, but nobody has read everything of Dumas, not even Dumas himself."

GHOSTWRITERS WHO HIRED GHOSTWRITERS

Probably there are a few, but I only know of one: sportswriter Tom Meany. When he was a ghostwriter for Christy Walsh, Babe Ruth's business manager, during the 1936 World Series, Meany was so busy with other assignments that he had to hire a ghost to ghost for him. "The only ghost writer I ever employed," Walsh later wrote (or had a ghostwriter write), "had a ghost writer of his own."

MURDERED WORDMONGERS

PERHAPS READERS will be able to supply the names of more authors murdered by people other than reviewers. I only remember the following unlucky nine. Not a mystery writer among them:

• François Villon, French poet (1431–1464?)—He died shortly after being banished from Paris for killing a priest or for attempted murder, and various legends have transported him to England and elsewhere on the continent in his last years, at least one story having him murdered by a band of cutthroats. No one really knows.

• Petrus Ramus, French religious author (1515–1572)—Ramus was assassinated by enemies and hacked to pieces.

• James Crichton, Scottish savant and author (1560–1582)—Crichton may have been run through the back by hirelings of Italian Prince Vicenzo Gonzaga because he won the favors of a lady sought by the prince; or the prince himself may have run him through while Crichton dallied in bed with said lady; or the prince may have stabbed him with his own sword when Crichton knelt and proffered it by the blade to his superior. In any event, there seems no doubt that Vicenzo done it, despite the fact that he was officially cleared of blame. Five years later, in fact, he interrupted someone else atop another lady he liked and had two archers shoot the poor wight full of arrows.

• Thomas Overbury, English poet (1581–1613)—When he opposed the marriage of his patron, Robert Carr, to the divorced Countess of Essex, the two lovers had him sent to the Tower of London as a prisoner on trumped-up charges. There agents of the Lady Essex slowly poisoned him; four of them later hanged for the murder, while Carr and his wife were convicted and pardoned.

• Meriwether Lewis, American explorer and author (1774–1809)—Best known for his leadership with Captain William Clark of the Lewis and Clark expedition to find an overland route to the Pacific; his sudden death in 1809 is still shrouded in mystery. Lewis had been traveling to Washington to prepare the expedition journals when he died alone in an inn near Nashville, Tennessee. He was probably murdered, though Jefferson assumed that his death was suicidal.

• Paul Leicester Ford, American novelist and scholar (1865–1902)—He was shot to death by his disinherited brother, *not* his brother Worthington Ford, the noted bibliographer and editor. Ford, a prodigy who had written and printed a book at age eleven, and the great-grandson of Noah Webster, was killed by his brother Malcolm in his Brooklyn home after an argument about Malcolm's financial difficulties. Malcolm, once considered the best all-round athlete in America, then killed himself.

• Maxim Gorky, Russian author (1868–1936)—In the Soviet treason trials of 1938 it was charged that Gorky was poisoned, though the evidence isn't conclusive.

• Isaac Babel, Russian author (1894–1939)—He was possibly murdered by Soviet secret police.

• Maxwell Bodenheim, American poet (1893–1954)—The dissolute Bodenheim and his alcoholic, derelict mistress, Ruth Fagin, a twenty-nine-year-old honors graduate of the University of Michigan, let a twenty-five-year-old dishwasher named Harold, who had been in and out of asylums and jails all his life, share their sordid five-dollar-a-week room on Third Avenue, in New York. One night Bodenheim awoke to find the man trying to rape Fagin. When he interfered, Harold reached for a .22 rifle and fatally shot him. Then the psychotic dishwasher stabbed Fagin to death with a kitchen knife, got drunk, and turned himself in to the police.

There has been some speculation that Ambrose Bierce was murdered in Mexico by bandits, but the Swedish author Karl Jonas Almqvist (1793–1866), who lived in America for a time, was *not* murdered. Almqvist may have been involved in the murder of a moneylender by poisoning, the reason he fled to the United States in 1851, where he lived for fourteen years working at odd jobs under various assumed names. He died broken and destitute in Bremen, Germany, where he was known as Professor Carl Westermann "from Westchester in Pennsylvania."

The Greek poet Terpander killed a rival in a brawl and was exiled. English playwright Ben Jonson also killed a man—an actor in his company. He escaped punishment by claiming *benefit of clergy* (see *Neck Verse, Benefit of Clergy*). Benvenuto Cellini describes in his autobiography how he killed one man with a dagger and maimed another. The renowned English philologist Eugene Aram was executed in 1759 for murdering a man who had seduced his wife, though it may be that money was the starving scholar's motive. (See also *Ages of Authors; Alcoholic Authors; Mad Poets.*)

LITERARY JAILBIRDS

Stone walls do not a prison make,
Nor iron bars a cage;
Minds innocent and quiet take
That for an hermitage;
If I have freedom in my love
And in my soul am free,
Angels alone, that soar above,
Enjoy such liberty.

THESE famous words by the Cavalier poet Richard Lovelace are from his "To Althea, from Prison," which he wrote in 1642 while serving seven weeks in the Gatehouse prison at Westminster for presenting a petition to the House of Commons on behalf of King Charles I. The poem also contains words praising Charles ("The sweetness, mercy, majesty / And glories of my King"), yet Lovelace was freed not by any action of the monarch but on a large bail of £4,000 to £40,000 that he posted. In 1648 Lovelace was again imprisoned, by the Commonwealth, and while in prison prepared for press another famous poem "To Lucasta, Going to the Wars," which contains the famous lyric "I could not love thee, Dear, so much / Loved I not Honour more." Lovelace named "Lucasta" for his beloved Lucy Sacheverell, who married another man when it was reported that the Cavalier poet was killed fighting for the French king in France. By the time Lovelace finished his second jail term his great fortune had been exhausted supporting the monarchy. It is said that he died in a cellar, without money to buy food, before his fortieth birthday in 1658.

Other literary political prisoners who wrote famous or infamous works in jail include Wön-Wang, duke of Chou, who was imprisoned by the Chinese emperor Chou-sin and while in prison compiled the *I-Ching* or *Book of Changes*; Wön-Wang's son overthrew the emperor and founded a new dynasty. Sir Walter Raleigh, imprisoned thirteen years in the Tower of London for high treason, wrote his *History of the World* there, and John Bunyan, jailed eleven years for his religious beliefs, wrote *Pilgrim's Progress* while imprisoned. Voltaire penned his poem "Henriade" in the Bastille; Thomas Paine wrote part of *The Age of Reason* in a Paris jail; Daniel Defoe wrote *Hymn to the Pillory* in jail; and Adolf Hitler, who wrote *Mein Kampf* in prison, was one of many politicians who took up the pen while incarcerated.

Probably the author to get in the most trouble for the slightest trifle was English poet William Collingham, who wrote:

> *The Rat, the Cat and Lovell the Dog,*
> *Rule all England under the Hog.*

In this couplet the "Rat" was royal adviser Ratcliff, the "Cat" minister Catesby, the "Dog" Viscount Lovell, and the "Hog" Richard III, whose crest was a boar. Collingham was executed for his wit.

Writers who served time for nonpolitical crimes include Cervantes, who started *Don Quixote* while in prison convicted of "causing shortages" as a navy quartermaster; François Villon, who wrote poems while serving terms for burglary and manslaughter; Oscar Wilde, who wrote *De Profundis, The Ballad of Reading Gaol*, and other works while serving a sentence for homosexuality; and John Cleland, who wrote *Fanny Hill* while in prison for debt. Sir Thomas Malory was a twice-convicted rapist, extortionist, and burglar, yet wrote the tender swan song of English chivalry, *Le Morte d'Arthur*, before dying in prison. Marco Polo, Roger Bacon, William Penn, Diderot, William Cobbett, Smollett, and O. Henry are still other authors who wrote masterworks in prison. In recent times, excellent books have been written by such prisoners as Jean Genêt, Eldridge Cleaver, and many Russian authors, and since the Kennedy assassination and Watergate almost everybody who goes to jail (or almost goes to jail) for a well-publicized crime writes a book about it, the results usually not quite up to *Don Quixote*, or even *Fanny Hill*.

According to a traditional tale, Rabelais had no money to pay his hotel bill or to get to Paris from a small town many miles away. Filling three packets with brick-dust, he labeled them "Poison for the King," "Poison for Monsieur," and "Poison for the Dauphin." His landlord immediately informed on this "poisoner" and he was transported to Paris by the police, explaining his joke there and being set free.

A MENAGERIE OF WILD (AND SOMETIMES CRAZY) WILDLIFE-LOVING WRITERS

OF ALL WILDLIFE writers possibly the wildest was taxidermist Charles Waterton (1782–1864), author of the classic *Original Instructions for the Perfect Preservation of Birds, etc., for Cabinets of Natural History*. Waterton slept with a live sloth (after kissing his pet chimp good night), kept a wildlife preserve devoted solely to scavengers such as buzzards, and gave an annual picnic for animals and lunatics only. The squire always went barefoot on his estate and frequently greeted guests by getting down on all fours, baring his teeth, growling fiercely, and finally sinking his teeth into their legs.

THE ANIMAL PERFORMERS

Edgar Allan Poe often wrote poems with his pet Siamese cat perched on his shoulder, and Restoration poet John Wilmot kept a pet monkey. Lord Byron certainly outdid both of them, usually traveling with "ten horses, eight enormous dogs, five cats, an eagle, a crow and a falcon," while Lord Chesterfield left handsome pensions to his many cats in his will. The green-haired Baudelaire is said to have walked a pet lobster on a leash down the boulevards of Paris, but the wrong man seems to be credited here. Says Arthur Symons of the poet Gérard de Nerval in *The Symbolist Movement in Literature*: ". . . when, one day, he was found in the Palais-Royal, leading a lobster at the end of a blue ribbon (because, he said, it does not bark, and knows the secrets of the sea), the visionary had simply lost control of his visions, and had to be sent to Dr. Blanche's asylum at Montmartre."

Sir Thomas More kept a monkey and many animal pets in his home, but Italian artist "Sodoma" (Giovanni Bazzi, 1477–1549) put him to shame, filling his house with "badgers, squirrels, apes, catamounts, dwarf asses, Barbary race horses, Elbe ponies, jackdaws, bantams, turtle doves, etc." Sodoma had a raven that he taught to speak, and it imitated his voice so well that visitors mistook it for him when it answered the door. "The other animals were so tame that they were always about him," one writer noted, "so that his house resembled a veritable Noah's Ark!"

Other odd literary pets include Christina Rossetti's wombat and Alexandre Dumas *père*'s vulture. Dumas purchased Jurgatha, as he called her, in Tunis and brought her back to Paris, where he tamed her and tried to teach her to speak like Polly—never succeeding, of course, because vultures are silent birds without voice boxes. Dumas had a menagerie of wild animals, including three monkeys he named after literary critics, but poet Dante Gabriel Rossetti, Christina's brother, managed to top him. On the verge of insanity in his last years, Rossetti preferred the company of wild animals to that of people. His house pets included an opossum that slept on the dining-room table, a raccoon that made its home in his dresser drawer, an armadillo that once gnawed its way into a neighbor's house, a peacock that died under a sofa, woodchucks, owls, a raven, a zebra, and a donkey.

PSEUDONYMOUS AUTHORS

T̶HE BEST-KNOWN American pseudonym is Mark Twain, with O. Henry running a close second. Worldwide, this distinction is probably shared by Lenin, Lewis Carroll, and Sholom Aleichem. Some of the noms de plume in the quiz below may not be familiar at all, but try to match the two columns anyway.

AUTHOR	PEN NAME
1. Washington Irving	A. Richard Saunders
2. Solomon Rabinovitch	B. Stendhal
3. Jean Baptiste Poquelin	C. Elia
4. Benjamin Franklin	D. Geoffrey Crayon
5. Charlotte Brontë	E. Maxim Gorky
6. Alexei Pyeshkov	F. Boz
7. Charles Dickens	G. Sholom Aleichem
8. Herman Melville	H. Currer Bell
9. Charles Lamb	I. Molière
10. François Rabelais	J. Alcofribas Nasier
11. Marie Henri Beyle	K. Salvatore R. Tarnmoor
12. Eric Blair	L. Leon Trotsky
13. Leo Davidovitch Bronstein	M. Lenin
14. Samuel Langhorne Clemens	N. Lewis Carroll
15. Hector Hugo Munro	O. O. Henry
16. Mary Ann Cross	P. George Sand
17. François Thibault	Q. Johnston Smith
18. Charles Lutwidge Dodgson	R. Saki
19. François Marie Arouet	S. Voltaire
20. Stephen Crane	T. Mark Twain
21. Armandine Aurore Dupin	U. Katherine Mansfield
22. Kathleen Beauchamp	V. George Eliot
23. William Sydney Porter	W. Anatole France
24. Alexander Pope	X. William March
25. William E. Campbell	Y. George Orwell
26. Vladimir Ilyich Ulyanov	Z. Martinus Scriblerus

ANSWERS: 1. D (also used Jonathan Oldstyle and Diedrich Knickerbocker) 2. G 3. I 4. A 5. H 6. E 7. F 8. K 9. C (name of a clerk in the customhouse where Lamb was employed) 10. J 11. B 12. Y 13. L 14. T 15. R (borrowed from a stanza of the *Rubáiyát of Omar Khayyám*) 16. V 17. W 18. N 19. S 20. Q 21. P 22. U 23. O 24. Z 25. X 26. M (he sometimes signed himself N. Lenin, but the variants V. I. Lenin, Vladimir Ilyich Lenin, or even Nicolai Lenin are all incorrect. Lenin itself is the pseudonym and when signed N. Lenin the N. doesn't refer to *Nicolai*—Lenin's father's name—but represents the Russian conventional symbol for anonymity, which perhaps derives from the Russian *nyet*, "no" or "not." *Lenin* itself has no meaning).

Now try matching these difficult examples. To make them even harder, I removed real first names and last names when they were the same as those of the pen names. One is a man using a woman's name:

AUTHOR	PEN NAME
1. Marie Joseph _____	A. Owen Meredith
2. Gabriel Téllez	B. Thomas Ingoldsby
3. Antonio Grazzini	C. Michael Arlen
4. Secondo Tranquilli	D. William Bolitho
5. _____ Yorke	E. Boris Pilnzak
6. Baroness Karen Blixen	F. Eugène Sue
7. _____ Lorenzini	G. Louis-Ferdinand Céline
8. Ray Stannard Baker	H. Sir Francis Palgrave
9. Dickran Kouyoumdjian	I. Mendele Mocher Sforim
10. Edward Bulwer-Lytton	J. Fiona MacLeod
11. W. B. Ryall	K. Jean Paul
12. _____ Cohen	L. Henry Green
13. Edna St. Vincent Millay	M. Christopher North
14. _____ Destouches	N. Tirso de Molina
15. John Williams	O. Ralph Connor
16. William Sharp	P. Marion Harland
17. Mary Terhune	Q. Isak Dinesen
18. _____ Südfeld	R. Anthony Hope
19. Richard Barham	S. David Grayson
20. John Wilson	T. Ignazio Silone
21. Johann Richter	U. Anthony Pasquin
22. _____ Vogau	V. Hans Fallada
23. _____ Hawkins	W. Carlo Collodi
24. Rudolf Ditzen	X. Nancy Boyd
25. Charles William Gordon	Y. Max Simon Nordau
26. Shalom Abramovich	Z. Il Lasca

ANSWERS: 1. F, French novelist 2. N, Spanish dramatist 3. Z, Italian author 4. T, Italian novelist—*tranquillity*, incidentally, also figures in the full name of the Roman biographer Suetonius, who is properly Caius Seutonius Tranquillus 5. L, English novelist 6. Q, Danish author 7. W, Italian journalist and author of *Pinocchio* 8. S, American author 9. C, Armenian author 10. A, English poet 11. D, English author 12. H, English author, née Cohen, father of the famous poet and anthologist Sir Francis Palgrave 13. X, American poet, sometimes used the pseudonym for prose 14. G, French author 15. U, English satirist 16. J, Scottish poet 17. P, American novelist 18. Y, German author 19. B, English humorist 20. M, Scottish author 21. K, German author 22. E, Russian novelist 23. R, English novelist 24. V, German novelist 25. O, Canadian novelist 26. I, Russian Yiddish novelist.

And if you knew all those, how about these authors, some of whom legally changed their names:

AUTHOR	BORN
1. Woody Allen	A. Henry Wheeler Shaw
2. Joseph Conrad	B. _____ Reizenstein
3. Clio	C. Arthur S. Ward
4. Robert Deitrich	D. Labrunie
5. Jules Romains	E. Emily Brontë
6. André Maurois	F. Ann Sophia Stephens
7. Acton Bell	G. Howard Hunt
8. Ellis Bell	H. Louis Farigoule
9. Sax Rohmer	I. William G. Patten
10. Audax Minor	J. Joseph Addison
11. Gérard Nerval	K. Teodor J. K. Korzeniowski
12. Burt L. Standish	L. John Treat Irving
13. Josh Billings	M. Josiah Holland
14. Sedulous	N. Émile Herzog
15. Elmer Rice	O. George Horatio Derby
16. Squibob	P. John Adams
17. Arthur Stirling	Q. Anne Brontë
18. Philenia	R. William Cobbett
19. Novanglus	S. Alexander Hamilton
20. Peter Porcupine	T. Gilbert Harrison
21. John Quod	U. Allen Stewart Konigsberg
22. Philemon Perch	V. Upton Sinclair
23. Timothy Titcomb	W. Sara Wentworth Morton
24. Pennsylvania Farmer	X. Richard Johnston
25. Jonathan Slick	Y. George Ryall
26. Publius	Z. John Dickinson

ANSWERS: 1. U 2. K 3. J 4. G 5. H 6. N 7. Q 8. E 9. C 10. Y 11. D 12. I 13. A 14. T 15. B 16. O 17. V 18. W 19. P 20. R 21. L 22. X 23. M 24. Z 25. F (the author of the first dime novel *Malaeska: The Indian Wife of the White Hunter* [1860], which sold 300,000 copies) 26. S (along with John Jay and James Madison).

Pen names past and present might indeed fill several scholarly books. Stendhal, for example, was only one of *171* pen names that Henri Beyle used, and we know that, before he adopted the name Lenin, Vladimir Ilyich Ulyanov used a great many pseudonyms, including Petrov, Karpov, Meyer, Frey, Starik, V. Ilyin, Vladimir Ilyin, and K. Tulin. We even know that "Suzy Says" of the *New York Daily News* is Aileen Mehle. But who knows

1. The pseudonymous author who adopted the name of a town?
2. The columnist Samuel Clemens satirized and believed (mistakenly) that he stole the pen name Mark Twain from?
3. Five pen names that are anagrams?
4. The Russian pen name that translates "most bitter"?
5. The pen name that means "peace to you"?
6. The pen name composed of what were once the two most common names in the New York telephone book?
7. The only pseudonymous author ever to win the Nobel Prize?
8. A pseudonym that resulted from mispronunciation?
9. The author who named himself after a bandit?
10. Ten humorous-sounding pen names?
11. The pen names of at least five mystery writers?

ANSWERS: 1. Marie Henri Beyle took Stendhal from the name of a German town. So did Mrs. Markham, Elizabeth Penrose, who took her pen name from Markham, England. 2. Windy, pompous river boat pilot Isaiah Sellers (1802–1864). 3. Voltaire (from Arouet l(e) j(eune), *u* being interchangeable with *v*, and *i* with *j*); Rabelais's Alcofribas Nasier; Fernán Caballero (Spanish novelist Cecilia

Böhl de Faber); Anastasius Grün (German author Anton Alexander von Auersperg); R'Hoone (an anagram of Balzac's first name, Honoré); Thorny Alio (John Taylor, the Water Poet); Ekalennā (the name of Anne Lake in reverse); Dalmocand (George MacDonald); Olphar Hamst (Ralph Thomas); Lewis Carroll (a Latinized form in reverse of the first two names of Charles Lutwidge Dodgson); Bysshe Vanolis (used by James Thomson, who in fashioning one of the oldest of pen names employed Shelley's second name with an anagram of Novalis, the pseudonym of German romantic poet Friedrich von Hardenberg); Alciunus (Calvinus, John Calvin); Onuphris Muralto (Horace Walpole); and "H. A. Large Lamb" (Alexander Graham Bell). 4. Maxim Gorky. 5. Sholom Aleichem. 6. Stephen Crane's Johnston Smith, which he used for his *Maggie: A Girl of the Streets* (1893). 7. Chilean poet Pablo Neruda (Ricardo Reyes), 1971. 8. Boz (Charles Dickens), derived from Dickens's younger brother's mispronunciation of the nickname Moses that Dickens had bestowed on him. 9. American poet Cincinnatus Hiner Miller used the pen name Joaquin Miller because his early writings defended Mexican bandit Joaquin Murietta. 10. Choose from Michael Angelo Titmarsh (William Makepeace Thackeray, who also used Ikey Solomon), Oliver Optic (American author William Taylor Adams), Jake Falstaff (American author Herman Fetzer), Peter Parley (American author Samuel Goodrich), Sam Slick (Nova Scotian humorist Thomas Haliburton), Ned Buntline (American dime novelist Edward Judson), Petroleum V. Nasby (American humorist David Locke), Ik Marvel (American author Donald Mitchell), Fanny Fern (American author Sara Parton), Peter Pindar (English satirical poet John Wolcot), Porte Crayon (American artist and author David Strother, who carried a crayon wherever he went), Josh Billings (American author Henry Wheeler Shaw), Squibob (American author George Horatio Derby), Peter Porcupine (English journalist William Cobbett), John Quod (American author John Treat Irving), Philemon Perch (American author Richard Johnston), Timothy Titcomb (American author Josiah Holland), Jonathan Slick (American author Ann Sophia Stephens). 11. Choose from, among many, many others Carter Dickson (English author John Dickson Carr), Sax Rohmer (English author Arthur Ward), S. S. Van Dine (American author Willard Wright), A. A. Fair (American author Erle Stanley Gardner), Maxwell Grant (American author Walter Gibson, creator of the Shadow), Ellery Queen (pseudonym of collaborators Frederic Dannay and Manfred B. Lee).

And that's about it, except to add that Italian artist Giovanni Bazzi was given the name "Sodoma" because of his sexual preferences, that feminist Marietta Holley (1836–1926) used the pseudonym "Josiah Allen's wife"; that Adolf Hitler's real name was *not* Schicklgruber, as so many sources have it (Hitler's *father* was illegitimate and Hitler's *father*, not Hitler, went by his mother's name); that John Paul Jones's real name was John Paul (he added the Jones to evade capture as a murderer); that Ben Franklin used *seven* pen names; that Sir Walter Scott, Thackeray, Defoe, Washington Irving, Jonathan Swift, and George Bernard Shaw each used *five*; that T. E. Lawrence, Lawrence of Arabia, changed his name to T. E. Shaw in his last years but did *not* use it as a pen name, though he did use the pseudonym J. H. Ross when he published *Seven Pillars of Wisdom*; and that John Kenneth Galbraith *may* have written a book under the pen name Mark Epernay. There are no great mysteries regarding pseudonyms today; even famous literary recluses like J. D. Salinger and Thomas Pynchon find it unnecessary to use them. Everyone knows by now that Genêt of *The New Yorker* was Janet Flanner, that Rebecca West was really Cicily Isabel Fairfield using the name of an Ibsen heroine she once played on the stage, that Mary Renault was actually Mary Challans. Novelist John le Carré is in reality David Cornwell; columnist Tom Wicker of *The New York Times* writes fine mysteries under the pseudonym Paul Connolly; former *Times* art critic John Canaday has written murder mysteries as Matthew Head, and former *Times* book review editor John Leonard wrote excellent criticisms for *Life* under the pen name Cyclops. It's hard to think of one real mystery pseudonym remaining today. We know, for example, that the "Unknown Philosopher" of history was in reality French Marquis Louis-Claude de Saint-Martin (1743–1803), and the mystery pseudonym Junius, for the famous English polemicist of the late seventeenth century, most likely conceals Member of Parliament Sir Philip Francis. As for "The Great Unknown," he was Sir Walter Scott, called that by his publisher because his Waverley novels were published anonymously. One of the few real mystery pseudonyms used today is "Newgate Callendar," the mystery-novel reviewer (or reviewers) for *The New York Times*, although Sue Donem (Pseu-donym), the author of a (panned) television mystery, is still hiding, too.

THE MYSTERY OF "ELLERY QUEEN"

*T*HE LATE Frederic Dannay, a member of the mystery-writing team known as Ellery Queen (the late Manfred B. Lee was his partner) told how the pseudonym was born in an issue of *New York* magazine, offering some insight into the varied ways authors choose pen names: " 'Ellery' was the name of one of my oldest boyhood friends in the small town in upstate New York where I grew up. I had never heard the name before, and I never heard it again till I came finally to the big city and heard of Ellery Sedgwick, the *Atlantic Monthly* editor, and William Ellery Leonard, the poet. It was such an odd name and I liked it so much that I suggested it, and Manny agreed. The second name was arrived at after many experiments. We tried to get a combination of syllables that had a mnemonic value, that once heard or seen would be remembered. We were only 23 years old then; it was 1928, and we had no notion that the word 'queen' had any other meaning: We've had some embarrassing incidents."

MOST COMMON PEN NAME

THERE ARE about 1,000 literary works in English alone of which the author is identified as "By a lady." Strange as it may seem, this is the world's most common pseudonym or anonym.

GODLIKE AUTHORS

NO ONE KNOWS the real name of the Greek philosopher Theophrastus (c. 371–c. 287 B.C.). So eloquent was this pupil of Aristotle's that he is remembered only by the name his master gave him, Theophrastus—meaning that he spoke like a god.

The French visionary preacher and pamphleteer Catherine Theot (1725–1794) believed that she was the mother of God and changed her name (Theot) to *Theos*, "God." She was guillotined during the French Revolution—not for heresy but for her support of Robespierre, whom she had called "her well-behaved son" and "the forerunner of the World."

Chilean poet Vicente Huidobro (1893–1948) often signed himself "The God of Poetry."

CHOOSING THE WRONG NAME

CHILEAN POET Pablo Neruda (1904–1973), born Neftali Ricardo Reyes Basualto, took the pseudonym Pablo Neruda in 1920. Only sixteen, with a father who didn't like the idea of his writing poetry, he picked the name at random from a newspaper to disguise his first efforts. He did not know that the name he chose was that of one of the most beloved of Czech poets, Jan Neruda (1834–1891), whose monument stands in Prague. Later, the Chilean legally adopted his pseudonym.

INITIALLY AUTHORS

*F*EW AUTHORS have consistently signed their work with initials instead of their real names. The most prominent example in recent times is probably *T.R.B.*, used by Richard Strout of the *Christian Science Monitor*, and, of course, *F.P.A.*, used by the late American humorist Franklin P. Adams, is very well known. *H.D.*, the initials with which Hilda Doolittle signed her poems are familiar too, as were the *H.H.* of American novelist Helen Hunt Jackson and the *L.E.L.* of English novelist Letitia Elizabeth Landon (1802–1838). *Q.*, the pen name of English author Sir Arthur Quiller-Couch, is the shortest initial-pseudonym; at least there could be none shorter. (Matthew Arnold used *A.* on his first book of poems.) *Æ* was the pseudonym of Irish poet George William Russell (1867–1935), and American columnist Bert Leston Taylor (1866–1921) signed himself *B.L.T* (no play on the sandwich intended), while Irish journalist and politician Thomas Power O'Connor signed his articles "Tay Pay" O'Connor, using the Irish pronunciation of his first two initials for a semipseudonym.

The anonymous English author of the play *Gammer Gurton's Needle* (1575), possibly John Still, used the pen name Mr. S., and American author Frederic Jesup Stimson (1855–1943) called himself J.S. of Dale. Then there was Oscar Wilde, who signed the *Ballad of Reading Gaol* "C.3.3." (prisoner of Cell 3, third landing) after he was convicted of homosexuality and imprisoned in Reading jail, where he wrote the classic poem. Other interesting initials make up the semipseudonym of E(mma) D(orothy) E(liza) N(evitte) Southworth (1819–1899), author of *The Maiden Widow* and some sixty other romances. In recent times O of the French novel *The Story of O* has become famous. This may be a pseudonym but there are said to be thirteen persons with the real last name O in the Brussels phone book.

Mencken reports that a "Ruth Dunbar, education editor of the *Chicago Sun Times*, was known as Viola before she had to initial her news stories." Other authors who encountered no such problems were Robert Lynd (1892–1970), who took the *y* from his last name to make the pseudonym *Y.Y.*; John Dewey, who as *N.Y.* used the finials of his names; Richard Bentley (1662–1742), known as *I.E.* from the second letters of his name; and Edward Hamilton Aitken, who formed the word *EHA* from his initials.

Author Robert L. Cope fashioned the word and pen names Arrelsea from his initials, but the best-known example of such a nom de plume is Smectymnuus, the name under which an anti-Episcopalian tract was published in 1641. Smectymnuus was a kind of acrostic made from the initials of the tract's authors: *S*tephen *M*arshall, *E*dward *C*alamy, *T*homas *Y*oung, *M*atthew *N*ewcomen, and *W*illiam *S*purston.

A.L.O.E., meant to stand for "A Lady of England," was the pen name of Charlotte Maria Tucker (1821–1893), the author of very popular children's books.

Authors known by initials in place of given names include D. H. (David Herbert) Lawrence, H. G. (Herbert George) Wells, G. K. (Gilbert Keith) Chesterton, E. M. (Edward Morgan) Forster, e. e. (Edward Estlin) cummings, T. S. (Thomas Stearns) Eliot, and H. L. (Henry Louis) Mencken.

Back in the late nineteenth century a writer using the pseudonym X.Y.Z. frequently advertised in the *Times* of London offering to do any kind of literary work for low wages. As a result his pen name became synonymous for "a hack of all work."

MOST DEDICATED BIOGRAPHER

SCHOLAR AND BIOGRAPHER Wilmarth Sheldon Lewis filled a library at Strawberry Hill in Farmington, Connecticut, with "what amounts to a day-by-day account of everything known of every day of British author Horace Walpole's life." Starting when he was twenty-six—he died at age eighty-five in 1979—Lewis amassed a collection at the Lewis Walpole Library that includes 7,000 Horace Walpole letters, five miles of microfilm, and a million file cards. "By his energy, his persistence, his lavish care," wrote historian J. H. Plumb, "W. S. Lewis had collected more information about a single human life [than has ever been done before]."

DR. MY-BOOK

BRITISH SURGEON Dr. John Abernethy (1764–1831) wrote a number of books on medicine, the best-known of which was *Surgical observations on the constitutional Origin and Treatment of Local Diseases* (1809). Very popular with his patients, he got the name Dr. My-book because like many an author he invariably told his patients, "Read my book," whenever a medical question came up.

AUTHORIAL AUTOGRAPHS

I SUPPOSE that most authors are pleased to sign books and give autographs until they are famous enough to attract hordes of autograph hunters. Hunting the autographs of authors has been a common pastime since Roman times, when the signatures of Cicero, Virgil, and others were in great demand and Pliny had an autograph collection worth $15,000. The rarest signatures today are those of Molière and Shakespeare; only five of the former and seven of the latter are known to be in collections around the world. Correspondents often write authors for their signatures and at least one entrepreneur mailed small checks in hopes that the literary celebrities would endorse them. Many authors have rebelled against autograph hunters. Mark Twain sent out this printed refusal:

MARK TWAIN

> I hope I shall not offend you; I shall certainly say nothing with the intention to offend you. I must explain myself, however, and I will do it as kindly as I can. Three hundred letters a year! One's impulse is to freely consent, but one's time and necessary occupations will not permit it. There is no way but to decline in all cases, making no exceptions; and I wish to call your attention to a thing which has probably not occurred to you, and that is this: that no man takes pleasure in exercising his trade as a pastime. Writing is my trade, and I exercise it only when I am obliged to. You might make your request of a doctor, or a builder, or a sculptor, and there would be no impropriety in it, but if you asked either for a specimen of his trade, his handiwork, he would be justified in rising to a point of order. It would never be fair to ask a doctor for one of his corpses to remember him by.

One autograph hunter, hoping to trap Tennyson, who rarely gave his autograph, wrote to the poet asking him which was the best English dictionary, *Webster's* or *Ogilvie's*. Tennyson cut the word *Ogilvie's* out of the man's letter, put it in an envelope, and sent it back to him.

Among the most generous of autographers was Henry Wadsworth Longfellow, who once honored a request for a hundred autographs to be used in a fair held to raise money for Civil War veterans.

SHAKESPEARE'S SIGNATURE

ACCORDING TO autograph expert Charles Hamilton, if one of the seven known signatures of William Shakespeare came on the market, or a new one was discovered, it would sell for $1,500,000, second only to a "Julius Caesar," which would be worth $2 million. As it stands now, no one really knows how

Shakespeare spelled his name. The seven unquestionable genuine signatures are very difficult to decipher. The name is spelled *Shakspeare* on the Bard's own monument, but *Shakespeare* on the tombs of his wife and daughter. Other early variations are *Shakspere* and *Shagspere* (on his marriage license). In 1869 a Philadelphian named J. R. Wise published a book called *Autograph of William Shakespeare . . . together with 4000 ways of spelling the name.*

AGES OF AUTHORS

*T*HE *Poète Maudit* School holds that the most great authors die young, victims of society in one way or another, while the Good Gray Poet Academy teaches that society honors its worthy authors, most of them living to ripe old ages. Neither is right, according to my study of some 2,000 authors, the overwhelming majority of whom died in their late middle years just like everyone else. But Good Gray Poets do seem to outnumber poets who died before their time—at least more than twice as many turned up here. To make this comparison lists were compiled of authors from the 2,000 who died by age thirty-five and those who lived past eighty-five. Arbitrary ages these, but as good as any for such a comparison. The limit at age thirty-five eliminates from consideration many authors who died young (Byron, thirty-six; Nathanael West, Rimbaud, and Robert Burns, thirty-seven; Apollinaire, Thomas Wolfe, and Pushkin, thirty-eight; Dylan Thomas, thirty-nine; Jack London and Poe, forty; Kafka, forty-one; Cesar Pavese, forty-two, Maupassant and Gogol, forty-three; Robert Louis Stevenson and F. Scott Fitzgerald, forty-four; D. H. Lawrence, forty-five; Oscar Wilde, forty-six, etc.). Age eighty-five eliminates such famous authors as Sean O'Casey, eighty-four; Ralph Waldo Emerson, seventy-nine; A. E. Housman and T. S. Eliot, seventy-seven; Robinson Jeffers, seventy-five; William Butler Yeats, seventy-four; Walt Whitman, seventy-three; and many others, not to mention octogenarian and nonagenarian authors alive and writing today. As for society, it rarely gave a damn either way, as can be seen most graphically from the terrible deaths most of the *poètes maudits* suffered. Tuberculosis, war, and suicide, in that order, killed most of these writers and even the suicides often took their lives as a direct result of poverty, persecution, or somebody else's stupidity. (Where the cause of death is unknown, assume this.) Read them and weep, if only for unfulfilled promise, unfinished work:

RALPH
WALDO
EMERSON

age at death   POÈTES MAUDITS

18—Thomas Chatterton, English poet (b. 1752)—the "marvellous boy" of Keats—committed suicide by drinking arsenic; his father—an eccentric *noted only for being able to put his entire fist in his mouth*—long outlived him.

19—John Knowles, English schoolboy poet (b. 1798) befriended by Robert Southey.

21—Henry White, English poet (b. 1785)—died of overwork.

22—James Crichton (the "Admirable Crichton"), Scottish savant and author (b. 1560)—assassinated by hirelings of a prince whose lady he had bedded.

23—Rupert Brooke, English poet (b. 1887)—killed in World War I.

25—Terence, Roman dramatist (b. 135).

26—John Keats, English poet (b. 1795)—died of tuberculosis.

28—William Hill Brown, author of "the first American novel" (b. 1765)—tuberculosis.

29—Christopher Marlowe, English playwright and poet (b. 1564)—probably killed in a tavern during an argument.

29—Stephen Crane, American author (b. 1871)—died of tuberculosis. Once he said: "I haven't time to learn to spell. I haven't time to dress [well] either; it takes an awful slice out of a fellow's life."

29—James Elroy Fletcher, English poet (b. 1884).

29—George Farquhar, Irish dramatist (b. 1678)—died of unrecorded illness caused by extreme poverty.

30—Catullus, Roman poet (84–54 B.C.)—died of unknown illness.

30—John Oldham, English-American satirical poet (b. 1653)—killed by Indians.

30—Percy Bysshe Shelley, British poet (b. 1792)—drowned while sailing near Spezia, Italy.

30—Henry Surrey, English poet (b. 1517)—executed on trumped-up charges of treason.

30—Sergei Esenin, Russian poet (b. 1895)—committed suicide by cutting his wrists.

30—Thomas Randolph, English poet and playwright (b. 1605).

PERCY BYSSHE SHELLEY

31—Nero, Roman emperor, "singer," "poet" (b. 37)—committed suicide, crying, "What an artist dies in me!"

31—Terence, Roman comic dramatist (b. 190 B.C.)—lost at sea.

31—Sylvia Plath, American poet (b. 1932)—committed suicide by inhaling gas from a kitchen oven.

31—Phillis Wheatley, American poet born in Africa and brought to America as a slave (b. 1753?)—a tragic marriage probably contributed to her death from unrecorded causes.

32—Francis Beaumont, English dramatist of Beaumont and Fletcher fame (b. 1584)—died of "overwork of the brain."

32—Frank Norris, American novelist (b. 1870)—died after an appendix operation.

32—Robert Greene, English dramatist (b. 1560)—died of "a surfeit of pickled herrings and Rhenish wine."

32—Joyce Kilmer, American poet (b. 1886)—killed in World War I.

32—Wilfred Owen, English poet (b. 1893)—killed in World War I.

32—Thomas Overbury, English poet (b. 1581)—slowly poisoned in the Tower by agents of the Lady Essex, whose divorce and remarriage he opposed.

33—Thomas Otway, English poet (b. 1652)—choked to death on a piece of bread he had begged money to buy.

33—John Reed, American author and revolutionary (b. 1887)—died of typhus in Russia, buried in the Kremlin.

33—François Villon, French poet (b. 1431)—died in poverty soon after being banished from Paris for attempted murder.

33—Artemus Ward (Charles Farrar Browne), American humorist (b. 1834)—died of tuberculosis.

33—John Suckling, English poet (b. 1609)—the inventor of cribbage, said to have committed suicide.

34—Heinrich von Kleist, German dramatist (b. 1777)—committed suicide.

34—Hart Crane, American poet (b. 1899)—jumped off a ship in mid-ocean.

34—Thomas Nash, English dramatist (b. 1567)—died in poverty after being forced into retirement for his satires.

35—Katherine Mansfield (Kathleen Beauchamp), English author (b. 1888)—died of tuberculosis.

35—Meriwether Lewis, American explorer and author (b. 1774)—was murdered, or possibly committed suicide, under mysterious circumstances.

35—Statius, Roman poet (b. 41).

After all that misery, it's a joy to list the Gray, if not always Good, Poets, who often make Walt Whitman look like a youngster. Many of them got so old because of a perversity to live despite everything and a few starved to death in their eighties, but let's not ruin an essentially happy statistical tale. Indeed, most of these authors were working well at advanced ages. Sophocles, for example, finished his *Oedipus* plays in his eighties; Goethe completed *Faust* at eighty-three; Freud was still writing at eighty-three; at eighty-three Winston Churchill wrote his *History of the English-speaking Peoples*; Somerset Maugham wrote *Points of View* when eighty-four; and George Bernard Shaw wrote his *Farfetched*

Fables at ninety-three. Robert Frost, Tennyson, and Walter Savage Landor wrote excellent poems when well into their eighties, and Thomas Hardy, who never published his poems until he was sixty, wrote some of the greatest lyrics in the language when in his eighties. There's hope for all us aging authors yet:

age at death

109—Jean Frédéric, Count de Waldeck (1766–1875)—published his second book when 100; dropped dead on a Paris street just after turning to eye a pretty woman.

107—Sa'ar, Persian poet (1184–1291)—said by some to have lived "only" to 100, but published all his major works in the last half of his life.

103—Alice Pollock, English novelist (1878–1981)—published *Portrait of My Victorian Youth* in 1971.

100—Charles Macklin, English actor and surprisingly good playwright (1697?–1797).

100—Bernard Le Bovier, French poet (1657–1757).

 99—Melville Cane, American poet (1879–1978).

 98—Rabbi Akiba, Jewish philosopher (d. 130?).

 98—Dr. Margarete Bieber, American historian and author (1879–1977)—her last book was published two years before her death.

 98—Eden Phillpotts, English regional novelist (1862–1960).

 98—Frank Swinnerton, English author (1884–1982).

 97—Edmond Hoyle—English author on games (1672?–1769).

 95—Guy Bolton, American playwright (1884–1979).

 95—James Martineau, English author (1805–1900).

 95—Agnes Repplier, American author (1855–1950).

 95—Norman Angell, English author (1872?–1967).

 94—Magdeleine de Scudéry, French author (1607–1701).

 94—Joseph Shipley, American author (1894–1988).

 94—Madeleine Sendery, French author (1607–1701).

 94—George Bernard Shaw, Irish author (1856–1950).

 94—Roscoe Pound, American educator and writer (1870–1964).

 94—Bliss Perry, American educator and author (1860–1954).

 94—Soho Tokutomi, Japanese author (1863–1957).

 94—Louis Grudin, American poet (1899–1993).

 94—P(elham) G(renville) Wodehouse, English novelist (1881–1975).

 93—Jean de Joinville, French chronicler (1224–1317).

 93—Knut Hamsun, Norwegian novelist (1859–1952).

 92—Joost van den Vondel, Dutch poet (1587–1679).

 92—Jean Henri Fabre, French author (1823–1915).

 91—Ernst Moritz Arndt, German poet (1769–1860).

91—Sarah Josepha Hale, American writer (1788–1879).

91—Irving Bacheller, American novelist (1859–1950).

91—Somerset Maugham, English author (1874–1965).

91—Julia Ward Howe, American poet (1819–1910).

91—Thomas à Kempis, German ascetic and writer (1380–1471).

91—Marion Harland (Mary Terhune), American novelist (1830–1922).

91—Tristan Bernard, French author (1866–1947).

91—Meredith Nicholson, American novelist (1866–1947).

91—Thornton Burgess, American children's writer (1874–1965).

91—Rebecca West, English author (1892–1983).

90—Sophocles, Greek tragedian (496–406 B.C.).

90—Sabine Baring-Gould, English novelist (1834–1924).

90—Izaak Walton, English author (1593–1683).

89—Robert Frost, American poet (1874–1963).

89—John Masefield, English poet (1878–1967).

89—Carl Sandburg, American poet (1878–1967).

89—Bronson Alcott, American philosopher (1799–1888).

89—Walter Savage Landor, English poet (1775–1864).

89—George Santayana, American philosopher and poet (1863–1952).

89—Cardinal John Henry Newman, English theologian and writer (1801–1890).

89—Mary Baker Eddy, American founder of Christian Science and author (1821–1910).

89—Anna Katherine Green, American mystery novelist (1846–1935).

89—Elizabeth Carter, English poet (1717–1806).

89—Henry Miller, American author (1891–1980).

88—Thomas Hardy, English author (1840–1928).

88—Hannah More, English writer (1745–1833).

88—Edwin Markham, American poet (1852–1940).

88—Alessandro Manzoni, Italian novelist (1785–1873).

88—Thomas Wentworth Higginson, American author (1823–1911).

88—Sidney Webb, English author (1859–1947).

88—Julian Hawthorne, American novelist (1846–1934), son of Nathaniel.

88—William Randolph Hearst, American journalist and publisher (1863–1951).

88—Simonides of Ceos, Greek lyric poet (556–468 B.C.).

88—George Saintsbury, English critic (1845–1933).

87—Ezra Pound, American poet (1885–1972).

87—Lyman Abbott, American author (1835–1922).

87—Edward Everett Hale, American author (1822–1909).

87—Lucretia Mott, American reformer and author (1793–1880).

87—Maurice Maeterlinck, Belgian poet (1862–1949).

87—Ida Tarbell, American author (1857–1944).

87—Emily Post, American writer on etiquette (1873–1960).

87—David Pinski, American Yiddish writer (1872–1959).

87—Paul Claudel, French author (1868–1955).

87—Margaret Campbell Deland, American novelist (1857–1945).

86—Charles Hamilton (pseudonym Frank Richards), English author (1875–1961).

86—Kathleen Norris, American novelist (1880–1966).

86—Ernest Seton, American writer and painter (1860–1946).

86—Donald Mitchell (pseudonym Ik Marvel), American author (1822–1908).

86—Agatha Christie, English author (1890?–1976).

86—Theodor Mommsen, German historian (1817–1903).

86—Colley Cibber, English dramatist (1671–1757).

86—John Evelyn, English diarist (1620–1706).

86—Thomas Carlyle, Scottish author (1795–1881).

86—Robert Bridges, English poet (1844–1930).

85—Gelett Burgess, American humorist (1866–1951).

85—John Greenleaf Whittier, American poet (1807–1892).

85—Xenocrates, Greek philosopher (396–314 B.C.).

85—Isaac Newton, English philosopher, mathematician, and author (1642–1727).

85—Harriet Beecher Stowe, American author (1811–1896).

85—H. M. Tomlinson, English novelist (1873–1958).

85—Beatrice Webb, English author (1858–1943).

85—Noah Webster, American lexicographer (1758–1843).

85—Oliver Wendell Holmes, American author (1809–1894).

85—Charles William Beebe, American author, (1877–1962).

85—William Beckford, English author (1759–1844).

85—Decimus Magnus Ausonius, Roman poet (310–395).

(See also *"Yet I Am Learning"* . . .)

HARDY'S LAST BOOK

*T*HOMAS HARDY was proud of his many years, and when preparing his book *Winter Words* for publication in 1928, he wrote in the preface, "So far as I am aware, I happen to be the only English poet who has brought out a new volume of verse on his _____ birthday. . . ." He had intended to write "eighty-ninth" in the blank space, but didn't quite make another birthday—the book appeared posthumously.

FAMOUS LITERARY LAST WORDS

R ELATIVELY FEW dying sayings show the presence of horror, or even great sorrow. As author Barnaby Conrad put it: "After reading thousands of death-bed utterances, one is struck and comforted by how comparatively pleasant dying is reported to be. Especially when compared with other ordeals. Such as living, for example." These are the most memorable last words, glad and sad, that I've come across from the mouths of authors:

• Charles Darwin: "I am not the least afraid to die."
• Johann Wolfgang von Goethe: "More light!"
• Hart Crane, leaping off a ship in mid-ocean: "Good-bye, everybody!"
• Edgar Allan Poe: "Lord help my poor soul." Or, according to another story: "My best friend would be the man who would blow my brains out with a pistol."
• George Bernard Shaw, to a nurse: "Sister, you're trying to keep me alive as an old curiosity, but I'm done, I'm finished, I'm going to die."
• Washington Irving: "Well, I must arrange my pillows for another weary night! When will this end?"
• Lord Byron: "Now I shall go to sleep," or "I must sleep now."
• A. E. Housman, on hearing a risqué tale: "Yes, that's a good one, and tomorrow I shall be telling it again on the Golden Floor."
• Thomas Carlyle: "So this is death—well—"
• Emily Dickinson: "Let us go in; the fog is rising."
• Rabbi Akiba was executed when ninety-eight with the basic tenet of Judaism on his lips: "Hear, O Israel! The Lord is our God, The Lord is one."
• Henrik Ibsen, to a nurse who said he seemed to be improving: "On the contrary!"

- Tolstoy: "But the peasants—how do the peasants die?"
- Henry David Thoreau: "Moose. Indians." (Before this he had been asked if he had made his peace with God and replied, "I was not aware that we had ever quarreled.")
- Cotton Mather: "Is this dying? Is this all? Is this what I feared when I prayed against a hard death? Oh, I can bear this! I can bear it!"
- Socrates: "Crito, I owe a cock to Asclepius; will you remember to pay the debt?"
- Jean Jacques Rousseau: "I go to see the sun for the last time."
- George Wilhelm Hegel: "Only one man ever understood me . . . and he didn't understand me."
- Benjamin Franklin, while being asked to shift his position: "A dying man can do nothing easy."
- Dylan Thomas: "I've had eighteen straight whiskies . . . I think that's the record."
- Rabelais: "I am going to the great perhaps," or "Let down the curtain, the farce is over."
- Lord Chesterfield, greeting a visitor: "Give Dayrolles a chair."
- Voltaire: "Let me die in peace."
- William Wordsworth: "God bless you! Is that you, Dora?"
- Peter Pindar (John Wolcot): "Give me back my youth!"
- Saki (H. H. Munro), killed by a sniper in WWII: "Put that bloody cigarette out."
- William Saroyan, in a suggested posthumous statement to the Associated Press five days before his death: "Everybody has got to die, but I have always believed an exception would be made in my case. Now what?"
- John Taylor, the Water Poet: "How sweet it is to rest!"
- Robert Louis Stevenson bequeathed his birthday (November 13) to his friend Annie Ide, who always complained that her own fell on Christmas Day.
- Friedrich von Schiller: "Many things are growing plain and clear to my understanding."
- Nero: "What an artist dies in me!"
- Charles Churchill, the English poet, who died of drunkenness: "What a fool I've been!"
- Robert Burns: "Don't let the awkward squad fire over my grave."
- Nicolas Boileau: "It is a great consolation to a poet on the point of death that he has never written a line injurious to good morals."
- Denis Diderot: "The first step toward philosophy is incredulity."
- Thomas Hobbes: "I am taking a fearful leap in the dark."
- Horace Greeley: "It is done."
- Dr. Johnson, to Miss Morris: "God bless you, my dear."

• Henry James: "So this is it at last, the distinguished thing."

• John Keats: "Severn—I—lift me up—I am dying—I shall die easy; don't be frightened, and thank God it has come."

• Charles Lamb: "My bedfellows are cramp and cough—we three all in one bed."

• John Locke, on hearing the Psalms read to him: "Oh! the depth of the riches of the goodness and knowledge of God. Cease now."

• Thomas Macaulay: "I shall retire early; I am very tired."

• Harriet Martineau: "I see no reason why the existence of Harriet Martineau should be perpetuated."

• Lady Mary Montague: "It has all been most interesting."

• Christian Nestell Bovee: "There is probably no hell for authors in the next world—they suffer so much from critics and publishers in this."

• P. T. Barnum: "How were the circus receipts today at Madison Square Garden?"

• Heinrich Heine, when a visitor asked if he should call a priest: "No, God will pardon me, that's his line of work." Heine's will read: "I leave my entire estate to my wife on the condition that she remarry; then there will be at least one man to regret my death."

• Isaac Newton: "I don't know what I may seem to the world. But as to myself I seem to have been only like a boy playing on the seashore and diverting myself in now and then finding a smoother pebble or prettier shell than ordinary, whilst the great ocean of truth lay all undiscovered before me."

• Plato: "I thank the guiding providence and fortune of my life: first that I was born a man and a Greek, not a barbarian nor a brute; and next, that I happened to live in the age of Socrates."

• O. Henry: "Turn up the lights; I don't want to go home in the dark."

• Disraeli, on being told that Queen Victoria would like to visit him: "What's the use? She would only want me to take a message to dear Albert."

• Sir Walter Scott, to his family: "God bless you all, I feel myself again."

• Wilson Mizner, on his deathbed as he came out of a coma and a priest tried to comfort him: "Why should I talk to you? I've just been talking to your boss."

• Max Baer: "Oh, God, here I go!"

• James Joyce: "Does nobody understand?"

• D. H. Lawrence: "I'm better now."

• Gertrude Stein: "What is the answer?" she asked, and on hearing no reply from Alice B. Toklas, she murmured: "In that case, what is the question?"

• Torlogh O'Carolan, asking for a cup of Irish whiskey: "It would be hard if two such friends should part at least without kissing."

• Dominique Bouhours, a grammarian: "I am about to—or I am going to—die. Either expression is used."

UNUSUAL ENDINGS

• The Greek lyric poet Anacreon (sixth century B.C.) choked to death on a grape pit. He is the man for whom the Anacreontic Society of London was named; the anthem of this club of amateur musicians, "To Anacreon in Heaven," provided the tune for "The Star-Spangled Banner."

• The Greek poet Terpander was singing one of his songs when somebody threw a fig at him that entered his mouth and lodged in his windpipe, "choking him to death in the very ecstasy of song."

• According to legend, the Greek playwright Aeschylus was killed when an eagle dropped a tortoise on his bald head, mistaking it for a rock.

• The Greek author Lucian, "The Blasphemer," is said to have been ripped to pieces by mad dogs for his impiety.

• Legend holds that the Greek dramatist Euripides was accidentally torn to pieces by a pack of dogs, or ripped apart by a mob of women who objected to one of his plays.

• Diogenes the Cynic was so cynical that he asked to be buried upside down, believing that the world would always be topsy-turvy.

• One legend has it that Aristotle (384–322 B.C.) drowned himself in a channel of water on the island of Euboea in the Aegean when he studied the channel and couldn't explain why its current changed direction some fourteen times a day. The phenomenon remains a mystery to science.

• Mithridates (132–63 B.C.), king of Pontus and a renowned man of letters, guarded himself against poisoning all his days by gradually acclimating his body to large amounts of poison; when he decided to commit suicide, he found that he had mithridatized himself too well. No poison in any amount would work and he had to order a slave to stab him to death.

• The ancient soothsayer Calchas died of laughter on learning that he had just outlived the predicted hour of his death.

• Heraclitus the Obscure (sixth-fifth century B.C.) died after covering himself with cow dung in an effort to get dry and warm.

• The Greek philosopher Zeno tripped and broke a toe when ninety. He pounded the ground with his fists, repeating a line from the *Niobe*: "I come, why call me so!" He then immediately hanged himself.

• Polybius, a Greek historian, died at age eighty-two after falling off his horse.

• One story has it that the Greek courtier Damocles, pursued by a tyrant, killed himself by diving into a cauldron of boiling water.

• While swimming at the Piraeus, the Greek dramatist Menander developed a cramp and drowned.

• Having lit his own funeral pyre at Olympus, the Roman cynic Peregrinus leaped into it and was consumed by the flames.

• The Roman author Lucretius was driven mad by an aphrodisiac and committed suicide when only forty-four.

• After writing a treatise on the pleasures of the palate, the Roman poet Quintus Ennius died of gout.

• When he was seventy-seven, finding that he suffered from an incurable disease, the Roman author Atticus starved himself to death.

• The Roman writers Seneca, Lucan, and Petronius were all ordered by Nero to commit suicide. Opening their veins, they slowly bled to death.

• The Roman poet Helvius Cinna was mistaken by a mob for one of Caesar's assassins and beaten to death.

• Apicius (first century A.D.), perhaps the world's first cookbook author, spent a huge sum—a hundred million sesterces, according to one source—on a fabulous banquet and then took a lethal dose of poison when he realized that he had only about ten million sesterces left (over half a million dollars), hardly enough to support himself.

• The Chinese poet Li Po (c.700–762), a "lighthearted winebibber," fell out of a boat and was drowned when he tried to kiss and embrace the moon's reflection in the water.

• Provençal troubadour Guilhen da Cabestan (fl.13th century) suffered an end similar to the tale of King Tereus in Greek mythology, who was served the flesh of his son by his vengeful wife, Procne. According to one story, Cabestan was killed by a jealous husband, who had the poet's heart cooked as a delicacy and served to his unfaithful wife. After his wife finished her meal the husband informed her that she had eaten the heart of her lover, and she threw herself out the window to her death.

• The Italian poet Petrarch (1304–74) apparently died in 1344 and was laid out for twenty-four hours in accordance with local law; after twenty hours he suddenly sat up in bed and instead of being buried lived another thirty years.

• British philosopher Francis Bacon (1561–1626) died of a cold contracted while he was stuffing a fowl with snow to see how long it would keep the dead body from putrefying.

• British poet and playwright Christopher Marlowe (1564–1593) was killed in a tavern during an argument over the bill with the man with whom he had just dined (although some say that Marlowe was a government agent and that the argument was political in nature).

• Ben Jonson (1573–1637) once remarked in jest that he wanted to be buried standing up. When he died, James I took him at his word and today he still stands below one square foot of Westminster Abbey.

• English author Robert Burton (1577–1640) died on the day he had astrologically predicted years before.

• British historian Thomas May (1595–1650) tied his drooping double chins tight with strips of cloth, which caused his death one day when he swallowed too much and choked.

• English author Sir Thomas Urquhart (1611–1660) died in a fit of laughter upon learning that King Charles II of England had been restored to the throne.

• Seventeenth-century Hungarian poet and national hero Miklos Zrinyi was killed by a wild boar.

• Cervantes and Shakespeare died on the same day, April 23, 1616.

• Molière (Jean Baptiste Poquelin, 1622–1673), the renowned French dramatist, died a few hours after playing the part of a hypochondriac onstage, where he had a fit of coughing blood but finished the performance. The comedy was entitled *La Malade Imaginaire*.

• American author James Otis (1725–1783), who had prayed that he would die in a "heaven-sent" manner, was struck down by a bolt of lightning.

• Fastidious British scholar Dr. Joseph Black (1728–1799) died seated with a bowl of milk on his lap and did not spill a drop.

• American poet Philip Freneau (1752–1832) froze to death in a snowstorm.

• English poet Lord Byron (1788–1824) died when doctors let over "four pounds" of his blood in treating him for malarial fever.

• When he died in 1824, German poet Hans Wilhelm von Thummel was buried in the hollow of an oak in Noebdentz, Germany; the tree containing his body still lives.

• When English poet Percy Bysshe Shelley (1792–1822) died of drowning, he was cremated on the beach on to which his body had washed. For some reason his heart would not burn and it was taken from the fire and given to his wife, Mary Wollstonecraft Shelley, who carried it with her in a silken shroud everywhere she went for the rest of her life.

• American poet William Cullen Bryant (1794–1878) died in June, the month he had selected for his death in his poem "June."

• Russian poet Alexander Pushkin (1799–1837) died in a duel, as did Russian poet Mikhail Lermontov (1814–1841), who had been inspired by Pushkin's death to write the poem "On the Death of a Poet."

• American author Nathaniel Hawthorne (b. 1804) felt all his life that the number 64 had a mystical significance for him and constantly scribbled it on his papers. He died in 1864.

• British novelist William Makepeace Thackeray (1811–1863) died of overeating.

• British poet Francis Thompson committed suicide because he believed that Thomas Chatterton, a suicide two centuries before, had appeared and ordered him to take his life.

• English philosopher and author Jeremy Bentham (1748–1832) left a large sum to London's University College on the condition that his preserved body—which was fitted with a wax head made by a French artist and "enclosed in a mahogany case with folding glass doors, seated in his armchair and holding in his hand his favorite walking stick"—be displayed every year at the annual board of directors meeting. This was done for ninety-two years, until the body was finally made a permanent exhibit at the College.

• Mark Twain was born when Halley's comet appeared in 1835 and died—as he had predicted—when it appeared again in 1910. "It will be the greatest disappointment of my life if I don't go out with Halley's Comet," he had written. "The Almighty has said, no doubt: 'Now here are two unaccountable freaks; they came in together, they must go out together.' "

• Sholom Aleichem (Solomon Rabinovitch) suffered from triskaidekaphobia, fear of the number 13, and his manuscripts never had a page 13. He died on May 13, 1916, aged sixty-three, but the date on his stone in Mount Carmel Cemetery, Glendale, New York, reads May 12a, 1916.

• Revolutionary French journalist Victor Noir (1848–1870) was killed in a duel with Prince Napoleon III. Sudden death caused an erection of his penis, and since his bronze statue was made exactly as he had lain on the field of honor, it shows the unmistakable bulge. For over a century now, women have visited his tomb in Paris's Perè Lachaise cemetery, considering it a fertility symbol.

• Charles Bonaparte (1851–1921), American founder of the Secret Service, an author, and the last of Napoleon's family in America, died of a fall when he tripped over his dog's leash.

• Scottish poet John Davidson (1857–1909) was loaned £250 by George Bernard Shaw to finish his trilogy *God and Mammon*. Davidson, a proud man, instead wrote a historical melodrama to repay the loan, and when the play failed, he was so mortified that he drowned himself in the English Channel.

• British poet Charlotte Mew (1869–1928) killed herself by drinking disinfectant.

• American poet Vachel Lindsay (1879–1931) also killed himself by drinking disinfectant.

• According to literary legend, British poet Lionel Johnson (1867–1902) died of injuries he suffered when he fell off a barstool.

• English novelist Arnold Bennett (1867–1931) died of typhoid fever he contracted from a glass of water he drank in Paris to demonstrate that the water there was perfectly safe.

• Russian poet Sergei Esenin (1895–1925) cut his wrists, wrote a last poem in his own blood, and hanged himself.

• As he lay on his deathbed, British poet A. E. Housman (1859–1936) remembered a passage from Arnold Bennett's novel *Clayhanger* describing *Cheyne-Stokes breathing*—gasping breathing that ceases for up to a minute, continues, and keeps alternating between gasping and breathlessness until death comes. Housman remembered Bennett's description of the "death breathing" named for William Cheyne and William Stokes, the physicians who first described it, and this may have been his *last* memory, for he remembered it when he began the same "death breathing" himself.

• British poet Rupert Brooke (1887–1915) died of blood poisoning from a mosquito bite. He left all his money and future royalties to three poets: Wilfred Gilman, Lascelles Abercrombie, and Walter de la Mare.

• British poet Robert Graves was officially listed as dead in the London *Times* in 1916, though he survived the severe chest wound he had received in battle.

• American novelist and Pulitzer Prize winner Ellen Glasgow (1874–1945) is buried with her dogs Billy, a French poodle, and Jeremy, a Sealyham, in Richmond, Virginia. The dogs, which died first and were the subjects of lengthy obituaries in local papers, were buried in her garden, but she left instructions in her will to have them exhumed when she died and their remains placed in her coffin. She also left instructions that she was to be buried nowhere near her father, whom she hated.

• American authors James Agee and Robert Lowell died in taxicabs.

• Ernest Hemingway read his own obituary in newspapers throughout the world when, unknown to reporters, he survived a plane crash in Africa in 1960. One obituary even said that he had crashed trying to fly the plane to the level that the leopard reached in his famous story "The Snows of Kilimanjaro." Mark Twain and Bertrand Russell also lived to read their own obits in the papers.

• Karl Marx and American author Edmund Wilson died at their desks.

• Evelyn Waugh, says W. H. Auden in *Forewords and Afterwords*, failed in an attempt at suicide because a school of jellyfish held him up and wouldn't let him drown.

(See also *The Ultimate Censor* and *Suicides Caused by Books*.)

LAST NOTE

WHEN EXILED Austrian novelist Stefan Zweig (1881–1942) and his wife, Lotte, committed suicide during World War II, on February 21, 1942, they bathed, dressed in their best, took massive doses of veronal, and lay down together to die in their bedroom, leaving beside them a touching "open declaration" that Zweig, that "European of yesterday," had written:

> Before parting from life of my own free will and in my right mind I am impelled to fulfill a last obligation; to give heartfelt thanks to this wonderful land of Brazil which afforded me and my work such kind and hospitable repose. With every day I have learned to love this country more and more, and nowhere else would I have preferred to rebuild my life from the ground up, now that the world of my own language has been lost and my spiritual homeland, Europe, has destroyed itself.
>
> But after one's sixtieth year unusual powers are needed in order to make another wholly new beginning. Those that I possess have been exhausted by the long years of homeless wandering. So I hold it better to conclude in good time and with erect bearing a life for which intellectual labour was always the purest job and personal freedom the highest good on this earth.

I salute all my friends! May it be granted them yet to see the dawn after the long night! I, all too impatient, go on before.

In a vase on the sideboard was a four-leaf clover.

BEST TRIBUTE TO A WRITER'S WIFE

*T*HE GREAT Italian stylist Pietro Bembo (1470–1547) wrote a letter to a friend telling of the death of his lover and mother of his three children:

I have lost the dearest heart in the world, a heart which tenderly watched over my life—which loved it and sustained it neglectful of its own; a heart so much the master of itself, so disdainful of vain embellishments and adornments of silk and gold, of jewels and treasures of price, that it was content with the single and (so she assured me) supreme joy of the love I bore it. . . . [Her dying words were] "I commend our children to you, and beseech you to have care of them, both for my sake and yours. Be sure they are your own, for I have never deceived you; that is why I take Our Lord's body just now with a soul at peace." Then, after a long pause she added, "Rest with God," and a few moments afterward closed her eyes forever, those eyes that had been the clear-shining faithful stars of my weary pilgrimage through life.

BEST EPITAPH FOR A WRITER
AND HIS WIFE

*I*TALIAN AUTHOR Baldassare Castiglione (1478–1529) mourned for his wife for ten years or so after she died in childbirth. When the gentlest of gentlemen was finally laid to rest in his own tomb, the bones of his wife were brought there to lie beside his own, under the following inscription he had written while he grieved for her: "I do not live now, o sweetest wife, for fate has taken my life from your body; but I shall live when I am laid in the same tomb with you, and my bones are joined with yours."

ELEVEN LITERARY GRAVEYARDS

*A*NY AUTHOR who can't get in the Poet's Corner (*q.v.*) might try Paris's Père Lachaise Cemetery, where probably more literary greats are buried than in any necropolis in the world, including the remains of Abelard and Héloïse, Balzac, Proust, Apollinaire, Daudet, Constant, Romains, Colette, Molière,

Wilde, and Gertrude Stein. It would be impossible to list the resting places of all the world's great writers here, so following are the cemeteries that rival Père Lachaise in the great number of famous literary people buried there.

• *Mount Auburn Cemetery*, Cambridge, Massachusetts—Longfellow, Oliver Wendell Holmes, James Russell Lowell, Amy Lowell, John Bartlett, Francis Parkman, Julia Ward Howe, Nathaniel Bowditch, William Ellery Channing, Charles Eliot Norton, and publishers (whose names still stand on Boston houses) George Mifflin, Charles Little, and James Brown.

• *Highgate Cemetery*, London, England—Coleridge, George Eliot, Karl Marx, Mrs. Henry Wood (author of the best-seller *East Lynne*), Radclyffe Hall (her *Well of Loneliness* was the first novel about lesbianism), Charles Dickens's parents and wife (he is in Westminster Abbey's Poet's Corner), and a memorial to John Galsworthy (who was cremated).

• *Sleepy Hollow Cemetery*, Concord, Massachusetts—Emerson, Hawthorne, Thoreau, Bronson Alcott, Louisa May Alcott, Harriet Mulford Stone (author of *The Five Little Peppers and How They Grew*).

• *The Woodlawn Cemetery*, the Bronx, New York—Melville, Victor Herbert, George M. Cohan (who pronounced his name *Cohen*, incidentally, despite what we've heard in a dozen movies), Nellie Bly (Elizabeth Cochrane Seaman).

• *Forest Hills Cemetery*, Boston, Massachusetts—Eugene O'Neill, e. e. cummings, Edward Everett Hale, William Lloyd Garrison.

• *Bunhill Fields*, London, England—Defoe, John Bunyan, Blake, John Wesley, George Fox. (*Bunhill* is a corruption of *Bonehill*.)

• *Cimitero degli Inglesi*, Florence, Italy—Elizabeth Barrett Browning, Frances Trollope, Walter Savage Landor, Arthur Hugh Clough.

• *Crown Hill*, Indianapolis, Indiana—James Whitcomb Riley, (Newton) Booth Tarkington, Kin Hubbard, Sarah T. Bolton.

• *Cimetière de Montparnasse*, Paris, France—Baudelaire, Maupassant, Sainte-Beuve, Jules Barbey d'Aurevilly.

• *Novo-Divichy Cemetery*, Moscow, Russia—Chekhov, Gogol, Lenin, Stalin, John Reed. (See also *Keats's Gravestone*.)

CEMETERIES FAMOUS IN FICTION

• *Stoke Pogis*, Buckinghamshire, England. The burial ground Thomas Gray wrote about in his "Elegy Written in a Country Churchyard."

• *Holy Trinity Cemetery*, Philadelphia, Pennsylvania. Said to be the "little Catholic churchyard in the heart of the city" in which the lovers in Longfellow's poem "Evangeline" are buried.

• *Glasnevin Cemetery*, Dublin, Ireland. The burial place of the fictional Paddy Dignam in James Joyce's *Ulysses*. Yeats's Maude Gonne (1866–1953) is also buried here.

• *Oakdale Cemetery*, Hendersonville, North Carolina. Home of the angel carved by stonecutter and sculptor William Oliver Wolfe, Thomas Wolfe's father, that inspired Wolfe to write *Look Homeward, Angel*. Wolfe (and O. Henry) are buried in Riverside Cemetery in Asheville, North Carolina.

HARDY'S HEART

*T*homas Hardy's heart was to be buried in Stinsford, England, his birthplace, after the rest of his body was cremated in Dorchester. All went according to plan until the great poet's sister's cat snatched the heart off her kitchen table and disappeared into the woods with it.

LANGSTON HUGHES'S MAILBOX

*W*HILE RECORDING the plight of homeless vagrants on the outskirts of Reno, Nevada, American poet Langston Hughes (1902–1967) took a long walk and came to a small mountain cemetery. On the cemetery gate there seemed to be a mailbox, though there was no house in sight. Upon reaching the gate he realized that what he saw was only an old board that had warped into the shape of a mailbox. The idea of a "mailbox for the dead," however, caught his fancy, and that night he began a story that would fit the title. During his writing he kept recalling his father, whom he had not seen for over thirteen years. The next day Hughes received a telegram informing him that his father had died the night before, at the same time the poet had been writing "A Mailbox for the Dead."

VIRGIL'S FUNERAL FOR A FLY
AND MONUMENT TO A GNAT

*L*EGEND has it that the Roman poet Virgil's (70–19 B.C.) "pet housefly" was given a funeral that cost over $100,000. Musicians, mourners, and eulogists were hired and Virgil's mansion was declared the fly's mausoleum. Later it was discovered that Virgil buried the fly so that he could prevent the state from confiscating his estate and distributing it to war veterans as payment for service—all family cemetery plots and mausoleums being exempt from such confiscation. History confirms that Virgil's property was confiscated and that he got it back, but tells us nothing abut his pet housefly. Many medieval legends arose about Virgil, and though this story may be true, it probably has its basis in Virgil's real troubles with his property, plus a story that he allegedly wrote called the "Culex." Spenser wrote a poem called "Virgil's Gnat," based on the "Culex," in which a sleeping shepherd is stung by a gnat, which bites him only to warn him that he is about to be attacked by a serpent. The shepherd kills the gnat and then slays the dragon, but the next night the gnat reproaches him for his cruelty and the remorseful shepherd builds a monument honoring the gnat.

LIVING MEMORIALS TO WRITERS

LASTHENIA

Among the students who attended the philosopher Plato's lectures at the Academy in Athens was a woman writer named Lasthenia, who stole in by disguising herself as a man. Little more is known of her, but centuries later her story inspired the naturalist Cassini to name the plant genus *Lasthenia* for Plato's pupil. The small genus contains but three species, two native to California and the other to Chile. Tender annual herbs, the showy flowers are yellow, on long, often nodding, peduncles.

NABOKOV'S PUG

This species of butterfly is named for the Russian-born author and lepidopterist Vladimir Nabokov (1809–1977), who discovered *Eupithecia nabokovi McDonough* "on a picture window of (publisher) James Laughlin's Alta Lodge in Utah" in 1943. (I haven't attempted to trace McDonough.) The author of *Invitation to a Beheading*, *Lolita*, *Pale Fire*, and many other novels emigrated from Russia shortly after the Revolution, residing in the United States and Europe. Like Gide he had an interest in butterflies from the time he was a young man. Once a Harvard research fellow in lepidopterology, Nabokov had a number of his discoveries named for him. *Butterfly* itself, incidentally, may be a spoonerism (*q.v.*) for *flutter-by*.

THE TWISS

*P*ERHAPS the most insulting literary memorial on record is to the name of English author Richard Twiss (1747–1821), who wrote an uncomplimentary travel book on Ireland. Some quick-witted Irishman promptly manufactured a chamberpot dubbed a Twiss, on the inside bottom of which was a portrait of the unlucky author, the picture captioned: *Let everyone piss / On lying Dick Twiss.*

CHAPTER THREE

Poets & Poetasters

"POETS ARE BORN, NOT MADE"

*T*RUE, UNTRUE, or partly true, this is an ancient belief, for it is a translation of the Latin *Poeta nascitur, non fit*. In his "To the Memory of . . . Shakespeare" (1623), in which he gave us the immortal lines "Sweet Swan of Avon!" and "He was not of an age but for all time," Ben Jonson wrote: "For a good poet's made, as well as born."

POETIC LICENSE

JOHN DRYDEN called *poetic license* "the liberty which poets have assumed to themselves in all ages, of speaking things in verse, which are beyond the severity of prose." Poetic license is the liberty taken by any writer, especially a poet, to fit the language to his needs, to deviate from conventional form, fact, and even logic to create a desired effect. Everything depends on the end justifying the means, that is, whether the poem (or other piece of writing) works. Luckily, Tennyson presented his poetic license after he wrote the line "Every moment dies a man / Every moment one is born." The literal-minded mathematician Charles Babbage had written him that "if this were true, the population of the world would be at a standstill" and urged him to change the line to: "Every moment dies a man / Every moment 1 1/16 is born."

POETIC JUSTICE

NOVELIST Henry Fielding, also a British justice of the peace, wrote an article for the satirical journal *The Champion* demanding that poet laureate Colley Cibber (1671–1757) be tried for murder of the English language. Fielding was apparently getting even for Cibber calling him "a broken wit."

SAPPHO AND OTHER SAPPHOS

LESBOS, a Greek island in the Aegean Sea off the west coast of Turkey, was a center of civilization in the seventh and sixth centuries B.C. There Sappho, the most famous poetess of her time, taught the arts of poetry to a select group of young women. The legend has never been proved but the romantic ardor of some of Sappho's lyrical poems probably accounts for the tradition that she and her followers engaged in homosexual love, female homosexuality being named for these lesbians, or residents of Lesbos.

Sapphism, from Sappho's name, is a synonym for lesbianism. The poetess, according to legend, threw herself into the sea when spurned by the handsome youth Phaon, but the story is generally regarded as pure invention. Sappho was probably married and had a son. Her simple, passionate verse, characterized by matchless lyricism and vivid use of words, originally formed nine books, only fragments of which (found made into papier-mâché coffins) are extant today because they were destroyed by puritans in the twelfth century. The "Tenth Muse," as she was known, used a four-lined verse form, called *sapphics* in her honor, and is in fact noted for her careful control over meter.

A *Sappho* means a great woman poet as well as a lesbian. Other writing Sapphos include:

The English Sappho, Mary Wortley Montagu (so named by Pope)
The English Sappho, Mary D. Robinson (1758–1800)
The French Sappho, Mlle. Scudéry (1607–1701)
The Scotch Sappho, Catherine Cockburn (1679–1749)
Sappho of Toulouse, Clémence Isaure (c.1450–1510)

FIRST THINGS FIRST

THE FRENCH CRITIC and poet Nicolas Boileau-Despréaux (1636–1711) once introduced a poet to a prospective patron, saying: "Sir, I present to you a person who will give you immortality; but you must give him something to live upon in the meantime."

NAME THOSE SWANS

POETS were called swans because it was said that Apollo, the god of poetry, turned into a swan and swans were believed to sing beautiful songs before they died. Try to identify these swans.

1. The Sweet Swan of Avon   A. Homer
2. The Swan of the Meander   B. John Taylor
3. The Mantuan Swan   C. Francesco Algarotti
4. The Swan of the Thames   D. Shakespeare
5. The Swan of Padua   E. Virgil
6. The Swan of Usk   F. Anna Seward
7. The Swan of Lichfield   G. Henry Vaughan

ANSWERS: 1. D 2. A 3. E 4. B 5. C 6. G 7. F

POET LAUREATE

*I*N GREEK LEGEND Apollo fell in love with and tried to seize Daphne, the daughter of a river, and at her own request she was turned into a bay laurel tree, which became sacred to Apollo. The god ordered that laurel be the prize for poets and victors, this leading to the belief that laurel leaves communicated the spirit of poetry (the ancients put laurel leaves under their pillows to acquire inspiration while they slept) and the tradition of laurel symbolizing excellence in literature. The first *laureates* were university graduates in poetry and rhetoric who were presented laurel wreaths and called "doctors laureate" and "bachelors laureate." Before the title poet laureate was conferred upon any poet in England there were a number of court poets: King Henry I (1068–1135) had a Versificator Regis (King's versifier) named Wale. Ben Jonson was granted a pension by James I in 1616 and was a poet laureate in the modern sense, and Chaucer, Skelton, and Spenser had been called laureates before him; but it wasn't until John Dryden was appointed poet laureate by Charles II in 1668 that the position became official. Dryden lasted twenty years, until he converted to Catholicism and was deposed. The seventeen official poets laureate since his time are:

Thomas Shadwell (1688–1692)
Nahum Tate (1692–1715)
Nicholas Rowe (1715–1718)
Laurence Eusden (1718–1730)
Colly Cibber (1730–1757)
William Whitehead (1757–1785)
Thomas Warton (1785–1790)
Henry James Pye (1790–1813)
Robert Southey (1813–1843)
William Wordsworth (1843–1850)
Alfred, Lord Tennyson (1850–1892)
Alfred Austin (1896–1913)
Robert Bridges (1913–1930)
John Masefield (1930–1967)
Cecil Day-Lewis (1968–1972)
Sir John Betjeman (1972–1984)
Ted Hughes (1984–   )

ALFRED, LORD TENNYSON

Currently the poet laureate is chosen by the sovereign from a list of names submitted by the prime minister when the position falls vacant. Appointments are for life and by custom the poet laureate composes odes for the sovereign's birthday and New Year's odes. Dryden was awarded a pension of £300 and a tierce of canary wine as laureate, but today the annual pension is £70 with £27 more given instead of the wine.

The youngest man to "receive the bays" was Laurence Eusden, appointed when he was only thirty; the oldest was Wordsworth, who was seventy-three when appointed. Tennyson held the office longer than anyone, nearly forty-two years. A number of noted authors rejected the laureateship—including Thomas Gray and Sir Walter Scott—and Robert Browning criticized Wordsworth for accepting it in a poem called "The Lost Leader" ("Just for a handful of silver he left us, / Just for a riband to stick in his coat"), influencing Wordsworth not to write any poetry at all while in office.

It is generally agreed that only Wordsworth and Tennyson among all the laureates can be accounted major poets. The worst poet among the group is undoubtedly Henry James Pye, who wheedled his way into the position by writing insipid poems praising mad George III. One poem that Pye wrote in the monarch's honor was so filled with allusions to birds or "feathered songsters" that it inspired George Stevens to write the famous punning lines:

> *When the Pye was opened*
> *The birds began to sing*
> *Wasn't that a dandy dish*
> *To set before the king.*

AMERICAN POETS LAUREATE

*T*HE UNITED STATES has had a national poet laureate since 1986. She presently is Rita Dove. Sixteen states have designated poets laureate. In the past these positions have been regarded as a joke among serious poets, their ranks described as filled by "hobbyists," but today several distinguished poets stand among them. Here is a complete directory, which I hope will be incomplete by the time this book is published:

Alabama—William Young Elliot
Alaska—Sheila Nickerson
Arkansas—Lily Peter
Delaware—E. Jean Lanyon
Florida—now conducting a search for a poet laureate
Georgia—Dr. John Lewis
Illinois—Gwendolyn Brooks
Kentucky—Lilli Chaffin, Agnes O'Rear
Louisiana—Henry Thomas Volz

Maryland—Lucille Clifton
Nebraska—now conducting a search for a poet laureate
New Hampshire—Richard Eberhart
North Carolina—now conducting a search for a poet laureate
North Dakota—Lydia O. Jackson, Henry Martinson
Oklahoma—Maggie Culver Fry
Oregon—William Edgar Stafford
Tennessee—Pek Gunn
Texas—Dorothy B. Elfstrom
West Virginia—Louise McNeill

Pulitzer Prize winners among these laureates are New Hampshire's Richard Eberhart and Gwendolyn Brooks of Illinois. William Edgar Stafford of Oregon has won a National Book Award.

Only Maryland ($1,000) and West Virginia ($900) pay their poets laureate anything. Brooklyn's poet laureate, Norman Rosten, receives $1 a year.

THE POET LARIAT

THE U.S. also had a "poet lariat," the venerable Bloodgood Cutter. Cutter was named the "poet lariat" by Mark Twain because of his "barbarous rhyme," which reminded Twain of the wild and woolly West. This self-proclaimed poet, who operated a grist and saw mill in Great Neck, New York, from 1817–1906, wrote such stirring lines as:

> *The photographer in front was seen*
> *A getting ready his machine.*

BEST-READ POET

ENGLISH AUTHOR Edward Trelawny once left Shelley standing by the mantel in his study reading at ten o'clock in the morning; when he returned that evening at six, he found the poet, who generally read sixteen hours a day, in the same position, still reading without having moved an inch.

TIMES HAVEN'T CHANGED

PUBLISHING a volume of poetry today is like dropping a rose-petal down the Grand Canyon and waiting for the echo.   —Don Marquis, in his column "The Sun Dial" (1920s)

PUBLISHING POETRY

W︎HEN PAT STRACHAN was a poetry editor at Farrar, Straus & Giroux, she estimated that there were only about 3,400 people in America who regularly bought either hardcover or paperback books of verse. (Another source lowers the number to 2,000.)

According to Poets and Writers, a New York clearinghouse for writers, the number of American poets (which it defines as people who have published ten or more poems in at least three literary magazines) is about 5,000 today.

Quadruple the poet figure (a very conservative estimate) and we have 20,000 poets with but 3,400 poetry readers to buy their books (some of the readers doubtless poets themselves).

Thus commercial houses all together publish only about sixty poetry titles a year.

And the *Atlantic Monthly* receives over 20,000 poems a year, printing about 50.

And *The New Yorker* publishes 150 poems a year from the 3,000 it receives a *week*.

MICHELANGELO, THE SINCERE POET

I︎T ISN'T widely known that Michelangelo was considered an excellent poet in his time. The artist's poetic compositions spanned most of his life and some 300 of his poems survive, the love poems he wrote to the poet Vittoria Colonna and nobleman Tommaso Cavalieri among the best of his day, "strong and sincere," according to one critic.

MICHELANGELO

Interestingly, the word *sincere* has its roots in the quarries where Michelangelo worked before he became an immortal sculptor and an accomplished poet. Roman quarrymen often rubbed wax on marble blocks to conceal their imperfections temporarily. Then the Roman Senate decreed that all marble be "without wax" or *sine cera*, this eventually becoming our word *sincere*, "without deception."

LET SLEEPING POETS LIE

In Xanadu did Kubla Khan
  A stately pleasure-dome decree:
Where Alph, the sacred river, ran
Through caverns measureless to man
  Down to a sunless sea.
        —Samuel Taylor Coleridge

T HE SEMILEGENDARY Greek poet Epimenides, who lived in the time of Solon, is said to have fallen asleep in a cave as a boy while tending his father's flocks and to have awakened fifty-seven years later possessed of all the learning and wisdom in the world. Epimenides lived to a great age, but all that is recorded of his work is a quotation in Titus sometimes attributed to him: "The Cretans are always liars, evil beasts, slow bellies"—which isn't very learned and is less wise. The legend of Epimenides inspired Washington Irving to create Rip Van Winkle.

It is said that Claude Joseph Rouget de Lisle, the French artillery officer who composed the "Marseillaise," or *Hymne des Marseilles*, as Parisians called it, fell asleep at the harpsichord on April 24, 1792, and "on waking he recalled the song as one recalls the impression of a dream, and then wrote down the words and music." The composer Tartini is supposed to have written the "Devil's Sonata" in the same way.

Most famous of all literary works inspired by a dream is Coleridge's "Kubla Khan" (1797). Since the story is usually garbled, here is Coleridge's account of his dream, which was a note prefixed to the original manuscript:

In the summer of 1797, the Author, then in ill health, had retired to a lonely farmhouse between Porlock and Linton, on the Exmoor confines of Somerset and Devonshire. In consequence of a slight indisposition, an anodyne had been prescribed, from the effects of which he fell asleep in his chair at the moment that he was reading the following sentence, or words of the same substance, in "Purchas's Pilgrimage":

"Here the Khan Kubla commanded a palace to be built, and a stately garden thereunto. And thus ten miles of fertile ground were inclosed with a wall."

The Author continued for about three hours in a profound sleep, at least of the external senses, during which time he has the most vivid confidence that he could not have composed less than from two to three hundred lines; if that indeed can be called composition in which all the images rose up before him as *things*, with a parallel production of the correspondent expressions, without any sensation or consciousness of effort. On awaking he appeared to himself to have a distinct recollection of the whole, and taking his pen, ink, and paper, instantly and eagerly wrote down the lines that are here preserved. At this moment he was unfortunately called out by a person on business from Porlock, and detained by him above an hour, and on his return to his room, found, to his no small surprise and mortification, that though he still retained some vague and dim recollection of the general purport of the vision, yet, with the exception of some eight or ten scattered lines and images, all the rest had passed away like the images on the surface of a stream into which a stone has been cast, but, alas! without the restoration of the latter!

Mary Shelley's *Frankenstein, or The Modern Prometheus*, Horace Walpole's *The Castle of Otranto*, and *The Phoenix* by A. C. Benson were also conceived in dreams.

"In the small hours one morning," Robert Louis Stevenson's wife wrote, "I was awakened by cries of horror from Louis. Thinking he had a nightmare I awakened him. He said angrily: 'Why did you awaken me? I was dreaming a fine bogey tale.' " The "bogey tale" turned out to be *Dr. Jekyll and Mr. Hyde*.

THE FIRST POETRY CONTESTS

*T*HE JAPANESE in the late seventeenth century held *hokku*, or *haiku*, contests that became a national craze, with so much money wagered on them that the government finally had to prohibit them. Long before this, in about 300 B.C., the Chinese poet Lu, noble minister to the Queen of Ch'in, was known "to hang a thousand pieces of gold at his gate as a reward to any man who should better his compositions by a single word." The Greeks held poetry contests at many of their religious festivals and the poet Sophocles won first prize in one of them when he was eighty-five. In an early Roman poetry contest Lucan was unlucky enough to win first prize over the Emperor Nero, who ordered him to stop writing poetry.

LOVING WORDS

I LOVE YOU the more in that I believe you have liked me for my own sake and nothing else. I have met with women whom I really think would like to be married to a Poem and be given away by a Novel.

—John Keats to Fanny Browne
in a letter of July 8, 1819

"HOW DO I LOVE THEE? LET ME COUNT THE WAYS"

THE FAMOUS LINE above from Elizabeth Barrett Browning's *Sonnets from the Portuguese* is one of the best known in English poetry, but up until recently no one thought to actually count the ways Miss Barrett loved Mr. Browning in sonnet XLIII. Author Randy Cohen did so and published the results in *New York* magazine, finding that she loved him "nine ways—unless 'with the breath, / Smiles, tears, of all my life' is considered to be three separate ways, in which case she loved him a total of eleven ways."

Sonnets from the Portuguese was written for Robert Browning and published, reportedly, only because Browning felt: "I dared not keep to myself the finest Sonnets written in any language since Shakespeare's." There is, of course, no Portuguese model for the sonnets and they were probably called *Sonnets from the Portuguese* because Browning's pet name for his wife was "my little Portuguese."

ODE ON A FAKE GRECIAN URN

Thou still unravished bride of quietness,
Thou foster-child of Silence and slow Time.

NO ONE would argue that Keats's poem isn't among the most beautiful and best-known of all time, but the vase that he wrote about might be called kitsch today. The story begins with the great English potter Josiah Wedgwood (1730–1795), who achieved his fame despite the fact that a childhood illness had caused the amputation of his right leg, barring him from using the potter's wheel. Wedgwood, the grandfather of Charles, was already renowned as a potter when he began to make the ubiquitous blue-and-white vases that still bear his name. These he copied from the famous "Grecian" Portland Vase that Sir William Hamilton, husband of Lord Nelson's great love, purchased when he served as ambassador to Naples, and sold to the Duchess of Portland before she donated it to the British Museum in 1784. The Portland Vase, however, wasn't a Greek vase as everybody thought, but a heavy-handed Roman imitation from the time of Augustus. The vase that John Keats saw and that inspired him to write his poem was a Wedgwood copy of a Roman copy of a Greek vase—a doubly fake Grecian urn:

Beauty is truth, truth beauty—that is all
Ye know on earth and all ye need to know.

A ROSE IS A ROSE IS A ROSE

WHAT Gertrude Stein really wrote in her poem "Sacred Emily" was "Rose is a rose is a rose is a rose," but her words have been misquoted as the above so often that she might as well have written "a rose is a rose is a rose." In her prose Gertrude Stein had no use for nouns: "Things once they are named the name does not go on doing anything to them and so why write in nouns." But in poetry, she felt: "You can love a name and if you love a name then saying that name any number of times only makes you love it more." And poetry is "really loving the name of anything."

BLIND BARDS

Bards were once blinded so they would not wander from the tribe. In recent memory a writer describes such a blindman in Rhodesia. The Slav word for bard was blind. —H. G. Wells, *Outline of History*

FEW MODERN SOCIETIES place such a value on bards, and bards that are blinded in prisons today are blinded so they won't see, not so they won't wander. The greatest blind authors in history are doubtless Homer and Milton, whose stories are well known. Louis Braille, who invented the Braille system of printing, and Helen Keller, the author of ten books, are also familiar figures. Not so familiar are publisher Joseph Pulitzer, for whom the Pulitzer Prize is named, who went blind at age forty; blind historian William Hickling Prescott, who had secretaries to read source material to him; and blind Argentine writer Jorge Luis Borges. James Thurber was blinded in one eye in a childhood accident and went all but completely blind in his later years, while James Joyce, Charlotte Brontë, and Aldous Huxley had very poor eyesight.

THE GENTLEST POETS

*T*HE ELEVENTH-CENTURY Hindu poet Tulsi Das is said to have been able to communicate with the creatures of the woods. He had been adopted by a mystic and survived after his parents, believing he had been born under an unlucky star, exposed him in the forest. Rabindranath Tagore, another great Indian poet, was so gentle a spirit that "squirrels climbed upon his knees and birds perched in his hands."

POET IN A CAGE

A robin redbreast in a cage
Puts all heaven in a rage.
      —William Blake

*T*HE CAGED BIRD'S human counterpart didn't live in dark ages past. Ezra Pound was kept in a cage by the United States Army at the Disciplinary Training Camp outside Pisa while awaiting trial for treason after World War II. The ungilded cage of steel standing in the middle of the prison yard had a tar-paper roof, bars all around, no shades or other coverings, and was brightly lighted at night. For six months, from May to October 1946, Pound lived and wrote in his cage, a guard always stationed outside. None of the prisoners was allowed to look or listen while the caged bird sang.

"MAD POETS"

'Tis very difficult to write like a madman,
but 'tis a very easy matter to write like a fool.
      —Nathaniel Lee

*A*LL POETS are mad," Richard Burton wrote in *The Anatomy of Melancholy*, but I could only come up with about a dozen mad poets, despite the popularity of the phrase, and I had to include a few novelists, a short-story writer, and a dramatist as well. In any case, a study of 2,000 authors revealed the following who were or could have been certified:

• Lucretius, Roman poet (99?–55 B.C.)—Driven mad by a love potion administered by his wife, he committed suicide.
• Nathaniel Lee, English dramatist (1653–1692)—Died insane in a drunken fit while escaping from Bedlam.

• Christopher Smart, English poet (1722–1771)—Perhaps drank himself mad; often knelt down and prayed in the middle of the street; was committed to a madhouse and later died "within the rules of the king's bench" (that is, while living in an area specified by a court that had imprisoned him for debt). A line he wrote in the madhouse: "Let Ross, House of Ross, rejoice with the Great Flabber Dabber Flat Clapping Fish with hands."

• William Collins, English poet (1721–1759)—Went mad and was under his sister's care for the last five years of his short life.

• Robert Southey, English poet laureate (1774–1843)—"Excessive mental work" and his wife's insanity affected his mental state in his latter years, when he lost his memory and died of what was called "softening of the brain."

• John Clare, English poet (1793–1864)—Became insane in 1837, when barely forty; died in an asylum.

• Charles Lamb, English author (1775–1834)—Spent a year in an insane asylum as a youth. His sister Mary Lamb (1764–1847) later killed their mother in a fit of insanity, and despite his own weak condition, Lamb took care of her all his life to keep her out of the asylum.

• Lady Rosina Bulwer-Lytton, English author (1802–1882)—Wrote a novel, *Cheveley, or The Man of Honour* (1839) in which her husband, Baron Bulwer-Lytton, was the villain; Rosina would also follow her husband around while he campaigned for political office and viciously heckle him; she was certified insane in 1858 and was in the care of a physician for a short time.

• Leopold von Sacher-Masoch, Austrian novelist (1836–1895)—Richard von Krafft-Ebing named *masochism* after the characters depicted in his novels; he died in an asylum after his wife had him committed for trying to strangle her, but she had had him declared legally dead ten years before this.

• Count Donatien Alphonse François de Sade, the French author (1740–1814)—The man who gave us *sadism* died at the lunatic asylum at Charenton, where he spent all but thirteen of his last thirty-seven years.

• Gérard de Nerval, French author (1808–1855)—Once wrote an analysis of his condition right after an attack of insanity; hanged himself with an apron string from a lamppost.

• Guy de Maupassant, French author (1850–1893)—Went insane in his last years and died in a sanitarium.

• Ezra Pound, American author (1885–1972)—Remanded to a hospital for the criminally insane after being indicted for treason in 1945, the indictment dismissed when Robert Frost and others interceded for him; released from St. Elizabeths in 1958, he went to Italy, where he died fourteen years later.

A case could also be made for Russian author Nikolai Gogol, who fell into a deep depression in his last year when a religious fanatic told him that his imaginative work was "sinful," destroyed a number of his manuscripts, and died. Jonathan Swift suffered from Ménière's disease all his life and for a time before his death was insane, while William Cowper, England's greatest poet in his lifetime, suffered mental breakdowns all his life, and Virginia Woolf was insane in her last year of life. The English authors Smart, Gray, Dr. Johnson, Boswell, Blake, and Lamb all suffered mental afflictions, too, at one time or another. Emily Dickinson was so reclusive that she would speak to visitors only from another room. Edgar Allan Poe, who wrote that he "became insane with long intervals of horrible sanity," might also qualify. Rimbaud explained it this way: "The poet makes himself a 'seer' by a long, immense, and rational derangement of all the senses. All forms of love, suffering, and madness. He exhausts all poisons in himself and keeps only their quintessences." It is futile to psychoanalyze seers. A poet as eminently sane as Yeats was considered balmy by some as he strode along the streets of Dublin, "mouthing poetry . . . swing[ing] his arms like a flail, unconscious of the alarm and bewilderment of the passersby." But, as Irish poet Katharine Tynan wrote, even the Dublin policemen eventually got used to him, saying "Shure, 'tisn't mad he is, nor yet drink taken. 'Tis the poethry that's disturbing his head," and left him alone.

The best lines I know by a mad poet were written in the lunatic asylum on Blackwells Island, New York, in the late nineteenth century by McDonald Clarke ("The Mad Poet of Broadway"):

> *Now twilight lets her curtain down*
> *And pins it with a star.*

THE NAMBY-PAMBY POET

Timely blossom, infant fair,
Fondling of a happy pair,
Every morn, and every night
Their solicitous delight,
Sleeping, waking, still at ease
Pleasing without skill to please.
Little gossip, blithe and hale,
Tattling many a broken tale.

AMBROSE PHILIPS (c.1675–1749), a sample of his seven-syllabled lines on children quoted above, had the bad luck to accidentally tread on Alexander Pope, easily the most venomous and malicious of the great English poets. Politics and envy had more to do with his misfortune than insipid versifying, for Philips was a Whig and Pope a Tory, and in 1713 the Whig *Guardian* praised the Whig pastoral poet as the only worthy successor of Spenser. This inane criticism enraged "the Wasp of Twickenham" and initiated a quarrel between the two poets that Samuel Johnson described as a "perpetual reciprocation of malevolence." Pope was particularly incensed because *his* pastorals had appeared along with Philips's in *Tonson's Miscellany* (1709)—he thought it obvious that he, if anyone, was Spenser's successor. The articles praising Philips in *The Guardian* implied a comparison with Pope's pastorals, being subtle veiled revenge on him because he had dedicated his poem "Windsor Forest" to Tory Secretary for War George Granville. So Pope ingeniously submitted an anonymous article to the periodical that ostensibly attacked his own poems. In it, as Dr. Johnson observed in *The Lives of the Poets*, he drew a "comparison of Philips's performance with his own, in which, with an unexampled and unequalled artifice of irony, though he himself always has the advantage, he gives the preference to Philips." Pope ridiculed *The Guardian*'s principles and disposed of Ambrose's pretensions in one bold stroke, but Philips was not to be deterred. Pope's rival continued to turn out his pastorals and even indited a few pieces to political powers like Sir Robert Walpole:

> *Votary to public zeal,*
> *Minister of England's weal*
> *Have you leisure for a song,*
> *Tripping lightly o'er the tongue,*
> *Soft and sweet in every measure,*
> *Tell me, Walpole, have you leisure?*

Such slavish deference won him coveted political appointments in Ireland, including a seat in Parliament there and a judgeship, not to mention Pope's further enmity. "Lo, Ambrose Philips is preferred for Wit," Pope sneered, and Ambrose in turn denounced him as an enemy of the government. But it was Philips's juvenile poems that did him most harm. He wrote several simple sentimental little poems (1725–1726) for the infant children of his friends Lord John Carteret and Daniel Pulteney including his "To Mistress Charlotte Pulteney," quoted above. These adulatory verses were addressed "to all ages and characters, from Walpole steerer of the realm, to Miss Pulteney in the nursery," and, if any further inspiration was necessary, may have inspired Pope to criticize Ambrose, among others, in his essay, "Martinus Scriblerus . . . or the Art of Sinking in Poetry" (1727). Pope scoffed that the verses were "little flams on Miss Carteret" and soon Pope's friend poet and composer Henry Carey joined in the fray. Carey, rumored author of the words and music of the British anthem "God Save the King," satirized Ambrose in the same book that included his popular song, "Sally in Our Alley," parodying Philips's juvenile poems and writing: "So the nurses get by heart Namby-Pamby's little verses." The author of *Chrononho-

tonthologos, a burlesque which he characterized as "the Most Tragical Tragedy that was ever Tragedized by any Company of Tragedians," even entitled his parody of Philips *Namby-Pamby*, taking the *amby* in each word from the diminutive of *Amb*rose and the alliterative *p* in the last word from Philips. Pope, ready for the kill, seized upon the contemptuous nickname and included it in the edition of his enormously popular poem "The Dunciad" that appeared in 1733. The phrase immediately caught the public fancy and, much to his distress, Ambrose Philips saw his name come to mean not only feeble, insipidly sentimental writing, but a wishy-washy, weakly indecisive person as well.

Philips wasn't really as bad as all that. In collaboration with his friend Swift he wrote *The Distrest Mother* (1712), a play taken from Racine, and certain of his poems have been included by anthologists as excellent examples of Augustan poetry, formal yet impassioned. As for his verses for children, several critics find them charmingly sentimental rather than saccharine or sickeningly sentimental, and Dr. Johnson, among others, says they are his pleasantest work. Some of Philips's poems are indeed flies in the amber of English verse, as one writer claims, but the man owes his enduring ignominy more to the almost unparalleled age of literary and political intrigue in which he lived and the childish love of intrigue and fame that characterized its great poet Alexander Pope. Not bad at all are poems like Philips's "The First Pastoral":

> *The flowers anew, returning seasons bring!*
> *But beauty faded has no second spring.*

Yet the unlucky poet is remembered by the word taken from Carey's poem about him:

> *Namby-Pamby's doubly mild,*
> *Once a man and twice a child . . .*
> *Now he pumps his little wits*
> *All by little tiny bits.*

TWIN POETS

Tirupati Winkatakawulu was the pseudonym of the Indian "twin poets" whose real names were Diwakarla Tirupati Sastri (1870–1950) and Cellapilla Wenkatasastri (1871–1921). The "twin poets" were good friends who wrote all their work together for over twenty-five years and called themselves by one name—the only known case of poets doing this. Great scholars as well as bards, they revived a broad interest in Indian Telugu literature with their many original poems and translations. The "twin poets" were also famous for their phenomenal memories, exhibited in the performance of *satawadhana*, where, according to one biographer, "a hundred interrogators were each given line-by-line a complete verse of four stanzas on a subject prescribed by each, the hundred verses finally repeated complete [by the twin poets] without missing a syllable." Wenkatasastri continued to write under the pseudonym for thirty years after his fellow poet died.

English authors Henry Vaughan (1622–1695) and Thomas Vaughan (1622–1666) are perhaps the only real twins known as distinguished poets in world literature. Henry, the elder and by far the greater, is known today as the Swan of Usk for his mystic religious poetry, while Thomas, who often wrote under the pseudonym Eugenius Philalethes, enjoyed a considerable reputation as a writer on magic and mysticism. Both men were imprisoned as Royalists in their youth, and they jointly authored the volume of poems *Thalia Rediviva: the Pastimes and Diversions of a Country Muse* (1678).

A PERFECTIONIST POET

VIRGIL was always diffident about his own poetic powers. When he died in 19 B.C., he left instructions that all twelve books of the *Aeneid* be burned because the manuscript wasn't polished enough. The work was saved when the Roman Emperor Augustus ordered that it be published despite Virgil's last wish. Later, Virgil's poem became so venerated that it was used to foretell the future by opening a volume at random to a page, that page supposedly predicting what was to come.

AN ODE ON TOOTH DISEASES

IN 1840 New York dentist Solyman Brown wrote and published a long ode, *Dentologia: A Poem on Diseases of the Teeth in Five Cantos*. One of the strangest of literary works, it gives after the poem a list of 300 qualified American dentists of the time.

POETS WHO CAME TO DINNER

DO YOU have a list of poets who overstayed their welcomes? If not, any such list would have to begin with that peerless poet Maxwell Bodenheim, who stayed at William Carlos Williams's house for several months faking a broken arm, cast and all, until Williams, a doctor, finally examined it and kicked him out. Poet Robert Lowell wasn't so audacious; he simply took poet Allen Tate literally when told that he'd have "to pitch a tent on the lawn" if he wanted to stay at his house. Lowell bought a tent at Sears and lived on Tate's lawn for the next two months, never realizing that Tate's words were just an expression meaning he had no room in his house.

POETS AND MUSIC

Music hath charms to soothe a savage breast (said Congreve, in allusion to Orpheus's flute), but surprisingly enough it doesn't always charm a poetic one. Byron, for example, had no ear for music, Pope "preferred a street barrel-organ to Handel's oratorios," Southey hated music, it gave "actual discomfort" to Samuel Rogers, Sir Walter Scott couldn't carry a tune, and Dr. Johnson "could scarcely discern one tune from another." Other authors who disliked music included Hume, Burke, Fox, Pitt, Newton, Lamb, Thoreau, and Emerson, who once wrote: ". . . it looked to me as if the performers were crazy, and all the audience make-believe crazy, in order to soothe the lunatics and keep them amused."

MUSIC OF THE SPHERES

Forward and backward rapt and whirled are
According to the music of the spheres.
　　　—Sir John Davies, *Orchestra* (1596)

*P*YTHAGORAS taught that the spheres or planets made harmonious sounds as they moved through space and Plato said that on each planet there sat a siren singing a sweet song that harmonized with the songs of all the other planets. Even farther back, in Biblical times, the Book of Job relates that "the morning stars sang together." The reasoning behind the belief is that "planets move at different rates of motion . . . and must make sounds in their motion according to their different rates," but "as all things in nature are harmoniously made, the different sounds must harmonize." At any rate, Chaucer, Milton, and Shakespeare all believed this theory and gave expression to it in poetry, although the phrase "music of the spheres" didn't find its way into the spoken language until the end of the eighteenth century.

ALL THIS FOR A SONG!

*T*HE WORDS, reflecting an often prevalent attitude toward poetry, were spoken by William Cecil, Lord Burleigh, England's Lord Treasurer under Queen Elizabeth, when the Queen ordered him to give £100 to Spenser as a royal gratuity for writing *The Faerie Queene*. Burleigh was later satirized in Richard Sheridan's *The Critic*, in which he comes on stage but never talks, just nodding because he is much too busy with affairs of state to do more. This inspired the expression "Burleigh's nod" and "as significant as a shake of Burleigh's head."

NAME THAT BARD

1. The Bard of Twickenham	A. Robert Burns
2. The Bard of Prose	B. Shakespeare
3. The Bard of Avon	C. William Wordsworth
4. The Bard of Ayrshire	D. William Cowper
5. The Bard of Rydal Mount	E. Shakespeare
6. The Bard of All Time	F. Boccaccio
7. The Bard of Olney	G. Alexander Pope

ANSWERS: 1. G　2. F　3. B or E　4. A　5. C　6. B or E　7. D

THOMAS GRAY'S ODE "The Bard" is based on the tradition that Edward I, after conquering Wales, ordered all Welsh bards killed because bards were supposed to denounce the king and predict all the evils that would befall him.

The souls of the dead never rested, according to an ancient Gaelic belief, until a bard sang an elegy over the deceased.

AN AUTHOR NAMED FOR A POEM

FREDERICK DOUGLASS (1817–1895), the former slave and abolitionist who edited the antislavery newspaper *North Star* and wrote the influential *Narrative of the Life of Frederick Douglass* (1845), was named for Lord James Douglas, the brave outlawed fictional hero of Sir Walter Scott's poem "The Lady of the Lake."

Booker T. Washington earned his unusual first name when a child because of his great love for books. Cicily Isabel Fairfield took her pen name, Rebecca West, from the name of an Ibsen character. Françoise Sagan, born Françoise Quoirez, took her pseudonym from Princesse de Sagan, one of Proust's minor characters.

A FOOD NAMED AFTER A POET'S CURLS

Schillerlocken is curled chips of smoked fish commemorating the curly locks of Johann Christoph Friedrich von Schiller (1759–1805). Schiller was one of the founders of modern German literature, only Goethe overshadowing him in his time. Forced to become a doctor, while serving in military school against his wishes, Schiller finally rebelled and lived as a fugitive for a while. A poet, dramatist, historian, and philosopher, Schiller also wrote ballads, many of which became German favorites as well. Schiller was an idealist who hated tyranny in any form and his philosophy influenced Einstein and Schweitzer among other famous Germans. The trilogy *Wallenstein* (1795) and *William Tell* (1804) are two of his masterworks and his renowned *Ode to Joy* (1785) was used by Beethoven in the chorale finale to his Ninth Symphony. Schiller, incidentally, often inspired himself to write by smelling a drawerful of rotten apples.

Another odd thing named for a poet was the Goethemobile, an automobile manufactured in 1902.

ENGLAND'S FATTEST MAJOR POET

ENGLAND'S POET LAUREATE John Dryden (1631–1700) was given the name "Poet Squab" by John Wilmot, the Earl of Rochester, because he was so fat.

But then Rochester, a former patron of Dryden, had the poet waylaid and beaten by masked thugs at Rose Alley in Covent Garden because he suspected that Dryden had anonymously attacked the king and himself in a book of the day. Dryden wasn't a very witty man—though he did once tell his wife that if she were a book he'd want her to be an almanac so that he could change her every year—and it is almost certain that he had nothing to do with the satiric attack.

"WITHOUT RHYME OR REASON"

Francis Bacon said that Sir Thomas More, chancellor to Henry VIII, once told a friend who had versified a rather poor book he had written: "That's better! It's rhyme now, anyway. Before it was neither rhyme nor reason." But More's witty remark isn't the basis for our expression meaning lacking in sense or any other justification, fit for neither instruction nor amusement. Used in English since the early sixteenth century the phrase is simply a translation of the medieval French saying *na ryme ne raison*.

POETASTERS

Swans sing before they die; 'twere no bad thing
Did certain persons die before they sing.
—Samuel Taylor Coleridge

Nineteenth-century Scottish poet William McGonagall is probably the only writer to have his work collected because it is so bad. In his introduction to McGonagall's selected poems, published by the Stephen Greene Press, James L. Smith writes that the poet is "unquestionably the great master of Il-literature in the language." McGonagall, who never lost faith in his greatness, and actually outsells Browning and Tennyson in Great Britain today, attracted audiences to his poetry readings because people who had read his poems wanted to pelt him with rotten tomatoes and eggplant. There have been others who have produced poems with more mechanical regularity than McGonagall; present-day Indian poet Sri Chinmoy composed 843 poems within a day in 1975, and another time turned out 16,031 paintings in a day. But no one's poetry has been as consistently bad as the Scottish bard's, which has been called "the worst poetry ever written, in any language, at any time." A sample of his work from "The Battle of Abu Klea":

> *Oh, it was an exciting and terrible sight,*
> *To see Colonel Burnaby engaged in the fight;*
> *With sword in hand, fighting with might and main*
> *Until killed by a spear thrust in the jugular vain.*

According to Ring Lardner, an ex-coroner once wrote an ode to his mother with the line: "If perchance the inevitable should come . . ."

A POETASTER WITHOUT PEER

JOHN DENHAM begged the King not to execute fellow poet George Wither (1588–1667) for treason. So long as Wither lived, Denham explained, he, Denham, "would not be accounted the worst poet in England."

BAVIUS AND MAEVIUS

VIRGIL sarcastically criticized the two minor Roman poets Bavius and Maevius in his Third Eclogue and Maevius was further criticized by Horace in his Tenth Epode, making their names forever synonyms for inferior poets or poetasters. In 1794 William Gifford wrote a fierce satire called *The Baviad* and followed it two years later with the *Maeviad*. The works attacked the Della Cruscan school of poetry, founded by sentimental young English poets living in Florence at the time. Ironically, the school bore the name of Florence's famous Accademia della Crusca (Academy of Chaff) whose object was purifying the Italian language, sifting away its chaff.

Virgil himself was much criticized in his time. One critic published eight volumes consisting of resemblances between lines in Virgil's poems and earlier Roman poems.

CHEAPEST POEM EVER SOLD

SOME, perhaps most, of the world's greatest poems have been published without the poet receiving a farthing, cent, or sou, and a great number weren't even published until years after the poets died. Such has always been the market for literature everywhere. But what about famous poems that have been paid for with a pittance, quality not considered here? Vachel Lindsay's pamphlet *Rhymes to Be Traded for Bread*, which he took on the road with him and did just that with, has to qualify, as does Julia Ward Howe's "The Battle Hymn of the Republic," for which the *Atlantic Monthly* paid $4. But perhaps Maxwell Bodenheim's "Strange Lady" sets some kind of a standard. The bohemian poet, addicted to alcohol, drugs, and sex, not necessarily in that order, wrote just about anything before his life ended in a sordid murder. The novels *Replenishing Jessica* and *Naked on Roller Skates* were among his masterworks. His poem "Strange Lady" originally sold for 25 cents. This was paid in the late 1920s by a passerby in Greenwich Village who spotted the verse pinned to the public toilet door that served as Bodenheim's showcase for his wares when he was flat broke.

Robert Graves said that there was no money in poetry, but that there was no poetry in money, either.

WELL-PAID POETS

THE MOST a poet ever got for a poem is the $312,000 Abul Qasim Mansur received from his sultan, who kept four hundred other poets besides him in constant attendance (see *Longest Poem in Any Language*). But the ninth-century Arab poet Hammad was given $237,500 and two slave girls by the Caliph Hisham just because he was able to recall and recite a poem the caliph could not remember. The Persian poet Merwan received 5,000 pieces of gold, *ten* slave girls, and a horse for one brief ode.

Pindar got $10,000 for the processional song in which he wrote the lines "renowned Athens, rich, violet-crowned, worthy of song, bulwark of Hellas, god-protected city." When he died, his seventh Olympian ode was inscribed in golden letters on a temple wall in Rhodes, the city the poem honored.

Pope made over £5,000 on his translation of Homer. Among the highest-priced of all American poems was Longfellow's "The Hanging of the Crane," which sold for $3,000 in 1873. The highest-paid American poet, or versifier, was Edgar Guest, who averaged about $130,000 a year at the height of his fame. Rudyard Kipling's poem "If" (1910) has been translated into twenty-seven languages, making it "The Most Successful Poem," according to the *Guinness Book of Records* (1992).

LIMERICKS

PEOPLE WERE composing limericks at least half a century before the name of Ireland's County Limerick was bestowed upon them in 1898. In fact, some authorities say that the limerick form was invented by Shakespeare. Iago does indeed sing an imperfect limerick in *Othello*:

And let me the canakin clink, clink;
And let me the canakin clink:
A soldier's a man;
A life's but a span;
Why, then, let a soldier drink.

Mad Tom (Edgar) in Shakespeare's *King Lear* also recites a limerick with faulty meter:

Saint Withold footed thrice the 'old:
He met the nightmare, and her nine fold;
*   Bid her alight*
*   And her troth plight,*
And aroint thee, witch, aroint thee!

Others (citing little evidence) say that the limericks were brought back to Ireland's Limerick in the early 1700s by Irish soldiers returning from the French war, while a third school contends that the form originated with the nursery rhymes found in *Mother Goose Melodies for Children*, which may have been published by Elizabeth Goose (or Vergoose) in 1719:

Hickory, dickory, dock!
The mouse ran up the clock.
The clock struck one—
The mouse ran down,
Hickory, dickory, dock!

All forms of the limerick appear in *Mother Goose Melodies*. Besides the five-line form with a nonsense line above, we find the variety that ends the first and fifth lines with a geographical name:

As I was going to Bonner,
Upon my word of honor
*   I met a pig*
*   Without a wig*
As I was going to Bonner.

And the form with a new rhyme sound in the fifth line:

There was an old soldier of Bister
Went walking one day with his sister,
*   When a cow at one poke*
*   Tossed her into an oak,*
Before the old gentleman missed her.

Mother Goose Melodies may not have been printed until 1760, long after those Irish soldiers returned to Limerick (see *The Real Mother Goose*), but there seems to be no doubt that both Shakespeare's efforts and the Mother Goose verses were in the air and strongly influenced the next two books to advance the limerick: *A History of Sixteen Wonderful Old Women* (1821) and *Anecdotes and Adventures of Fifteen Gentlemen* (1822). It was the latter book that author-artist Edward Lear (1812–1888), who once gave drawing lessons to Queen Victoria, cited as the source of his idea for the form in his still popular *Book of Nonsense* (1846). One of Lear's first limericks goes:

> *A flea and a fly in a flue*
> *Were imprisoned, so what could they do?*
> *Said the flea, "Let us fly!"*
> *Said the fly, "Let us flee!"*
> *So they flew through a flaw in the flue.*

In another limerick, Lear continued to use the five predominantly anapestic lines rhyming *a a b b a*, but he printed the third and fourth lines as one line, which is still permissible today:

> *There was a Young Lady of Lucca,*
> *Whose lovers completely forsook her;*
> *She ran up a tree and said Fiddle-dee-dee!*
> *Which embarrassed the people of Lucca.*

Lear's nonsense verses were labeled "learics" by M. Russell, a Jesuit wit of the day, the new word a play on the poet's name, on the fact that what he wrote weren't dignified *lyrics*, and on the *leering* grins some such verses even then produced. It wasn't until fifty-two years after Lear's book was published that the one-stanza poems, by now immensely popular, were dubbed *limericks*. One theory has it that the name arose then because a popular contemporary song had a chorus that went, "We'll all come up, come up to Limerick." It seems that there was also a party game played at the time in which each guest would invent and recite a *learic*, the whole group singing the chorus about "coming up to Limerick" between recitations. This may be true, but it is just as likely that the *learic* became the limerick because people believed that the verses were invented in Ireland, the land of poetry.

THE FLESHLY SCHOOL
OF POETRY AND THE SNARK

*T*HE SNARK never was until Lewis Carroll created him in his mock-heroic nonsense poem "The Hunting of the Snark" (1876). Its name a portmanteau word formed from *snake* and *shark*, the *snark* was an elusive creature and just when its hunters thought they had tracked it down they found that their quarry was the very dangerous *Boojum* (another word Carroll coined). *Snark-hunter* has since been applied to dreamers and visionaries. The poet and painter Dante Gabriel Rossetti always believed that Carroll was caricaturing him in "The Hunting of the Snark," but this wasn't the case. Rossetti had been viciously attacked from a moral point of view by the poet Robert Buchanan in an article in the *Contemporary Review* called "The Fleshly School of Poetry." Published in October 1871 under the pseudonym Thomas Maitland, the article accused Rossetti, Swinburne, William Morris, and several others of being decadent, morally irresponsible, and obsessed with the sensual and carnal. The piece created great controversy, Swinburne replying at length to the charges in his *Under the Microscope* (1872), and Rossetti, who got the brunt of the criticism, never really recovered from it. His tendency toward gloomy brooding increased, he avoided people, overused narcotics, and became paranoid enough for friends to fear his sanity. Rossetti had many delusions like one about the snark until his death in 1882, at age fifty-four. (See also *Poems from the Grave*.)

GRUES

Grues are grisly little comic poems with sadistic content and trick last lines. They are sometimes called "Little Willies" in honor of the "hero" of so many, but the name grue, coined by Robert Louis Stevenson from *gruesome*, is more appropriate. Though their content is never worse than the daily news, most grues are anonymous:

> *Willie poisoned father's tea;*
> *Father died in agony.*
> *Mother looked extremely vexed;*
> *"Really, Will," she said, "what's next?"*

Sometimes a grue will even offer a little social comment:

> *Daddy and his tidy spouse*
> *Killed all the kiddies in the house.*
> *Mommy said, when Daddy cried,*
> *"Come on, let's get the ones outside!"*

Not many writers have signed their names to grues. Even the most accomplished "gruester" of them all, Henry Graham, wrote his *Ruthless Rhymes for Heartless Homes* under the pseudonym Col. D. Streamer. Here are three samples of Graham at his best, or worst:

BABY

Baby in the caldron fell,—
See the grief on mother's brow!
Mother loved her darling well.
Darling's quite hardboiled by now.

THE STERN PARENT

Father heard his children scream,
So he threw them in the stream,
Saying as he drowned the third,
"Children should be seen, not heard!"

TENDER HEARTEDNESS

Billy, in one of his nice new sashes,
Fell in the fire and was burned to ashes.
Now, although the room grows chilly,
I haven't the heart to poke poor Billy.

RHYMING SLANG AND RHYMING TERMS

*T*RUE RHYMING SLANG originated with Cockney street vendors and criminals in the nineteenth century. It is a cryptic device, a secret language or argot where words are formed by substituting a phrase whose last word rhymes with the word the speaker wants to keep secret—as *holy friar* (liar); *storm and strife* (wife). Often only one rhyming word is used, as in *pies* (eyes), and sometimes to make the code even less obvious, the rhyming word is dropped; for instance, *storm and strife* for wife would become simply *storm*. Partridge's *Dictionary of Slang and Unconventional English* and other works are filled with thousands of examples of Cockney and Australian rhyming slang. Here are just a few:

apples and pears—stairs
Aristotle—a bottle
Bo-Peep—sheep
bows and arrows—sparrows
china plate—mate
Duke of York—talk
fisherman's daughter—water
Lady Godiva—fiver (five pounds)
love and kisses—the Mrs.

Mother Hubbard—cupboard
Oliver Twist—fist
plates of meat—feet
plates—feet
Robin Hood—good
sixty-four—whore
sugar and honey—money
twist and twirl—girl
weeping willow—pillow

Rhyming slang has never caught on in America, but we do use many rhyming terms, both intentional and unintentional. The uncontrived accidental or unintentional ones include, among many others: *BVDs, claptrap, crumbbum, deadhead, double-trouble, gyp joint, hi-fi, hotshot, hustle-bustle, nitwit, pickle puss, plug-ugly, rootin' tootin', scuttlebutt, slaphappy,* and *worrywart.* There are even more intentional or "jive" rhyming terms. They include: *boogie-woogie, chillerdiller, eager beaver, footsie wootsie, glad rags, hell's bells, hootchie cootchie, in like Flynn, jeepers creepers, la-di-da, lamebrain, legal eagle, loose as a goose, passion ration* (WWII teenage slang for a boyfriend), *wheeler-dealer,* and *zoot suit.* None of these rhyming terms rhymes with a word it is attempting to conceal; the full rhyme or alliteration simply makes the expression itself more colorful and memorable. Sometimes they can be carried to extreme lengths, as with the thirteen-word: "like the farmer and the tater, plant you now and dig you later." Some originally had longer stories behind them as with the phrase "wham, bam, thank you Ma'am," an expression for hurried loving, which was once the punch line of a story about a rabbit who made love to an iron statue of a female rabbit.

THE HORSECAR SCHOOL OF POETRY

*N*ew York Tribune editorial writer Isaac H. Bromley was seated in a streetcar during the summer of 1875 when he noticed the following sign:

The conductor, when he receives a fare, will punch, in the presence of the passenger,

> A blue trip-slip for an eight-cent fare,
> A buff trip-slip for a six-cent fare,
> A pink trip-slip for a three-cent fare.

Musing on these words at the office, Bromley produced the following poem in a few moments:

> *The conductor when he receives a fare,*
> *Will punch in the presence of the passin jare*
> *A blue trip-slip for an eight-cent fare*
> *A buff trip-slip for a six-cent fare,*
> *All in the presence of the passin jare.*
> *Chorus:*
> *Punch, brothers, punch with care & c.*

The *Tribune* published the poem, it was reprinted by many newspapers, and according to reporter Joseph B. Bishop in his *Notes and Anecdotes of Many*

Years (1925), it became so popular that hardly a passenger across the country didn't repeat it on getting aboard a streetcar. "Everybody fell victim to the jingle," Bishop wrote. "It was set to music, parodied, and quoted everywhere and on all occasions." Mark Twain caught the infection and wrote an amusing account of his sufferings, which was published in the *Atlantic Monthly*, in February 1876, under the title of "A Literary Nightmare," in which he maintained that the only way by which he could rid himself of the jingle was to give it to somebody else. This publication gave rise to a quite general belief that Mark Twain was himself the poem's author, and that belief persists to the present day. In *Scribner's Monthly*, of April 1876, Bromley himself, under the fictitious name of Winkelried Wolfgang Brown, published a true account of the authorship, claiming for himself the honor of founding a new school of verse to be known for all times as "Horsecar Poetry." Its fame spread to other lands and it was translated into other tongues. *The Western*, a St. Louis magazine, found relief in a Latin anthem, with the chorus:

> *Pungite, frates, pungite,*
> *Pungite, cum amore,*
> *Pungite pro victore*
> *Diligentissime pungite.*

It reached Paris and appeared as follows in the *Revue des Deux Mondes*:

> *Le Chant du Conducteur*
> *Ayant été payé, le conducteur*
> *Percera en pleine vue du voyageur,*
> *Quand il reçoit trois sous un coupon vert,*
> *Un coupon jaune pour six sous c'est l'affaire.*
> *Et pour huit sons un coupon couleur*
> *De rose, en pleine vue du voyageur.*
> *Choeur:*
> *Donc, percez soigneusement, mes frères,*
> *Tout en pleine vue des voyageurs, & c.*

THE SPASMODIC SCHOOL OF POETRY

THE ENGLISH POET Sydney Dobell's long, unfinished *Balder* (1854) is considered perhaps the most extreme example of the Spasmodic School, a term applied in his day to violent, wordy dramatic poems characterized by obscurity and wild imagery. Two of its lines went: "Ah! Ah! Ah!/Ah! Ah! Ah! Ah! Ah! Ah! Ah! Ah! Ah! Ah!" When he wrote his poem *The Roman* (1850), Dobell inverted his first name to form the pseudonym Sydney Yendys.

CLERIHEWS

Sir Humphry Davy
Abominated gravy
He lived in the odium
Of having discovered sodium.

THAT WAS the first clerihew written by Edmund Clerihew Bentley (1875–1956). The English detective story writer composed his first irreverent quatrain while only a schoolboy, according to his classmate G. K. Chesterton, "when he sat listening to a chemical exposition, with his rather bored air and a blank sheet of blotting paper before him." Bentley, one of the few men, if not the only man, ever to have a word honor his middle name, wrote a full volume of these "severe forms of free verse" over his lifetime, including:

Sir Christopher Wren
Said "I'm going to dine with some men.
If anybody calls
Say I'm designing St. Paul's."

And:

Alfred de Musset
Used to call his cat pusset.
His accent was affected.
That was to be expected.

Bentley's favorite clerihew was:

It was a weakness of Voltaire's
To forget to say his prayers,
And which, to his shame,
He never overcame.

But others are partial to:

George the Third
Ought never to have occurred
One can only wonder
At so grotesque a blunder.

THE REAL MOTHER GOOSE

THE FAMOUS BOOK of nursery rhymes often called *Mother Goose's Melodies* is said to have been printed at Boston in 1719 by Thomas Fleet, from verses his mother-in-law, Mrs. Elizabeth Goose, created or remembered and repeated. There is no doubt that Mrs. Goose (1665–1757) existed. She was born Elizabeth Foster in Charlestown, Massachusetts, and at the age of twenty-seven married Isaac Goose (formerly Vergoose) of Boston, inheriting ten stepchildren and bearing six children of her own. One of her daughters married the printer Fleet, who had a shop on Pudding Lane in Boston. At this point the facts become unclear, yielding, at any rate, to a good story. According to John Fleet Eliot, a great-grandson of Thomas Fleet, Mrs. Goose took care of all her seven grandchildren and the printer was "almost driven distracted" by her unmelodic singing and constant storytelling—a practice she had no doubt perfected with her own sixteen children. By word of the great-grandson we have it that Fleet finally decided to profit from his annoyance and published Elizabeth Goose's songs and stories—among which were the first real limericks—in a book that contained other rhymes, too, but which he called *Songs for the Nursery*, or *Mother Goose's Melodies for Children*. Yet although the great-grandson wrote in 1860 that Fleet's book had been in the library of the American Antiquarian Society at Worcester, no one has ever been able to find a copy of it.

While the American Mother Goose did exist, and may have written children's verses and stories, lack of evidence has forced most scholars to conclude that the book of nursery tales and verses entitled *Mother Goose's Melodies* was first published in 1760 by London publisher John Newbery, who is generally conceded to have originated the publication of children's books and for whom Oliver Goldsmith wrote the children's story "Goody Two Shoes." The tales in the collection came from older English and French sources, including such classics as "Old King Cole," "Sing a Song of Sixpence," and "Little Jack Horner." As for its title, this apparently was taken from Charles Perrault's *Contes de ma Mère l'Oye (Tales of My Mother Goose)* which was published in 1697 and contained some of the same tales. Perrault himself may have been inspired by a real Mother Goose, however! For it is said that Sir Walter Scott once traced a fabulous storyteller named Mother Goose "to a period of remote antiquity in Italy"—no record of his sleuthing is now at hand.

AN UNEXPURGATED NURSERY RHYME

Lucy Locket lost her pocket
Kitty Fisher found it;
There was not a penny in it,
But a ribbon round it.

P ROBABLY the only two prostitutes celebrated in a nursery rhyme are the ladies above. Lucy Locket and Kitty Fisher were celebrated courtesans in the time of the lascivious Charles II, so celebrated that their names were used by the anonymous inventor of the innocuous rhyme, which was first a bawdy popular song. Kitty Fisher was also depicted as Kitty Willis in Mrs. Cowley's *Belle's Stratagem* and she was painted several times by Sir Joshua Reynolds. Lucy Locket was the model for Lucy Lockit in John Gay's *Beggar's Opera* (1728), a play said to have made Gay rich and Rich (the producer) gay (not in today's sexual meaning of the word). Incidentally, the song "Kitty Fisher's Locket" provided British troops with the music for "Yankee Doodle Dandy."

MARY DID INDEED HAVE A LITTLE LAMB

Mary had a little lamb,
    Its fleece was white as snow
And everywhere that Mary went
    The lamb was sure to go;
He followed her to school one day,
    That was against the rule;
It made the children laugh and play
    To see a lamb in school.

T HERE SEEMS to be no doubt that the Mary and little lamb in the well-known nursery rhyme were real, but there is some uncertainty about who wrote the poem. Sarah Josepha Hale first published the twenty-four-line verse over her initials in the September 1830 issue of *Juvenile Miscellany*. In time it became known that the poem was based on the true experiences of eleven-year-old Mary Sawyer, who had a pet lamb that followed her to the schoolhouse at Redstone Hill in Boston one day in 1817. In fact, Mary Sawyer a half-century later confirmed the story during a campaign to save the famous Old South Church of Boston from being torn down. The prototype for Mary (by then Mrs. Mary Tyler) unraveled a pair of stockings she said had been made from her lamb's wool, cut the wool into short strands, tied these with ribbons, and fastened them to cards which she sold at ten cents each to raise money for the church. The cards told the story of her pet following her to school but claimed that a young man named John Roulstone chanced to observe the strange pair trotting toward the schoolhouse and was inspired to write the famous poem. Mrs. Hale flatly denied this, but the restored Redstone Hill schoolhouse that Henry Ford bought to preserve as a landmark in 1926 bears a memorial plaque naming Roulstone as the author of the first three quatrains of the poem and Mrs. Hale as the author of the last twelve lines.

POET IMPROVISATORS

P ETRARCH is supposed to have introduced the game of inventing poems on the spot for a particular occasion and to have received a laurel crown for extemporizing in verse. Others among many famous for this talent were Italian poet Angelo Mazza (1741–1817), reputedly best of all; Francisco Gianni (1759–1822), whom Napoleon made imperial poet to celebrate his victories in verse; English poet Thomas Hood, author of "The Bridge of Sighs"; William Cowper; and Alexandre Dumas, *père*.

FRANCESCO PETRARCH

Nathaniel Lee was visited by Sir Roger L'Estrange in the madhouse. L'Estrange couldn't conceal the sorrow he felt for the gifted poet, but Lee sensed and spurned his pity, improvising:

> *Faces may alter, names can't change*
> *I am strange Lee altered, you are still Le-strange.*

NECK VERSE, BENEFIT OF CLERGY

K IPLING'S TALE "Benefit of Clergy," makes punning use of the second expression by applying it to the marriage ceremony instead of a death sentence. Benefit of clergy was until 1827 a procedure in English law whereby a criminal arrested for a felony was exempt from trial in the secular courts if he could recite a passage from the Bible—the passage becoming known as "neck verse."

After reciting the verse, whether he was accused of murder, rape, or burglary—all capital offenses—he would be turned over to an ecclesiastical court, which could not invoke the death penalty for such crimes, and his neck would be saved from the hangman or axman. Originally this privilege was granted only to the clergy, but as it was based on the Biblical injunction "Touch not my anointed, and do my prophets no harm" (Psalms 105:15), it was extended to anyone who could read or write, that is, could *become* an ordained clergyman. This early-day "diplomatic immunity" of course discriminated against the uneducated poor. The *neck verse* that had to be recited was from the first verse of Psalms 51: "Have mercy upon me, O God, according to Thy loving kindness: according unto the multitude of Thy tender mercies blot out my transgressions." This verse is commonly called the Miserere because its opening words in Latin are *Miserere mei Deus.*

An old doggerel verse defines benefit of clergy:

If a clerk has been taken
For stealing of bacon,
For burglary, murder or rape;
If he could but rehearse
(Well prompt) his neck verse,
He never could fail to escape.

TRUE TO HIS WORDS

I am known to the horse-troop, the night and the desert's expanse
Not more to paper and pen than the sword and the lance.

Nοτ long after the ancient Persian poet Ahmad ibn Husein wrote this couplet, he was attacked by robbers. When he tried to escape, his slave reminded him of his words. He fought and he was killed.

EMBLEMATIC POEMS

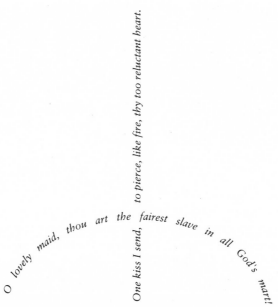

Those charms to win, with all my empire I would gladly part

EMBLEMATIC or shaped poems like the anonymous one above date back to Grecian times, but they flourished in sixteenth- and seventeenth-century Europe, Edward Benlowes and George Herbert leading the list of the great "word torturers" who made them. Poems have been shaped into crowns, crosses, altars, wings, eggs, violins, wineglasses, hatchets, hearts, goblets, spectacles, saddles, and frying pans, among just a few objects.

SONG OF THE DECANTER

*There was an old decanter
and its mouth was gaping
wide; the rosy wine had
ebbed away and left
its crystal side;
and the wind
went humming
—humming up
and down: the
wind it flew, and
through the reed-
like hollow neck the
wildest notes it blew.
I placed it in the window,
where the blast was blow-
ing free, and fancied that its
pale mouth sang the queerest
strains to me. "They tell me—puny
conquerors! the Plague has slain his ten,
and war his hundred thousand of the very
best of men; but I"—'twas thus the Bottle spake—
"but I have conquered more than all your famous
conquerors, so feared and famed of yore. Then come,
ye youths and maidens all, come drink from out my cup,
the beverage that dulls the brain, and burns the spirits up;
that puts to shame your conquerors that slay their scores
below; for this has deluged millions with the lava
tide of woe. Tho' in the path of battle darkest
streams of blood may roll, yet while I killed the
body, I have damned the very soul. The
cholera, the plague, the sword such ruin
never wrought, as I in mirth or
malice on the innocent have
brought. And still I breathe
upon them and they shrink before
my breath, while year by year my
thousands go my dusty way of death."*

—Warfield Creath Richardson, 1899

Many poets, including modern masters like Apollinaire, constructed emblematic poems. Following are three more.

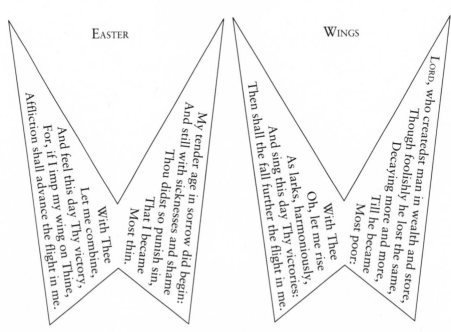

EASTER

WINGS

My tender age in sorrow did begin:
And still with sicknesses and shame
Thou didst so punish sin,
That I became
Most thin.
With Thee
Let me combine,
And feel this day Thy victory,
For, if I imp my wing on Thine,
Affliction shall advance the flight in me.

Lord, who createdst man in wealth and store,
Though foolishly he lost the same,
Decaying more and more,
Till he became
Most poor:
With Thee
Oh, let me rise
As larks, harmoniously,
And sing this day Thy victories:
Then shall the fall further the flight in me.

—Anonymous

THE ALTAR.
A BROKEN ALTAR, Lord, Thy servant rears,
Made of a heart, and cemented with tears:
 Whose parts are as Thy hand did frame;
 No workman's tool hath touch'd the
 same.
 A HEART alone
 Is such a stone,
 As nothing but
 Thy power doth cut.
 Wherefore each part
 Of my hard heart
 Meets in this frame,
 To praise Thy name:
 That, if I chance to hold my peace,
 These stones to praise Thee may not
 cease.
Oh, let thy blessed SACRIFICE be mine,
And sanctify this ALTAR to be Thine.

—George Herbert

THE CROSS.

Blest they who seek,
While in their youth,
With spirit meek,
The way of truth:
To them the sacred Scriptures now display
Christ as the only true and living way.
His precious blood on Calvary was given
To make them heirs of endless bliss in heaven;
And e'en on earth the child of God can trace
The glorious blessings of his Saviour's grace.

For them He bore
His Father's frown;
For them He wore
The thorny Crown;
Nailed to the Cross,
Endured its pain,
That His life's loss
Might be their gain.
Then haste to choose
That better part,
Nor dare refuse
The Lord thy heart,
Lest He declare,
"I know you not,"
And deep despair
Should be your lot.
Now look to Jesus, who on Calvary died,
And trust on Him alone who there was crucified.

—George Herbert

SHORTEST POEM IN ENGLISH

THE *Oxford Dictionary of Quotations* cites the anonymous "On the Antiquity of Microbes" as the shortest poem ever written. It consists of three words:

> *Adam*
> *Had 'em.*

But there are several shorter anonymous poems, such as "On the Condition of the United States after Several Years of Prohibition":

> *Wet*
> *Yet.*

LONGEST AND MOST PROFITABLE POEMS IN ANY LANGUAGE

THE LONGEST POEM written by a single poet is probably the 456,047-line *Promethee* by Canadian Roger Brien (b. 1910). The longest and most profitable poem composed by a single poet was begun in A.D. 999 by the Persian author Abul Qāsim Mansur, who used the pen name Firdausī. The *Shah-nama* or *Book of Shahs* was written for Sultan Mahmud, who promised Firdausī a gold dinar ($4.70) for every couplet he wrote of the 60,000-couplet epic that is a complete history of Persia's kings from 700 B.C. to A.D. 700. This would have come to $282,000 for the poem, but when Firdausī delivered it in the year 1010, the Sultan reneged and gave him only 60,000 silver dirhams (about $30,000). Legend has it that the scornful poet gave half of the fee to a sherbet salesman and half to a bath attendant before leaving for another kingdom. Later, the story goes, Sultan Mahmud had a change of heart when a visiting troubadour quoted a beautiful couplet from the poem by Firdausī and ordered that 60,000 gold dinars worth of indigo be sent to the poet along with his apologies. As the caravan pulled into Firdausī's village, however, it met a funeral procession carrying the poet's body to the grave. If Firdausī's family received the indigo, that would mean that over $312,000 was paid for the one poem.

The *Mahabharata*, which appeared in India from about 400 to 150 B.C., is, at 220,000 lines and nearly 3 million words, far longer than the *Shah-nama*, but it was not written by one person. One poem in English on the life of King Alfred by John Fitchett (1766–1838) took forty years to write and contains 129,807 lines, but the poem's last 2,585 lines were written by Fitchett's editor after the poet's death.

The Kirghis folk epic *Manas*, which has never been translated into English, runs to about 500,000 lines but consists of three separate parts written at different times.

COMPUTER POETRY

PROGRAMMERS can now feed a basic vocabulary into a computer's memory along with rules about a poem's structure and the machine will write poems. Thus far the results aren't worthy of Edgar Guest, as this cybernetic haiku composed at the Cambridge Language Research Institute shows:

All white in the buds
I flash snowpeaks in the Spring.
Bang the sun has fogged.

Dr. William R. Bennett, Jr., a professor of physics and computer expert at Yale University, in 1979 tackled the old hypothesis that if enough monkeys pecked randomly at typewriters long enough they could eventually write the complete works of Shakespeare. Yes, they could, he calculated, but it would take almost an eternity. Dr. Bennett figured that "if a trillion monkeys were to type ten randomly chosen characters a second it would take, on the average, more than a trillion times as long as the universe has been in existence just to produce the sentence *'To be or not to be, that is the question.'*"

A computer that had been programmed with the writings of James Joyce, D. H. Lawrence, some twentieth-century women authors, and the "angry young men" of the sixties "wrote" a novel called *Bagabone, Hem I Die Now* (Vantage, 1980).

BLACKMAIL BY POEM

FAMED ORNITHOLOGIST Alexander Wilson, whose nine-volume *American Ornithology* is a classic and who has the Wilson's petrel, phalarope, plover, snipe, and thrush named after him, was an itinerant tinker and poet before he immigrated to America in 1794. Two years earlier he was accused of writing a poem about a mill owner, alleging that the man used false measures in determining the week's output of cloth, and then demanding five guineas to refrain from publishing the poem. Though he may have been innocent, he was fined and jailed several months for libel and blackmail.

BLACK BART, THE PO-8

THIS WAS the nom de plume of Charles E. Boles, the daring stagecoach robber who held up stagecoaches in the 1870s, and did it alone on foot (he had no use for horses) with an unloaded shotgun! A consummate artist at his chosen work, Black Bart wasn't a bad poet, either. He wrote many poems, the following sample certainly his rationalization for his crimes:

> *I've labored long and hard for bred*
> *For honor and for riches*
> *But on my corns too long you've tred*
> *You fine-haired Sons of Bitches.*

Black Bart will have to do until America produces a Villon. Unfortunately, little is known of him. The man who signed his poems PO-8 seems to have disappeared after being released from jail in 1888.

OF PATES AND POETS

> *Poets are almost always bald*
> *when they get to be about forty.*
> —John Masefield

THE POET'S CORNER

PART OF THE south transept of Westminster Abbey, where many great authors are buried, the Poet's Corner was so named by Oliver Goldsmith, later buried there himself; it had been called "the poetical Quarter" before then. In the Corner are, among others, the tombs of or monuments to Chaucer, Spenser, Ben Jonson, Shakespeare, Samuel Butler, Drayton, Milton, Davenant, Cowley, Prior, Gay, Addison, Thomson, Goldsmith, Dryden, Dr. Johnson, Sheridan, Burns, Southey, Coleridge, Campbell, Macaulay, Longfellow, Dickens, Thackeray, Tennyson, Browning, and Hardy. In the case of Hardy, his heart is buried in his native Dorset. One of the oddest stories about the Poet's Corner concerns Thackeray's bust there. The novelist's daughter had always "deplored the length of the whiskers on each side of the face of her father's bust," believing that the Italian sculptor Marachetti had made them far too long. Finally, as an old woman, she managed to persuade officials to let another sculptor move the bust into a secluded alcove and chip away at the sideburns until they were the right length. This accomplished, an appropriately bewhiskered Thackeray was restored to his proper niche in the nave.

OLIVER GOLDSMITH

THE LAST WORD

A<small>FTER</small> Ella Wheeler Wilcox (1850–1919) published her poem "Solitude" in 1883, John A. Joyce claimed that he had written it twenty years earlier. Mrs. Wilcox offered $5,000 for any printed version of the poem dated earlier than her own and none was ever produced. Joyce, however, had the last word when he died in 1915, aged seventy-two. The most famous lines from the poem are attributed to him on his gravestone in Oak Hill Cemetery, Washington, D.C.:

> *Laugh and the world laughs with you*
> *Weep and you weep alone.*

POEMS FROM THE GRAVE

W<small>HILE HIS WIFE</small>, Elizabeth, was dying of tuberculosis, Dante Gabriel Rossetti had been unfaithful to her and he felt great remorse for this the rest of his life. When the beautiful Elizabeth died of an overdose of laudanum in 1862, only two years after their marriage, the painter buried with her the little book in which he had handwritten all his poems, placing the volume close to her lips and wrapping it with her long golden hair. There the poems were meant to stay, for as Rossetti had said to his dead wife at graveside, speaking as though she could hear him, the poems had either been written to her or for her. Yet after seven years Rossetti regretted having renounced poetry and wanted back the only perfect copy of poems he thought were the most beautiful he could ever write. Finally obtaining official permission, the poet had his wife's grave in Highgate Cemetery opened one night and in the light of a great fire built by the side of the grave (to prevent infection) the buried poems were taken from the coffin, drenched with disinfectants, and dried leaf by leaf. Rossetti noticed that his wife's golden hair had continued to grow after death, filling the coffin, and the scene so unnerved him that despite the fact that he wrote about it in his sonnet "Life in Love," he left instructions in his will that he be cremated and not buried beside Elizabeth. A year after their disinterment, in 1870, Rossetti's *Poems* were published to excellent reviews, becoming a living monument to his wife.

MOST HONORED POETS

*E*L-AAMA ET TOTELI, the Blind Poet of Tudela, read his poems at a Seville competition, and all the other poets tore their own verses to pieces without reciting them.

When the venerated blind arch poet Abu'l-Ala al-Ma'arri died in 1057, 180 fellow poets attended his funeral and 84 of them, one for each year in his life, recited poems at his grave.

CHAPTER FOUR

Wits, Wags & Literary Weasels

BREVITY IS THE SOUL OF WIT

S INCE BREVITY is the soul of wit, and tediousness the limbs and outward flourishes, I will be brief," Polonius says in *Hamlet*. But Shakespeare did not mean *wit* in the sense of a witty remark when he wrote this. He used *wit* here in its older meaning of "wisdom," and what Polonius is really saying is that wise men know how to put things succinctly—which the Bard knew was a dramatically ironic thing for a windy fellow like Polonius to say. The newer meaning of *wit* was known in Shakespeare's time; he himself used it in *Much Ado About Nothing*: "They never meet but there's a skirmish of wit between them." Yet "brevity is the soul of wit" meant "brevity is the soul of wisdom" for many years before it took on its present, universal meaning. Swinburne's "An Epigram" (1802) is both witty and wise:

> *What is an Epigram? A dwarfish whole,*
> *Its body brevity, and wit its soul.*

ADDRESSEE KNOWN

Several friends, not knowing where in the world Mark Twain had wandered, sent him a birthday card addressed: "Mark Twain, God knows where." Within the month, they received an unsigned letter postmarked from Italy, reading only, "He did."

ANECDOTE

W<small>E OWE</small> the above word to Justinian, Byzantine emperor from A.D. 527 to 565, who wrote a book of brief tales about life in his court. These true stories were satirical, scandalous, and sometimes off-color. Justinian—better known for the Justinian legal code—probably didn't intend them for publication, but they were published by Procopius, a secretary to one of Justinian's generals, as a supplement to his history of the times. Procopius entitled the book *Anekdota*, this Greek word meaning "unpublished, secret." The title of the book later became the term *anecdote*, meaning a brief factual story like the ones *Anekdota* contained.

Anecdotage, "the state of being advanced in age and strongly inclined to tell reminiscent anecdotes," is probably a happy coinage of John Wilkes in about 1835.

PUNOLOGY PRO AND CON

> *However critics may take offense*
> *A double meaning has double sense.*
> —Thomas Hood

P<small>ROBABLY</small> the most widely quoted remark about puns was made by English critic John Dennis (1657–1734), who once told a punster that "any man who would make such an execrable pun would not scruple to pick my pocket." He was speaking to English composer Henry Purcell, who had rung the bell for the *drawer*, or waiter in a tavern. When no one answered, Purcell tapped the table top and asked Dennis "Why is this table like the tavern?," answering "Because there is no *drawer* in it."

Dennis's remark, often attributed to Dr. Johnson, is frequently given incorrectly as "He who would make a pun would pick a pocket," which means something entirely different from what Dennis said. Nevertheless, many writers *have* scorned the pun over the years. Charles Lamb wrote, "A pun is a pistol let off at the ear, not a feather that tickles the intellect." Others have called it "the lowest form of wit," to which, Willard Espy reports (in an entry in *The Game of Words* called "Pun My Word,"), one punster replied, "Yes, for it is the foundation of all wit."

Good puns can be very witty indeed, and they are a universal form of humor that go back to Homer's time or earlier. They are, of course, a figure of speech involving a play on words, the humorous use of a word emphasizing different meanings or applications. English writers from Shakespeare to James Joyce, one of the most compulsive of punners, have used them, perhaps the most famous of the Bard's puns being the lighthearted Mercutio's remark as he is dying: "Ask for me tomorrow and you shall find me a grave man" (*Romeo and Juliet*). One writer who counted found 1,062 puns in Shakespeare's works, while another took eighty-nine pages to list the puns in his plays.

Charles Lamb felt that the worst puns are the best: "This species of wit is the better for not being perfect in its parts. What it gains in completeness it loses in naturalness. The more exactly it satisfies the critical, the less hold it has upon some other faculties. The puns which are most entertaining are those that will least bear an analysis."

A much-quoted pun is found in this humorous verse by nineteenth-century poet Anita Owen:

> *O dream eyes*
> *They tell sweet lies of Paradise;*
> *And in those eyes the lovelight lies*
> *And lies—and lies—and lies!*

Although puns are almost always solely humorous today, they were formerly used seriously, especially to achieve bitterness or irony. When the mad Lear, for example, says to the blinded Gloucester "you see how this world goes," and Gloucester replies, "I see it feelingly," the pun heightens the horror. John Donne puns seriously in his "Hymn to God the Father," using the word *Son* to mean both the *sun* and *Christ* and using the word *done* as a play on his own name:

> *I have a sin of fear, that when I have spun*
> *My last thread, I shall perish on the shore;*
> *But swear by Thy self, that at my death Thy Son*
> *Shall shine as he shines now, and heretofore;*
> *And having done that, Thou hast done;*
> *I fear no more.*

Another long-remembered pun is Sir William Harcourt's reply to Tennyson when the poet said his first pipe of tobacco was always the best of the day. Recalling a famous line from Tennyson's poem "The Princess," Harcourt replied, "Ah, the earliest pipe of half-awakened *bards*." Tennyson's poem reads

> *Ah, sad and strange as in dark summer dawns*
> *The earliest pipe of half-awakened birds.*

Addison says that puns are not true wit because they can't be translated into other languages, which is obviously not true, for puns can be translated—when they can't the fault is often in the translator. One author notes that the "unspeakable" pun "Confucius say, 'Seven days on honeymoon make one whole week' " has been translated into Chinese, though I don't wholly believe him.

The word *pun* is first recorded in about 1660, after the Restoration, when a number of clipped words such as *mob, nob,* and *snob* came into fashion as slang. It is not a contraction of the word *pundit,* but may be short for the obsolete *pundigrion,* which means the same and is of unknown origin, or may be related to the Italian *puntiglio,* "a quibble" or "a fine point." "What of Whims and Shams, Punns and Flams, Stultiloquious Dialogs?" an early author wrote. "Having pursued the History of a Punn," pronounced Addison in the *Spectator,* "I shall hear define it to be a Conceit arising from the use of two Words that agree in the Sound but differ in the Sense." Pope was of the opinion that in a pun "a word, like the tongue of a Jackdaw, speaks twice as much by being split," while Swift (who used many puns) in his broadside "God's Revenge against Punning" wrote that "One Samuel, an Irishman, for his forward attempt to pun, was stunted in stature."

But the pun never set on the British empire. Wrote British poet Hilaire Belloc, "When I am dead, / I hope it may be said: / 'His sins were scarlet, / but his books were read.' " Other diverse authors who loved puns include Pericles, Aristophanes, Euripides, Sophocles, Rabelais, Milton, Petrarch, Erasmus, Lamb, Hood, Moore, Sir Thomas More, Cotton Mather, Jeremy Bentham, Lewis Carroll, and Vladimir Nabokov. Even authors who hated puns, such as Dr. Johnson and Oliver Wendell Holmes, used them one or more times. There are puns in the Pentateuch. In the *Odyssey* the Cyclops is blinded by Ulysses, who answers "No One" when he is asked his name by his captor and escapes after searing the monster's eye. In the morning the Cyclops tells his brethren that No One has hurt him.

Punning is sometimes called *paronomasia,* though this term doesn't mean exactly the same thing. In *Poplollies and Bellibones* Susan Sperling gives twenty synonyms for *pun,* some dating back to the fifteenth century and obsolete today: *bull, carriwitchet, clench, clinch, crotchet, figary, flam, jerk, liripoop, pundigrion, quartorquibble, quibble, quiblin, quiddity, quillet, quip, quirk, sham, whiblin, whim.*

PUNS AND LOVERS .

*H*UMORIST George Selwyn, "the first of the fashionable wits" and a member of the notorious Hellfire club, was told that a father, son, and grandson all had had the same mistress, passing her on from one generation to another.

"There's nothing new under the sun," the man remarked. "Nor under the grandson," Selwyn added. (It was Selwyn, incidentally, who was asked by politician Charles Fox if he had attended the hanging of a highwayman also named Charles Fox. "Oh, no, I never go to rehearsals," Selwyn drawled.)

FUNNY BONE

They have pull'd you down flat on your back,
And they smack, and they thwack,
Till your "funny bones" crack,
As if you were stretched on the rack,
  At each thwack!
Good lack! what a savage attack!

REVEREND RICHARD HARRIS BARHAM, well known for his punning, wrote the above in *The Ingoldsby Legends* (1840) and it is the first mention of the expression *funny bone* in literature. The funny bone—Americans called it the crazy bone in the past—is technically the medial condyle of the humerus, that is, the enlarged knob on the end of the bone of the upper arm which lies below the ulnar nerve at the elbow. Since the ulnar nerve is exposed at the elbow, the unpadded nerve hits the humerus as if against an anvil when we strike it on something, causing sharp, tingling pain. Nothing is very funny about this—it inspires cursing rather than laughter—but Barham or some punster before him probably saw the pun *humorous* in the *humerus* bone and dubbed it the funny bone, adding one of the few puns that have become words to the language.

"LAND OF NOD"

JONATHAN SWIFT, as fond of puns as the next man and better at them than most, is responsible for this expression meaning the land of sleep. In his *Polite Conversation* (1738) Swift wrote that he was "going into the land of Nod," that is, going to sleep. The "land of Nod," which suggests the nodding of a sleepy head, was a pun on the "land of Nod" or "land of wandering," the place where Cain was exiled after he slew Abel (Genesis 4:16).

JONATHAN SWIFT

THE FIRST JOKE BOOK

A famous teacher of Arithmetic, who had long been married without being able to get his wife with child—One said to her, Madam, your husband is an excellent Arithmetician. Yes, replied she, only he can't multiply.

*T*HOUGH INCLUDED in *Joe Miller's Jest Book* this old joke couldn't have been written by Joe Miller, nor could any of the hoary jests in the collection. The English comic actor and barfly Joseph or Josias Miller (1684–1738), a favorite at Drury Lane Theatre in parts such as Hamlet's first gravedigger, was an illiterate. He married his wife, in fact, only so that she could read his parts for him. When Miller died leaving his family in poverty, his friend playwright John Mottley gathered a collection of jokes attributed to him—and there were many, either because he was famed for his wit, or because it was something of a joke to credit this "grave and taciturn" actor with any joke making its rounds of the pubs. The proceeds of the seventy-two-page book went to Miller's family, and being the only joke book extant for many years, it went into numerous editions over the next two centuries. Eventually the original 272 jokes increased to well over 1,500. Because the jokes were widely quoted and imitated on the stage so long, any stale joke began to be called a "Joe Miller." The full title of the joke book was *Joe Miller's Jests: or, The Wits Vade-Mecum, being a collection of the most brilliant jests, the polite repartees, the most elegant bon mots, the most pleasant short stories in the English language. First carefully collected in the company, and many of them transcribed from the mouth of the facetious gentleman whose name they bear.* Some writers have gone so far as to say that it is the basis for all stage and screen humor, and professional comedians such as Fred Allen have acknowledged their indebtedness to the collection. But poor Joe Miller probably had very little to do with it at all.

AN OLD CHESTNUT

*E*NGLISH PLAYWRIGHT William Dimond wrote a melodrama, *The Broken Sword* (1816), which is all but forgotten, along with its characters, plot, and dialogue and the author himself isn't remembered in most guides to literature. Yet Dimond has found immortality of sorts in the expression *an old chestnut*, a stale joke or story, which probably derives from an incident in his play. *The Broken Sword*'s principal character is crusty old Captain Xavier, who is forever spinning the same yarns about his highly unlikely experiences. He begins to tell the following one to Pablo, another comic character:

CAPTAIN XAVIER: I entered the woods of Colloway, when suddenly from the thick boughs of a cork tree—
PABLO: A chestnut, Captain, a chestnut!
CAPTAIN XAVIER: Bah, I tell you it was a cork tree.
PABLO: A chestnut; I guess I ought to know, for haven't I heard you tell this story twenty-seven times?

Fame didn't come immediately. The lines lay at rest in Dimond's play for almost seventy years before American actor William Warren, Jr., repeated them at a stage testimonial dinner in Boston, after hearing another speaker tell a stale joke. Other actors present adopted Warren's *chestnut*, elaborated on it, and it became the time-worn *old chestnut*.

PRACTICAL JOKERS

THE MOST delightful of impoverished authors was the Japanese novelist Jippensha Ikku (d. 1831). Poor and owning no furniture, Ikku hung his walls with pictures of the furniture he would have if he could afford to buy it; he made offerings to the gods in the same way. When his publisher came to call on him, Ikku prepared a bath for him, donned the man's clothes—he had no good clothes of his own—and then went out properly attired to make social calls. As a last wish the novelist requested that certain packets be placed on his corpse when he was cremated. After the pyre was lighted, it developed that the packets contained firecrackers.

Unlikely as it may seem from his poetry, T. S. Eliot was another practical joker. He particularly liked handing out exploding cigars to critics.

AMPHIGORY

*A*mphigory derives from the Greek for "circle on both sides" and means a burlesque or parody, usually a kind of nonsense verse that seems to make sense but doesn't. Swinburne's "Nephelidia," a parody of his own style, is an example, as the opening lines show:

> *From the depth of the dreamy decline of the dawn*
> *through a notable nimbus of nebulous noonshine,*
> *Pallid and pink as the palm of the flag-flower that*
> *flickers with fear of the flies as they float,*
> *Are they looks of our lovers that lustrously lean from*
> *a marvel of mystic miraculous moonshine,*
> *These that we feel in the blood of our blushes that*
> *thicken and threaten with throbs through the throat?*

A CUTTING REMARK

*T*HERE IS French fraternity for you!" Edmund Burke exclaimed, suddenly plunging a dagger into the floor of the House of Commons. "Such is the poniard which French Jacobins would plunge in the heart of your sovereign!"

Author Richard Brinsley Sheridan, then sitting as an M.P., responded to this theatricality: "The gentleman has brought his knife with him; but *where's the fork?*"

MOST GLOWING LITERARY REFERENCE

*W*HEN Clare Boothe Luce, whose sharp tongue hardly qualified her for sainthood, asked author Charles Murphy for a reference to help her get an apartment at the exclusive Watergate East in Washington, D.C., Murphy provided the following mock hagiology for the management:

> I could hardly feel more comfortable had I been called upon to vouch for the piety of the recently sainted Sister Elizabeth Seton; for the courage of a Molly Pitcher; the zeal of a Susan B. Anthony; for the rectitude of a Carry Nation; for the rural grace of an Emily Dickinson; or for the acumen of a Hetty Green . . . you and Watergate East will become the gathering place of sages. It will acquire the healing powers of Lourdes. Vestal virgins will descend on the north bank of the Potomac to kindle

the sacred fire on the hearth which Major L'Enfant in his disillusionment left cold. And the District of Columbia itself, once so gracious, will abandon its simpleminded craving to become just another state. It will declare itself a heavenly body.

BATTLE LINES

T. O'CONOR SLOANE III, long an editor at Doubleday, tells the following story:

> Many years ago, when Robert Giroux was editor-in-chief of Harcourt, Brace, he told me this little anecdote. He was expecting a visit from T. S. Eliot one day, and he knew that Carl Sandburg was going to be in the offices at the same time. Mr. Giroux made what arrangements he could to keep the two from meeting face to face, because he knew that the poets were not mutual admirers. When he returned to his office from lunch, to his horror he saw Sandburg and Eliot there, glaring at each other from opposite corners. "Your face has deep lines," Sandburg was saying to Eliot. I later told this little story to Melville Cane, the lawyer and poet. He said, "If I had been Eliot, I would have said to Sandburg, 'I can't say the same for your poetry.'"

THE DEVIL'S DICTIONARY

*D*ENIED EXISTENCE by the chief publishing houses in this country," ran the dedication to *Tales of Soldiers and Civilians*, Ambrose Bierce's masterwork, "this book owes itself to Mr. E. L. Steele, *merchant*, of this city." Old malevolent "Bitter Bierce," his pen dipped in wormwood and acid, disappeared into Mexico in 1913, at age seventy-one, to seek "the good, kind darkness" and was never heard from again. He had perhaps the most sardonic wit in the history of

American letters. From his vitriolic pen came *The Cynic's Word Book* (1906), later retitled *The Devil's Dictionary*, which is justly famous for its ironic definitions, a few of which are given below:

Alone—in bad company
Love—a temporary insanity curable by marriage
Marriage—a master, a mistress and two slaves, making in all, two
Positive—mistaken at the top of one's voice
Saint—a dead sinner, revised and edited

SHAKESPEARE, RICHARD BURBAGE, AND FRIEND

WITH THE passing of time there have been many variations, one more risqué than the other, on the old joke about Shakespeare, actor Richard Burbage, and their lady friend. The incident may or may not have occurred, but here is the original story from the diary of seventeenth-century English author John Manningham:

Upon a time when Burbage played Richard the Third there was a citizen grew so far in liking him, that before she went from the play she appointed him to come that night unto her by the name of Richard the Third. Shakespeare, overhearing their conversation, went before, was entertained and at his game ere Burbage came. Then, message being brought that Richard the Third was at the door, Shakespeare caused return to be made that William the Conqueror was before Richard the Third.

VOLTARIAN WIT

THE UNIVERSAL genius of the Enlightenment, Voltaire (François-Marie Arouet, 1694–1778) with sharp wit and clever mockery attacked the cruelties and absurdities of his time in the name of social and moral progress. No one mind, quick and exact, more changed the world.

• It is said that the Chevalier de Rohan-Chabor, encountering him in a theater lobby, intoned, "Monsieur de Voltaire, Monsieur Arouet—what really is your name?" Replied Voltaire: "My name begins with me, yours ends with you." He won that round, but two months later Rohan hired six hoodlums to beat him. Directing them from his carriage, he instructed: "Don't strike his head; something good may yet come out of that."

• When a young man Voltaire wrote the most unusual of his works, a poem called "The Padlock" (1716). It was written to his mistress "Mme. B.," never further identified, and the padlock he raged about was a chastity belt her suspicious seventy-year-old husband had made Mme. B. wear to "lock the free sanctuary," "trouble our good time," and "abuse our desires," as Voltaire put it.

• He told of how a commentator on Lucretius by the name of Creech noted on his manuscript: "N.B. Must hang myself when I have finished." Added Voltaire: "He kept his word, that he might have the pleasure of ending like his author [Lucretius]. Had he written upon Ovid, he would have lived longer."

• According to one old story, Voltaire participated in an orgy with a group of dissolute Parisians. When invited to participate again, he replied, "No thank you, my friends. Once: a philosopher; twice: a pervert!"

• He could hardly get a word in edgewise when Diderot came to visit him, the great encyclopedist speaking from the time he came until he left. As soon as Diderot was out the door, Voltaire observed, "That man is a great wit, but nature has denied him one great gift—that of dialogue."

• Meeting him in Brussels, the poet Jean Baptiste Rousseau complimented Voltaire on his verse but criticized him for his impiety. It was at this time that Voltaire took a look at Rousseau's "Ode to Posterity" and made his famous remark: "Do you know, my master, that I do not believe this ode will ever reach its address?"

• After reading a copy of the *Discours* sent to him by Jean-Jacques Rousseau, Voltaire replied: "I have received, Monsieur, your new book against the human race. . . . You paint in true colors the horrors of human society; . . . no one has ever employed so much intellect to persuade men to be beasts. In reading your work one is seized with a desire to walk on four paws. However, as it is more than sixty years since I lost the habit, I feel, unfortunately, that it is impossible for me to resume it. . . ." But then he was always jealous of Jean-Jacques Rousseau, calling him "A mad dog who bites everybody," among other scurrilities. He once quipped that the first half of Rousseau's *Julie, ou la Nouvelle Héloise* was written in a brothel and the second in a madhouse.

• Casanova visited the Swiss poet Albrecht von Haller, who told him, "Monsieur Voltaire is a man who deserves to be known, although, contrary to the laws of physics, many people have found him greater at a distance." Several days later Casanova visited Voltaire, who asked him where he last came from. "From Roche," Casanova told him. "I did not want to leave Switzerland without having seen Haller . . . I kept you to the last as a *bonne bouche* [a tidbit]." "Were you pleased with Haller?" Voltaire inquired. "I spent the three happiest days of my life with him," Casanova said. "I congratulate you," Voltaire said. "I am glad you do him justice," said Casanova. "I am sorry he is not so fair toward you." "Ah-hah!" Voltaire cried. "Perhaps we are both mistaken."

• He did not approve of theological writings. "I have two hundred volumes on the subject," he remarked, "and, what is worse, I have read them. It is like going the rounds of a lunatic asylum."

• The Bishop of Annecy wanted Voltaire executed for his anticlerical writings. "That rascally bishop still swears that he will have me burned in this world or the other," Voltaire remarked to d'Alembert. "To escape being burned I am laying in a supply of holy water."

• A young poet called on Voltaire and asked him if he had any use for "a young atheist ready to serve you." "I have the honor of being a deist employer," Voltaire replied, "but though our professions are so opposed, I will give you supper today and work tomorrow. I can make use of your arms, though not of your head."

• The French critic Elie Catherine Fréron (1719–1776) made the mistake of attacking Voltaire and the encyclopedists. Voltaire, not a man to be tampered with, let go a barrage of overkill upon him in wicked epigrams, in his tragedies, in the virulent satire *Le Pauvre Diable*, and in an anonymous work called *Anecdotes sur Fréron* (1760). What hurt the critic most was Voltaire's making him the principal character in his comedy *L'Éscossaise*. In this comedy Fréron's magazine, *L'Année Litteraire* (*The Literary Year*) is called *L'Ane Litteraire* (*The Literary Ass*). The play also depicts Fréron as a scoundrel, spy, toad, hound, snake, lizard, and man with a heart of filth, among other things. Voltaire later circulated a quatrain about the critic: "The other day, down in a valley, / A serpent stung Fréron. / What think you happened then? / It was the serpent that died."

• Writing to Mademoiselle Quinault, Voltaire was the first to point out what has become almost a literary maxim. "The only reward to be expected for the cultivation of literature," he wrote, "is contempt if one fails and hatred if one succeeds."

THE GREAT CHAM

*T*HANKS in great part to his biographer Boswell, more anecdotes have been recorded about Dr. Samuel Johnson (1709–1784) than any other literary figure that comes to mind. The greatest part of these show an incisive wit that set a style for British men of letters. There are so many, in fact, that even Boswell came nowhere near gathering them all.

• The Great Cham of Literature advised his former teacher that he would complete his groundbreaking *Dictionary* in three years (though it actually took eleven). "But the French Academy, which consists of forty members, took forty years to compile their dictionary," he was told. "Sire, thus it is," Johnson explained. "This is the proportion. Let me see; forty times forty is sixteen hundred. As is three to sixteen hundred, so is the proportion of an Englishman to a Frenchman."

• He defined *Grub Street* in his *Dictionary* as "Originally the name of a street in Moorfields in London, much inhabited by writers of small histories, dictionaries, and temporary poems; whence any mean production is called grub-street." Though he never resided in Grub Street, he selected that home of needy writers of dictionaries like himself by attaching to the entry a Greek quotation meaning: "Hail, Ithaca! After toil and bitter woe, I am glad to reach your soil."

• "Your manuscript is both good and original," he told a prospective author, "but the part that is good is not original, and the part that is original is not good."

• Boswell told Johnson that he might dislike puns so much because he couldn't make them. "If I were punished for every pun I shed," Johnson replied, "there would not be left a shed for my puny head."

• Of his many remarks about Scotsmen perhaps the most famous was his reply when Boswell told him, "I do indeed come from Scotland, but I cannot help it. . . ." Johnson replied: "That, sir, I find, is what a very good many of your countrymen cannot help."

• Another time Boswell wondered aloud how he could describe a terrible inn where he and Johnson had stayed in Bristol. "Describe it, sir?" Johnson said. "Why, it was so bad that Boswell wished to be in Scotland."

• While touring Scotland with Boswell he visited the MacDonald clan; one of the young MacDonald ladies sat on his knee and kissed him on the cheek. "Do it again," Dr. Johnson told her, "and let us see who will tire first."

• He liked the Irish almost as little as the Scots. "The Irish are a fair people," he said, "they never speak well of one another."

• He bet that he could repeat verbatim a complete chapter of Horrebow's *National History of Ireland*. It proved to be Chapter LXXII, "Concerning Snakes," which read in its entirety: "There are no snakes to be met with throughout the whole island."

• Boswell censured a certain widower for marrying a second time, claiming this showed disrespect for the man's dead wife. "Not at all, sir," Dr. Johnson disagreed. "On the contrary, were he not to marry again, it might be concluded that his first wife had given him a disgust for marriage, but by taking a second wife he pays the highest compliment to the first by showing that she made him so happy as a married man, that he wishes to be so a second time."

• While enjoying a particularly good meal with Dr. Johnson, Boswell asked him if he didn't think that a good cook was more essential to a community than a good poet.

"I don't suppose," Johnson replied, "that there's a *dog* in the town that doesn't think so."

• The actor David Garrick asked Johnson to name life's greatest pleasure. "[He] answered fucking and the second was drinking," Garrick recalled. "And therefore he wondered why there were not more drunkards, for all could drink tho all could not fuck."

• "Drinking drives away care. Would you not allow a man to drink for that reason?" Boswell once asked the Great Cham.

"Yes, sir, I would," Dr. Johnson replied. "If he sat next to you."

• "If your company does not drive a man out of his house," he said to Boswell one day, "nothing will."

• "I would rather be attacked than unnoticed," he told Boswell. "For the worst you can do to an author is to be silent to his works." Another time he remarked, "Never mind whether they praise or abuse your writings; anything is tolerable, except oblivion."

• Of music Dr. Johnson remarked that it was the only sensual pleasure without vice.

• "Do you like music?" a lady friend once asked Johnson.

"No, madam," replied the Great Cham, "but of all noises, I think music is the least disagreeable."

• Once he was told that a piece being played by a famous musician was very difficult. "Difficult do you call it, sir?" he replied. "I wish it were impossible."

• One of Dr. Johnson's circle was complaining about the playwright Samuel Foote being kicked in Ireland. "He is rising in the world," Johnson said. "When he was in England no one thought it worthwhile to kick him."

• Another time he observed of Foote: "If he be an infidel, he is an infidel as a dog is an infidel; that is to say, he has never thought upon the subject."

• After a performance of *Irene* his friend Garrick took him backstage to the dressing rooms of the actors. When asked to go backstage another time, he replied: "No, David, I will never come back. For the white bubbies and the silk stockings of your actresses excite my genitals."

• He could be childlike. While visiting friends, he advised them that he would like to "take a roll down" a steep hill behind their house. Emptying his pockets, he lay atop the hill and propelled himself sideward, rolling over and over like a joyous boy until he reached bottom.

• Johnson correctly believed that the celebrated poems allegedly written by the Scottish bard Ossian were actually forgeries written by their translator James Macpherson. And he thought little of them. "Do you think, sire," Dr. Robert Blair asked him, "that any man of a modern age could have written such poems?"

"Yes, sir," he replied, "many men, many women, and many children."

• Said Dr. Johnson, "Rousseau, sir, is a very bad man. I would sooner sign a sentence for his transportation than that of any felon who has gone from the Old Bailey these many years. Yes, I should like to have him work in the Plantations."

"Sir," asked Boswell, "do you think him as bad a man as Voltaire?"

"Why, sir," Johnson replied, "it is difficult to settle the proportion of inequity between them."

• A certain Miss Brooks had written a tragedy entitled *The Siege of Sinape* and wanted the Great Cham to read and correct it because she was too busy and had too many irons in the fire. Johnson replied, "In that case, madam, I would say: Put your tragedy where your irons are."

• Though the magistrate Sir John Hawkins devoted much of his life to the arts, Johnson found him stingy and unsociable. One night Hawkins refused to pay his share of the dinner check at their club. "Sir John, sir," Johnson later told a friend, putting down Hawkins for the ages, "is a very unclubable man."

• Mrs. Elizabeth Montagu was the head of a London literary salon contemptuously dubbed the bluestockings because one of its impecunious male members (Mr. Benjamin Stillingfleet) wore common blue worsted hose instead of gentleman's black silk hose. She had a falling out with Dr. Johnson and broadcast the word that he was persona non grata in her little circle. "Mrs. Montagu has dropt me," Johnson remarked when he heard the news. "Now, sir, there are people whom one should like very well to drop, but would not wish to be dropt by."

• At one of Mrs. Montagu's literary gatherings, a group of young women surrounding Dr. Johnson wondered how to treat this great, gruff bear whose hostility they had heard so much about. Finally Johnson assured them, "Ladies, I am tame, you may stroke me."

• "To endeavour to make *her* ridiculous," he said of the radical historian Mrs. Catherine Macaulay, "is like blackening the chimney."

• In a move to expose literary pretension, Dr. Johnson read a long difficult poem to a noted critic, who expressed unreserved admiration for the work. The Great Cham then told him that he had omitted every other line.

• "No man but a blockhead ever wrote except for money," he told Boswell.

• He was told that a man who had been most unhappy in marriage married immediately after his shrewish wife died. "It was a triumph of hope over experience," he said.

• Johnson was asked by his friend Maurice Morgann to compare the talents of the poets Christopher Smart and Samuel Derrick, both of whom he thought little of, though history has not upheld his opinion of the insane Kit Smart. In any case, Dr. Johnson's answer did not help either of the poets. "Sir," he replied, "there is no setting the point of precedency between a louse and a flea."

• The insane poet Christopher Smart (see above) was a brilliant classical scholar and innovative poet but little recognized in his own time. Smart's derangement usually took the form of praying in public, "falling upon his knees and saying his prayers in the street, or in any other unusual place," as Johnson put it. Though Johnson did not appreciate his "poor friend's" genius, he didn't think Smart should be confined to the madhouse. "I did not think he ought to be shut up," he told his friend Dr. Burney after Smart's death. "His infirmities were not noxious to society. He insisted on people praying with him; and I'd as lief pray with Kit Smart as anyone else. . . ."

• "Sir, what is poetry?" he was asked.

"Why, sir, it is much easier to say what it is not. We all *know* what light is; but it is not easy to *tell* what it is."

• A pretentious shopkeeper asked Johnson to write an epitaph for the man's daughter, advising him that she had always been modest and polite to her inferiors. "An admirable trait," Dr. Johnson said, "but it might not be so easy to discover who the lady's inferiors were."

• Henry Hervey, an army officer of noble birth, was very kind to Dr. Johnson when the author was a struggling young writer in London, often inviting him to dinner at a time when Johnson had little if anything to eat. Dr. Johnson never forgot his generosity, despite his shortcomings. "Harry Hervey," he said years later, "was a vicious man, but he was very kind to me. If you call a dog Hervey, I shall love him."

• Critics are continually placed in the position of having to say something clever and this is a heavy tax on them, a friend told Dr. Johnson.

"It is indeed," Johnson replied, "a very heavy tax on them, a tax which no man can pay who does not steal."

• Johnson hated baby talk and once gave a ride in his coach to a poor woman walking in the rain with her baby on the condition that she wouldn't indulge in it in his presence. When the woman forgot her promise and cooed to her waking child, "The little dearie, is he going to open his eyes-pysies then," Johnson had the coach stopped and ordered her out into the rain again.

• "Sir," he told Boswell, "you have but two topics, yourself and me. I am sick of both."

• "I hate a fellow," he said, "whom pride, or cowardice, or laziness drives into a corner, and who does nothing when he is there but sit and *growl*; let him come out as I do, and *bark*."

• Discussing Bishop Berkeley's theory of the nonexistence of matter, Boswell remarked that though he considered it untrue, he wasn't able to refute it. Kicking a large stone, Johnson said, "I refute it thus."

• He was not much impressed by literary innovation. "A new manner [of writing]!" he exclaimed when the subject arose one evening. "Buckinger had no hands, and he wrote his name with his toes at Charing-cross for half a crown apiece; that was a new manner of writing!"

• "A man should begin to write soon," he remarked, "for if he waits until his judgement is matured, his inability, through want of practice to express his conceptions, will make the disproportion so great between what he sees, and what he can attain, that he will probably be discouraged from writing at all."

• He was of the opinion that "whoever thinks of going to bed before twelve o'clock is a scoundrel."

• "Fly fishing may be a very pleasant amusement," he is said to have remarked, "but angling or float fishing I can only compare to a stick and a string, with a worm at one end and a fool at the other."

• When Frances Sheridan, the mother of Richard Brinsley Sheridan, published her *Memoirs of Miss Sydney Biddulph* (1763), a novel with an unhappy ending, Johnson was one of the few critics not to receive it warmly. "I know not, madam," he told her, "that you have a right, upon moral principles, to make your readers suffer so much."

• No one could understand why Pope had written the lines:

> *Let modest Foster, if he will, excell*
> *Ten metropolitans in preaching well.*

"What do you think?" Dr. Johnson was asked. "Sir, he hoped it would vex somebody," Johnson replied.

• When the Great Cham was seriously ill, Bennet Langton brought him texts to read on Christian charity. "What is your drift, sir?" Johnson inquired.

• Author Hannah More wondered why Milton, who had written *Paradise Lost*, wrote such awful sonnets. "Milton, madam," replied Dr. Johnson, "was a genius that could cut a Colossus from a rock, but could not carve heads upon cherrystones."

• After reading Goldsmith's apology in the London *Chronicle* for beating Evans the bookseller, Dr. Johnson observed, "It is a foolish thing well done."

• Of literary criticism he remarked, "You may scold a carpenter who has made a bad table, though you cannot make a table. It is not your trade to make tables."

• "Shakespeare never had six lines together without a fault," he exclaimed. "Perhaps you may find seven, but this does not refute my general assertion."

• "If I had no duties, and no reference to futurity," he remarked, "I would spend my life in driving briskly in a postchaise with a pretty woman."

• Late in life he observed, "As I know more about mankind I expect less of them, and am ready now to call *a good man* upon easier terms than I was formerly."

STERNE DROLLERIES

BRITISH HUMORIST Laurence Sterne's life was hardly a humorous one. The son of a wandering soldier-father and an often malevolent mother, he made an unhappy marriage in which all of his children save one were stillborn. Even before Sterne became a pastor in 1738 he had contracted tuberculosis. His only solace seems to have been the women he flirted with or chased. In 1759, soon after *Tristram Shandy* was rejected by a printer, his wife had a mental breakdown. A year later he awoke to find himself famous with the publication of the first volume of his book, but his happiness was short-lived, for in 1762 his health began to deteriorate, worsening every year until his death. It is said that his last words were "Now it is done," after which "he put his hand up as if to stop a blow, and died in a minute." Trouble followed even after his death in 1768, when only fifty-five: his body was stolen by grave robbers a few days after burial and sold to anatomists at Cambridge, where a friend recognized it on the dissecting table at an anatomy lecture and had it returned to the grave. During his life, however, Sterne always attacked his troubles with his rapier wit.

• "Men of wit," the Duke of Newcastle once admonished Sterne, "are not fit to be employed, being incapable of business."

"They are not incapable of business, my Lord," Sterne replied to the prime minister. "A sprightly generous horse is able to carry a pack-saddle as well as an ass, but he is too good to be put to the drudgery."

• By the eighteenth century, book dedications had become slavish, as authors vied for patrons. Writers got up to fifty guineas for a dedication at the time, and some included more than one dedication in a book—Edward Young's *The Complaint, or Night Thoughts* (1742–1745), for example, had a dedication for each of the seven nights of the week. It was with such examples in mind that Sterne parodied literary dedications in *Tristram Shandy* (1760–1767), inscribing the dedication page with the words "To be let or sold for fifty guineas."

• The novelist asked a woman if she'd read his *Tristram Shandy*. "I have not," she replied, "and to be plain with you, I am informed it is not proper for female perusal." Sterne pointed at her three-year-old son rolling on the floor in his white tunic. "My dear good lady," he said, "do not be gulled by such stories. The book is like your young heir there. He shows at times a good deal that is usually concealed, but it is all in perfect innocence!"

• It is said that Sterne's *A Sentimental Journey* (1768) is the first English novel to survive in its author's handwriting. The dash that ends *Sentimental Journey* has the distinction of being the only dash to end a novel and the only dash that is listed as a euphemism for the vagina in a slang dictionary (Farmer and Henley's *Slang and Its Analogues*, 1890). The novel ends: " . . . so that, when I stretched out my hand, I caught hold of the fille-de-chambre's ——."

• Reverend Sterne shocked his congregation on the Sunday following his Saturday marriage to Elizabeth Lumley in 1741. He preached a sermon that took its text from Luke 5:5, "We have toiled all night and have taken nothing."

THE ENGLISH ARISTOPHANES

*F*INDING THAT HIS more prominent victims had his satiric impersonations of them suppressed under the licensing laws of the British theater, playwright Samuel Foote (1720–1777), known to his contemporaries as the English Aristophanes, would invite the audience to join him for tea the next day, promising some diverting comedy. While the tea was being made he would render his uproarious mimicry of prominent people. Life for Foote always seemed to be a script in which he had the best lines.

• When a habitually drunk nobleman asked the dramatist and actor in what disguise he should go to a costume ball, Foote suggested, "Why don't you go sober, My Lord."

• "It's a very good match she has made," an actor said of an actress with a bright scarlet past. "And they say she made to her husband a full confession of all her past affairs."

"What honesty she must have had!" another remarked.

"Yes," Foote added, "and what a memory!"

• He tearfully asked when his recently deceased friend Sir Francis Delavel would be buried. "Not till the end of next week," he was told, "as I hear the surgeons intend first to dissect his head." "And what will they get there?" he said, still crying. "I am sure I have known Frank these five and twenty years, and I never could find anything in it."

• A friend asked Foote's advice after having been thrown out of a second-floor window for cheating at cards. "Do not play up so high," suggested Foote.

• "I've given my dear wife a thousand pounds," a friend told the playwright. Foote shook his head sagely. "She is truly your dear wife," he replied.

• Foote was asked by Charles Howard if he had read Howard's book *Thoughts, Essays, and Maxims.*

"No, I wait for the second volume," Foote replied.

"And why so?" asked Howard.

"Because I have heard that *Second Thoughts* are best."

• "Why do you always sing that same tune?" the playwright asked an acquaintance.

"Because it haunts me," the man replied.

"No wonder," Foote said. "You continually murder it."

THE WORLD'S GREATEST WIT

Many would rate British author and politician Richard Brinsley Sheridan (1751–1816) the greatest literary wit of all time. A good-sized book could be made of "Sherry's witticisms, of which a short selection follows.

• In 1776 Sheridan had acquired a share in the famous Drury Lane Theatre and produced his plays there. He rebuilt the theater eighteen years later. In 1809 the new Drury Lane Theatre was destroyed by fire and Sheridan sat at the Piazza coffeehouse watching it burn to the ground. "How can you bear your misfortune so calmly?" a friend inquired. Replied Sheridan, "A man may surely be allowed to take a glass of wine by his own fireside."

• One of the biggest hits Sheridan produced at the new Drury Lane Theatre was Frederick Reynolds's play *The Caravan*, in which the trained dog Carlo jumped nightly into a pool to save a drowning child. After opening night, an elated Sheridan, sure he had a hit that would save him from financial ruin, rushed backstage shouting, "Where is my Preserver?" Reynolds, the play's author, modestly stepped forward to receive the great man's plaudits. "Pooh, not you—*the dog*," Sheridan said. Another evening during *The Caravan*'s long run a principal actor ran up to Sheridan indicating that something terrible had happened.

"What is it?" Sheridan asked.

"I've lost my voice, can't you tell!" the actor finally said.

"Oh, is that all?" Sheridan replied. "I thought something had happened to the dog."

• Sheridan's son Thomas couldn't understand his father's love of politics, though he later became a politician himself. "If I were in Parliament," Thomas told him one evening, "I would write on my forehead, 'To Let.' " Sheridan made a point of studying the boy's head for a moment and replied, "Add 'Unfurnished.' "

• Edward Gibbon was at first full of praise for Sheridan's parliamentary speech during the trial of Warren Hastings, noting that Sheridan had complimented him. "Mr. Sheridan's eloquence commanded my applause," the historian noted, "nor could I hear without emotion the personal compliment which he paid me in the presence of the British Nation. Sheridan said, 'I do say, that if you search the history of the world, you will not find an act of tyranny or fraud to surpass this; if you read all past histories, peruse the annals of Tacitus, read the luminous pages of Gibbon. . . .' "

Gibbon, however, was not so happy when he heard Sheridan's reply to his remarks.

"I did not say luminous," he told a fellow Whig, "I said *vol*uminous."

• Sheridan rose to make a point of order when a fellow M.P. stopped to pour a glass of water in the middle of a long, boring speech.

"What is your point, sir?" the Speaker said.

"Why, I think, sir," Sheridan replied, "that it is *out of order* for a windmill to go by water."

• During a parliamentary debate Sheridan was asked to apologize for insulting another M.P. "Mr. Speaker," Sheridan replied, "I said the honorable member was a liar it is true and I am sorry for it. The honorable member may place the punctuation where he pleases."

• Social status meant everything to Sheridan. He badly wanted to become a member of the exclusive Whig club Brook's, but two members, the earl of Bessborough and George Selwyn, wanted to exclude him because he was associated with the theater. Members had to be elected unanimously and night after night the two men blackballed him, but finally Sheridan was for some reason elected. According to one old story, Sheridan accomplished this by sending Selwyn a note saying that his daughter had suddenly fallen ill, and sending the earl a note saying that his house was on fire. Before the men got back and realized that they had been hoaxed, Sheridan was elected.

• Two noblemen greeted Sheridan playfully, one of them quipping, "I say, Sherry, we were just discussing whether you were a rogue or a fool."

Taking each man by the arm, Sheridan replied, "Why I believe I am midway between both."

• While he was visiting friends in the country, a persistent woman tried to get Sheridan to take her for a walk. The playwright pleaded bad weather, but she looked up at the sky and advised him that it was clearing. Sheridan, too, looked out the window. "Yes," he replied after a brief scrutiny, "enough for one, but not enough for two."

• "Won't you come into the garden?" he asked a beautiful young woman. "I would like my roses to see you."

• The playwright had told a joke to the earl of Lauderdale, who began laughing hysterically and said he'd be sure to repeat it over and over. "Pray don't, my dear Lauderdale," Sheridan replied. "A joke in your mouth is no laughing matter."

• Sheridan was known throughout England for the great sums he owed and as often as not failed to pay back. One time when he stood for Parliament, mobs sang this popular ditty in the streets.

> *Oh, Sherry! red Sherry!*
> *You'd make us all merry.*
> *With your drolls, your stage tricks and curvets;*
> *But don't, on old Davy*
> *Draw drafts for the Navy:*
> *Nor pay 'em as you pay your debts.*

• "I'll cut you off without a shilling!" Sheridan said to his son Thomas in the heat of an argument.

"Ah, father," Thomas quickly replied, "but where will you borrow the shilling?"

• A tailor dunned Sheridan for at least the interest he owed on a bill. Replied Sheridan, "It is not my interest to pay the principal, nor my principle to pay the interest."

• Without money, as usual, Sheridan wondered how he would pay for the coach he had hired over two hours ago. Then the playwright spied his friend Joseph Richardson, celebrated for his persistent argumentativeness, strolling down the street. He gave Richardson a lift and managed to start an argument with him. Eventually, pretending to be very angry, Sheridan shouted that he could not remain in the same coach with a person who used such foul language. Asking the coachman to let him out, he stuck the still-arguing Richardson with the fare.

• Sheridan was always joking, even to the point of masquerading as a policeman one time in Bath and arresting people. His last joke was made on the day of his death, July 7, 1816, at about noon. He looked up at a woman friend several hours before he died and spoke words he had put in the mouth of his creation Mrs. Justice Credulous: "I don't die, Bridget, I don't like death."

THE WIT OF JOHN WILKES

SEVERAL OF the most famous quips in history are attributed to champion of English-American liberty, politician, and author John Wilkes, after whom a county in North Carolina and half a city (Wilkes-Barre, Pennsylvania) are named. Wilkes, described by Byron as "a merry, cockeyed, curious looking sprite," made up for his physical shortcomings with a ready Irish wit and suave manner. Though small and squint-eyed, he was able to launch his career with an expedient marriage. "I married a woman twice my age," he wrote shortly after his wedding night. "It was a sacrifice to Plutus, not to Venus." Of course, the marriage didn't last. Once he had obtained the funds he needed, Wilkes abandoned the domestic life.

After separating from his wife, he began his dual career in earnest. First he joined the Hellfire Club—a secret fraternity which included in its membership such peccant officials as Lord Orford, Lord Sandwich, and Charles Churchill. At this time Wilkes may have writetn and had printed the obscene "Essay on Woman," a parody of Pope's "Essay on Man," which was to plague his political career as much as the orgies for which the Hellfire Club was infamous. Wilkes hardly slept while a member of the Hellfire Club, where wild parties with naked masked women, drinking bouts, and weird religious ceremonies were routine.

Eventually, Wilkes directed all his energies to affairs of state. He tried intently to get elected to Parliament. During his first campaign, the opposition imported a boatload of voters from another district. Wilkes promptly bribed the ship's captain to deliver his cargo to Norway. Persistent, he was. "I'd sooner vote for the devil than John Wilkes," a constituent once told him. "And what if your friend is not running?" Wilkes replied.

Another great Wilkes riposte was his answer to a smug Catholic who asked him, "Where was your religion before the Reformation?" Replied Wilkes: "Where was your face before you washed it this morning?" But his most famous witticism, probably the most famous political put-down in history, made his onetime friend Lord Sandwich its victim. It appears that the earl had verbally attacked Wilkes, shouting, "You, Wilkes, will either die on the gallows or from

syphilis!" The great wit Wilkes simply turned, tapped his snuff-box, and looked Sandwich full in the eye. "That depends, my Lord," he said, matter-of-factly, "on whether I embrace your principles or your mistress."

Eventually, even crusty old Dr. Johnson—who had said he would rather dine with Jack Ketch, the public hangman, than with Jack Wilkes—came to admire John Wilkes. By the time the great libertine and libertarian died at the age of seventy in 1797, he had come to be as universally respected as he had earlier been reviled.

THE SMITH OF SMITHS

*H*ISTORY HAS known few wittier conversationalists than British clergyman and author Sydney Smith (1771–1845), who seemed to have a witty remark for every occasion and held no occasion sacred. Only Chesterton could rival "the Smith of Smiths" as a religious wit. In his diary author Tom Moore wrote that Smith was so funny he could actually make people in a room cry with laughter.

• "I never read a book before reviewing it," Smith once commented. "It prejudices a man so."

• Another time clergyman-author Smith won an argument with a man who angrily declared, "If I had a son who was an idiot, I would make him a parson."

"Your father was of a different opinion," Smith said.

• Smith saw two women angrily shouting at each other, heads stuck out their windows on opposite sides of St. Paul's Close. "They will never agree," he observed, "as they are arguing from different premises."

• "You never expected justice from a *company*, did you?" he asked a friend. "They have neither a soul to love nor a body to kick."

• Smith studied the outfit worn by eccentric British author Harriet Grote, which was topped off by a Turkish turban. "Now I know the meaning of the word 'grotesque,' " he finally said.

• Referring to his friend and cofounder of the *Edinburgh Review*, the invariably severe critic Lord Francis Jeffrey, who was once challenged to a duel by Thomas Moore for his strictures, Smith made this observation: "No one minds what Jeffrey says: . . . it is not more than a week ago that I heard him speak disrespectfully of the equator." (Harriet Martineau said Mrs. Smith told *her* that when Captain [later Sir John] Ross had approached Jeffrey, interrupting his daily ride, about supporting an expedition to the North Pole, he had snapped "Damn the North Pole!" When an upset Ross reported this to Smith, he replied soothingly, "Never mind him damning the North Pole. *I* have heard him speak disrespectfully of the equator.")

• It was his practice, he told friends, to "take short views, hope for the best, and trust in God."

• George Canning, a witty parodist himself, became prime minister in 1827, much to Smith's dismay. Smith couldn't understand how the Tory had been elected. "Canning in office is like a fly in amber," he remarked. "Nobody cares about the fly: the only question is, 'How the devil did he get there?' "

• "Correspondences," he wrote to a Mrs. Crowe, "are like small-clothes [knee-britches] before the invention of suspenders. It is impossible to keep them up."

• "I am just going to pray for you at St. Paul's," he told a caller, "but with no very likely hope of success."

• He once boasted that his sermons were "long and vigorous, like the penis of a jackass."

• "I look upon Switzerland," he wrote to Lord Holland, "as an inferior sort of Scotland."

• He didn't appreciate rural life. "I have no relish for the country," he wrote to a young lady, "it is a kind of healthy grave." Another time he complained that his parish in Yorkshire "was so far out of the way, that it was actually twelve miles from a lemon."

• "I have, alas, only one illusion left," he was heard to say, "and that is the Archbishop of Canterbury."

• "Marriage," he said, "resembles a pair of shears, so joined that they can not be separated; often moving in opposite directions, yet always punishing anyone who comes between them."

• He put his recipe for salad into rhyme for his friends:

> *Let onion atoms lurk within the bowl,*
> *And, scarce-suspected, animate the whole.*

• "Poverty is no disgrace to a man," he observed, "but it is confoundedly inconvenient."

• The imperious hostess Lady Holland once in-structed him, "Sydney, ring the bell for the butler." To which he replied, "And shall I sweep the room, too?"

• "Lord Dudley was one of the most absent [minded] men I have ever met with in society," he con-fided. "One day he met me in the street and invited me to meet myself: 'Dine with me today; dine with me, and I will get Sydney Smith to meet you.' I admitted the temptation he held out to me, but said I was engaged to meet him elsewhere."

• Of the wide-ranging philosopher William Whewell, he said, "Science is his forte, and omniscience his foible."

• "Don't tell me of the facts," he declared, "I never believe facts; you know [Prime Minister] Canning said nothing was so fallacious as facts, except figures."

• "What you don't know would make a good book," he told an arrogant acquaintance.

• Of a moralistic acquaintance, Smith quipped, "[He] deserves to be preached to death by wild curates."

• When it was proposed that St. Paul's be surrounded with a wooden pave-ment, he suggested, "Let the Dean and Canons lay their heads together and the thing will be done."

• "What a pity it is," he remarked, "that we have no amusements in England but vice and religion."

• In his last, pain-filled days, he had light heart enough to write to a friend, "If you hear of sixteen or eighteen pounds of human flesh, they belong to me. I look as if a curate has been taken out of me."

• He died "at peace with himself and all the world," his wife, all of whose friends had advised against marrying him, wrote in her memoirs. Concluding her reminiscences she wrote: "And now dear Children I have done. After passing nearly half a century with *such* a man I am alone . . . the Light of my Life is extinguished."

THE DEADLY LAMB

A MAN OF great charm, much loved by all who knew him, British essayist, poet, and critic Charles Lamb (1775–1834) suffered from mental illness all his life, but neither this nor his persistent stammer prevented him from delivering some of the best bon mots of his or any other time.

• A loud hiss came forth from somewhere in the audience while Lamb was delivering a lecture. After a brief silence, Lamb, showing no emotion, simply said: "There are only three things that hiss—a goose, a snake, and a fool. Come forth and be identified."

• In an 1823 letter to a friend, Lamb succinctly described the relationship between nineteenth-century authors and their publishers or booksellers: "These fellows hate us."

• The poet, who had a hearty appetite, was invited to dine with poet Thomas Hood. "We have a hare," Hood told him. "And how many friends?" Lamb anxiously asked.

• A talkative woman at a dinner party was irritated at Lamb's inattention. She finally tugged at his arm and declared, "You seem to be none the better for all I am telling you."

"No, madam," Lamb replied, "but this gentleman on the other side of me must be—for it all went in one ear and out the other."

• Songwriter and journalist Barry Cornwall made a witty remark to Lamb. "V-very well, my dear boy, v-v-very well," Lamb stammered. "B-Ben, Ben Jonson has said worse than that—and b-b-better."

• Lamb was watching a game of cards over the shoulder of a friend whose personal hygiene offended everyone in the room. "George," he finally said, unable to bear him any longer, "if dirt were trumps, what a hand you'd have."

• "Really, Mr. Lamb, you come very late!" said an official at the East India House in reprimanding Lamb for his poor work habits.

"Y-yes," Lamb replied, "b-but consi-sider how ear-early I go!"

• Lamb once described his friend Samuel Taylor Coleridge as "an archangel slightly damaged." Coleridge, unquestionably a great poet, was addicted to opium and was a man of many enthusiasms, which he rarely failed to broadcast in a strong voice cultivated by his preaching throughout England's West Country. One day, bragging of his oratorical abilities, he asked Lamb, "Did you ever hear me preach?"

"I never heard you do anything else," Lamb replied.

• Wordsworth sometimes diverged from the everyday language he espoused and used archaic "poetical" terms. One time Lamb read aloud the first line of a new Wordsworth poem, "The Force of Prayer": "What is good for a bootless bene?" Immediately his sister Mary cried out, "A shoeless pea!"

• Lamb had observed a man doing something he strongly disliked when an unknowing friend offered to introduce him to the fellow. "Don't introduce me to that man!" he exclaimed. "I want to go on hating him, and I can't hate a man whom I know."

• He was more specific than the myriad writers who've said they don't give two cents for critics. "For critics," he told a friend, "I care the five-thousandth part of the tythe of a half-farthing."

• Dr. Parr asked him how he puffed so much smoke out of his pipe and he replied, "I toil after it as other men after virtue." A dedicated pipe smoker, he once said he would like "to draw his last breath through a pipe and exhale it as a pun."

• "This very night I am going to leave off tobacco!" he wrote to Thomas Manning in 1815. "Surely there must be some other world in which this unconquerable purpose shall be realized."

• Commenting on William Hazlitt's marriage to the widow Isabella Bridgewater, which was astonishing to his friends because he had just divorced his wife and gotten over a disastrous love affair with Sarah Walker, Lamb wrote to Robert Southey: "I was at Hazlitt's marriage, and had like to have been turned out several times during the ceremony. Anything awful makes me laugh. I misbehaved once at a funeral." The marriage ended a few years later.

• Lamb, Coleridge, and Thomas Holcroft were fiercely arguing about which was best: "Man as he was, or man as he is to be." Remarked Lamb, "Give me man as he is *not* to be."

• "Nothing puzzles me more than time and space," he told a friend, "and yet nothing troubles me less, as I never think about them."

• He jotted down this verse in a copy of *Coelebs in Search of a Wife* (1809), a book of sharp moral observations by Hannah More about the protagonist's search for the proper wife.

If I ever marry a wife,
  I'll marry a landlord's daughter
For then I may sit in the bar,
  And drink cold brandy and water.

• Coleridge had written in "This Lime-tree Bower, My Prison" (1797):

For thee my gentle-hearted Charles, to
    whom
No sound is dissonant which tells of life.

Reading the poem, Lamb wrote to him: "For God's sake (I never was more serious) don't make me ridiculous any more by terming me gentle-hearted in print . . . substitute drunken dog, ragged head, seldom-shaven, odd-eyed, stuttering, or any other epithet which truly and properly belongs to the gentleman in question."

JERROLDIAN JIBES

AMONG THE MOST successful playwrights of his time, British author Douglas Jerrold (1803–1857) seems in retrospect wittier than any of the characters he left to posterity. This close friend of Dickens's, who often wrote under the pseudonym Q, has never been given the attention he deserves.

• On the first night of his first play, *Fifteen Years of a Drunken Life* (1828), Jerrold was kidded about his nervousness by a seasoned, successful playwright. "I," he intoned, "never feel nervous on the first night of my pieces."

"Ah, my boy," replied Jerrold, "you are always certain of success. Your pieces have all been tried before."

• Publisher Richard Bentley told Jerrold that before he named his noted magazine *Bentley's Miscellany* he had planned to call it *The Wit's Miscellany*. "Well, that would have been going to the other extreme," Jerrold replied.

• Jerrold didn't have a very happy married life. One time someone at a party asked him who was dancing with his wife. "God knows, my dear boy," Jerrold replied. "Some member of the Humane Society, I suppose."

• "If an earthquake were to engulf England tomorrow," he remarked to friends, "the English would manage to meet and dine somewhere among the rubbish, just to celebrate the event."

• A very thin man had been boring Jerrold all evening with his rambling stories. "Sir," Jerrold finally said, "you are like a pin, but without either its head or its point."

• One afternoon, a well-known bore approached Jerrold on the street, ready to buttonhole him. "Well, well, Jerrold," he began. "What's going on?"

"I am," said Jerrold, and left.

• Jerrold's contemporary, Albert Smith, wrote a piece for *Blackwood's Magazine* and signed it A. S. Jerrold didn't much admire Smith. "What a pity," he said, reading the initials, "that Smith will tell only two-thirds of the truth."

• Jerrold agreed with Thomas Carlyle's criticisms of life in the nineteenth century but found him wanting in the alternatives he offered. "Here is a man," he said, "who beats a big drum under my windows, and when I come running downstairs, has nowhere for me to go."

• "He is a kind man," Jerrold said to a friend, speaking of a mutual acquaintance.

"Why, he has been away from his family for years and never sent them a farthing," his friend said. "You call that kindness?"

"Yes, I do," replied Jerrold. "Unremitting kindness."

• A notorious sponger asked a mutual friend to borrow money for him from Jerrold. "How much does he want this time?" Jerrold asked. "Oh, just a four and two naughts will put him straight," his friend advised. "Put me down for one of the naughts," Jerrold replied.

• Jerrold was a captive audience at his club, caught between a raucous admirer of the prince of Orange and an enraged admirer of William III. "Bah to you, sir!" one man finally shouted. "I spit upon your prince of Orange!"— only to have his opponent jump up and scream, "And I, sir, spit upon your King William!" This went on for a few minutes, until Jerrold rang the bell and shouted to a waiter, "Here, boy—spittoons for two!"

• Jerrold was not the outdoor type. "The only athletic sport I ever mastered," he confessed, "was backgammon."

• He was told that a hack writer planned to dedicate his next book to him. Alarmed, Jerrold replied, "Ah, that's an awful weapon he has in his hands!"

WILDE WIT

Oscar Wilde once told André Gide, "I have put my genius into my life; I have put only my talent into my work." Though he only lived forty-six years, Wilde is remembered as one of the greatest wits in English history. Perhaps only James Whistler ever got the better of Wilde in an exchange of ripostes. Once, Wilde remarked "Oh, I wish I'd said that!" on hearing a clever remark and Whistler replied: "You will, Oscar, you will." Another time Whistler wrote: "What has Oscar in common with Art? Except that he dines at our tables and picks from our platters the plums for the puddings he peddles in the provinces, Oscar—the amiable, irresponsible, esurient Oscar—with no more sense of a picture than of the fit of a coat, has the courage of the opinions . . . of others." To which Wilde replied: "As for borrowing Mr. Whistler's ideas about art, the only thoroughly original ideas I have heard him express have had reference to his own superiority as a painter over painters greater than himself." Which inspired Whistler to retort: "A poor thing, Oscar!—but, for once, I suppose your own."

At any rate, only George Bernard Shaw's witticisms would rival Wilde's, and G.B.S. lived more than twice as long. A few brief examples of Wilde Wit:

- "I can resist everything but temptation."
- "The only things one never regrets are one's mistakes."
- "Experience is the name everyone gives to his mistakes."
- "The basis of optimism is sheer terror."
- On being shown Niagara Falls by a Chamber of Commerce type: "It would be more impressive if it flowed the other way."
- "Nothing succeeds like excess."
- On fox hunting: "The unspeakable in full pursuit of the uneatable."
- "The difference between journalism and literature is that journalism is unreadable and literature is not read."
- "One should always play fair when one has the winning cards."
- "Scandal is gossip made tedious by morality."
- "A cynic is a man who knows the price of everything and the value of nothing."
- On going through customs in New York City: "I have nothing to declare except my genius."
- "Nothing spoils a romance so much as a sense of humour in the woman."
- "A thing is not necessarily true because a man dies for it."
- On choosing the world's 100 best books: "I fear that would be impossible, because I have written only five."
- "George Bernard Shaw hasn't an enemy in the world, and none of his friends like him."
- "When the gods wish to punish us, they answer our prayers."
- "Life is far too important a thing ever to talk seriously about."
- After a huge fee for an operation was mentioned: "Ah, well, then, I suppose I shall have to die beyond my means."
- Last words, as he called for champagne: "I am dying as I have lived, beyond my means."

MORE WILDE WIT

- In his student days Wilde attended a lecture by Walter Pater. The great scholar and man of letters was speaking in his usual whisper of a voice. "I hope you all heard me," Pater said to the group at lecture's end.

"We *over*heard you," Wilde responded.
- When warden of New College, Reverend William A. Spooner (see *Spoonerisms*) reprimanded Wilde, then a student in his second year at Oxford, and as a punishment made him copy the twenty-sixth chapter of Acts in Greek. After he felt Wilde had worked long enough, Spooner told him to stop, but Wilde continued writing. "Did you hear me tell you, Mr. Wilde, that you needn't write anymore?" Spooner asked.

"Oh, yes, I heard," Wilde replied, "but I was so interested in what I was copying that I could not leave off. It was all about a man named Paul, who went on a voyage and was caught in a terrible storm, and I was afraid that he would be drowned; but do you know, Mr. Spooner, he was saved; and when I found that he was saved, I thought of coming to tell you."

• According to one acquaintance, Wilde looked "gigantic, smooth shaven and rosy, like a great priest of the moon." He scorned sport. One time he was asked if he ever took any exercise. "I am afraid I play no outdoor games at all," he replied. "Except dominoes. I have sometimes played dominoes outside French cafes."

• "Who am I to tamper with a masterpiece?" Wilde said when asked to make minor changes in one of his plays.

• "A poet," he said, "can survive anything but a misprint."

• Henry Arthur Jones was the most popular and one of the most prolific dramatists of the 1890s, but Wilde disliked his pamphleteering or perhaps considered this writer of comedies a too-successful rival. In any case, he formulated these three rules of playwrighting: "The first rule for a young playwright to follow is not to write like Henry Arthur Jones. . . . The second and third rules are the same."

• Sir Lewis Morris, author of a volume of rather mediocre verse entitled *The Epic of Hades*, was complaining to Wilde about being ignored for the poet laureateship. "It is a complete conspiracy of silence against me—a conspiracy of silence!" he cried. "What ought I do, Oscar?"

"Join it," Wilde replied.

• Wilde and a friend were discussing the work of Sir Thomas Hall Caine, Rossetti's great friend and the author of many sensational novels. "Mr. Hall Caine, it is true, aims at the grandiose," Wilde remarked, "but then he writes at the top of his voice. He is so loud that one cannot hear what he says."

• James Payn, the English author and editor, had written 100 novels, all of which Wilde found obscure and inconsequential. "Mr. James Payn is an adept in the art of concealing what is not worth finding," he once observed.

• In a letter to Robert Ross (1899), Wilde wrote, "Henry James is developing, but he will never arrive at passion, I fear."

• Wilde was asked if he knew the Irish novelist and poet George Moore. "Know him?" he replied, "I know him so well that I haven't spoken to him in ten years."

• Sarah Bernhardt once bested Wilde. Immediately after arguing with the actress about the interpretation of a role in one of his plays, Wilde took out a cigarette. "Do you mind if I smoke, madam?" he asked.

"I don't care if you burn!" said the Divine Sarah.

• Wilde so irritated the captain of the *Arizona*, on which he sailed to the

United States for his lecture tour in 1881, that the captain later swore, "I wish I had had that man lashed to the bowsprit on the windward side."

• Someone in the audience got the better of Wilde when he spoke in Boston. "You're Philistines who have invaded the sacred sanctum of Art," Wilde told the audience.

"And you're driving us forth with the jawbone of an ass," that someone shouted back.

• Members of Wilde's London club knew that his latest play had flopped, but tried to appear ignorant of the fact when the writer arrived late that evening.

"Oscar, how did your play go tonight?" asked one member.

"Oh," Wilde replied loftily, "the play was a great success but I'm afraid the audience was a failure."

• Wilde once confessed that he spent an entire morning pondering a line from which he finally took out a comma. However, he added, he put it back in by the end of the afternoon.

• In order to ingratiate oneself with high society, he said, "one has either to feed people, amuse people, or shock people."

• The worst of Wilde is seen in his treatment of his loving wife, Constance. Wilde grew disgusted with her as she changed from a slim pretty girl to a heavy, "blotched" matron. One time he reportedly said that after kissing her, "I used to wash my mouth and open the window to cleanse my lips in the pure air."

• During the trial of the marquis of Queensberry for libel, Wilde denied that he had written the allegedly obscene story "The Priest and the Acolyte." "Was that story immoral?" he was asked by the court. "It was much worse than that," Wilde replied. "It was badly written."

• At another point in Wilde's celebrated libel suit, the author made an irrelevant remark about his physician.

"Never mind your physician," said the lawyer cross-examining him.

"I never do," said Wilde archly.

• "Oscar, do you think Marie Corelli is a great writer?" asked a friend visiting Wilde in jail.

"From the way she writes," Wilde replied, according to one version of the story, "*she* ought to be in here."

• William Butler Yeats told a story of Wilde's visit to a Dieppe brothel with poet Ernest Dowson after Wilde's release from prison:

Dowson impressed upon him the necessity of acquiring a more wholesome taste. They emptied their pockets onto the cafe table, and though there was not much, there was enough, if both heaps were put into one. Meanwhile the news had spread, and they set out accompanied by a cheering crowd. Arrived at their destination, Dowson and the crowd remained outside, and presently Wilde returned. He said in a low voice to Dowson, "The first in ten years, and it will be the last. It was like cold mutton . . ." and then aloud, so that the crowd might hear him, "But tell it in England, for it will entirely restore my character."

• When one is surrounded by disciples, Wilde remarked toward the end, there is always a "Judas who writes the biography."

• One of Wilde's last and best bon mots came while he lay dying in his seedy Paris hotel room, where he had registered as Sebastian Melmoth (the name of a wanderer in a gothic novel by his great-uncle Charles Maturin). His friend Robert Ross was at his bedside when Wilde pointed at the garish walls surrounding him. "My wallpaper and I are fighting a duel to the death," he said. "One or another of us has to go."

SHAVIAN WIT

GEORGE BERNARD SHAW didn't like the way *Shawian* sounded and so Latinized his name to Shavius and coined the word *Shavian* from it. *Shavian*, meaning characteristic of the work or style of George Bernard Shaw, soon bred the phrases "Shavian wit" or "Shavian humor," referring to the dramatist's brilliant lines.

GEORGE
BERNARD
SHAW

Shaw was as celebrated for his wit in real life as in his plays. The portly G. K. Chesterton, for example, once thought he had scored when he told the stringy Shaw, "Looking at you, one would think there was a famine in England." But not after Shaw replied, "Looking at you, one would think you caused it." Then there was the time Shaw received an invitation from a celebrity hunter reading: "Lady Blank will be home Thursday between four and six." He returned the card with the message "Mr. Bernard Shaw likewise" written underneath. Or take his advice to William Douglas-Home: "Go on writing plays, my boy. One of these days a London producer will go into his office, and say to his secretary, 'Is there a play from Shaw this morning?' and when she says 'No,' he will say, 'Well, then we'll have to start on the rubbish.' And that's your chance, my boy." But for all his wit, the bearded Irishman could be bettered. The actress Cornelia Otis Skinner got the best of Shaw in the following exchange of telegrams after a revival of *Candida*—Shaw: *Excellent Greatest.* Skinner: *Undeserving such praise.* Shaw: *I meant the play.* Skinner: *So did I.* And even Mrs. Shaw occasionally outdid the master. "Isn't it true, my dear, that male judgement is superior to female judgement?" Shaw once asked his wife. "Of course, dear," she replied. "After all, you married me and I you."

PSHAW ON SHAW

*T*HE EXCLAMATION of impatience or contempt is usually pronounced *shaw*, though I often heard it spoken as *shah* when people still used it. Oscar Wilde once asked George Bernard Shaw what title he'd give to a magazine he proposed starting. "I'd want to impress my own personality on the public," Shaw replied, banging his fist on the table. "I'd call it *Shaw's Magazine*: Shaw—Shaw—Shaw!"

"Yes," Wilde said, *"and how would you spell it?"*

MORE SHAW

• Londoners first became aware of Shaw's name in a series of scurrilous interviews published in an evening paper. The interviewer claimed that he had forced his way into Shaw's apartment and browbeat and insulted him into talking. People couldn't understand why this Shaw put up with a boorish newspaper man: Why didn't he bodily eject him, or at least call the police—do *something*? No one could figure it out—until it was revealed that the "interviews" were written by none other than the formerly unknown Shaw himself.

• A young Irish actress asked Shaw why he'd come to England instead of seeking his inspiration in Ireland, the land of his birth. "I could not stay there, dreaming my life away on the Irish hills," he explained. "England had conquered Ireland, so there was nothing for it to do but come over and conquer England. Which, you will notice, I have done rather thoroughly."

• When Shaw and Fabian union organizer Annie Besant decided to marry, Mrs. Besant, an atheist, drew up a marriage contract to replace the traditional religious vows. But when she presented the long, tedious document to Shaw he began laughing hysterically and refused to sign it. "Good God!" he finally managed to say. "This is worse than all the vows exacted by all the churches on earth." The two never married.

• To H. G. Wells, he once wrote, "The longer I live the more I see that I am never wrong about anything, and that all the pains I have so humbly (!) taken to verify my notions have only wasted my time."

• Shaw printed the following as his review of a play when he was drama critic for the *London Saturday Review*:

> I am in a somewhat foolish position concerning a play at the Opera Comique, whither I was bidden this day week. For some reason I was not supplied with a program; so that I never learned the name of the play. At the end of the second act the play had advanced about as far as an ordinary dramatist would have brought it five minutes after the first rising of the curtain; or say, as far as Ibsen would have brought it

ten years before that event. Taking advantage of the second interval [intermission] to stroll out into the strand for a little exercise, I unfortunately forgot all about my business, and actually reached home before it occurred to me that I had not seen the end of the play. Under these circumstances, it would ill become me to dogmatize on the merits of the work or its performance, I can only offer the management my apologies.

• After switching occupations from critic to playwright, Shaw addressed a dinner of London critics. "I used to be a critic," he told them. "I still regard it as one of the professions I keep in reserve. I gave it up because the profession of playwright which I adopted is very much easier, very much more illustrious and much more attractively renumerative. You will notice I don't say it was better paid."

• Though married, G.B.S. carried on a passionate correspondence over the years with the actress Mrs. Patrick Campbell, a widow. Later in their lives Mrs. Campbell begged Shaw to let her publish 128 of his love letters to her. An indignant Shaw cabled her: "I will not, dear Stella, at my time of life, play the horse to your Lady Godiva."

• One perhaps apocryphal story has it that Eleanora Duse wrote Shaw telling him that every eugenical principle cried that they should have a baby. "Think what a child it would be," she added, "with my body and your brain!"

Wrote Shaw in reply, "Think how unfortunate it would be if the child were to have my body and your brain."

• "People must not be forced to adopt me as their favorite author," he remarked to Alma Murray, "even for their own good."

• Lady Randolph invited G.B.S. to lunch and he wired back, "Certainly not; what have I done to provoke such an attack on my well-known habits?"

The lady countered with another telegram: "Know nothing of your habits; hope they are not as bad as your manners."

• "Oh, Mr. Shaw, what made you ask me to dance?" said a dowager to G.B.S. at a benefit affair.

"This *is* a charity ball, isn't it?" Shaw replied.

• A visitor asked why Shaw kept no vases of flowers. "I thought you were so fond of flowers," he said.

"So I am," Shaw retorted. "I'm very fond of children, too. But I don't cut off their heads and stick them in pots all over the house."

• Mrs. Pat Campbell got the starring role in Shaw's *Pygmalion* because all the reigning London actresses refused to say the taboo word *bloody* that the playwright put in the mouth of Eliza.

• "Did you know that 'sumac' and 'sugar' are the only two words in English that begin with *su* and are pronounced *shu*?" historian B. H. Liddell Hart said to Shaw.

"Sure," replied Shaw.

• Shaw came across a book of his in a second-hand bookstore. The volume had been inscribed to a friend, beneath whose name G.B.S. had written, "With the compliments of George Bernard Shaw." Shaw bought the book and sent it back to his friend, writing under the original inscription, "With renewed compliments, G.B.S."

• One opening night Shaw stepped forward on stage to accept the plaudits of the audience. Amid all the applause, however, a lone dissenter shouted out, "Shaw, your play stinks!" G.B.S. hardly missed a beat after the brief silence that followed. "My friend," he said almost immediately, "I agree with you completely, but what are we two"—he gestured toward the audience—"against the great majority?"

• Captain Shotower in Shaw's *Heartbreak House* (1917) was modeled on either Commander Charles Ashwell Boteler Pocock or Gordon Craig, both of whom led full and fascinating lives. Both of these possible prototypes refused on his deathbed, in Shaw's words, "to take the bread of Extreme Unction unless he could have some cheese with it."

• When playwright St. John Ervine lost a leg in World War I, the outrageous Shaw wrote him, offering this strange consolation: "For a man of your profession two legs are an extravagance. . . . The more the case is gone into the more it appears that you are an exceptionally happy and fortunate man, relieved of a limb to which you owed none of your fame, and which indeed was the cause of your conscription; for without it you would not have been accepted for service."

• "Obscenity," he said in defending authors from censorship, "can be found in every book except the telephone directory."

• Shaw did not like receiving manuscripts to read from aspiring authors and made it a policy to insult people who imposed upon him in this way. To a young man who sent him a long boring novel, he wrote: "The covers of your book are too far apart."

• "You must not suppose," Shaw told a correspondent, "because I am a man of letters, that I never tried to earn an honest living."

• Mrs. Patrick Campbell liked to taunt the vegetarian Shaw about his prowess as a lover. "Some day you'll eat a pork chop, Joey," she once told him, "and then God help all women."

• Though a staunch vegetarian, Shaw refused an invitation to a testimonial where the bill of fare was strictly vegetarian. Said G.B.S., "The thought of two thousand people crunching celery at the same time horrifies me."

• Friends told him that his vegetarianism would kill him, and he replied that at least his funeral could be attended by a procession of all the animals he had never eaten. "And they will look better than most pallbearers I have seen," he added.

• He was asked during the Great War to let his name be used as an example of vegetarianism in newspaper ads to help ease the meat shortage. Refusing, he explained, "There are millions of vegetarians in this world but only one Bernard Shaw. You do not obtain eminence quite so cheaply as by eating macaroni instead of mutton chops."

• In an early edition of *Who's Who* G.B.S. gave his hobbies as "cycling and showing off."

• A shrewd literary negotiator, he was once overheard saying to a motion picture producer, "There's no use in our talking about it [anymore] because, obviously, you're a great artist and I'm just a businessman."

• Sam Goldwyn telephoned Shaw, trying to drive down his price for the film rights to several of his plays. Argued Goldwyn, "Think of the millions of people who would get a chance to see your plays who would otherwise never see them. Think of the contribution it would be to art."

"The trouble is, Mr. Goldwyn," said Shaw, "that you think of nothing but Art and I think of nothing but money."

• Producer Gabriel Pascal acquired the film rights to Shaw's plays after far richer men had failed. Pascal had made a successful film in London and then emigrated to Hollywood, where he could get no work. Arriving back in London, he impulsively called on Shaw, whom he had never met, without an invitation, and told him he wanted to film his plays. "How much capital do you have?" Shaw asked him. "Fifteen shillings and sixpence—but I owe a pound," Pascal replied.

Delighted with Pascal's admiration, effrontery, and wit, Shaw gave him a pound to pay his debts and signed a contract.

• Shaw was standing alone in a corner at a cocktail party. "Are you enjoying yourself, Mr. Shaw." his hostess anxiously asked him. "Certainly," he replied. "There is nothing else here to enjoy."

• Wrote Shaw to Oswald Garrison Villard in 1921, "You are right in your impression that a number of people are urging me to come to the United States. But why on earth do you call them my friends?"

• George Bernard Shaw despised the Eros fountain the sculptor Sir Alfred

Gilbert had erected in London's Piccadilly Circus. Later, Gilbert was charged with taking payment for another sculpture that he never even began. When the sculptor's friends came to the playwright seeking his support, an outraged Shaw refused to do anything except help Gilbert drown himself in the fountain he'd built.

• When Shaw visited William Randolph Hearst's opulent, baroque estate at San Simeon, he turned to a companion and said, "This is probably the way God would have done it if He'd had the money."

CHURCHILLIAN WIT

Writing is an adventure," Winston Churchill said in explaining his avocation. "To begin with, it is a toy and an amusement. Then it becomes a mistress, then it becomes a master, then it becomes a tyrant. The last phase is that just as you are about to be reconciled to your servitude, you kill the monster and fling him to the public." Churchill's wit, however, came easy, and needless to say, was rarely bested.

• Noticing the pompous Sir Stafford Cripps pass by him one day, he turned to a friend and observed, "There, but for the grace of God, goes God."
• Shortly after Churchill had switched from the Conservative side of the House of Commons to the Liberal side, early in his career, a brazen young woman approached him in one of England's corridors of power.

"There are two things I don't like about you, Mr. Churchill," she said.

"And what are they?" he asked.

"Your new politics and your new mustache."

"My dear madam," Churchill replied, "pray do not disturb yourself. You are not likely to come in contact with either."

• "There is a good saying to the effect that when a new book appears one should read an old one," he remarked. "As an author I would not recommend too strict an adherence to this saying."

• "Well, I hope he doesn't have feet of clay, too," Churchill said of Greek prime minister Plasteras.

• He found it difficult to tolerate the pomposity of Charles de Gaulle, leader of the Free French during World War II. "Of all the crosses I have to bear," he once told a friend, "the heaviest is the Cross of Lorraine."

• Churchill was accosted by a voter after winning an election to Parliament. "I presume we may expect you to continue to be humbly subservient to the powerful interests that control your vote," the man said.

"I'll thank you to keep my wife's name out of this," Churchill replied.

• "Have you read my recent book?" Churchill's cousin and political opponent Lord Londonderry asked.

"No," Churchill replied, "I only read for pleasure or profit."

• Churchill wasn't very impressed with Clement Atlee, his successor as prime minister in 1946. He once told a friend Atlee was "a sheep in sheep's clothing." Another time he made this observation: "He [Atlee] has the gift of compressing the largest amount of words into the smallest amount of thought."

• "May I have some breast?" he asked his American hostess at a buffet luncheon.

"In this country, Mr. Churchill, we say, white meat or dark meat," his hostess replied, a little prissily.

Churchill apologized and the next day sent her an orchid along with a card reading, "I would be most obliged if you would pin this on your white meat."

• When told that by the year 2100 women would rule the world, he replied, "Still?"

• "Sarah," he told his daughter in commenting on the state of the world, "we have to a large extent succeeded in erasing the lion and the tiger from the human soul. But we have not succeeded in removing the donkey."

• One morning during Churchill's last days in Parliament, he was shuffling slowly to his seat when the following was heard between two back-benches:

"What a pity."

"They say he's nearly blind."

After which, those closest to the former prime minister heard him mumble, "They also say he's deaf."

• "I am ready to meet my Maker," he said on his seventy-fifth birthday. "Whether my Maker is prepared for the ordeal of meeting me is another matter."

• Churchill could be nearly impossible to work for. Late in his life one of his loyal valets received one undeserved reprimand too many and stood up to him. A loud argument ensued and when it subsided, Churchill said, "You were very rude to me, you know."

"Yes," the manservant replied, "but you were rude, too."

"Yes," Churchill groused, "but I am a great man."

Later the servant would say: "There was no answer to that. He knew, as I and the rest of the world knew, that he was right."

The manservant continued working for him.

BLITHE SPIRIT

BRITISH PLAYWRIGHT Noel Coward (1899–1973) tried to keep his homosexuality a secret, lest receipts from his plays should diminish. In the 1960s a biographer tried to convince him that he could reveal his sexual nature in a much more tolerant era, citing the example of drama critic T. C. Worsley, who had done so with no trouble. "There is one essential difference between me and Cuthbert Worsley," Coward replied. "The British public at large would not care if Cuthbert Worsley had slept with mice." The author of *Blithe Spirit*, *Private Lives*, and many other smart, sophisticated comedies was among the fastest and most facile of modern wits. "I write at high speed," he once said, "because boredom is bad for my health."

• "I've always thought I'd be particularly good in Romeo," he remarked to a friend. "As the nurse."

• One time he was mistaken for actor Rex Harrison. He replied, rather indignantly, "Do I look as if I sold Bentleys in Great Portland Street?"

• It is said that when his childhood friend actress Gertrude Lawrence married Robert Aldrich, Coward cabled her this poem: "Dear Mrs. A / Hooray, hooray /At last you are deflowered. I love you this and every day / Yours truly, Noel Coward."

• He was a great practical joker. It's said that he once sent identical anonymous notes to the twenty most prominent Londoners: "All is discovered. Escape while you can." All twenty left town by morning.

• Coward corrected singer Elaine Stritch when she pronounced the city of Babel to rhyme with scrabble.

"It's *bayble*, Stritch," he advised.

"I've always said *babble*," she countered. "Everyone says *babble*. It means mixed-up language, doesn't it? Gibberish. It's where we get *babble* from."

"That's a fabble," Coward said.

• "Mr. Coward, have you anything to say to the *Sun*?" a reporter asked him one cloudy day.

"Shine," he pleasantly replied.

• Coward had a six-month-old elephant delivered to songwriter Cole Porter's Beverly Hills house with an attached note reading "This trunk call says it all. To Coley from Noely."

Not one to be bettered, Porter soon sent a live alligator to Coward's house with the attached note: "Here are some teeth to match your tongue. To Noely from Coley."

• The playwright, a friend, and the friend's young son were walking by the shore when they passed two copulating dogs. "What are they doing?" the child asked innocently.

"It's like this, dear boy," Coward explained. "The one in front is blind and the kind one behind is pushing him."

• "Did you see my last play, *Private Lives?*" Coward asked the actress Lady Diana Manners.

"Yes," she replied, "Not at all amusing. Speaking of plays, did you see me play the role of the Virgin in *The Miracle?*"

"Yes," said Coward. "*Very* amusing."

• Coward heard that a rather obtuse acquaintance had "blown his brains out." "He must have been a marvelously good shot," the playwright observed.

AMERICA'S GREATEST HUMORIST

NATIVE AMERICAN humor came from many sources, no one person fathering or mothering it, but Mark Twain (Samuel Clemens, 1835–1910) was the first American writer to refine it into an art. For half a century his books, lectures, and after-dinner speeches made him the most quoted humorist in the country, an honor he may still hold today.

• At the top of a letter he wrote in 1865 describing how he first decided to make his life's work "serious scribbling to excite the laughter of God's creatures," he scrawled this sentence as an apparent afterthought: "You had better shove this in the stove—for if we strike a bargain I don't want any absurd 'literary remains' & 'unpublished letters of Mark Twain' published after I am planted."

• During his lean days as a reporter in San Francisco, Twain was approached by a lady friend who saw him gazing into a shop window, a cigar box under his arm. "I'm sorry to see you carrying that cigar box, Mr. Clemens," she said. "I'm afraid you're smoking too much."

"It isn't that," Twain replied. "I'm moving again."

• Twain's knees were shaking so violently that few people in the audience believed he would be able to deliver his first lecture, but he won the day when he began, "Julius Caesar is dead, Shakespeare is dead, Napoleon is dead, Abraham Lincoln is dead, and I am far from well myself."

• Only once did he fail as an after-dinner speaker. In 1877 he was asked to speak at John Greenleaf Whittier's seventieth birthday dinner in Boston. His speech, in which he was supposed to represent the West paying homage to the East, centered on three overbearing tramps who visited a camp of California prospectors. The three tramps were Ralph Waldo Emerson, Oliver Wendell

Holmes, and Henry Wadsworth Longfellow—who sat dignified as ever in the audience. None of them thought his conception funny and their reaction spread to the other guests. Except for a solitary hysterical man there was utter silence, and Mark Twain stood there so embarrassed that for one of the few times in his life he was unable to think of anything funny to say.

• Among his most famous speeches was his address on New England weather at a dinner of the New England Society in New York in 1876:

> There is a sumptuous variety about the New England weather that compels the stranger's admiration—and regret. The weather is always doing something there; always attending strictly to business; always getting up new designs and trying them out on people to see how they will go. But it gets through more business in Spring than in any other season. In the Spring I have counted one hundred and thirty-six different kinds of weather inside of twenty-four hours.

• He answered a "Toast to the babies" at a Chicago banquet in 1879: "We haven't all had the good fortune to be ladies; we haven't all been generals, or poets, or statesmen; but when the toast works down to babies, we stand on common ground."

• Speaking to the Young People's Society of the Greenpoint (Brooklyn) Presbyterian Church in 1901, he advised, "Always do right. This will gratify some people, and astonish the rest."

• When a friend invited him to dinner, Twain, who just arrived home off the banquet lecture circuit, wrote in reply: "Dear Lee—I can't. I am in a family way with three weeks undigested dinners in my system, and shall just roost here and diet and purge till I am delivered. Shall I name it after you? Yr. friend, Sam'll. Clemens."

• A customs inspector found a bottle of bourbon in his suitcase. "I thought you said there was only clothing in there," he questioned.

"I did," Twain replied. "You're looking at my nightcap!"

• "Don't you adore babies?" an elderly lady, holding her infant niece in her arms, asked Twain.

"No, I hate them," Twain replied, vastly enjoying his outrageous joke. He went on to tell her that when he was recovering from typhoid, his little nephew had come into his room and kissed him. "I made up my mind," he said in his best serious manner, "that if I lived I would put up a monument to Herod."

• He observed in his notebook, "Familiarity breeds contempt—and children."

• Remarked American literary critic Van Wyck Brooks, "His wife not only edited his works but edited him."

• Though he quipped that working in bed is dangerous, "because so many people die there," Twain did a lot of his own writing in bed, as photographs of him show. Large parts of *Huckleberry Finn, Tom Sawyer*, and *A Connecticut Yankee in King Arthur's Court*, among other works, were written between the sheets, with pillows propped up behind his head.

• On the road for one of his lecture tours Twain went to a barber shop in a small town.

"You picked a good time to come, stranger," the barber said, "Mark Twain's going to read and lecture tonight. I suppose you'll go?"

"Oh, I guess so."

"Have you got a ticket?"

"Not yet."

"Then you'll have to stand. Everything is sold out."

"How annoying," Twain sighed. "I never saw such luck! I always have to stand when that fellow lectures."

• Several scholars were arguing heatedly about whether or not Shakespeare had written the plays and sonnets attributed to him. Finally, Twain butted in. "It wasn't William Shakespeare who really wrote those plays," he explained, "but another Englishman who was born on the same day at the same hour as he, and who died on the same day, and, to carry the coincidences still further, was also named William Shakespeare."

• "It could probably be shown by facts and figures," Twain once mused, "that there is no distinctively native American criminal class except Congress."

• Twain took a rival publisher, Estes and Lauriat, to court when they printed *Huckleberry Finn* before even his own publishing company could print it. When Judge Le Baron Colt ruled against him in the United States Circuit Court in Boston, the author was so enraged that he publicly condemned Colt. The judge, he said, has allowed the defendant "to sell property which does not belong to him but to me—property which he has not bought and I have not sold." Therefore, he went on, "under this same ruling I am now advertising the judge's homestead for sale; and if I make as good a sum out of it as I expect I shall go on and sell the rest of his property."

• "Dear Charley," he wrote to his publisher Charles Webster in early 1885, "the Committee of the Public Library of Concord, Massachusetts, have given us a rattling tip-off puff which will go into every paper in the country. They have expelled Huck [Huckleberry Finn] from their library as 'trash suitable only for the slums.' That will sell 25,000 copies for us sure." (It sold 50,000 the first year.)

• While giving a speech on honesty he told this story:

When I was a boy, I was walking along a street and happened to spy a cart full of watermelons. I was fond of watermelon, so I sneaked up quietly to the cart and snitched one. Then I ran into a nearby alley and sank my teeth into the melon. No sooner had I done so, however, than a strange feeling came over me. Without a moment's hesitation, I made my decision. I walked back to the cart, replaced the melon—and took a ripe one.

• A friend asked Twain why he had so many books piled all over his house but no books lined on shelves. "You see," Twain explained, "it's so very difficult to borrow shelves."

• When Twain asked a neighbor for the loan of a book, the man said that he was more than welcome to it, but he had to read it there, as he made it a rule never to let any book out of his library. Some time later the neighbor asked to borrow Twain's lawnmower. "Certainly," Twain told him. "You're more than welcome to it. But I must ask you to use it here. You know I make it a rule."

• Twain was in a foul mood one morning. Unable to find a clean shirt to wear, he unleashed a stable of expletives only he could have strung together. His wife, Livy Langdon, standing in the doorway, decided to teach him a lesson and slowly repeated each vile curse he had uttered. But when she was done, Twain simply sighed and said, "My dear, you have the words, but you don't have the music."

• A gushing fan seized Twain's hand and kissed it in admiration of his work. "How God must love you!" she cried.

"I hope so," Twain said, smiling, but after the lady left, he added, "I guess she hasn't heard of our strained relations."

• At a dinner party guests were discussing heaven and hell and how one must act to merit either place. One matron turned to Mark Twain and demanded to know his opinion on the matter. "Madam, you must excuse me," Twain replied gravely. "I am silent of necessity: I have friends in both places."

• Twain, an agnostic himself, was asked if he was going to hear the celebrated agnostic Robert Ingersoll's lecture at the Hartford Opera House. "No," Twain replied. "I understand that Ingersoll will talk about what he thinks of Moses. But I would be far more interested in hearing what Moses thinks of Ingersoll."

• A Mormon arguing with Twain defied him to cite any biblical passage expressly forbidding polygamy.

"Nothing easier," Twain told him. " 'No man can serve two masters.' "

• After hearing a dramatic sermon one Sunday, Twain told the preacher it was a good one but that he had a book at home that contained every word of it. "Impossible," the preacher snorted. "I'd certainly like to see that book, if it exists." Within a week the preacher received a bulky package from Twain containing an unabridged dictionary.

• "Before I die," said a ruthless businessman to Twain, "I mean to make a pilgrimage to the Holy Land. I will climb Mount Sinai and read the Ten Commandments aloud at the top."

"I have a better idea," Twain suggested. "You could stay home in Boston and keep them."

• "Do you think it will stop?" William Dean Howells asked Twain as they were leaving church one Sunday and it began to rain heavily. "It always has," said Twain.

• "Quitting smoking is easy," the great cigar-smoker remarked. "I've done it a hundred times."

• An acquaintance told Twain she hadn't been feeling well for a week or so, and he advised her to buy a certain magnetic health belt.

"I bought the belt and have worn it constantly," she wrote him a few weeks later, "but it didn't help me one bit."

Twain wired back, "It helped me. I own stock in the company."

• "In a world without women what would men become?" Twain was asked.

"Scarce, sir," Twain said, "mighty scarce."

• "My grandfather was cut down in the prime of his life," Twain told a haughty woman who had been bragging about her ancestors. "In fact, my grandmother used to say that if he had been cut down fifteen minutes earlier, he could have been resuscitated."

• "Mr. Clemens, I would give ten pounds not to have read your *Huckleberry Finn*," an Englishman who encountered him on a train told a startled Twain. When Twain looked up, he added, "So that I could again have the great pleasure of reading it for the first time."

• While visiting James McNeill Whistler's London studio, Twain bent as if to touch one canvas. "No," Whistler warned, "don't touch that! Don't you see it isn't dry yet!"

"It's all right," Twain said. "I have gloves on."

• Twain claimed a certain admiration for British empire builder Cecil Rhodes, who had made his fortune in the Kimberley diamond fields and later was forced to resign as prime minister of Cape Colony, Africa, after being pronounced guilty of serious breaches of duty. "I admire him," Twain remarked, "I frankly confess it; and when his time comes I shall buy a piece of the rope for a keepsake."

• An arrogant Frenchman remarked to Twain that whenever an American had nothing to do he could endlessly amuse himself by trying to find out who his grandfather was. "And whenever a Frenchman has nothing to do," Twain countered, "he can amuse himself endlessly by trying to find out who his *father* was."

• Weak French coffee was a Twain *bête noire*. After drinking a cup one time he told a friend it was made by "rubbing a chicory bean against a coffee bean and dropping the chicory bean in the water."

• Twain was charged $8, a good deal of money then, for a boat tour of the Sea of Galilee. "Do you wonder that Christ walked?" he asked.

• "All you need in this life is ignorance and confidence," Twain wrote in an 1887 letter to Mrs. Foote, "and then success is sure."

• A traditional story has it that in 1897 an American newspaper bannered Twain's death. When another paper sent a reporter to check the story Twain came to the door of his Connecticut home and gave him the following statement: "James Ross Clemens, a cousin of mine, was seriously ill two or three weeks ago, but is well now. The reports of my illness grew out of his illness. The reports of my death are greatly exaggerated." Nothing any scholar says will change this tale, which is by now part of American folklore, but the true story is that a reporter from the *New York Journal* called on Twain while the author was staying in England—to check out a rumor that Twain was either dead or dying in poverty. Twain explained to the reporter that his cousin had been seriously ill in London and that reports of his own illness grew out of his cousin's illness, that "the report of my death was an exaggeration."

• "When I was younger," he confided toward the end of his life, "I could remember anything, whether it had happened or not; but my faculties are decaying now and soon I shall be so I cannot remember any but the things that never happened. It is sad to go to pieces like this, but we all have to do it."

F. P. A. F A V O R I T E S

F.P.A., as Franklin Pierce Adams (1881–1960), the American humorist and Algonquin Round Table habitué, was known, professed to dislike writing and considered it hard work. One time an interviewer told him of an author who was "terribly eager" to begin writing every day. Replied F.P.A., "The only people who like to write terribly are those that do." Adams himself never wrote terribly, and his column, "The Conning Tower," encouraged many eager and excellent American humorists.

• Adams was a punctual man. "Promptness is a worthy cause," he once told an editor, "but costly. You call the doctor and he says he'll be at your home between three and four to have a look at your wife. You wait. He arrives at seven. You have an appointment with the dentist for 3:00 P.M. sharp. At 3:00 P.M. sharp you are waiting in his reception room. So are six other patients waiting their turn. You buy tickets for the theater. The curtain will rise on the dot of eight, or so the announcements say. Fifteen minutes earlier you are in your seat and already have memorized the pages of program notes. You also have read all the ads and decided on which sandwich you'll order later at Sardi's. At 8:17 the curtain rises. Slowly. I have wasted a year and a half of my life waiting for curtains to rise, and seven years waiting for people who were late."

• Alexander Woollcott asked that his friend give him a shower when he moved into his new apartment. "I'd actually appreciate your bringing china, linen, and silver," he made it known. Accordingly, F.P.A. brought him a mustache cup, a handkerchief, and a dime.

• *New York World* editor Herbert Bayard Swope was questioning a foreign visitor at his home about German poetry when the name of Henrich von Kleist came up. "Who's Kleist?" Swope demanded. F.P.A., seated nearby, answered, "The Chinese messiah."

• Adams wasn't noted for his good looks. One morning humorist Irvin Cobb entered a room where a moosehead was mounted over the mantel. "My God, they've shot F.P.A.!" he cried.

• After watching young Helen Hayes play Cleopatra on Broadway in *Caesar and Cleopatra*, F.P.A. remarked to a friend that she appeared to be suffering from "fallen archness."

• Adams and his wife doted on their white angora cat Miztah, with whom *New Yorker* editor Harold Ross planned to mate his cat Missus—until she mysteriously disappeared one spring night. The two Adams often went so far as to spell out words in front of their cat to keep him from becoming conceited: "See how H-A-N-D-S-O-M-E he is!"

• Adams, Harpo Marx, and other members of the Thanatopsis Poker Playing and Inside Straight Club were playing in a hotel room when a waiter entered in the middle of a big hand, tripped, and fell, spilling a mess of food all over the table. Nobody stopped cursing until Harpo Marx quipped, "Well, the waiter drops out," and F.P.A. added, "Yeah, he only had a tray."

• An interminable bore went on and on with a story until he came to the inevitable point where he said, "Well, to cut a long story short . . ."

"Too late," F.P.A. advised.

THE WIT OF RING LARDNER

*T*HOUGH HE WROTE some of the funniest stories in the English language, American author Ring Lardner (1885–1933) was a quiet, solemn man who rarely smiled or laughed. "A noble dignity flowed from him," F. Scott Fitzgerald once said. And his friend, sportswriter Hugh Fullerton, said he "looked like Rameses II with his wrappings off." He so disliked jokes that whenever anyone warned him, "Stop me if you've heard this one," he invariably cried "Stop!" But this kind man with the "phonographic ear for American speech" had the driest wit of any of the great American writers of his time.

• He was by nature aloof and detached. At a Dorothy Parker party he told everyone who didn't know him that he was a recent emigrant from Poland so that they wouldn't expect him to speak.

• At a Friar's Club dinner a fellow member asked Lardner to read a syrupy poem by the man's late brother, who had passed away twenty years ago. On finishing, Lardner turned to the man and inquired, "Did your brother write this before or after he died?"

• Asked to contribute to a symposium on how the wives of prominent men had helped them, Lardner did not give any of the usual hackneyed answers to the trite question. He replied:

In 1914 or 1915, I think it was July, she cleaned my white shoes. She dusted my typewriter in 1922. Late one night in 1924, we got home from somewhere and I said I was hungry and she gave me a verbal picture of the location of the pantry. Another time I quit cigarettes and she felt sorry for me. Once on a trip just as I was nearly crazy trying to guess whether I should take the lower or upper berth she solved the problem by crawling into the lower berth.

• Of his friends the Scott Fitzgeralds he said, "Mr. Fitzgerald is a novelist. Mrs. Fitzgerald is a novelty."

• Lardner was well into his cups at the Lambs Club when a wild-haired, wild-eyed actor passed the bar. The writer looked up and said nothing, but when the actor passed by a second time, he stopped him and inquired, "How do you look when I'm sober?"

• Perhaps the most famous of Lardner's quips was inspired by the writer's move with his family from Chicago to New York, where he began his syndicated column. Somehow the Lardners went astray in the Bronx. The famous exchange came when the author's son asked him if they were lost, Lardner later re-creating the scene in his short story "The Young Immigrants," told from a child's viewpoint:

> "Are you lost, Daddy?" I asked tenderly.
> "Shut up," he explained.

• After visiting "Silent Cal" Coolidge at the White House, Lardner confided to friends, "I told him my funniest story, and he laughed so hard you could hear a pin drop."

THE WELL-GROOMED WIT OF HEYWOOD BROUN

ANOTHER OF THE famed Algonquin wits, Heywood Broun (1888–1939) served as drama critic for the *New York Tribune* and panned his share of plays, writing of *Just Outside the Door* (1915) that "wherever the long arm of coincidence intrudes, the author seizes it and shakes hands." Broun was a sloppy dresser well known among his friends for the carelessness and disarray of his personal appearance, which often alarmed strangers. One time he and a number of war correspondents were presented to General Pershing. Eyeing him with some concern, the general inquired, "Have you fallen down, Mr. Broun?" Someone said that only his wit was well-groomed.

• As a cub reporter for the *New York World*, Broun was sent to interview Utah's Senator Smoot, but Smoot refused, telling him, "I'm sorry, I have nothing to say."

"I know," Broun replied, "now let's get down to the interview."

• Caught in a downpour and soaked to the skin, Broun ran into the Algonquin, where he ordered a glass of wine to warm himself. He tasted the wine, didn't like it, but quickly downed the liquid, quipping, "Oh, well, any port in a storm."

• "Don't look now," he told Tallulah Bankhead on one of her opening nights, "but your show's slipping."

• His bad jokes came to be expected by his friends. Here's a sample: "If a philosopher lectured on Descartes in a bordello what would I say?—I would say the philosopher was putting Descartes before de whores."

• Morris Ernst, who knew Broun from when he was a boy, and was well aware of his hypochondria, once described his friend as "a one-man art show of cardiograms." Before undergoing an operation for a hernia the confirmed hypochondriac wrote the following limerick while waiting in his hospital bed:

> *There was a young man with a hernia*
> *Who said to his surgeon "Gol-dernya,*
> *When carving my middle*
> *Be sure you don't fiddle*
> *With matters that do not concernya."*

THE BEST OF BOB BENCHLEY

AUTHOR AND DRAMA critic Robert Benchley (1889–1945) is one of the few Americans who could be ranked among the world's greatest humorists. He and his good friend Dorothy Parker were the most celebrated wits of their time, and Benchley is the only author ever to win an Academy Award for a film he starred in—his *How to Sleep*, which he wrote and solely performed, winning the 1936 Oscar for the best live-action short subject.

• During his Harvard days, Benchley took a final examination in which he was asked to "discuss the arbitration of the international fisheries problem in respect to hatcheries, protocol, and dragnet and travel procedure as it affects (a) the point of view of the United States and (b) the point of view of Great Britain."

Benchley answered as follows: "I know nothing about the point of view of Great Britain in the arbitration of the international fisheries problem and nothing about the point of view of the United States. Therefore, I shall discuss the question from the point of view of the fish."

• Benchley was known to drink; in fact, he was known to drink more and to be able to hold more than anyone else in his circle.

"What do you drink so much for?" Scott Fitzgerald, of all people, once lectured him. "Don't you know alcohol is slow poison?"

"So who's in a hurry?" Benchley replied.

• For the title of a 1928 book, the master of low comedy chose *20,000 Leagues Under the Sea, or David Copperfield*.

• Standing on the balcony of Delmonico's restaurant and looking out at Fifth Avenue one spring evening in 1923, Marc Connelly suddenly pointed to Benchley and shouted to the pedestrians below: "People, people! Your new prince!" As Connelly put it in his autobiography: "Without a flicker of hesitation, Benchley stepped forward to the balustrade. He lifted his hands to silence un-shouted cheers, then, as smoothly as though he had gone over the speech with an equerry, he assured his listeners in broken German that he did not want them as a conquered people to feel like slaves under a yoke but as chastened human beings aware that their future depended on the acceptance of a regime which they might resent but that would do its best to govern them in a kindly fashion. Benchley promised that as soon as they evidenced self-restraint, he would order curfews lifted, begin freeing political prisoners, and in time restore to qualified Americans the right to vote for local officials. 'And now,' he concluded, 'my prime minister and I will retire to discuss matters of state. And you have all been so cute, next Saturday night I will. permit fireworks and dancing in the streets.' "

• He liked to collect books with odd titles. These he kept on a special shelf, books such as *Talks on Manure, Keeping A Single Cow, Forty Thousand Sublime and Beautiful Thoughts, In and Out with Mary Anne, Perverse Pussys*.

• Dorothy Parker asked Benchley why he didn't leave the office at *Vanity Fair* and review plays himself, since he was so fond of drama. "No, I'll stay at the desk," Benchley said. "I do most of my work sitting down—that's where I shine."

• Parker and Benchley set up business together as freelance writers after leaving *Vanity Fair*, renting a small office and marking the door "The Utica Drop Forge and Tool Company, Benchley and Parker, Presidents." Their cable address was "Parkbench." Benchley later described the tiny office: "One cubic foot less of space and it would have constituted adultery."

• During a session of charades at a friend's house Benchley was given the name of Hungarian playwright Ladislaus Busfekete to act out. Snorting, he dropped to the floor, circled the room on all fours, crawled out the French doors and out the front door, got up, brushed himself off, and hailed a cab to take him home.

• The first time he visited Venice, Benchley was on assignment for the *New Yorker*. "Streets full of water," he wired Harold Ross, "please advise."

• Alexander Woollcott told the story of Benchley leaving a Manhattan eatery and asking a uniformed man in the doorway to hail him a taxi. "I'm not a doorman," came the indignant reply, "I'm a rear admiral in the United States Navy!"

"In that case," Benchley countered, "get me a battleship."

• During a stay in Paris a doorman gave Benchley, a generous tipper, very poor attention. But as the writer left on his last day the man fawned all over him, finally opening the door of Benchley's taxi, holding out his hand, and saying, "You're not going to forget me, sir?"

Benchley grabbed his hand and shook it heartily.

"No," he promised. "I'll write you every day."

• The Broadway and Hollywood actor Charles Butterworth was a little man with a deadpan delivery. Once, he, Benchley, and friends were watching a tennis tournament at a woman's nudist camp in California. All eyes remained glued on the action, and not a word was said until Butterworth, breaking up even Benchley, turned and asked, "Who's winning?"

• James Thurber told the story of the time the proud owner of an "indestructible" watch showed it to Benchley and Dorothy Parker. They banged it on the table, threw it on the floor, and stomped on it. Finally, the owner picked it up and held it to his ear. "I can't believe it—it has stopped!" he said incredulously.

"Maybe you wound it too tight," Benchley and Parker said in unison.

• Leaving a party on Riverside Drive early in the morning, Benchley wandered over to Grant's Tomb, not realizing that several friends were following him. After a while his friends saw him pick something up, write a few words on a slip of paper, and then place the object back on the ground again. When he left, his friends came closer. There, outside the tomb, stood an empty milk bottle with a note in it, reading "One milk, no cream—U. S. Grant."

• Benchley attended the premiere of *The Squall*, a turkey about gypsies who spoke in broken English. He bore the pain as long as he could, until a young gypsy girl came on stage and delivered the immortal lines, "Me Nubi. Nubi good girl. Nubi stay."

Benchley immediately rose.

"Me Bobby," he said. "Bobby bad boy. Bobby go." And he left the theater.

• Usually a man of impeccable judgment, Benchley made a bad mistake as theater adviser to millionaire John Hay Whitney. "I could smell it when the postman came whistling down the lane," he told the millionaire about a play he had received that was based on several popular *New Yorker* magazine stories. "Don't put a dime in it." Luckily, Whitney decided to back *Life with Father* anyway, and it ran for seven and a half years.

• Toward the end of a Hollywood party in the late 1930s, Benchley began backing away from playwright Robert Sherwood and suddenly cried, "Those eyes—I can't stand those eyes looking at me!" Everyone thought a joke was coming, but the humorist was dead serious. Pointing at Sherwood, he said, "He's looking at me and thinking of how he knew me when I was going to be a great writer. . . . And he's thinking *now* look at what I am!"

• At the end of his career, when he was no longer reviewing plays, Benchley went to a Broadway opening with a friend. He fell asleep during the first act, but when a telephone rang on stage he awoke with a start, shouting, "Will someone please answer that—I think it's for me!" The next day one review read, "Show terrible but Benchley superb in small part."

• The first time Dorothy Parker attempted suicide, swallowing a bottle of barbiturates, Benchley visited her in the hospital to try and cheer her up. "Dottie," he said, looking at her sadly, "if you don't stop this sort of thing, you'll make yourself sick."

• Benchley's columns sometimes reflected his darker side, as in this tragic 1930 bit: "I would like to protest the killing by a taxicab, on December 10th of Wesley Hill, the Angel Gabriel of *Green Pastures*. . . . There was really no sense in that, Lord, and you know it as well as I do."

• "I can hear him laughing now," Benchley's wife said upon reaching the Nantucket graveyard where his ashes were to be buried—and then inspecting the open burial urn she was transporting. As a kind of cosmic farewell joke, the ashes in the urn had blown away en route, and she had been driving for miles with an empty vessel.

A KAUFMAN COLLECTION

*F*ROM HIS earliest days, playwright George S. Kaufman (1889–1961) had a precocious wit and vocabulary. When he was only four, his mother told him that his aunt would be visiting soon. "It wouldn't hurt to be nice to her, would it?" she asked. "That depends," Kaufman replied, "on your threshold of pain." And he got better as he got older; he is as much remembered today for his incisive wit as for his enduring plays.

• Once another wit at the Algonquin Round Table made an anti-Semitic remark to Kaufman "in the spirit of fun." The playwright retaliated with mock indignation. "For my part, I've heard enough slurs," he cried. "I am now leaving this table, this dining room, this hotel—never ever to return!" Pausing, he glanced at Dorothy Parker, whose mother was Jewish and father was Christian. "And I trust Miss Parker will walk out with me," he added. "Halfway."

• One afternoon at the Round Table, Kaufman was asked to supply a definition of satire. "Satire," he replied, "is what closes on Saturday night."

• Some of Kaufman's best ripostes were made during sessions of the Thanatopsis poker club, which took its name from the club in Sinclair Lewis's *Main Street* and had as its members such bright literary lights as Ring Lardner, Alexander Woollcott, Harold Ross, and Marc Connelly. Kaufman, an expert player, once dropped out of a hand with a pair of tens showing, punning, "I will now fold my tens and silently steal away."

• Kaufman worried about the lyrics of Irving Berlin's "Always." " 'Always' seems like such a long time," he told the composer. "Why don't you make it, 'I'll be loving you on Thursday.' "

• Alexander Woollcott had created the eponymous cocktail the Alexander, made with cream, crème de cacao, and other dreadful ingredients. The "lethal mixture . . . tasted like ice cream," Helen Hayes said. "I drank one down and took another and drank it down, and I was blind." Searching for something to say, fearing everyone would think her drunk if she didn't, Miss Hayes remembered that she would be moving soon to a smaller apartment and wanted to get rid of her large piano. But her words came out, "Anyone who wants my piano, is willing to it." After a long, terrible silence, Kaufman said, "That's very seldom of you, Helen."

• "What's my motivation for doing it?" a young Method actor asked when Kaufman told him to make a certain stage movement. "Your job," Kaufman replied.

• "There's no scenery at all," said an actress, describing a new play she was rehearsing. "In the first scene, I'm on the left side of the stage and the audience has to imagine I'm eating dinner in a restaurant. Then in scene two, I move over to the right side of the stage, and the audience has to imagine I'm in my drawing room."

"And the second night," Kaufman said, "*you* have to imagine there's an audience out front."

• Kaufman's bridge partner, who played terribly all afternoon, asked to be excused to go to the men's room. "Gladly," Kaufman replied. "For the first time today I'll know what you have in your hand."

• The author of a panned Broadway show had the misfortune to run into Kaufman shortly afterward. "I understand," Kaufman said, "that your play is full of single entendre."

• Popular singer Eddie Fisher, appearing on a television show, told Kaufman that women refused to date him because he looked so young. He asked Kaufman's advice, and the author replied:

> Mr. Fisher, on Mount Wilson there is a telescope that can magnify the most distant stars up to twenty-four times the magnification of any previous telescope. This remarkable instrument was unsurpassed until the construction of the Mount Palomar telescope, an even more remarkable instrument of magnification. Owing to advances and improvements in optical technology, it is capable of magnifying the stars to four times the magnification and resolution of the Mount Wilson telescope —Mr. Fisher, if you could somehow put the Mount Wilson telescope *inside* the Mount Palomar telescope, you *still* wouldn't be able to detect my interest in your problem.

• Charlie Chaplin was said to be richer than he was famous. One day he remarked to Kaufman that his blood pressure was down to 108. "Common or preferred?" Kaufman inquired.

• Kaufman was outraged at Paramount Pictures' offer of $30,000 for the film rights to one of his plays. He countered by offering $40,000 for Paramount.

• The playwright met with Broadway producer Jed Harris at Harris's Waldorf Astoria suite, and for some reason known only to himself, Harris squatted naked on the floor for the whole meeting. If he meant to shock Kaufman it didn't work, for the great wit didn't say a word about his nakedness until he was leaving. Then, with hand on the doorknob, Kaufman stared at Harris and advised, "Jed, your fly is open."

• After the flop of his adaptation of the French farce *Someone in the House*, Kaufman suggested the following advertising slogan to the producer: "Avoid crowds, see *Someone in the House* at the Knickerbocker Theatre."

• After reading a manuscript filled with spelling errors, Kaufman told the author: "I'm not very good at it myself, but the first rule about spelling is that there is only one *z* in *is*."

• Waiters were Kaufman's pet hate; he believed they were actually trained to exasperate him and other customers. His many remarks about the breed culminated with his mock epitaph for a dead waiter: "God finally caught his eye."

• "After all, it's only a small, insignificant theater," explained a summer stock producer who had used a Kaufman play without paying royalties.

"Then you'll go to a small, insignificant jail," Kaufman replied.

• "How do I get our leading lady's name in the *Times*?" the press agent for a musical asked Kaufman when he was drama critic at that newspaper. "Shoot her," Kaufman advised.

• All through dinner the woman at his side didn't shut up, giving him her opinions on a wide variety of subjects and never letting him get a word in edgewise. When dessert was served, Kaufman finally turned to her and said, "Madam, don't you have any unexpressed thoughts?"

• When Kaufman was scriptwriter for the Marx Brothers' *Cocoanuts*, Groucho tried to slip one of his jokes into a scene. Kaufman thought it was terrible. "They laughed at Fulton and his steamboat, too," Groucho groused. "Not at matinees," Kaufman said.

• S. N. Behrman had been given a farewell party on the eve of his planned departure from Hollywood to New York. He didn't leave the next day, because the studio asked him to do some emergency rewriting. When Kaufman ran into him on the lot, he quipped, "Ah, forgotten but not gone."

• After Clifford Odets had written a rather anemic play, Kaufman asked him, "Odets, where is thy sting?"

THE LONGEST COMPENDIUM OF PARKERISMS

AMERICAN AUTHOR Dorothy Parker (1893–1967) surely ranks with Oscar Wilde, George Bernard Shaw, Richard Brinsley Sheridan, and several others as one of the ten greatest literary wits in history. Born Dorothy Rothschild in what is now Long Branch, New Jersey, she married Eddie Parker in 1917, kept her married name after their divorce, and was commonly called Miss Parker. She certainly had the sharpest tongue at New York's celebrated Algonquin Round Table. Her famous quips include the mock epitaphs "This is on me" and "Pardon my dust." It should be noted that Miss Parker is *not* responsible for the three bon mots most often attributed to her: "Let's slip out of these clothes and into a dry martini" (Robert Benchley); "Everything worthwhile doing is either immoral, illegal, or fattening" (Alexander Woollcott); and "I'd rather flunk my Wasserman test / Than read the poems of Edgar Guest" (Anonymous). Following is one of the largest collections of the bon mots of a woman who "could make a fool immortal with her jibes."

• She was born two to three months premature on August 22, 1893. But all the rest of her life she never got anywhere on time, a fact that all her friends and she herself recognized. "My premature birth," she once said, "was the last time I was early for anything."

• The author told her companions at the Algonquin Round Table that she had been early on one other occasion in her life. Her first husband, Eddie Parker, had lied to her about the time, so they arrived at a funeral a half-hour early. She claimed that Eddie began fooling with a knob under the casket and suddenly machinery was heard cranking and humming. The casket and corpse began moving and finally slid through a little door that opened into the fires of the crematorium. She and her husband fled out a side door before anyone else arrived.

• Her first writing job was as a caption writer for *Vogue*, the fashion magazine. Her wit was evident in the very first caption she wrote, which appeared under several photos of women's underwear: "Brevity is the Soul of Lingerie, as the Petticoat said to the Chemise."

• Her friend Franklin Pierce Adams's "The Conning Tower" column was the first to publish Parker's celebrated couplet "News Item":

> *Men seldom make passes*
> *At girls who wear glasses . . .*

Later, S. Omar Barker qualified the couplet: "Whether men will make passes at girls who wear glasses / Depends quite a bit on the shape of the chassis."

• Clare Boothe Brokaw, who later became Clare Boothe Luce, had joined the staff of *Vanity Fair* and encountered Miss Parker in the lobby one morning. "Age before beauty," said the sharp-tongued Clare, holding the door open. "Pearls before swine," Dorothy Parker said, entering first. Clare Boothe Luce later denied this story, and a similar quip was used in one of Alexander Woollcott's pieces, but it has nevertheless become part of the Parker legend. Recalled Mrs. Robert Benchley when she was eighty years old: "I was right there, the time in the Algonquin, when *some little chorus girl* and Dottie were going into the dining room and the girl stepped back and said, 'Age before beauty,' and Dottie said very quickly, 'Pearls before swine.' I was right there when she said it."

• Another time a mutual friend was extolling the virtues of Clare Boothe Luce to her. "Actually, she's awfully kind to her inferiors," the friend said.

"Where does she find them?" Miss Parker asked.

• When Dorothy Parker was a young and struggling writer working in a small New York office, she was so lonely that she had a sign lettered on the door reading MEN.

• For a time Miss Parker worked as a writer for Metro-Goldwyn-Mayer, a Hollywood studio not noted then for its kind treatment of writers. One afternoon she threw open a window in the little cottage Metro provided her and screamed to passersby: "Let me out of here! Let me out of here! I'm as sane as you are!"

• She was advised that a young playwright had lifted some bright lines from her short stories for his latest play. On meeting him, she asked what the play was about. "Well, it's very hard to describe," he said, "except that it's a play against all 'isms.' "

"Except plagiarism?" Miss Parker asked.

• "Looking at a list of our authors who have made themselves most beloved and therefore most comfortable financially," Miss Parker once said, "it shows that it is our national joy to mistake for the first rate, the fecund rate."

• "He's a writer for the ages," she said of one overrated author. "For the ages of four to eight."

• Miss Parker's play *Close Harmony*, which she wrote with Elmer Rice, was a failure at the box office. Sometime during the fourth week of its short run, she wired Robert Benchley: CLOSE HARMONY DID A COOL $90 AT THE MATINEE STOP ASK THE BOYS IN THE BACK ROOM WHAT THEY WILL HAVE.

• "Don't you think she ought to wear a brassiere in this scene?" a producer asked her, pointing at his leading lady.

"God, no," she replied. "You've got to have something in this show that moves."

• Ruth Gordon and George Oppenheimer used thinly disguised characters based on Dorothy Parker in their plays *Over 21* and *Here Today*, which both appeared on Broadway. At the time, a publisher offered Miss Parker a large advance to write her autobiography. "No chance," she replied. "Gordon and Oppenheimer would sue me for plagiarism!"

• "Most good women," she remarked, "are hidden treasures who are only safe because nobody looks for them."

• She found most of the many guests at Alexander Woollcott's country place particularly tedious one weekend and couldn't think of a good thing to say about them. "Where do you suppose all of these people go when they leave Alec's?" somebody asked her.

"Back into the woodwork," she replied.

• Another guest at a party told her that she thought their host was outspoken. "By whom?" she replied.

• Miss Parker was asked why she hadn't seen Kaufman and Hart's *Merrily We Roll Along* (1934), in which the character Julia Glenn is modeled on her. She replied, "I've been too fucking busy and vice versa."Another version of the story has her saying the same to a telephoner who called to chat at the wrong time.

• Despite her joy of sex, she found that men weren't worth it. Completely disillusioned with the opposite sex by her last years, she quipped, "The fucking you get isn't worth the fucking you get."

• "The best way to keep children home," she explained, "is to make the home atmosphere pleasant—and let the air out of the tires."

• As a lark she and Robert Benchley subscribed to undertaking trade journals. From them she learned that morticians sprayed tuberose perfume on corpses, and she began ordering a tuberose scent from London to use as her own perfume.

• "Excuse me, everybody, I have to go to the bathroom," she said one afternoon, rising from her chair at the Round Table. She then bent down to Robert Benchley, confiding, "I really have to make a phone call, but I'm too embarrassed to say so."

• "Every year," she once complained, "back spring comes, with nasty little birds, yapping their fool heads off, and the ground all mucked up with arbutus."

• British actor Herbert Marshall was entertaining a circle of admirers at a party and kept advising them of how busy he was, continually referring to his crowded schedule, which he pronounced "shedshoole" in the British manner. "If you don't mind my saying so," an annoyed Miss Parker finally said, "I think you are full of skit."

• "I can't talk about Hollywood," she once told a journalist. "When I got away from it I couldn't even refer to the place by name. 'Out there,' I called it. You want to know what 'out there' means to me? Once I was coming down a street in Beverly Hills, and I saw a Cadillac about a block long, and out of the side window was a wonderfully slinky mink, and an arm, and at the end of the arm a hand in a white suede glove wrinkled around the wrist, and in the hand was a bagel with a bite out of it."

• "This must be a gift book," she said of Lucius Beebe's *Shoot If You Must.* "That is to say, a book which you wouldn't take on any other terms."

• The eminent black writer W. E. B. Du Bois was given a ninety-second birthday party featuring entertainment by African spear dancers. During the performance a few spears came dangerously close to Du Bois's head. "Watch it, mate," said Dorothy Parker, seated next to him, "or you'll never see ninety-three."

• Kate's wonderful, isn't she?" a friend said of Katharine Hepburn's Broadway performance in *The Lake*, between acts at the Martin Beck Theater. "Oh, yes," Miss Parker agreed. "She runs the gamut of emotions all the way from A to B." These words became as celebrated as any of her ripostes, but years later she told Garson Kanin that she didn't think there was a finer actress anywhere than Katharine Hepburn; she had made the remark for the same reason she said many things—because it was funny, a joke. Miss Hepburn, however, agreed with her assessment of *The Lake*.

• An acquaintance cornered Parker at a dinner party and raved on for what seemed hours about her husband. "Why, he's marvelous," she concluded, "and do you know, I've kept him for eight whole years!"

"Don't worry," Miss Parker said, "if you keep him long enough he'll come back in style."

• Miss Parker and Stockton Rush were staying at a friend's house, where they had drunk to excess at a party the night before. Staggering down to breakfast the next morning, a hungover Rush remarked, "Would it be all right if I cut my throat?"

"Move over on the blade and make room for me," Miss Parker told him.

• Assured by a loud drunk that he was a good person and a man of real talent, she replied, "Look at him, a rhinestone in the rough."

• A priggish matron called Miss Parker, telling her, "I really can't come to your party. So many foolish people will be there and I really can't bear fools."

"That's strange," she replied. "Your mother could."

• One bright afternoon, as a notoriously stupid Hollywood producer swaggered by them on the street, she commented to a companion, "He hasn't got enough sense to bore assholes in wooden hobbyhorses."

• After being shown an apartment on Riverside Drive by a high-powered real estate agent, she turned to him and said, "Oh, dear, this is much too big. All I need is room to lay a hat and a few friends."

• Returning from London, a noted actress complained to the press that she'd somehow gotten splinters in her derriere over there. "I suppose she got them sliding down a barrister," Miss Parker remarked.

• Parker excelled at the Round Table word game in which players had ten seconds in which to make a pun from a multisyllabic assigned word. Given *horticulture* one day, she quickly responded, "You can lead a horticulture, but you can't make her think."

• Wyatt Cooper remarked to her that Christine Jorgensen, who had had a much-publicized sex change operation in Denmark, was soon to visit her mother in America. "And what sex, may I ask, is the mother?" Miss Parker inquired.

• When someone made a remark about all the pretty girls at a Yale prom, Dorothy Parker observed, "If all these sweet young things were laid end to end, I wouldn't be the slightest bit surprised."

• The author and her friends were discussing a promiscuous acquaintance. "You know she speaks twenty-seven languages," Miss Parker said, "and she can't say *no* in any of them."

• The marriage of two friends who had long lived together inspired Parker's congratulatory telegram reading WHAT'S NEW?

• Mrs. Robert Sherwood had had a difficult pregnancy. When she finally gave birth, Dorothy Parker telegraphed her: GOOD WORK, MARY, WE ALL KNEW YOU HAD IT IN YOU.

• Early in 1920 she had an illegal, medically controlled abortion in a New York hospital, to which she was admitted with "stomach trouble." The next day Robert Benchley visited and found her in pain and despondent, but she tried to make a joke of her condition. "Serves me right," she told Benchley, "for putting all my eggs in one bastard."

• Miss Parker was asked to leave William Randolph Hearst's palatial San Simeon estate, either for drinking or for sleeping with another guest. Thinking this hypocritical, since Hearst drank and loved there with his mistress, actress Marion Davies, she wrote the following in the visitor's book on leaving:

> *Upon my honor,*
> *I saw a Madonna*
> *Standing in a niche,*
> *Above the door*
> *Of the famous whore*
> *Of a prominent son of a bitch.*

• It wasn't in conversation but in her short story "The Little Hours" that Dorothy Parker made her much-quoted remark, "And I'll say of Verlaine too, he was always chasing Rimbauds!"

• Invited to a party attended mostly by homosexuals, Miss Parker got drunk, covered herself with drapery, and climbed out on to the balcony waving a bottle of champagne. "Come and get me boys," she cried. "I'm a man."

• She loved animals, over the years keeping an assortment of dogs and cats, a baby alligator, and a messy canary that she named Onan, because it "spread its seed all over the place." She named one of her dogs Woodrow Wilson, a president who had disappointed her, explaining that he too "was full of shit."

• Alexander Woollcott's cat was old and suffering and he wanted to have it put to sleep. "But I don't know how to go about it," he told Dorothy Parker one afternoon at the Algonquin.

"Try curiosity," she advised.

• She took one of her dogs to a Hollywood party that she found "dreadfully boring." When the dog vomited on the carpet, she turned to her hostess and explained, "It's the company."

• Alexander Woollcott claimed that when her dog had a "distressing malady" she "issued bulletins about his health. Confidential bulletins, tinged with scepticism: 'He said he got it from a lamp post.' "

• Actress Ruth Gordon told of Dorothy Parker being invited to the home of a California wildlife lover who attracted animals to his yard evenings by putting out a large platter of meats far from the house. The animals, however, didn't show up the first time Miss Parker visited. "Please come again," her host insisted. "I can't account for tonight. It won't happen again." Miss Parker made a second visit and was again handed a pair of binoculars, but again the animals didn't appear, though she waited until nearly midnight. "Oh, I don't understand it," the host cried. "How could it happen?"

Miss Parker shook her head in commiseration. "I thought," she said sadly, "we'd at least get the after-theater crowd!"

• Asked by Vincent Sheean what her husband, Alan Campbell, would do without her now that they had broken up, Miss Parker summed up her analysis of him in a sentence. "Don't worry about Alan," she said. "When Alan falls he always lands up on somebody's feet."

• Said the author of her mother-in-law, Hortense Campbell, a woman she considered something of a poseur: "Hortense is the only woman I know who pronounces the word *egg* with three syllables."

• When she remarried actor and screenwriter Alan Campbell in 1950, someone observed that most of the guests at the wedding hadn't spoken to each other for years. "Including the bride and groom," said Miss Parker.

• On the morning of June 14, 1963, she awoke to find her husband, Alan Campbell, dead beside her, the victim of an apparent heart attack. A neighbor who accompanied her to the mortuary asked if there was anything she could do to help. "Get me a new husband," Miss Parker replied.

"Dottie, I think that is the most callous and disgusting remark I ever heard in my whole life," said the neighbor after a long silence.

"So sorry," said Miss Parker with a sigh. "Then run down to the corner and get me a ham and cheese on rye and tell them to hold the mayo."

• Summoned to appear before the House of Representatives Un-American Activities Committee in 1952, she spent the evening before the dread day in a Washington, D.C., bar. There a loudmouth annoyed her, voicing his approval of Hollywood producers who worked "against the Reds." Miss Parker rose and stared at him icily. "With the crown of thorns I'm wearing," she said as she turned and left, "why should I be bothered with a prick like you."

• Toward the end she thought little of her celebrated wit. "Damn it, it was the twenties," she once recalled, "we had to be smarty. I wanted to be cute— that's the terrible thing. I should have had more sense. A smartcracker, they called me. I was the toast of two continents—Greenland and Australia."

• "There's a hell of a distance between wisecracking and wit," she told an interviewer. "Wit has truth to it, wisecracking is simply calisthenics with words."

• "These were no giants," she said of the Round Table late in her life. "Think who was writing in those days—Lardner, Fitzgerald, Faulkner, and Hemingway. Those were the real giants. The Round Table was just a lot of people telling jokes and telling each other how good they were."

• Her doctor told a despondent Dorothy Parker that if she didn't stop drinking she'd be dead in a month. "Promises, promises," she replied.

• Confined in an oxygen tent after a suicide attempt, she still had presence of mind enough to ask, "May I have a flag for my tent?"

• "If I had any decency, I'd be dead," she said a few years before she died. "Most of my friends are."

• Somerset Maugham summed her up: "It is as difficult to say anything about Dorothy Parker that has not been said as it is about the Venus of Milo. Helen could make a scholar famous with a kiss; she can make a fool immortal with a jibe."

MIZNERISMS

Wilson Mizner (1876–1933) wasn't as well known as Dorothy Parker, F.P.A., George S. Kaufman, Heywood Broun, Robert Benchley, Ring Lardner, or any of the Algonquin Wits (who met for lunch regularly at New York's Algonquin Hotel), but the Hollywood screenwriter was one of America's greatest wits. Just a sample of his many witticisms follow:

• "A drama critic is a person who surprises the playwright by informing him of what he meant."

• "You're a mouse studying to be a rat."

• "He's the only man I know who had rubber pockets so he could steal soup."

• "Steal from one author and it's plagiarism; steal from many and it's research."

• "Hollywood is a trip through a sewer in a glass-bottomed boat."

• "The first hundred years are the hardest" (sometimes attributed to T. A. Dorgan).

• A sign he posted when manager of New York's Hotel Rand: "Carry out your own dead."

• "Be nice to people on your way up because you'll meet 'em on your way down."

• On hearing that boxer Stanley Ketchel had been shot to death by a jealous husband: "Tell them to start counting ten over him and he'll get up."

• "All the movie heroes in Hollywood are in the audience."

• In describing former boxer Tom Sharkey and a saloon with swinging doors that he owned: "He was so dumb that he crawled under them for two years before he found out they swung both ways."

THURBERIAN WIT

WRITE SHORT dramatic leads to your stories, James Thurber's editor told him during his early days as a newspaper reporter. Shortly after, Thurber turned in a murder story which began:

"Dead. That's what the man was when they found him with a knife in his back at 4 P.M. in front of Riley's Saloon at the corner of 52nd and 12th Streets."

ANCIENT FORGERIES

• To advance his political career the Greek statesman Solon wrote and inserted new verses in the *Iliad*.

• The idea for *Troilus and Cressida* came from a forged "diary" of a supposed soldier in the Trojan War that was actually composed in A.D. 4.

• In 1582 a forger composed "the last *Consolatio* of Cicero," his work so good that the forgery wasn't discovered for two centuries.

• The "Celtic epic" *Fingal* was actually written by James Macpherson (1736–1796), a Scottish scholar who claimed that this poem and others were written by a Gaelic poet named Ossian. For a time the "Ossianic Controversy," as it was called, sharply divided literary England, Dr. Johnson and his allies denouncing Macpherson and others praising him.

• Alcibiades Simonides (b. 1818) was a brilliant Greek scholar who fooled kings and archaeologists with his forgeries of ancient documents. He was first caught red-handed by an old gardener in a Turkish pasha's garden, where he had insisted that an "ancient manuscript" was buried in a box under a fig tree. The manuscript was there all right, but the gardener testified that he had planted the fig tree only twenty years before, that the soil was thoroughly dug up at the time, and there had been no sign of a box. His exposure, however, didn't prevent Simonides from perpetrating forgeries almost to the day he died.

THE PSALMANAZAR HOAX

GEORGE PSALMANAZAR (1679?–1763) was a pseudonymous literary faker whose real name still isn't known. Psalmanazar, a Frenchman, fashioned his pseudonym from that of the Biblical character Shalmaneser. Claiming to be a native of Formosa (Taiwan) and even inventing a complete "Formosan" language that he spoke, he attracted the attention of Scottish army chaplain William Innes, who saw through his imposture but became his confederate. Innes "converted" him in order to get credit for a "conversion" and in 1703 Psalmanazar went to London, where incredulous authorities hired him to teach "Formosan" at Oxford and write a dictionary of "Formosan." The following year the impostor wrote *The Historical and Geographical Description of Formosa*, which described the odd customs of the "Formosans"—that they ate only raw meat, including the flesh of executed criminals, and they annually offered as a sacrifice to the gods 18,000 hearts cut from the breasts of boys under the age of nine. In 1706 Catholic missionaries to Formosa exposed Psalmanazar and after a time he confessed his fraud, renouncing his past life in 1728 and going on to become an accomplished scholar. But there remained something of the impostor in this friend of Dr. Johnson. The title of his autobiography, published posthumously in 1764, was *Memoirs of —— commonly known by the Name George Psalmanazar.*

THE BICKERSTAFF HOAX

NEARLY ALL of Jonathan Swift's works were published anonymously and he received payment only for *Gulliver's Travels* (£200). In the case of the Bickerstaff Hoax, Swift made no profit and used the pen name Isaac Bickerstaff. The Dean grew prudently indignant in 1708 when an ignorant cobbler named John Partridge, claiming to be an astrologer, published an almanac of astrological predictions, so he parodied the book under the title "Prediction for the ensuing year by Isaac Bickerstaff." In his parody, Swift foretold the death of John Partridge on March 29, 1708, and when that day arrived he published a letter affirming his prediction and giving an account of Partridge's death. Partridge indignantly protested that he was very much alive, but Swift wrote what he called a "Vindication," *proving* that Partridge was dead. Poor Partridge was doomed to a literary death as a result, especially when other writers perpetuated the joke. So famous did the pseudonym Isaac Bickerstaff become that Richard Steele used it as his pen name in the *Tatler*. Benjamin Franklin later emulated Swift's hoax in America. (See *Almanacs*.)

THE JEALOUS LITERARY HOAXER

FOR SOME REASON the English author William Lauder hated John Milton and tried to prove that a great part of the poet's work was stolen from modern Latin poems. He went to the trouble of translating passages from Milton into Latin and inserting them into Latin poems, publishing his work as "proof" of Milton's thievery. Even Dr. Johnson was fooled, writing a preface and postscript to Lauder's *An Essay on Milton's Use and Imitation of the Moderns* in 1750 and it wasn't until the next year that a scholarly book exposed this most ill-intentioned of literary hoaxers.

THE QUART BOTTLE PLAYHOUSE HOAX

IN 1749 the Duke of Portland bet that if "a man advertised the most impossible thing in the world, he will find fools enough to fill a play house and pay handsomely for the privilege of being there." His friends took him up on the wager and they advertised in the newspapers that on the next Monday, January 16, on the stage of Mr. John Potter's playhouse, a man would "jump into a quart bottle placed on a table . . . in the sight of all spectators." On the appointed night the playhouse was "crowded to suffocation" with people who had paid up to 7s. 6d. a seat. When the man failed to appear and jump into the bottle, the mob went wild and totally destroyed the theater, burning it to the ground after stealing everything in it. Yet some people believed the duke and his friends when they advertised again that the man would have appeared if someone watching him rehearse hadn't corked him up in his bottle and carried him off to parts unknown.

THE ROWLEY HOAX

H ERE IS BOTH a hoax and a tale of literary ratiocination involving the little word *its*. Before the seventeenth century *its* wasn't used to indicate the possessive case, *it* and *his* serving this purpose (as in, "For love and devotion toward God also hath it infancie" or, "Learning hath his infancy"). From ages twelve to sixteen, English poet Thomas Chatterton (1752–1770) wrote, among other forgeries, a number of poems purporting to be the work of an imaginary fifteenth-century monk, Thomas Rowley. These poems were published after the destitute, despairing Chatterton tore up most of his work and committed suicide by drinking arsenic. They were soon hailed as works of poetic genius. But eight years later critic Thomas Tyrwhitt revealed that the poems were forgeries, finding, among other errors, that one of Chatterton's lines read: "Life and its good I scorn."

Chatterton's tragic death at the age of eighteen inspired Keats to dedicate "Endymion" to him, while Ruggiero Leoncavallo composed an opera about him and Alfred de Vigny wrote a play called *Chatterton*.

MÉRIMÉE POSES AS A WOMAN

THE FRONTISPIECE portrait of "Clara Gazul," the purported author of *Le Théâtre de Clara Gazul* (1825), was actually a faked portrait of the twenty-two-year-old French author Prosper Mérimée wearing a mantilla! Mérimée had written the six short plays he attributed to "Spanish actress Clara Gazul," but thought that his first published work would be successful if people thought a celebrity had written it. Before his hoax was exposed, *Le Théâtre de Clara Gazul* was widely acclaimed.

There is another case of a man posing as a woman all his writing life. Fiona Macleod was the pen name of William Sharp, the Scottish poet and man of letters who was such a brilliant talker that he was known as "Conversation" Sharp. Under his own name, Sharp wrote a number of noted biographies and several novels. But it was as Fiona Macleod that he triumphed in his double life; the mystic stories and sketches he wrote under that name made him the most prominent Scottish writer of the modern "Celtic twilight" movement. Sharp kept his authorship of the Fiona Macleod books secret while he lived—even going to the extent of writing letters to magazines over the name of Fiona Macleod and supplying an entry to *Who's Who* for her. His secret was not revealed until after his death, in 1905. Sharp once confided to a friend that whenever he wrote as Fiona Macleod, he dressed as a woman. When the sententious scholar William Paton Ker was told this, he replied, "Did he?—the bitch!"

THE IRELAND HOAX

WHILE WORKING as a clerk in a lawyer's office William Henry Ireland (1777–1835) discovered blank Elizabethan parchments and used them and a faded brown ink he concocted to forge a number of documents purporting to be in the handwriting of William Shakespeare. Ireland, only seventeen at the time, claimed that he received the documents from an old "gentleman of fortune" who "had many old papers which had descended to him from his ancestors" but wanted to remain anonymous. When Ireland's father, an engraver and bookseller, pronounced the first documents authentic and notified scholars of the find, his forger-son proceeded to turn out scores of Shakespeare documents, including letters to the Earl of Southampton, a "Profession of Protestant Faith," and even a love letter to Anne Hathaway enclosing a lock of hair. The young man published his findings in book form and exhibited them, charging admission and gulling people like Pitt, Burke, Boswell, and the Prince of Wales. Ireland's masterworks, however, were two new "Shakespeare" plays: *Vortigern and Rowena* and *Henry II*. Playwright Richard Sheridan actually purchased *Vortigern* for £300 and half of any royalties, producing it at Drury Lane on April 2, 1796. By this time many people had sensed that Ireland's "discoveries" were forgeries and the play proved it. A complete fiasco, it was created as a joke by the actors and practically hooted off the stage by the audience, never to be played again. Its failure and an exposé by Shakespearean scholar Edmund Malone at the end of the year caused Ireland to confess his forgeries in print. The only punishment he received was the condemnation of literary critics, and he went on to write several forgettable novels.

THE MOON HOAX

NONE OF THE ASTRONAUTS who have walked on the moon have seen any evidence of life there, but in 1835, according to *New York Sun* reporter Richard Adams Locke, the eminent British astronomer Sir John Herschel trained a new, powerful telescope on the moon and observed some fifteen species of animals there, including what seemed to be a race of winged men. Locke's article, supposedly reprinted from the actually defunct Edinburgh *Journal of Science*, raised the circulation of James Gordon Bennett's newspaper from 2,500 to 20,000, and inspired one ladies' club to raise money to send missionaries to the moon. The book that the *Sun* reporter made from the article sold over 60,000 copies, and was studied assiduously by a scientific delegation from Yale. Locke finally admitted his hoax the following year, calling it a satire on absurd scientific speculations that had gotten out of hand. His friend Poe, who never believed a word of the story, nevertheless admitted that it had anticipated most of his own "Hans Pfaall," and was the reason he left the story unfinished.

HAWTHORNE'S HOAX

As a PREFACE to his famous story "Rappaccini's Daughter" Nathaniel Hawthorne originally wrote a paragraph claiming that the tale was written by a Frenchman named Aubépine and constituting a brief appreciation of the French author. Some readers immediately recognized that Aubépine meant "hawthorn" in French and that Hawthorne was actually discussing his own work.

THE BIRD THAT NEVER WAS: THE OESOPHAGUS HOAX

When Mark Twain wrote his satire on Sherlock Holmes stories "A Double-Barrelled Detective Story," he began the tale as follows:

> It was a crisp and spicy morning in early October. The lilacs and laburnums, lit with the glory-fires of autumn, hung burning and flashing in the upper air, a fairy bridge provided by kind Nature for the wingless wild things that have their homes in the tree-tops and would visit together; the larch and the pomegranate flung their purple and yellow flames in brilliant broad splashes along the slanting sweep of the woodland; the sensuous fragrance of innumerable deciduous flowers rose upon the swooning atmosphere; far in the empty sky a solitary oesophagus slept upon motionless wing; everywhere brooded stillness, serenity, and the peace of God.

The "solitary oesophagus" in the passage was solitary all right, for it never existed outside of Twain's teeming imagination. He had of course invented the bird—which know-it-alls were quick to describe to friends—and later remarked that few readers ever questioned him about it.

TWAIN AND THE *TIMES* HOAX

Mark Twain sent this letter to *The New York Times*, signing W. D. Howells's name to it:

> To the Editor: I would like to know what kind of goddam govment this is that discriminates between two common carriers and makes a goddam railroad charge everybody equal and lets a goddam man charge any goddam price he wants to for his goddam opera box.
>
> W. D. Howells

Enclosing a copy of the letter, he then wrote to his friend explaining his action:

> Howells, it is an outrage the way the govment is acting so I sent this complaint to N.Y. Times with your name signed because it would have more weight.
>
> Mark

O. HENRY'S HALF-STORY

O. Henry, still one of the most underrated of American writers, was always hard up for money, often because he was being blackmailed by a man who knew that he had been in jail—in fact, he would frequently come into the Doubleday offices just about quitting time and demand $25 or $50 advances, never revealing of course that the money was going to the blackmailer. In any event, he constantly needed money and didn't trust publishers very much. When a publisher named Hampton solicited a story from him for his *Hampton's Magazine*, O. Henry demanded $500, paid in advance. Hampton wanted to pay nothing until he read the story and so they compromised: the author would get $250 for the first half of the story and $250 more on delivery of the second half. O. Henry soon turned in the first half, but Hampton never paid the first $250 or even answered the author's letters. The perfidious Hampton, it turned out, published the first half of the story without paying for it, with an offer of $250 to anybody who could complete it.

IMAGINARY BIOGRAPHIES

In William Beckford's *Biographical Memoirs of Extraordinary Painters* (1824) we find biographies of imaginary artists such as Og of Bason. *Appleton's Cyclopedia of American Biography*, first published in 1886, for many years contained eighty-four biographies of nonexistent persons sent in by an unknown correspondent; it wasn't until 1936 that they were all weeded out. Noel Coward did a bit of the same in his *Terribly Intimate Portraits* (1922), giving us imaginary biographies of people like Jabey Puffwater and E. Maxwell Snurge. Later, he pulled similar stunts in *Spangled Uniform* and *Chelsea Buns*.

IMAGINARY BOOK REVIEWS

Many critics have been fooled by phony books and poems, but the only instance I've come across of a critic writing imaginary book reviews is Gerald Johnson, who, according to Martin Gardner, reviewed "six imaginary books . . . perceptively" in *The New York Times* on January 2, 1949. Gardner adds that many whimsical authors—Rabelais, Huysmans, and James Branch Cabell (with his "distinguished German scholar" Gottfried Johannes Biilg)—liked to "refer to the books of non-existent authors." Jorge Luis Borges has done the same in recent times.

CHAPTER FIVE

Of Editors & Agents

THE IDEAL EDITOR

MY DEFINITION of a good editor," American novelist John Cheever said, "is a man who I think charming, who sends me large checks, praises my work, my physical beauty, and my sexual prowess, and who has a stranglehold on the publisher and the bank."

FAULKNER'S FORMULA

YOU KNOW, I think Albert [Erskine] is the best book editor I know," William Faulkner told Random House publisher Bennett Cerf.

"Golly, Bill, coming from William Faulkner that's quite an encomium," Cerf said. "Have you told Albert?"

"No, I haven't, Bennett," Faulkner replied after a moment. "When I've got a horse that's running good, I don't stop to give him some sugar."

THINGS AIN'T CHANGED MUCH

*I*N HIS *The Fool of Quality* (1765–1770) Irish novelist Henry Brooke wrote of an editor he knew who said of his authors: "I can get one of these gentlemen . . . on whose education more money has been spent . . . than would maintain a decent family to the end of the world—I can get one of them to labor like a hackney horse from morning to night at less a wage than I could hire . . . a porter or shoeboy for three hours."

EVERY AUTHOR IS A SON OF A BITCH

*T*HE NOTED publisher and editor Horace Liveright (1886–1933), who published the early work of Ernest Hemingway and other great writers, made a deal with Theodore Dreiser to sell the movie rights to *An American Tragedy* (1925), his commission being 50 percent of anything over $50,000. Once the difficult sale was made, Dreiser cursed him for taking his commission, threw a cup of coffee in his face, and stalked out of the restaurant where he had been invited by Liveright to celebrate the sale. Liveright turned to his associate, Bennett Cerf, wiping the coffee off his face. "Bennett," he said, "let this be a lesson to you. Every author is a son of a bitch."

REJECTION QUIPS AND SLIPS
(THAT IS, LAPSES)

*M*ORE than one writer has literally papered his or her walls with rejection slips. William Saroyan, for example, had a pile of rejection slips as high as his desk before he sold his first story. But few authors ever see the readers' reports editors write regarding their rejected children. Here are a few of the most famous misjudgments among them.

• While an editor at *La Nouvelle Revue Française*, André Gide rejected Marcel Proust's *Remembrance of Things Past*, saying of the pages, "They're full of duchesses, not at all our style." Later he wrote an apologetic letter to Proust admitting that the rejection was "one of the most painful regrets and remorses in my life."

• The respected editor of the *Pictorial Review*, Herbert R. Mayes, who went on to edit many other magazines, turned down a prepublication offer to serialize *Gone with the Wind*. "A period novel!" he cried. "About the Civil War! Who needs the Civil War now—who cares?"

• In rejecting Vladimir Nabokov's *Lolita* one reading editor predicted, "It will not sell," adding that the novel was "totally perverse," "nauseating," and should "be buried under a stone for a thousand years."

• "Good God, I can't publish this," an editor who rejected *Sanctuary* told William Faulkner. "We'd both be in jail!"

• Said an editor of George Orwell's *Animal Farm*, "It is impossible to sell animal stories in the U.S." (But then Orwell himself didn't think *1984* would sell, and it has so far sold about 20 million copies.)

• The reader's report went: "The idea of men adrift on a raft does have a certain appeal, but for the most part this is a long, solemn and tedious Pacific voyage." The book was *Kon Tiki*.

• Another editor who turned down *Kon Tiki* (a year on the *New York Times* best-seller list): "Who wants to read about a crazy bunch of Scandanavians floating around the ocean in a raft?"

• When James Joyce sent Ezra Pound the Shawn chapters of *Finnegans Wake* for possible use in a literary magazine he was planning, Pound wrote back: "Nothing, so far as I can make out, nothing short of divine vision or a new cure for the clap can possibly be worth all the circumambient peripherization."

• Pound highly praised Joyce's *Ulysses* in the backwoods vernacular he often affected. "Wall, Mr. Joyce," Pound wrote to him, "I recon' your a damn fine writer, that's what I recon'. An' I recon' this her work o' yourn is some concarn'd litershure. You can take it from me, an' I'm a jedge." But he could be insensitive and condescending to his friend, as when he received a manuscript of poems from Joyce five years later, in 1927, and urged him to file the new poems in the family Bible or photograph album and forget about them. Joyce published the poems anyway, but Pound's opinion probably influenced him in choosing their title, *Pomes Penyeach*.

• An editor who rejected *Madame Bovary* advised Flaubert: "You have buried your novel under a heap of details which are well done but utterly super-fluous."

THE NAKED TRUTH

W̲H̲I̲L̲E̲ W̲O̲R̲K̲I̲N̲G̲ for Simon & Schuster, Clifton Fadiman reviewed a sub-mission consisting entirely of nude photographs of a certain Miss Jones, who was proposing an illustrated book of yoga exercises. His one-sentence reader's report: "I see nothing in the manuscript except Miss Jones."

UNREAD MANUSCRIPTS

W̲H̲E̲N̲ Walter Hines Page (1855–1918), later ambassador to Great Brit-ain, edited *The World's Work*, he received the following letter from a would-be contributor: "Sir: You sent back last week a story of mine. I know that you did not read the story, for as a test I had pasted together pages 18, 19, and 20, and the story came back with these pages still pasted; and so I know you are a fraud and turn down stories without reading them."

Replied Page, "Madame: At breakfast when I open an egg I don't have to eat the whole egg to discover it is bad."

This riposte has also been attributed to *Saturday Evening Post* editor George Lorimer.

TRUMAN CAPOTE, ART EDITOR

I̲N̲ *Here at the New Yorker* Brendan Gill tells the story of Truman Capote working as "a sort of self-appointed art editor" when he was a young assistant at the magazine. According to the possibly apocryphal tale, when Capote opened the mail, if he "didn't like a drawing, he dropped it over the far edge of the big table at which he worked." Years later the table was moved and "behind it were found hundreds of drawings that Capote had peremptorily rejected."

S . A . S . E .

D̲O̲N̲'̲T̲ M̲A̲K̲E̲ the mistake of enclosing a self-addressed envelope big enough for the manuscript to come back in," Ring Lardner told a young writer. "This is too much of a temptation for the editor."

A REJECTION FROM DICKENS

IN 1850 Charles Dickens started his weekly magazine, *Household Words*, which he edited until his death (the name was changed to *All the Year Round* in 1859). He published the first work of many famous writers, including Wilkie Collins and George Meredith, but had to read much dross for the gold. One time a poet named Laman Blanchard sent him an interminably long poem entitled "Orient Pearls at Random Strung." Dickens mailed it back with the note: "Dear Blanchard, too much string—Yours. C.D."

POSTAGE SAVER

A STORY in the trade has it that an editor of a literary magazine hated a story he received so much that he didn't return it in the conventional manner. It was sent back in a much smaller envelope, the ashes of the manuscript falling out when the author opened it.

HOW TO REJECT A REJECTION

WHEN *La Nouvelle Revue Française* editors rejected a batch of his poems in 1923, the French avant-garde poet and theorist Antonin Artaud rejected the rejection. He wrote back:

> The question of the acceptability of these poems is a problem which concerns you as much as it does me. I am speaking, of course, of their absolute acceptability, of their literary existence. I suffer from a horrible sickness of the mind. My thought abandons me at every level. From the simple fact of thought to the external fact of its materialization in words. Words, shapes of sentences, internal directions of thought, simple re- actions of the mind—I am in constant pursuit of my intellectual being. Thus as soon as I can grasp a form, however imperfect, I pin it down, for fear of losing the whole thought. I lower myself, I know, and I suffer from it, but I consent to it for fear of dying altogether. . . . This is why, out of respect for the central feeling which dictates my poems to me and for those strong images or figures of speech which I have been able to find, in spite of everything I propose these poems for existence.

RING TWICE FOR REJECTION

W HY title a book about adulterous sex *The Post-man Always Rings Twice*? Its author, James Cain, claimed that he so named the book because his postman brought him many letters of editorial rejection, always ringing twice when he left them.

AUTHOR'S REVENGE

T HE VERY FRANK author's acknowledgment in Lowell Edmunds's *The Silver Bullet*, a study of the martini, reads: "I should like to blame the editors of *Notes and Queries* for rejecting the extremely concise and dignified query on the Martini I sent them and I should also like to blame the editor of the *New York Times Book Review* for failing to print my author's query. May these editors find that their gin has turned to gasoline or may they drink too many Martinis and then swallow a toothpick, as Sherwood Anderson is said to have done."

SWEETER REVENGE

S ERVING as an editor of the *Partisan Review* in 1945, the poet Delmore Schwartz rejected as "unrealistic" a short story submitted by Calder Willingham, then a young, unknown author. When Schwartz received a long letter from Willingham denouncing the rejection, he answered it as best and as calmly as he could. Several years passed and Willingham won fame with his novel *End as a Man*. Schwartz bought a copy of the novel in paperback and was startled to find a whorehouse in the novel named the Hotel Delmore. From then on he could read no more of Willingham's work, but he did tell a mutual friend that the hotel naming must have been a subconscious expression of deep resentment. Not so, Willingham told the friend; he had been completely aware of what he was doing when naming the house of ill fame after Schwartz, although the name had been "exactly right from an artistic standpoint."

NO THANKS TO . . .

B ORROWING MONEY from his mother, e. e. cummings self-published a much-rejected book of poetry in 1935. Its dedication went: "No thanks to: Farrar & Rinehart, Simon & Schuster, Coward-McCann, Limited Editions,

Harcourt, Brace, Random House, Equinox Press, Smith & Haas, Viking Press, Knopf, Dutton, Harper's, Scribner's, Covivi, Friede"—all publishers who had rejected his manuscript.

REJECTED EDITORS

GUY DE MAUPASSANT, Rudyard Kipling, Sinclair Lewis, and Eugene O'Neill were among the literary giants criticized by their editorial employers for their prose style. Maupassant was almost denied a promotion. Kipling was advised by the *San Francisco Examiner* editor who fired him that he just didn't "know how to use the English language." Lewis was told by publisher Frederick A. Stokes: "You are not cut out to be a writer, that's all there is to it." As for O'Neill, he received the following note from his editor when he worked as a reporter for the *New London* (Conn.) *Telegraph* in 1912: "This is a *lovely* story, but would you mind finding out the name of the gentleman who carved the lady and whether the dame is his wife or daughter or who? And phone the hospital for a hint as to whether she is dead or discharged or what? Then put the facts into a hundred and fifty words and send this literary batik to the picture framers."

POLITICALLY INCORRECT

IN 1979 the editor of the Russian humor magazine *Niangi* was fired for not being serious enough.

EDITORIAL ERRORS

THE ONLY difference between an editor and a publisher is that an editor has to be able to spell," English author Anthony Blond wrote. But some haven't been able to, and worse:

• The most costly editorial error in history occurred when the U.S. space probe *Mariner I*, bound for Venus, headed off course, and had to be destroyed at a cost of $18.5 million. The rocket had responded erratically because an anonymous flight computer programmer had left out a comma from *Mariner*'s computer program.
• *Umbrage* derives from the Latin *umbra* (shadow or shade), the same root that gives us the word *umbrella*. The expression means to take offense, suggesting someone "shadowed in offended pride, retreating into the darkness of proud

indignation." There is a tale about the editor of a small newspaper who quickly read a wire-service story during World War II stating that the Russians had taken *umbrage* at something, as they often did. Not knowing what the phrase meant, he headed the story RUSSIANS CAPTURE UMBRAGE.

• A 1978 newsletter edited at a branch of Mensa, an organization for high-IQ people, had the spellings "recieved," "attornies," and, of course, "intelligense."

• Russian author Fyodor Dostoyevsky had no patience with grammars and stylebooks. When he edited *The Citizen* he angrily instructed the newspaper's proofreaders: "Every author has his own style and consequently his own grammatical rules. I put commas where I deem them necessary, and where I deem them unnecessary others must not put them! . . . [And] remember that I never use superfluous commas: Never add or remove a single one!" On the other hand, Dostoyevsky's editor on the *Moscow Gazette* made a number of cuts and changes in the manuscript of *Crime and Punishment*, and the author was mostly grateful for them. "I do not regret *all* the deletions, . . ." he wrote to his editor. "Some of them actually improve the passage. I have been painfully aware for twenty years now of a fault in my writing—long-windedness—but I am quite unable to rid myself of it."

• The famous French *Encyclopedie* edited by Denis Diderot actually began as a 1745 translation by John Mills of Englishman Ephraim Chamber's *Cyclopaedia*. The vast revision made by Diderot of Mills's translation was mutilated by the king's printer, Lebreton. After Diderot had corrected the last proof sheet Lebreton, fearing royal displeasure, secretly and hastily cut out anything that seemed daring or likely to give offense to the monarch. Diderot, beside himself with rage and grief, could do nothing.

• American humorist Eugene Field carried a lifelong grudge against proofreaders, whose ineptness, he felt, had marred too much of his work. While working for the *Denver Tribune* he hung a sign on the wall over his desk, reading GOD BLESS OUR PROOFREADER, HE CAN'T CALL FOR HIM TOO SOON.

• As editor of a California gold-town news-paper, Bret Harte wrote the obituary of a prominent local woman, noting that "she was distinguished for charity above all other ladies of this town." On reading the proofs he noticed that the printer had rendered this: "She was distinguished for chastity above all the other ladies of this town." Harte corrected the error, referring the compositor back to the original copy by putting a large query (?) in the margin. The

next day he picked up the paper and read to his horror that the lady was "distinguished for chastity (?) above all the ladies of this town."

• The poet and literary journalist J. C. Squire (1884–1958) wrote an article about Shakespeare's *A Midsummer Night's Dream*. Finding that the name Hermia was misspelled "Hernia" in the proofs, he let the mistake stand, inserting an asterisk and the note: "I cannot bring myself to interfere with my printer's first fine careless rupture."

• A cub reporter asked his editor, "How do you spell *pinochle*?" The next day the editor read the lead of the reporter's story: "An inspired Illinois team yesterday reached the pinochle of success."

• The poet Alfred Noyes (1880–1958) submitted a poem to the *Irish Times* about a soldier returning home, its first lines reading

> *All night he lies beneath the stars,*
> *And dreams no more out there.*

The *Times* printed the first line as

> *All night he lies beneath the stairs,*

• "In all the proof that has reached me," the author Gordon Dorrance wrote to his publishers, "windrow has been spelled window. If, in the bound book, windrow still appears as window, then neither rain nor hail nor gloom of night nor fleets of riot squads will prevent me from assassinating the man who is responsible. If the coward hides beyond my finding, I shall step into Scribners and merely shoot up the place Southern style."

• The large number of compound words (manvoice, womansmelling, etc.) in William Faulkner's *Light in August* upset the copy editor, and the book's galleys are full of editorial questions about them. Next to the inquiries are Faulkner's invariably angry replies: "Stet"; "O.K. damn it"; "O.K. as set, god-damn it"; and finally, "O.K. as set / and written / Jesus Christ!"

• As for the fabled Thomas Wolfe, he knew that editorial cuts were absolutely essential for him. Legend has it that the complete manuscript of *Look Homeward, Angel* that Wolfe sent to his editor Maxwell Perkins measured three feet high, or some 6,000 pages. Actually it was about a third of that, and the novel still had to be cut extensively. Often Wolfe would agree to cut only if he were allowed to write what he called a "transitional sentence." The transitional sentences would turn into transitional paragraphs, pages, and chapters, but his work was usually pruned into shape by his editors.

THE MOST NOVEL EXPLANATION FOR POOR PROOFREADING

SOME SAY the reason for [so many misprints in British books today] is the increasingly liberal attitude of the Church of England. Not enough parsons are unfrocked these days. These [highly educated] unfortunates of earlier days were often happy to find themselves employment in printing houses, correcting proofs."　　　　　　　　　　　　　　　　　—*London Daily Telegraph*,
April 24, 1979

EPITAPH OF A DEAD AUTHOR

I suffered so much from printer's errors
That death for me can hold no terrors
No doubt this stone has been misdated
Oh, how I wish I'd been cremated.
　　　　　　　　　—Anonymous

TYPOGRAPHICAL INSPIRATION

THE FIRST numbers of the famous *Story Magazine* were edited by Whit Burnett and Martha Foley on the island of Majorca, off the coast of Spain, and were printed locally. As the local printer's font had no *w*, all those early issues of *Story* had little holes on the pages where *w*'s should have been. This inspired Miss Foley to write and print a story in the magazine without a single *w.* Later in the year, Edward O'Brien included her tale in his annual *Best Stories* anthology.

EDITORIAL HYPE

*F*INDING a spider in the folds of a newspaper edited by Mark Twain, an advertiser wrote to him asking if this signified good luck or bad luck. Twain replied, "Finding a spider in your paper was neither good luck nor bad luck for you. The spider was merely looking over our paper to see which merchant is not advertising, so that he can go to that store, spin his web across the door, and live a life of undisturbed peace afterward."

KING TUT'S TYPEWRITER

*T*HE MOST imaginative of Canadian newspaper editor Charles Langdon Clarke's ingenious hoaxes, which included "the unearthing of the whale that swallowed Jonah," was the story he printed in 1922 after archaeologist Howard Carter discovered the tomb of Egyptian pharaoh Tutankhamen. KING TUT'S GOLDEN TYPEWRITER, Clarke headlined the story, and he went on to describe the instrument, never bothering to explain how a typewriter could possibly type hieroglyphics! The story seemed so authentic (despite the fact that the typewriter was invented in the

nineteenth century) that rival newspapers picked up on it before Clarke admitted to the hoax.

REORIGINATED AND ANALYTICALLY CONDENSED

*I*N DECEMBER 1843, only weeks after "A Christmas Carol" had been published, an English magazine published what was entitled "A Christmas Ghost Story Re-originated from the Original by Charles Dickens Esquire and Analytically Condensed." Dickens sued, pointing out that "even the language is the same" in the "ghost story," where the language wasn't "degraded." The disreputable publishers, however, using an ancient and still common ploy, quickly declared bankruptcy and Dickens, though he won a moral victory, lost about £700 in legal fees.

CONTINUED NEXT WEEK

D ANIEL DEFOE, the creator of *Robinson Crusoe*, probably the first modern novel, is said to also have invented the newspaper serial story, which led to such modern-day forms as the soap opera, in the weekly *Review* that he published and edited beginning in February 1704.

EDITORIAL PRUDES AND PROFLIGATES

• G. K. Chesterton liked to tell the story of a Victorian editor's complaint about a serial novel his sister-in-law Mrs. Cecil Chesterton had written: "You have left your hero and heroine tied up in a cavern under the Thames for a week, and they are not married!"

• Magazine editor Frank Munsey told O. Henry, who owed him several stories, that he would receive no more advances unless he advised Munsey what he needed the money for. O. Henry immediately mailed him an envelope containing one long blonde hair. The advance was granted.

• Theodore Dreiser's story "Glory Be, McGlathery" was written and published after magazine editor Arthur Vance challenged him: "I'll make you a proposition, Theodore! If you will write a story that hasn't a prostitute or a kept woman in it, I promise to buy it and pay our top price."

• George Horace Lorimer, the longtime editor of the *Saturday Evening Post*, had an ironclad rule never to allow even a hint of impropriety to appear in his magazine. Readers were thus shocked when the first installment of Katherine Brush's serial *Red-headed Woman* ended with the heroine having a drink at her boss's house while his wife was away and the second installment began with them having breakfast together. To answer the flood of indignant mail from readers Lorimer prepared a form letter: "The *Post* cannot be responsible for what the characters in its serials do between installments."

• Horace Liveright, publisher of Sherwood Anderson, Dreiser, Hemingway, T. S. Eliot, Ezra Pound, Dorothy Parker, Edgar Lee Masters, Robinson Jeffers, Bertrand Russell, and so many other greats, was a serious and generous man when it came to literature, but his editorial offices were called "the asylum" by people who worked there. To set the tone, Liveright—who lived up to his name—had in his office a hidden bedroom where he conducted his daily affairs; when he pushed a button on the wall, a section of bookcase swung out to reveal a bed all done up in lace. He found this necessary to keep his affairs secret from both his wife and his mistress.

• Brendan Gill writes in *Here at the New Yorker* that publisher and editor Harold Ross had a firm rule for newly hired editors: "Don't fuck the contributors." The corollary to this was "Moreover, we won't hire the people you *do* fuck." (Though Gill adds, "Certain exceptions to the edict spring to mind.")

• Ross once phoned author Robert Coates about his *New Yorker* review of Hemingway's *Death in the Afternoon*. "[Alexander] Woollcott tells me there's a hell of a bad word in the book—bathroom stuff," he told Coates.

"What word is that?" Coates asked.

"I can't tell you over the phone," Ross said.

• Poet Richard P. Blackmur described working as an editor for Henry Luce at *Time-Life* publications as working in "a kind of fur-lined purgatory."

EDITORIAL REVISION

*T*HE SCENE in Hardy's novel *Tess of the D'Urbervilles* (1891) where Angel Clare wheels Tess and her dairymaid friends across a flooded lane in a wheelbarrow did not originate with Hardy. Rather, it was the result of censorship. The novelist had had Angel carry the girls across in his arms, but according to Hardy's wife, his editor thought "it would be more decorous and suitable . . . if the damsels were wheeled across the lane in a wheelbarrow." In any case, the book created a sensation when it was published, and many critics called it immoral.

The editors of the *Ladies' Home Journal* once cabled Rudyard Kipling that he had to change lines in a story where the character drank a glass of wine. A disgusted Kipling wired back: "Make it malted milk."

THE LAW AND THE LADY

*I*N THE PAST editors often arbitrarily cut "erotic" passages from novel manuscripts, even if the author's contract specified that his book was to be published verbatim from his manuscript. This happened to Wilkie Collins, whose *The Law and the Lady* (1875) was so bowdlerized. The edited version of the passage in question read: "He caught my hand in his and covered it with kisses. In the indignation of the moment I cried out for help." The "objectionable" original version read: "He caught my hand in his and covered it with kisses. He twisted himself suddenly in the chair, and wound his arm around my waist. In the terror and indignation of the moment, seriously struggling with him, I cried out for help."

EDITORIAL CUT

*F*EW DARED disagree with archconservative editor and publisher Colonel Robert Rutherford McCormick of the *Chicago Tribune*, whose anger knew no bounds. One time the Rhode Island legislature passed a bill that displeased the Colonel, who strode out into the Tribune lobby and cut one star out of the American flag hanging there.

EDITORIAL CUTS

*I*N PROMOTING Simon & Schuster's children's book *Doctor Dan the Bandage Man*, publisher Richard Leo Simon decided to give away six Band-Aids with each copy. "Please ship half-million Band-Aids immediately," he wired a friend at Johnson & Johnson. He soon received the reply: "Band-Aids on the way. What the hell happened to you?"

"JUST GET IT PRINTED"

THE RUSSIAN lyric poet Afanasy Fet (A. A. Shenshin) was reprimanded by some small-minded puritan for letting his poems be printed in an "improper" magazine. Replied Fet, "If Schmidt [the lowest St. Petersburg hack of the day] had been publishing a dirty sheet, bearing the title of a four-letter word, I would have let him publish my poems in it. Poetry purifies."

EDITORS ANONYMOUS

• No one knows what anonymous editor invented this common definition of publishing, but it is widely accepted throughout the industry: "The largest floating crap game in the world."

• "You know how it is in the kids' book world," observed a longtime children's-book editor: "It's just bunny eat bunny."

• A would-be humorist sent a batch of jokes to an anonymous magazine editor. A few months later he got the following letter from the editor. "Dear sir: Your jokes received. Some we have seen before, some we have not seen yet."

• A towering book manuscript came back to the author with the anonymous one-line rejection note: "I'm returning this paper—someone wrote on it."

• "The characters in the story are purely fictional and bear no resemblance to any person, living or dead," an author wrote in a note attached to his manuscript. Not much time passed before his story came back with the penciled rejection: "That's what's wrong with it."

• A newspaper editor in upstate New York at the turn of the century was criticized at a town meeting for his bad grammar and diction. "So I been criticized somewhat for grammar," he replied. "Well, I got three good reasons for it. To begin with, I don't know any better. If I did, none of you would know the difference; and more than that, if I spoke and wrote any better than I do, I'd be managing editor of a big New York paper at a decent salary and you farmers would lose the best damned editor in Herkimer County."

• For all his working career the editor of a small-town New England paper had saved an old-fashioned wooden scarehead type of about 60-point size, never using it no matter how much he was implored to do so. But one summer he went off on a fishing trip and while he was gone a terrible cyclone hit the town, nearly devastating it. Figuring that this disaster rated the 60-point scarehead, his assistants got it down and set up a sensational front-page headline. But the editor was hardly happy when he returned and saw the result. "Balls of fire!" he cried. "What d'ye mean by taking down that type for a cyclone! All these years I've been savin' that type for the Second Coming of Christ!"

ACQUISITIONS EDITORS

AN EDITOR-IN-CHIEF at a leading publishing house was told that two editors at another house had had four and five wives, respectively. "Acquisitions editors acquire," he replied.

BUYING OFF CRITICS

ALEXANDER POPE once asked Bernard Lintot, his editor and publisher, how he dealt with critics. The poor ones, Lintot replied, could be bought off with food and drink. As for prosperous critics: "I can silence . . . the rich ones for a sheet apiece of the blotted manuscript, which costs me nothing. They'll go about with it to their acquaintances, and pretend they had it from the author, who submitted to their correction: this has given some of them such an air that in time they come to be consulted with, and dedicated to, as the top critics of the town."

EDITORS BENNETT OF THE *HERALD*

JAMES GORDON BENNETT and his sensational *New York Herald* changed the course of American journalism, for better or worse. But Bennett had no friend in the young, immoderate editor of the *New York Aurora*. The *Aurora*'s Walt Whitman wrote this short description of Bennett in 1842: "A reptile marking his path with slime wherever he goes, and breathing mildew at everything fresh and fragrant; a midnight ghoul, preying on rottenness and repulsive filth; a creature, hated by his nearest intimates, and bearing the consciousness thereof upon his distorted features, and upon his despicable soul; one whom men avoid as a blot to his nature—whom all despise, and whom no one blesses—all this is James Gordon Bennett."

The son and successor of the *Herald*'s founder, James Gordon Bennett the younger (1841–1918), was an eccentric who ran the paper well but had little or no regard for money. Once he gave the guard on a train a $14,000 tip. Another time he threw a batch of money into a roaring fireplace to watch it burn and when a young man salvaged the notes, angrily flung them back into the flames. When he found someone seated at his favorite table in a Monte Carlo restaurant, he bought the place for $40,000, evicted the diners, sat down to eat—and when he left gave the restaurant back to its original owners as a tip.

An anonymous "Old Philadelphia Lady" living in Paris wrote the younger Bennett one of the most famous letters in newspaper history:

> To the Editor of the *Herald*:
>   I am anxious to find out the way to figure the temperature from centigrade to Fahrenheit and vice versa. In other words, I want to know, whenever I see the temperature designated on the centigrade thermometer, how to find out what it would be on Fahrenheit's thermometer.
>
> Old Philadelphia Lady
Paris
December 24, 1899

The letter became famous after it was unintentionally reprinted the next day, a mishap that made the eccentric Bennett so mad that he published it every day until he died. Readers canceled their subscriptions, even threatened to kill the old woman, but Bennett nevertheless ran her letter for the next *eighteen years and five months*, a total of 6,718 continuous days in all.

REAL NEWS

LECTURING a young reporter, a hardened city editor quoted the old saw that a dog biting a dog is commonplace while a man biting a dog is real news. "Now go out and dig up a story," he concluded. Later that day the reporter proudly handed him a piece headed HYDRANT SPRAYS DOG.

WHO, WHAT, WHERE, WHEN, WHY, AND HOW

NEWSPAPER EDITOR Samuel Bowles (1829–1878) devoted most of his life to the Springfield *Republican* in Massachusetts, making it a virtual school for the "new journalism" of the time. His advice to a young reporter became a maxim for conciseness, pungency, and the importance of the lead in a newspaper story. "Put it all in the first paragraph," he told the young man.

Bowles was so jealous of the accuracy of his paper that when the *Republican* mistakenly reported the death of a local man in its obituary columns, he refused to print a correction. He did, however, arrange to have the man's name listed in the paper's birth notices the next morning.

EDITORIAL AUTHORITY

THE LEGENDARY Western gunslinger, gambler, and sheriff William "Bat" Masterson worked as a sports reporter and editor on the *New York Morning Telegraph* in the early 1900s and was considered a great boxing and horse racing authority. One day a Texas editor named Dinklesheets burst into the bar at the old Waldorf Astoria, shouting that he was going to settle an old score with Bat. "Bat's going for his cannon!" someone cried and the bar cleared out, Dinklesheets first. Masterson later confided in his quiet, unruffled way that he had only been reaching for a pack of cigarettes.

GREELEY THE GREAT

THOUGH BORN in New Hampshire, Horace Greeley lived in New York from the time he was twenty-three, when he founded the *New Yorker*, a critical review not to be confused with today's magazine of the same name. Most historians consider Greeley to be the greatest of American editors. Though he cried "Go West, Young Man" in his *New York Tribune*, which he founded in 1841, he himself remained in New York's serene, rustic Gramercy Park neighborhood, where he even kept goats in his backyard. A forgetful man, Greeley would often stroll through the neighborhood mulling over some problem in his mind, and on one occasion, "his mind intent on great affairs," he walked into the home of his next-door neighbor, poet William Allen Butler, mistaking it for his own.

• Greeley's infamous illegible handwriting caused him trouble when he penned the following letter:

Dear sir:

I am overworked and growing old. I shall be 60 on next February the 3rd. On the whole, it seems I must decline to lecture henceforth except in this immediate vicinity. If I go at all, I cannot promise to visit Illinois on that errand, certainly not now.   Yours truly,
                                                                          Horace Greeley

Soon after he received this reply:

Dear sir:

Your acceptance to lecture before our association next winter came to hand this morning. Your penmanship not being the plainest, it took some time to translate it; but we succeeded and would say your time, February 3rd, and the terms, $60, are entirely satisfactory. As you suggest, we may be able to get you other engagements.   Respectfully,
                                                                          M. B. Castle

• In times past the word *news* was treated as a plural, Queen Victoria once writing to the king of Belgium: "The news from Austria are very sad and make me very anxious." Greeley demanded, legend says, that his reporters on the *New York Tribune* always treat *news* as a plural noun. "Are there any news?" he cabled a reporter one time. "Not a new," the reporter wired back.
• "Sure I buy the *Tribune*," a fellow train passenger told Greeley. "I use it to wipe my arse with."
"That's why you have more brains in your arse than in your head," the *Tribune* editor replied.
• While Greeley was hard at work at the *Tribune* a temperance fanatic burst into his office. "What is it?" Greeley growled, and the man made his pitch for a contribution to the cause. "No, I won't give anything," Greeley replied and he went on writing.
But the man insisted. "Why, Mr. Greeley, won't you give me $10 to save an immortal soul from hell?" he asked.
"No," Greeley repeated, "not half enough people go to hell now."
• A politician collared the American editor at a convention and proudly confided to him that he was a "self-made man."

"That, sir," Greeley replied, "relieves the Almighty of a terrible responsibility."

• One time a group of artists was discussing Horace Greeley when author Henry Class interrupted. "Greeley," he said, "was a self-made man who worshipped his creator."

• Greeley suffered from a dreadful insomnia that got worse during his campaign for president in 1872. After he lost the election to President Grant he went immediately to the bedside of his dying wife and for several weeks hardly slept at all. This resulted in the delirium that led to his death that same year.

. . . 3 3 8 . . . 3 3 9 . . . 3 4 0 T H O U S A N D

W HEN American newspaper magnate Frank A. Munsey (1854–1925), founder and editor of *Munsey's* weekly magazine, purchased the *New York Daily News* in 1901, he bought it in cash from the widow of its founder, Benjamin Wood. Munsey paid Mrs. Wood with 340 thousand-dollar bills.

ALL THE NEWS THAT DOES NOT SOIL THE BREAKFAST CLOTH

A DOLPH S. OCHS purchased *The New York Times* in 1896 and raised it to the eminent position it enjoys today. Instead of getting into the "yellow journalism" competition of the day, he chose the high road, adopting the two slogans to make his intentions clear. One, still used, was the famous "All the news that's fit to print." The other was "It does not soil the breakfast cloth."

IMPERIAL HEARST

W ILLIAM RANDOLPH HEARST (1863–1951), American newspaper publisher, editor, and model for *Citizen Kane*, is responsible for the term *yellow journalism*. In 1896 Hearst hired R. F. Outcault away from the *New York World* to draw his comic character the Yellow Kid for Hearst's *New York Journal*. But the *World* continued the Yellow Kid cartoon, the first color comic, using another artist to draw the antics of the sassy little kid in his bright yellow nightgown. From the resulting sensational battle between the two Yellow Kids, plus the use of *yellow* to describe sensational books since at least 1846, came the term *yellow journalism*, or *yellow press*, for sensational, unscrupulous reporting, which was coined in 1898 and applied to Hearst's Spanish-American War stories.

• In 1898 Hearst sent combat art-ist Frederick Remington to Cuba. "There is no trouble here," Remington insisted in a telegram, wanting to come home. Hearst supposedly replied (he later denied the story), "You furnish the pictures and I'll furnish the war."

• In early 1890 Kentucky's Gov-ernor-elect William Goebel was shot and killed as a result of feuding over the state election. Ambrose Bierce wrote a quatrain about the shooting that appeared in Hearst's *New York Journal* on February 4, 1901:

The bullet that pierced Goebel's breast
Cannot be found in all the west;
Good reason, it is speeding here
To stretch McKinley on his bier.

The distasteful poem attracted little notice until seven months later, when anarchist assassin Leon Czolgosz shot President McKinley, who died on Septem-ber 14, 1901. Some went so far as to blame Bierce's prophetic poem for inciting Czolgosz. But it developed that the assassin had never read the poem and wasn't carrying a copy of Hearst's inflammatory anti-McKinley *Journal* in his pocket when he shot the president. Instead, Czolgosz told reporters that a lecture given by anarchist leader Emma Goldman had inflamed him. For his part, Bierce rather lamely claimed that his quatrain had been written as a warning against the inade-quate security measures taken to protect American presidents at the time.

• Hearst spent some $7 million before his chain of papers showed a profit and reigned supreme in yellow journalism, but his tactics were as important as his bank-roll. In 1932, to cite just one of many examples, his *New York Mirror* illustrated a concocted story about British hunger marchers storming Buckingham Palace with what was really a 1929 photo showing a crowd of well-wishers waiting outside the palace for news of the condition of ailing King George V (who recovered).

• Hearst's mother had been used to her son's eccentricities at least since he was expelled from Harvard for giving a chamber pot to each of his profes-sors—each chamber pot bearing a professor's portrait. Once someone told her that William was losing a million dollars a year in the *Journal*'s circulation war with Pulitzer's *World*. "Is he?" Mrs. Hearst shrugged. "Then he will only last about thirty years."

• Hearst's *Journal* editors, suspecting that the *New York World* was ransacking its obituary columns, faked an obituary for one Reflipe W. Thanuz. The *World* promptly stole it, only to have their rival point out that *Reflipe W.* was "we pilfer" spelled backward and that *Thanuz* was a phonetic spelling of "the news." When enough time had passed, the *World* avenged itself by planting the name Lister A. Raah in a news story. After printing it the *Journal* learned that this was an anagram of "Hearst is a liar."

• Novelist Gertrude Atherton was one of the few people on the staff of Hearst's *San Francisco Examiner* who wasn't a heavy drinker. Her colleagues included Ambrose "Bitter" Bierce and managing editor Sam Chamberlain, who had earned the sobriquet Sam the Elegant (for his style of dress), Sam the Drunken, and who once got drunk in San Francisco and turned up at a bar in Antwerp! "Poor man," Atherton once said of Hearst, "he prided himself on having the most brilliant editorial staff in the United States, but he paid high for the privilege: every one of them was a periodical or steady drinker, and there was a memorable occasion when all of them were down at Los Gatos taking— or pretending to take—the Keeley cure, and he had to get out the paper himself with the aid of the printers. He used to say that no one suffered more from the drink habit than he, although he never drank, himself."

ONE-MAN MAGAZINE

*T*HE VIENNESE satirist and critic Karl Kraus (1874–1936) published his famous radical magazine *Die Fackel (The Torch)* from 1899 until his death, writing the whole of it from 1911 on. On the back cover was the warning: "It is requested that no books, periodicals, invitations, clippings, leaflets, manuscripts or written information of any sort be sent in. No such material will ever be returned, nor will any letters be answered. Any return postage that may be enclosed will be turned over to charity." Kraus had his rules, like any editor, but they weren't usually like the rules of most editors. Once he confided, "I have decided many a stylistic problem first by head, then by head or tails."

EDITORIAL INTEGRITY

*W*HEN his former mistress tried to blackmail him by making public their affair, Edward Wyllis Scripps (1854–1926), founder and editor of the Scripps chain of newspapers, held a news conference, giving the story to rival papers and running it in his own *Cincinnati Post* the next day. Rather than lose circulation, as everyone had expected, *Post* sales increased.

FALLING IN LOVE WITH LITERATURE

*T*HE MONOCLED, worldly Grant Richards (1872–1948) was an editor and publisher who devoted his life to literature rather than making money from literature. He supported a great many authors, including Housman, Dreiser, and Firbank—Dreiser rewarding him by basing the character Barfleur in *A Traveller at Forty* (1913) on him. Twice-bankrupted, Richards was far from financially prudent and was so honest he is said to be the first publisher to quote unfavorable reviews in advertising his books. Richards's *Memories of a Misspent Youth* (1932) recounts his career. Wrote George Bernard Shaw to him about the book: "You should have called your book *The Tragedy of a Publisher Who Allowed Himself to Fall in Love with Literature*."

MENCKENIANA

*T*HOUGH it is hard to imagine the legendary, iconoclastic Sage of Baltimore as a cautious man, H. L. Mencken was an extreme hypochondriac who took few chances with his health. When he was editing an article, for example, he'd often wash his hands five or six times, so much did he fear contacting strange germs.

• He once suggested a novel way to improve higher education: burn down the universities and hang all the professors. But that was before he married a Goucher College professor of English.

• When Joseph Conrad's agent asked $600 for letting Mencken's *The Smart Set* run the author's latest story, Mencken took a look at the magazine's books and budget and wired back: "For $600 you can have the *The Smart Set*."

• Alexander Woollcott recalled that Mencken had a "happy formula" for answering controversial letters. He simply replied, "Dear sir (or Madame): You may be right."

• Mencken wasn't asked this question, he invented it: "If you find so much that is unworthy of reverence in the United States, why do you live here?" Then he answered his own question with another question. "Why do men go to zoos?"

• Mencken published an article on the bathtub called "A Neglected Anniversary" in the *New York Evening Mail* on December 28, 1917. In this piece he gave a spurious history of the bathtub, stating that it was first introduced to Americans in 1842, that three years later Boston made bathing in bathtubs illegal, and that President Fillmore installed the first tub in the White House, among other deliberate lies. Mencken planned his dirty work as "a piece of spoofing to relieve the strains of the war years," but almost everyone took it seriously and to this day many of Mencken's inventions are presented as fact in books and magazine articles.

• Despite the fact that his *Smart Set* offices were in New York City he continued to live in Baltimore and rarely visited New York. "Trying to be a philosopher in New York is like trying to sing in a boiler factory," he complained.

• When editing the *Smart Set* Mencken would answer the telephone with the greeting (containing perhaps a germ of sincerity), "The great critic Henry Mencken speaking."

• Someone wrote him: "Fifteen years ago you said just the reverse in an article—you are now saying exactly the opposite! How do you explain such a change?"

Replied Mencken, "Formerly I was not as wise as I am now."

• The Anti-Saloon League of Virginia seriously contended in its *Bulletin*, "His initials are H. L., meaning the first and last letters of the word Hell." Said a religious paper in Texas, "If a buzzard laid an egg in a dung hill and the sun hatched a thing like Mencken, the buzzard would be justly ashamed of its offspring." Far from ignoring the myriad insults like these he collected and published them in a book entitled *Menckeniana: A Simplexicon*.

• "H. L. Mencken," said avant-garde writer Maxwell Bodenheim, "suffers from the hallucination that he is H. L. Mencken—there is no cure for a disease of that magnitude."

• He claimed he was the world's champion mixologist and once hired a mathematician to figure out that 17,864,392,788 different cocktails could be mixed from the stock of a first-class bar. When he sold the Canadian film rights to his famous hoax on the origins of the bathtub, "A Neglected Anniversary," he demanded and received as payment two cases of Labatt's Ale a month for as long as he lived.

• To a reporter who questioned him about his celebrated drinking he replied: "I've made it a rule never to drink by daylight and never to refuse a drink after dark."

• Not long before Mencken died in 1956, eight years after a stroke had made him incapable of reading or writing, depriving him of his life's blood, a friend mentioned a writer who had died in 1948. "Ah, yes," Mencken said, "he died the same year I did."

HALF ON DELIVERY

A{\small T THE HEIGHT} of O. Henry's career the *New York World* paid him the then grand sum of $100 for each of his short stories. But he often failed to deliver his tales on deadline and his editor refused to pay him in advance, making a deal with the author to pay him $50 for delivering the first half of each story and $50 on receipt of the completed tale. Some critics believe that this is why the beginnings of a number of O. Henry stories seem unrelated to the endings. Whenever the author badly needed money, they contend, he would hurriedly write any beginning that came to mind and often ignore it later, when he had more time to finish the story.

AHEAD OF HIS TIME

A{\small S AN EDITOR} and columnist for the *Chicago Daily News*, Ben Hecht hired a legman to help him dig up new stories. Hecht had to fire his new assistant after a month or so, however, because "nothing he writes makes any sense." The legman was Henry Luce, who went on to found *Time* magazine.

FORTY MAD-DOGS HOOFER

ALTHOUGH he was a great editor as well as an important writer, Ford Madox Ford (1873–1939) ran the *English Review* very inefficiently, like "an infant in charge of a motor car," as Violet Hunt put it. One day the American poet Ezra Pound was visiting the *Review* offices and looked around, shaking his head. "Ford," he said, "if you were placed naked in a room without furnishings, I could come back in an hour and find total confusion."

• Ford began signing his books "Ford Madox Ford" in place of "Ford Hermann Hueffer" (his actual name) with the publication of the *Marsden Case* (1923). Ford claimed that his publisher suggested the new name, telling him his books would sell better if his name were pronounceable. "And how does one pronounce your beastly name?" he said. "Hoo-fer? Hweffer? Hoifer? Hyoofer? It's impossible to know." Tired of Ezra Pound calling him "Forty Mad-dogs Hoofer," among other mispronunciations, Ford agreed to the change and made it legal. But he would yet have to cope with Osbert Sitwell calling him "Freud Madox Fraud."

• "Only two classes of books are of universal appeal," he said, "the very best and the very worst."

• Robert Frost once said that writing free verse is "like playing tennis with the net down." That is just about the way Ford and Ezra Pound played tennis. A friend described a typical game between them: "[They looked] readier to spring at each other's throats than the ball. . . . It seemed to matter little how often they served fault after fault. They just went on till the ball was where they wanted, then one or the other cried 'Game' or 'Hard luck,' 'My set,' or 'That's love-all' or 'Six sets to one!' It was beyond anyone to umpire or score."

• Author and artist Wyndham Lewis would go to great lengths, if not any length, to get his work published. One tale has it that he wanted to publish his short story "The Pole" in the influential *English Review* edited by Ford. Entering Ford's house—Ford always left doors unlocked—Lewis found him in the bathtub and read the entire story aloud while Ford bathed. In any case, Ford did publish the story in the *English Review*.

UPBLOWN JOURNALESE

SEND two hundred words upblown nurse," Evelyn Waugh's editor cabled him regarding a rumor that an English nurse had been killed in an Italian air raid in Ethiopia. Finding that the story had no basis in fact, Waugh cabled back, "Nurse unupblown."

BOOK RETURNS

*I*T WAS esteemed publisher Alfred Knopf (1892–1984) who first uttered these words, now common wisdom among publishers, about book returns from bookstores: "Gone today, here tomorrow."

PERKINS OF SCRIBNERS

*P*ROBABLY the best-known of American book editors, Maxwell Perkins (1884–1947) was notoriously absentminded. One story has a distinguished-looking man entering his office while he sat talking to a young writer he had just ushered in. Perkins looked up and began snapping his fingers trying to remember the older man's name. "Charles Scribner," snapped his employer.

• While housecleaning in the spring of 1935, Perkins's wife came upon several boxes and barrels of old books, and she paid a book dealer $5 to cart them away. The books turned out to be signed first editions of works by Scribners's authors, including F. Scott Fitzgerald, that were worth thousands of dollars. Luckily a friend of Perkins's spotted the books on a stand outside a Second Avenue bookstore and, figuring that they were the editor's, bought them back from the bookdealer for $25 and presented them to Perkins.

• Perkins's boss Charles Scribner (1854–1930) was a gentleman of the old school. Reading the manuscript of *The Sun Also Rises*, the conservative publisher grew concerned about the four-letter words Hemingway used. As he read, he recorded these words on a daily calendar, leaving it on his desk when he went out to lunch. While she straightened his desk that noontime, his rather prudish secretary came across the calendar. It was headed "Things To Do Today," with the words *"piss . . . shit . . . fuck"* listed below.

• While at a literary cocktail party Perkins argued that no one attending such affairs ever really listened to what anyone else had to say. To prove his point he said, on shaking his hostess's hand in the midst of the crowded room, "I'm sorry I'm late, but it took me longer to strangle my aunt than I expected."

"Yes, indeed," his hostess replied. "I'm so happy you have come."

• Perkins wanted to buy two of the then-struggling young Erskine Caldwell's stories for *Scribner's Magazine*. "Would two-fifty be all right? For both of them?" he asked.

"Two-fifty?" Caldwell said. "I don't know. I thought maybe a little more than that."

"You did?" Perkins replied. "Well what would you say to three-fifty then? That's about as much as we can pay, for both of them. In these times magazine circulation is not climbing the way it was, and we have to watch our costs. I don't think times will get any better soon, and maybe worse yet. Economic life isn't very healthy now. That's why we have to figure our costs so closely at a time like this."

Caldwell sighed resignedly. "I guess that'll be all right," he said. "I'd thought I'd get a little more than three dollars and a half, though, for both of them."

• F. Scott Fitzgerald's career was almost nipped in the bud when Scribners sent a copy of his first novel, *This Side of Paradise*, to its sales manager, who had a great reputation for spotting potential best-sellers. The man's method was to let his sister pass judgment on all new books. This time the lady not only disliked the book but despised it so much that she used a pair of tongs to throw it into the fire! Luckily, Perkins prevailed at Scribners.

• "Editors are extremely fallible people, all of them," Perkins once said. "Don't put too much faith in them."

THE MAGIC OF TITLES

*I*N HIS delightful *And I Worked at the Writer's Trade* (1988) the late Malcolm Cowley tells the story of the now-defunct Macaulay Publishing Company, headed by Lee Furman, who "believed in the magic of titles." At one editorial meeting in 1933, Furman urged his staff, "Let's have a big novel written to order and let's give it a tremendous title—you know, something that will make people think of *The Good Earth* or *All Quiet on the Western Front*. Any bright ideas?" Replied poet Isidor Schneider, serving as the company's advertising manager, "What about *All Noisy on the Eastern Behind*?"

Among the most unusually named of all the American magazines published over the last three centuries is *Smith's*. It was some anonymous genius's idea to so name the magazine in the mid-nineteenth century, not in honor of anyone, but to attract a readership from among the myriad Americans named Smith.

NEWSPAPER NAMES

*I*TALY boasts some of the most improbable newspaper names found anywhere. A Naples daily is for some reason called *Roma*, while a Genoa paper is called *Il Secolo XIX* (*The Nineteenth Century*). Milan's respected *Corriere della Sera* (*Evening Courier*) is a morning paper.

MOST BORING HEADLINE

Wʜɪʟᴇ an editor for *The Times* in the 1920s, journalist Claud Cockburn (1904–1981) won a contest for "the most boring headline" with the following entry: ꜱᴍᴀʟʟ ᴇᴀʀᴛʜǫᴜᴀᴋᴇ ɪɴ ᴄʜɪʟᴇ: ɴᴏᴛ ᴍᴀɴʏ ᴅᴇᴀᴅ.

ROSS OF THE *NEW YORKER*

Wʜᴇɴ ᴏɴʟʏ fourteen years old Harold Ross (1892–1951), later the renowned founder and longtime editor of the *New Yorker*, worked as a reporter on the *Salt Lake City Tribune*. One of his assignments was to interview a bordello madam. He began by asking her, "How many fallen women do you have?"

• Harold Ross was perhaps the only private in the U.S. Army to have calling cards. His card read: "Pvt. H. W. Ross / Company C / Eighteenth Engineers Railway U.S. Army / United States Expeditionary Force in France."

• Ross ran the *New Yorker* on a meager budget in the early days. Once he asked Dorothy Parker why she hadn't come into the office to write a piece she had promised him. She had, Dorothy replied, but "someone else was using the pencil."

• "You can't quit," he told E. B. White when White threatened to leave the *New Yorker*. "This isn't a magazine—it's a Movement!"

• When James Thurber submitted his famous parody of Henry James, "The Beast in the Dingle" (which he first entitled "The Return of the Screw"), to Harold Ross, the *New Yorker* editor rejected it, commenting, "I only understand 15 percent of its illusions."

• "Ross gave me a job [on the *New Yorker*]," Thurber once recalled, "because he convinced himself I was an old pal of E. B. White. I tried to tell him I had met White for the first time on the way in to his office, but he wouldn't listen. I thought I was hired to be a writer, but for three weeks all I did was sign slips of paper they thrust under my nose. Finally, I asked, 'What am I signing here, anyhow?' 'That,' said my secretary, 'is the payroll.' That's when I found Ross had made me managing editor. When I asked him why, he said firmly, 'Because everybody starts at the bottom here.' It took me eight years of solid writing to persuade Ross to make somebody else his confounded managing editor."

• "His ignorance," Dorothy Parker said of Ross, "was an Empire State Building of ignorance. You had to admire it for its size."

• Humorist Ring Lardner once told the gullible Ross that he wrote his stories by jotting down "a few widely separated words or phrases on a piece of paper" before he "went back and filled in the spaces." Ross always believed him.

• "I'm a profane *** by nature," he told an interviewer in explaining how he managed to avoid guest spots on radio programs, "and whenever one of those *** round tables or something called up, I'd say, 'Hell, yes, I'll be glad to sit in on your *** panel, or whatever the *** you call it!' The word soon got around that I couldn't draw a breath without cursing and the *** hucksters never bothered me again."

• Ross butted into a conversation about Willa Cather. "Willa Cather?" he said. "Willa Cather? Did he write *The Private Life of Helen of Troy?*"

• Speaking to Sherwood Anderson one afternoon he happily advised him, "There hasn't been a good short story written in America, Anderson, since O. Henry died."

• Dubuque, Iowa, is named for the first settler, a French-Canadian lead miner named Julien Dubuque. But what about the famous symbol of prudery, *the little old lady in Dubuque?* The phrase seems to have originated in this sense with Harold Ross, when he promised in a prospectus of the *New Yorker* that his magazine would *not* be edited for "the old lady in Dubuque." According to Brendan Gill, in his fascinating *Here at the New Yorker* (1975), Ross may have been inspired by "Boots" Mulgrew, a former Broadway musical comedy skit writer forced by drinking and financial problems to retreat from New York to his birthplace. Mulgrew soon after began contributing squibs to a widely read *Chicago Tribune* column called "A Line o' Type or Two." These pieces, describing "the provincial absurdities of Dubuque," were signed with the pseudonym "Old Lady in Dubuque," and Gill suggests that "Ross read them, admired them, and, whether consciously or not, got the old lady in Dubuque fixed in his mind as a natural antagonist."

A PERSON-TO-PERSON CALL FOR MR. ROSS

*T*RYING to discourage editors from making personal telephone calls on the *New Yorker* phones, Harold Ross installed a pay booth in the reception area.

The next day he found the booth ripped out by the wires and arranged like a coffin in his own editorial sanctum. Inside it, a wreath on his head and a calla lily in one hand, rested James Thurber.

EDITOR ELIOT

LONG an editor at the London publishing firm of Faber and Faber, the great poet T. S. Eliot, who became a British subject in 1927, had a firm rule about editorial praise. "An editor should tell the author his writing is better than it is," Eliot believed. "Not a lot better, a little better."

When lunching with Eliot in the spring of 1946, American publisher Robert Giroux, then an editor at Harcourt, Brace, asked the poet if he agreed with the old saw that most editors are failed writers. "Perhaps," Eliot replied, "but so are most writers."

An incurable practical joker, Eliot was never in better form than when he worked as an editor for Faber and Faber. One of his favorite pranks was to seat visiting authors in chairs with whoopee cushions and offer them exploding cigars.

This possibly apocryphal palindrome is said to have been uttered by an American publisher on visiting Faber and Faber: "Was it Eliot's toilet I saw?"

MORE POETIC EDITORS

• William Cullen Bryant (1794–1878) edited the *New York Evening Post* for almost fifty-five years of his seventy-year literary career, which began with the publication of his famous blank-verse poem "Thanatopsis" when he was sixteen.

• Edgar Allan Poe (1809–1849) for a short time edited the *Southern Literary Messenger*. The year he edited the magazine was by far the most profitable one in his literary career—he made $800.

• Walt Whitman (1819–1892) edited the *Brooklyn Eagle*, among other New York papers, and for a brief time, *The New Orleans Crescent*. He always managed to praise and print his own work in his columns.

• Jean Sevé, a friend of the avant-garde poet Guillaume Apollinaire

(1880–1918), is thought to have financed Apollinaire's first magazine, *Festin d'Esope* (*Aesop's Feast*). To show his gratitude, Apollinaire signed the name Jean Sevé to a small paragraph he printed in the magazine satirizing the grandiose paintings of the illustrious Gérôme, a much respected member of the Academy. After the piece was published, Apollinaire met his friend in a bar. "Have you read the magazine?" he asked, beaming. "Are you pleased with your bit about Gérôme?"

"Yes, I've read it," Sevé said, more sorrowful than angry. "Didn't you know that Gérôme is my uncle?"

THE FIRST MIDDLEMEN

THE FIRST professional author's agent appears to have been Alexander Pollock Watt, an Englishman who had as his clients Thomas Hardy, Rudyard Kipling, Arthur Conan Doyle, and Bret Harte, among other greats. Watt published a list of his clients, along with testimonials, in 1893. The firm he founded, A. P. Watt and Son, is still in business.

THE ROLE OF THE AGENT I

THE RELATION of the agent to the publisher," claimed one anonymous publisher, "is the same as that of the knife to the throat."

THE ROLE OF THE AGENT II

IN *Pomfret Towers* English novelist Angella Thirkell (1890–1961) wrote that "an agent is someone whom you pay to make bad blood between you and your publisher." (Agentless herself, she left an estate of over £85,000.)

THE HEART OF AN AGENT

ALL the sincerity in Hollywood can be put into a gnat's navel and you'd still have room for three caraway seeds and an agent's heart.   —Fred Allen

AN AGENT STRIKES BACK

IT IS INTERESTING to think how . . . book publishing is so widely regarded as . . . one of the last great gentlemanly businesses. . . . Let me tell you, things have been pulled on me—in the gentlemanly publishing business—that are more venal than *anything* that was ever tried on me in Wall Street."

—Mort Janklow, agent and attorney,
quoted in Thomas Whiteside's
The Blockbuster Complex (1984)

AUTHOR HUNTING

WHEN THACKERAY'S *The History of Henry Esmond* (1852) was reprinted in Random House's Modern Library series, the editors received this letter from a Hollywood agency addressed to William Makepeace Thackeray, Esq.:

Dear sir:

We have read your recent book *The History of Henry Esmond, Esq.* and believe it possesses material adaptable for motion pictures.

We are recognized agents for writers at all studios and as such would like to represent you in the sale of both your own personal services and your literary products.

In the event you have already made a commitment to some agent for the above book, we nevertheless are impressed with your potential possibilities as a screen writer and would be interested in both your services and future stories.

We would appreciate your advising us by return mail whether or not you are represented here in Hollywood; and in the event that you are not and desire us to represent you, we would be happy to forward to you a copy of our agency agreement with writers for your information and guidance.

The editors decided to have a little fun, writing back:

Thank you for your letter telling me that you believe that my recent book, *The History of Henry Esmond*, possesses material adaptable for motion pictures. This effort is a rather crude attempt, I fear, but I am now working on a new novel which I think will be a natural for pictures. I am thinking of calling the new book *Vanity Fair*.

I will be interested in hearing what you think of this title.

Sincerely yours,
William Makepeace Thackeray

The agency immediately replied:

Acknowledging receipt of your letter of December 28, in reply to our previous communication, we feel that the title which you are thinking of giving your new book, namely *Vanity Fair*, is a good one. We would greatly appreciate receiving a manuscript on this story. Perhaps you could also send us a manuscript at this time, or if not, a copy of the book, *The History of Henry Esmond*.

We would like to submit this, if we are authorized to do so by you, to the studios for their consideration.

BEST-LAID PLANS

*I*N THE reference library of Doubleday & Co. is a lavish illustrated edition of Edwin Markam's *The Man with the Hoe*, published in 1900. On the flyleaf is an inscription by publisher F. N. Doubleday: "The edition was made to please the author and get his next book. It did neither."

AUTHORIAL EGO

*W*HEN William Dean Howells edited the *Atlantic Monthly* he found himself in the unenviable position of having to choose between running a poem by Emerson or one by Oliver Wendell Holmes, mainly because Emerson had held the proofs of his poem too long. Howells finally wrote Emerson proposing either to print his poem in the *next* issue or to have it appear in the current number along with Holmes's poem. In Howells's words: "He wrote me back to 'return the proofs and break up the forms.' I could not go to this [last] iconoclastic extreme . . . but I could return the proofs. I did so, feeling that I had done my possible, and silently grieving that there could be such ire in heavenly minds."

P.R. PEOPLE

*I*T IS SAID that the American publicity writer Eddie Benay (fl.1920) coined the term *public relations* in May 1920—as a respectable way to describe his profession in the announcements heralding his marriage.

WORD OF MOUTH

P.R. MAN Harry Reichenbach turned Elinor Glyn's *Three Weeks* into a best-seller by sending anonymous letters protesting the book to post offices all over the country. The Postmaster General finally stepped in, barring the book from the mails, and sales soared.

EDITORIAL GHOSTS

CLEVELAND AMORY told of a ghostwriter hired by a publisher to write the "autobiography" of a prominent political figure. When the book was published, a New York newspaper assigned a well-known lawyer to review it, and he hired the same ghostwriter to write the review—which was of course a glowing one.

PUTTING DOWN THE EDITORS

• The distinguished journalist Frederick Greenwood (1830–1909) was given a copy of the sensational newspaper *The News of the World* by its new editor. Several days later the editor asked him what he thought of the tabloid. "I looked at it and then I put it in the wastepaper basket," he replied, "and then I thought, 'If I leave it there the cook may read it,' so I burned it."

• The powerful newspaper publisher Baron Beaverbrook (William Maxwell Aitken) was called upon by David Lloyd George.

"Is the lord at home?" Lloyd George asked the butler.

"No, sir, the lord is out walking."

"Ah," replied Lloyd George. "On the water, I presume."

• Statesman and author Robert Cecil, the marquess of Salisbury, was asked by its editors what he thought of the popular newspaper the *Daily Mail*. Replied Lord Salisbury, "By office boys for office boys."

• Rudyard Kipling, like Mark Twain, Hemingway, Robert Graves, and several other writers, lived to see his obituary mistakenly published in a newspaper. That same day he wrote to the paper, "I've just read that I am dead. Don't forget to delete me from your list of subscribers."

• When told that his editor on the *New York World* was ill, author Irwin Cobb remarked, "I hope it's nothing trivial."

• Sure that his beloved *World* was the answer not only to Earth's but also to all the *universe's* troubles, the egocentric American newspaper publisher and editor Joseph Pulitzer, whose will established the Pulitzer Prizes in journalism and letters, once considered erecting an advertising sign in New Jersey that would be visible on Mars. He only abandoned his plan when an associate asked, "What language would we print it in?"

• On an early visit to America, Thomas Mann prepared a speech in English praising his publisher, Alfred Knopf. "He is not only a publisher," Mann said to guests gathered at a testimonial dinner, "he is a creature, too." (He had meant to say "creator.")

• A foolhardy magazine editor sent a note to Jack London's hotel demanding a story the American author was late in delivering. "Dear Jack London," it read.

"If I don't receive the story within 24 hours, I'll come up to your room and kick you downstairs, and I always keep my promises."

For once London did not retaliate with his fists.

"Dear Dick," he wrote back. "If I did all my work with my feet, I'd keep my promises, too."

• One time the publisher Condé Nast told Dorothy Parker that he was going on a cruise. "And Dorothy, I wish you would come with me," he said. "Oh, I wish I could!" she replied, but as soon as he walked out of earshot, she added, "Oh, God, make that ship sink!"

• An efficiency expert hired by Condé Nast decreed that any employee late for work at *Vanity Fair* had to fill out a form explaining his or her tardiness. In minute handwriting staffer Robert Benchley filled out a form one morning, explaining that all the elephants at the Hippodrome had escaped and had been attempting to board a steamship leaving for Boston. To prevent a terrible marine disaster he had had to round them up and herd them back to the Hippodrome, this explaining why he was eleven minutes late for work.

At about the same time *Vanity Fair* issued a directive ordering members of its editorial staff under no circumstances to discuss their salaries with other staff members. Benchley and Dorothy Parker responded by marching throughout the building wearing billboards specifying exactly how much they made.

• Bennett Cerf prefaced this Publisher's Note to Gertrude Stein's *The Geographical History of America or the Relation of Human Nature to the Human Mind*:

This space is usually reserved for a brief description of a book's contents. In this case, however, I must admit frankly that I do not know what Miss Stein is talking about. I do not even understand the title.

I admire Miss Stein tremendously, and I like to publish her books, although most of the time I do not know what she is driving at. That, Miss Stein tells me, is because I am dumb.

I note that one of my partners and I are characters in this latest work of Miss Stein's. Both of us wish we knew what she was saying about us. Both of us hope too that her faithful followers will make more of this book than we were able to!

When Cerf interviewed her on his national radio program, he commented, "I'm very proud to be your publisher, Miss Stein, but as I've always told you, I don't understand very much of what you're saying."

"Well, I've always told you, Bennett," she replied, "you're a very nice boy but you're rather stupid."

• An editor offered Vladimir Nabokov $200 for 2,000 words on the question "Does the writer have a social responsibility?" Wrote Nabokov in reply: "My answer to your question . . . is NO. You owe me 10 cents, Sir."

LAYING UP THE PUBLISHER

THE SUCCESS of her famous story "The Lottery" inspired Shirley Jackson to study witchcraft, and she became convinced that she had supernatural powers. On one occasion she apparently did. After a quarrel with her publisher, Alfred Knopf, she learned that he was going skiing that weekend. Making a wax image of him, she stuck a pin in one leg of the image. Knopf broke that leg skiing.

EDITORIAL RIVALRIES

• The editor of the *Laramie Boomerang*, American humorist Bill Nye, feuded with the editor of the *Sweetwater Gazette*. "Aside from the fact that he is a squinteyed, consumptive liar, with a breath like a buzzard and a record like a convict, I don't have anything against him," Nye said. "He means well enough, and if he can evade the penitentiary and the vigilance committee for a few more years, there is a chance he'll end up his life in a natural way. If he doesn't tell the truth a little more plentifully, however, the Green River people will rise as one man and churn him up till there won't be anything left of him but a pair of suspenders and a wart."

• When the *New York Post* and *New York Sun* were feuding early in this century, an editor on the *Post* called the *Sun* "a yellow dog." Answered a *Post* editor, most aloofly, "The *Post* calls the *Sun* 'a yellow dog.' The attitude of the *Sun*, however, will continue to be that of any dog toward any post."

• In 1923 the editor of the *Topeka Capital* charged that William Allen White's Emporia *Gazette* "is the best-loved paper in Kansas because its editor never looks in yesterday's files to see if what he proposes to write today is consistent."

Replied White, "Consistency is a paste jewel that only cheap men cherish."

A DANGEROUS BUSINESS

• Ben Franklin's grandson Benjamin Franklin Bache (1769–1798), proud to be called Lightning Rod, Jr., bitterly attacked President Washington and Federalist policies in his *Philadelphia Aurora*. Angered by one of Bache's editorials, veterans of Washington's army wrecked the newspaper office. When Bache said that compared to any of the great generals of European history Washington wasn't fit to lead a sergeant's guard, he was arrested by American authorities under the Alien and Sedition Acts, though he died before he could be tried. The infamous Alien and Sedition Acts were, in fact, partly aimed at Bache and his *Aurora*.

• A devout Quaker, the poet John Greenleaf Whittier dedicated just as much of his life to the antislavery movement as to his poetry, often risking his life for the cause. In the fall of 1835 he and an English abolitionist were attacked by a mob in Concord, New Hampshire. Five years later, in Philadelphia, the offices of his newspaper *The Pennsylvania Freeman* were burned to the ground by an angry mob.

• The noted editor of *Scribner's Magazine* from 1887 to 1914, Edward L. Burlingame rejected probably the most notorious rejected author in American literary history. In June 1881 Charles Guiteau stormed into the Scribner's offices screaming that he would kill Burlingame for rejecting his manuscript. Staffers managed to eject Guiteau, who a month later assassinated President Garfield.

• Vituperative scandal-mongering William Cowper Brann's violent treatment of the moral and social problems of his day as editor of the *Iconoclast* in Waco, Texas, made him a notorious national figure. In 1898 he finally became involved in a dispute with the local religious college and was killed in a pistol duel after being bushwhacked by one of its incensed supporters—but not before he whirled and killed the man with his own gun.

STRANGE EDITORIAL ENDINGS

• The rich Roman aristocrat Titus Pomponius Atticus (109–32 B.C.) was also an editor and publisher who kept a large staff of slaves trained in copying and binding manuscripts. Atticus served as Cicero's publisher and advised him on both literary and personal matters. He was stricken with an incurable illness in his seventy-seventh year and starved himself to death.

• A prolific man of letters who contributed to the *Spectator*, the *Tatler*, and the *Guardian* and later published and edited his own weekly, the *Bee*, Eustace Budgell was a confidant of Joseph Addison's, his mother's cousin, and other English notables. Budgell, however, was an extravagant eccentric who lost over £20,000 in the infamous South Sea stock scheme and spent huge amounts of money to get elected to Parliament. When his friend and fellow deist Dr. Matthew Tindal died, it seemed that Budgell's financial worries were over, for a legacy of some £2,000 was left him in Tindal's will. But Tindal's nephew charged that Budgell had inserted the bequest in the will, and the courts agreed with him. Budgell was ridiculed in Pope's satire *Epistle to Dr. Arbuthnot* (1735): "Let Budgell charge low Grub Street in his quill, / And write whate'er he pleased—except his will." Scandal plagued him for two years as he vainly tried to prove his innocence in various lawsuits. Finally, on May 4, 1737, after filling his pockets with rocks from the beach, he hired a boat at Somerset-Stairs and, while the waterman rowed them under the bridge there, threw himself overboard. Budgell had tried to persuade his natural daughter, the actress Anne Eustace, to kill herself with him, but she had refused. Found on his desk was a slip of paper on which he had written of his act of suicide: "What Cato did, and Addison approved, cannot be wrong."

• The notorious Ohio Copperhead politician and newspaper editor Clement Laird Vallandigham was banished behind Confederate lines for the duration of the Civil War for supporting the South and declaring that the war being fought was not to save the Union but to free the blacks and enslave the whites. After the war Vallandigham became a prominent lawyer in his home state. His unusual end came in 1871, when he was defending a man charged with murder. Vallandigham's defense was that the murdered man had actually killed himself while trying to draw his pistol. When he demonstrated his theory to his associates in his hotel room—rising from a kneeling position, drawing his pistol from his pocket and pulling the trigger—he shot and killed himself. He had inadvertently used a loaded pistol. His defense theory later worked in court, however, and his client went free.

• The wealthy expatriate American publisher Harry Crosby (1898–1929), a friend to Hemingway and other writers, shot himself to death in Paris toward the end of the Lost Generation era. Crosby lived life to the fullest, no matter what it cost. Even his practical jokes were expensive. One time he surreptitiously stocked bookstalls along the Seine with rare editions, priced ridiculously low, just to witness the chaos he created when patrons tried to buy the rare volumes from the booksellers.

• Soon after he was dismissed from his post as the longtime editor of *Cosmopolitan* magazine in 1954, Ray Long committed suicide. Thus began the most violent period in American magazine history. Next, Long's successor, Harry Payne Burton, was fired and took his own life with an overdose of sleeping pills. Then, an assistant editor who had hoped for the job of *Cosmopolitan* editor hanged herself when she didn't get the post. Finally, the woman in charge of the magazine's editorial production jumped or fell off a ship in the Atlantic and drowned.

• It is hard to think of a more ironic end than that of the founder of *Organic Gardening* magazine, J. J. Rodale, who did so much to advance the cause of organic farming and good health in America. Rodale died while appearing on the Dick Cavett television talk show in 1971, soon after stating, "I'm so healthy that I expect to live on and on." Just as the show ended, before he could leave his chair, he slumped over with a fatal heart attack.

EDITORIAL EPITAPH

THIS EPITAPH for an editor can be found in an English churchyard:

> *Here lies an editor!*
> *Snooks if you will;*
> *In mercy, Kind Providence,*
> *Let him lie still!*
> *He lied for his living; so*
> *He lived while he lied;*
> *When he could not lie longer,*
> *He lied down and died.*

CHAPTER SIX

Critics, Censors, Bowdlerizers & Book Burners

WRITERS BE DAMNED!

FEW CRITICS have been as immoderate as Jacques Vaché, the Dadaist who climbed up on the stage of a Paris theater, pulled out a revolver, and threatened to shoot anyone who applauded a play he disliked. Fortunately, literary critics usually confine themselves to words. Only a handful of the best of these often wrong-headed and wrong-hearted little "pieces of hate," as Heywood Broun called them, can be listed here and I begin with Shakespeare to show that no one's feelings should really be hurt:

Ben Jonson, on hearing Shakespeare's boast that he had never blotted out a single line: "Would he had blotted out a thousand."

"Shakespeare never has six lines together without a fault."
—Samuel Johnson

"Shakespeare undoubtably wanted taste."
—Hugh Walpole

"With the single exception of Homer, there is no eminent writer, not even Sir Walter Scott, whom I can despise so entirely as I despise Shakespeare, when I measure my mind against his. . . . It would positively be a relief to me to dig him up and throw stones at him."
—George Bernard Shaw
in *Dramatic Opinions and Essays* (1907)

Edmund Waller on Milton's *Paradise Lost*: "If its length is not considered a merit it hath no other."

The *Quarterly Review*, the same vicious sheet that killed Keats, predicted that Dickens would have "an ephemeral popularity followed by oblivion."

The *Boston Intelligencer* reviewing Walt Whitman's *Leaves of Grass*: "This book should find no place where humanity urges any claim to respect and the author should be kicked from all decent society as below the level of brute . . . it seems to us that he must be some escaped lunatic, raving in pitiable delirium." A column in the *New York Times* called Whitman a "half beast . . . who roots among the rotten garbage of licentious thoughts."

Thomas Carlyle on refusing to meet the poet Algernon Swinburne: "I have no wish to know anyone sitting in a sewer and adding to it."

"In his youth, Wordsworth sympathized with the French Revolution, went to France, wrote good poetry, and had a natural daughter. At this period he was a 'bad' man. Then he became 'good,' abandoned his daughter, adopted correct principles, and wrote bad poetry."
—Bertrand Russell

Lord Chesterfield refused to support Samuel Johnson while he was at work on his great dictionary, but reviewed the book favorably on its completion. Johnson wrote to him: "Is not a patron, my lord, one who looks with unconcern on a man struggling for life in the water, and when he has reached ground encumbers him with help?"

Dr. Johnson, later, on the collected letters of Lord Chesterfield: "They teach the morals of a whore, and the manners of a dancing master."

Johnson once again on Lord Chesterfield: "This man I thought had been a Lord among wits; but I find, he is only a wit among Lords."

The French critic Sainte-Beuve was challenged by an author to a duel and given the first choice of weapons. "I choose spelling," he said. "You're dead."

Antoine de Rivarol on a two-line poem: "Very nice, but there are dull stretches."

> *Cibber! write all thy Verses upon Glasses,*
> *The only way to save 'em from our Arses.*
> —Alexander Pope

Wrote Thomas Babington Macaulay of Bertrand Barère's work: "A man who has never been within the tropics does not know what a thunderstorm means; a man who has never looked on Niagara has but a faint idea of a cataract; and he who has not read Barère's *Memoirs* may be said not to know what it is to lie."

Algernon Swinburne wrote of Emerson: "A gap-toothed and hoary-headed ape . . . who now in his dotage spits and chatters from a dirtier perch of his own finding and fouling: coryphaeus or choragus of his Bulgarian tribe of autocoprophagous baboons . . ."

Swinburne had worse to say about Whitman: "Under the dirty clumsy paws of a harper whose plectrum is a muck-rake, any tune will become a chaos of discords. . . . Mr. Whitman's Eve is a drunken apple-woman, indecently sprawling in the slush and garbage of the gutter amid the rotten refuse of her overturned fruit-stall: but Mr. Whitman's Venus is a Hottentot wench under the influence of cantharides and adulterated rum."

George Bernard Shaw on Gounod's *Redemption*: "If you will only take the precaution to go in long enough after it commences and to come out long enough before it is over, you will not find it wearisome."

Jonathan Swift claimed that an Irish bishiop criticized *Gulliver's Travels* on the grounds that it "was full of improbable lies, and for his part he hardly believed a word of it."

One critic, his name goes unrecorded, burned Thomas Hardy's *Jude the Obscure* and sent him the ashes.

H. H. Munro (Saki) on George Bernard Shaw: "Bernard Shaw had discovered himself and gave ungrudgingly of his discovery to the world."

R. K. Munkittrick wrote on a rejection slip to a poet who had submitted several poems to *Judge*: "Please curb your doggerel."

A fledgling poet sent editor Eugene Field a long tedious poem entitled "Why Do I Live?" Wrote Field on the rejection slip: "Because you send your poem by mail."

"This isn't a kindergarten for amateur writers," said the editor who fired Rudyard Kipling from his job as a reporter for the *San Francisco Examiner*. "Sorry, Mr. Kipling, but you just don't know how to use the English language."

"Then comes Sir Walter Scott with his enchantments, and by his single might checks this wave of progress, and even turns it back; sets the world in love with dreams and phantoms; with decayed and degraded systems of government; with the silliness and emptiness, sham grandeurs, sham gauds, and sham chivalries of a brainless and worthless long-vanished society. He did measureless harm; more real and lasting harm, perhaps, than any other individual that ever wrote."   —Mark Twain

"Mr. Henry James writes fiction as if it were a painful duty."
—Oscar Wilde

Voltaire was told of an author who said spiteful things about him, despite Voltaire's kind words about the man: "Perhaps," Voltaire replied, "we are both mistaken."

"This is not a novel to be tossed aside lightly. It should be thrown with great force."   —Dorothy Parker

H. G. Wells described Henry James as: "A magnificent but painful hippopotamus resolved at any cost . . . upon picking up a pea."

Alexander Woollcott, signing a first edition copy of his *Shouts and Murmurs*: "Ah what is so rare as a Woollcott first edition?" Franklin Pierce Adams (F.P.A.): "A Woollcott second edition."

Alphonse Daudet was asked to write an essay congratulating Émile Zola on finishing the twentieth volume of his Rougon-Macquart family series. "If I were to write that article," he replied, "it would be to advise Zola, now that the family-tree of the Rougon-Macquarts is complete, to go and hang himself from the highest branch."

"Mr. Zola is determined to show that, if he has not got genius, he can at least be dull."   —Oscar Wilde

"George Moore wrote brilliant English until he discovered grammar."
                    —Oscar Wilde

Drama critic Robert Hendrickson on a poor performance of *Hamlet*: "There has long been a controversy over who wrote Shakespeare's plays—Shakespeare or Bacon. I propose to settle it today by opening their graves. Whoever turned over last night wrote *Hamlet*."

"It was one of those plays in which all the actors unfortunately enunciated very clearly."   —Robert Benchley

Director George S. Kaufman in a telegram sent between acts to actor William Gaxton, who played the President in *Of Thee I Sing*: "I am watching your performance from the rear of the house. Wish you were here."

"*Hook and Ladder* is the sort of play that gives failures a bad name."
—Walter Kerr

Eugene Field on a poor performance of *King Lear*: "———played the King as though someone had led the ace."

Dorothy Parker reviewing A. A. Milne's *The House at Pooh Corner*: "Tonstant Weader fwowed up."

Wolfgang Pauli on a paper written by a physicist colleague: "This isn't right. This isn't even wrong."

"George Meredith is only a prose Browning—and so was Browning."   —Oscar Wilde

"Wagner's music is better than it sounds."
—Bill Nye
(often attributed
to Mark Twain)

The British *Times Literary Supplement* in reviewing *The Cherry Pit*, written by a direct descendant of Sir John Harrington, Elizabethan poet and inventor of the first flush toilet: "Mr. Harrington is less successful than his ancestors at dealing with fundamentals."

"It took me fifteen years to discover I had no talent for writing, but I couldn't give it up because by that time I was famous."
—Robert Benchley

The world's shortest review: a one-word summary of a play called *Wham!* about which critic Wolcott Gibbs wrote: "Ouch!"

"Hemingway, remarks are not literature."
—Gertrude Stein

Gertrude Stein, to her dog: "Play Hemingway. Be fierce."

"Mr. James Payn is an adept in the art of concealing what is not worth finding."   —Oscar Wilde

Talleyrand was caricatured as an old woman in Mme. de Staël's novel *Delphine*. On meeting the author at a party he observed: "That is the book, is it not, in which you and I are exhibited in the disguise of females?"

George Jean Nathan about a contemporary playwright: "He writes his plays for the ages—the ages between five and twelve."

Wolcott Gibbs on Alexander Woollcott: "He wasn't exactly hostile to facts, but he was apathetic about them."

Robert Benchley reviewing an unfunny stage comedy: "Some laughter was heard in the back rows. Someone must have been telling jokes back there."

"There are two ways of disliking poetry. One way is to dislike it, the other is to read Pope."   —Oscar Wilde

"To me, Poe's prose is unreadable—like Jane Austen's. No, there is a difference. I could read his prose on a salary, but not Jane's."
—Mark Twain

To Virginia Woolf, James Joyce's *Ulysses* was: "The work of a queasy undergraduate scratching his pimples."

MORE BRICKBATS FOR THE BARD

• Playwright Robert Greene on Shakespeare: "There is an upstart Crow, beautiful with our feathers, that with his *Tygers hart wrapt in a Players hyde*, supposes he is well able to bombast out a blanke verse as the best of you: and being an absolute *Johannes factotum* is in his owne conceit the onely Shakescene in a countrey." (Greene parodied here a line from *3 Henry VI*: "Oh Tiger's heart wrapt in a woman's hide.")

• Poet John Dryden: "[Shakespeare] writes in many places below the dullest writers of ours or any precedent age. Never did any author precipitate himself from such heights of thought to so low expressions. . . . He is the very Janus of poets; he wears almost everywhere two faces; and you have scarce begun to admire the one ere you despise the other."

• Samuel Pepys hated many of Shakespeare's plays and called *A Midsummer Night's Dream* "the most insipid, ridiculous play that I ever saw in my life."

• John Dennis thought Shakespeare "utterly devoid of celestial fire."

• Pope sneered at the Bard when he wrote: "Shakespeare (whom you and every play-house bill / Style the divine, the matchless, what you will) . . ."

• Addison failed to include Shakespeare in his *Account of the Greatest English Poets*.

• Hume considered Shakespeare "a disproportioned and misshapen giant."

• Byron sneered at: "One Shakespeare and his plays so doting, / Which many people pass for wits by quoting."

• Sardou called Hamlet an "empty wind-bag hero" and wrote that there is "nothing good in the play . . . except the scene with the actors."

• Voltaire wrote: "Shakespeare is a drunken savage with some imagination whose plays can please only in London and Canada" and "Shakespeare is the Corneille of London, but everywhere else he is a great fool." Elsewhere he compared him to "a mean or vicious ape."

"DAMN WITH FAINT PRAISE"

ALEXANDER POPE invented this phrase when satirizing the scholar and author Joseph Addison as "Atticus" in 1723. The full paradox is seldom quoted anymore but Pope wrote that Atticus would

> *Damn with faint praise, assent with civil leer,*
> *And, without sneering, teach the rest to sneer.*

"ALWAYS SCRIBBLE, SCRIBBLE, SCRIBBLE! EH! MR. GIBBON?"

HENRY DIGBY BESTE, in his *Personal and Literary Memorials* (1829), tells the full story of this famous remark made to English historian Edward Gibbon.

The Duke of Gloucester, brother of King George III, permitted Mr. Gibbon to present him with the first volume of *The History of the Decline and Fall of the Roman Empire*. When the second volume of that work appeared, it was quite in order that it should be presented to His Royal Highness in like manner. The prince received the author with much good nature and affability, saying to him, as he laid the quarto on the table, "Another damn'd thick, square book! Always scribble, scribble, scribble! Eh! Mr. Gibbon?"

This insulting remark about the greatest historical work in English (though Gibbon generally saw history as "little more than the crimes, follies and misfortunes of men") has also been attributed to the Duke of Cumberland. In his autobiography Gibbon writes of his "final deliverance," how he finished the last lines of his book—almost a quarter of a century in the making—between eleven o'clock and midnight on June 27, 1787, in the summerhouse of his garden at

Lausanne: "After laying down my pen, I took several turns in a *berceau*, or covered walk of acacias, which commands a prospect of the country, the lake, and the mountains. The air was temperate, the sky was serene, the silver orb of the moon was reflected from the waters, and all nature was silent. I will not dissemble the first emotion of joy on recovery of my freedom, and, perhaps, the establishment of my fame."

MOST DIPLOMATIC CRITIC

CRITICISM OF A sonnet France's Louis XIV wrote, given to the King by the court poet Boileau: "Sire, nothing is impossible for your Majesty. You set out to write some bad verses and you have succeeded."

ACROSTICS AND CRITICS

CRITICISM OCCUPIES the lowest place in the literary hierarchy; as regards form, almost always; and as regards "moral value," incontestably. It comes after rhyming games and acrostics, which at least require a certain inventiveness.
—Gustave Flaubert, in a letter to a friend

REVIEW OF *LADY CHATTERLEY'S LOVER*

Field and Stream magazine's reviewer felt, tongue in cheek, that D. H. Lawrence's account of an English gamekeeper's daily life "is full of considerable interest to outdoor-minded readers, as it contains many passages on pheasant raising, the apprehending of poachers, ways to control vermin and other chores and duties of the professional gamekeeper. Unfortunately, one is obliged to wade through many pages of extraneous material in order to discover and savour these sidelights on the management of a midland shooting estate."

The Ape turn'd Sportsman

THE MOUTHS OF ADDERS

ONE OF OUR greatest modern playwrights, Tennessee Williams, had his first play, *Battle of Angels* (1940), hissed off the stage, and its producers even took the unprecedented step of apologizing to the audience. Over a century before, Charles Lamb saw his first play hissed off the stage and actually joined in the hissing so that he wouldn't be recognized as the author by the violent audience. Lamb, however, had the last word about the hissing, writing:

> Mercy on us, that God should give his favorite children, men, mouths to speak with, discourse rationally, to promise smoothly, to flatter agreeably, to encourage warmly, to counsel wisely; to sing with, to drink with, and to kiss with; and that they should turn them into mouths of adders, bears, wolves, hyenas, and whistle like tempests, and emit breath through them like distillations of aspic poison, to asperse and vilify the innocent labour of their fellow creatures who are desirous to please them. God be pleased to make the breath stink and the teeth rot out of them all therefore!

"THEY WILL NOT LET MY PLAY RUN, AND YET THEY STEAL MY THUNDER"

Our author, for the advantage of this play, had invented a new species of thunder, . . . the very sort that is presently used in the theatre. The tragedy itself was coldly received, not withstanding such assistance, and was acted but a short time. Some nights after, Mr. Dennis, being in the pit at the representation of *Macbeth*, heard his own thunder made use of; upon which he rose in a violent passion and exclaimed, "See how the rascals use me! They will not let my play run, and yet they steal my thunder."

*T*HIS EARLY account of the origin of the expression *steal my thunder*, from the *Biographia Britannica*, is accurate in all respects, according to most authorities. Restoration playwright John Dennis (1657–1734) had invented a new and more effective way of simulating thunder on the stage (by shaking a sheet of tin) for his play *Appius and Virginia* (1709). The play soon closed, but a rival company stole his thunder, inspiring his outburst and giving us the expression "steal my thunder." (See also *Punology Pro and Con*.)

MURDERED BY THE CRITICS

A POEM BY Annibale Caro failed to attain an adequately Petrarchan style, sixteenth-century Italian critic Ludovico Castelvetro charged. Caro and his defenders disagreed, a literary feud breaking out during which the critic apparently murdered one of the poet's supporters. Excommunicated from the Church, Castelvetro fled Rome and wandered Europe in exile the rest of his life.

ROBERT BROWNING AVENGES HIS WIFE

*R*EADING THE *Life and Letters of Edward FitzGerald*, Robert Browning came upon the following passage in a letter the translator of the *Rubáiyát* had written to a friend:

> Mrs. [Elizabeth Barrett] Browning's death is rather a relief to me, I must say. No more *Aurora Leighs*, thank God. A woman of real genius, I know, but what is the upshot of it all! She and her sex had better mind the kitchen and her children, and perhaps the poor. Except in such things as little novels, they only devote themselves to what men do much better, leaving that which men do worse or not at all.

FitzGerald was dead and Browning's wife had died twenty-eight years before, but the poet's fury at the cruel words he read inspired him to write one of his last and most memorable poems:

I chanced upon a new book yesterday;
I opened it; and where my finger lay,
'Twixt page and uncut page, these words I read—
Some six or seven, at most—and learned thereby
That you, FitzGerald, whom by ear and eye
She never knew, thanked God my wife was dead.
Ay dead, and were yourself alive, good Fitz,
How to return your thanks would task my wits.
Kicking you seems the common lot of curs,
While more appropriate greeting lends you grace;
Surely, to spit there glorifies your face—
Spitting—from lips once sanctified by hers.

PUFFERY

In HIS PLAY *The Critic* (1779) English dramatist Richard Sheridan created a cast of characters including the bogus, verbose critic and author Mr. Puff. Sheridan named Mr. Puff after the English word *puff*, meaning inflated praise, which is suggestive of the sound made by puffing wind from the mouth and was commonly applied to exaggerated newspaper ads at the time. But Mr. Puff added a new dimension to the word in Sheridan's satire of the malignant literary criticism of the day. Puff talks with the spiteful critics Dangle and Sneer about the absurd, bombastic "tragedy" he has written called *The Spanish Armada*, pushing his play all the while, for he has reduced the art of *puffery* to a science. At one time he even catalogs the puff: "Yes, the puff preliminary, the puff collateral, the puff collusive and the puff oblique, or puff by implication. These all assume, as circumstances require, the various forms of letter to the editor, occasional anecdote, impartial critique, observation from correspondent, or advertisement from the party." So absurdly does Mr. Puff overpraise or blow up his work that his name entered the language in the form of *puffery* as a word for the kind of criticism produced by literary cliques, the mutual back-scratching or log-rolling that is usually subtler, but still as common today among the Sneers and Smears of literature as it was in Sheridan's time. Thanks to Mr. Puff we also have a synonym for a *blurb (q.v.).*

CRITICIZING THE CRITICS

As for you, little Envious Prigs, snarling, bastard, puny Criticks, you'll soon have railed your last: Go hang yourselves.
　　　　　　　　　　　—Rabelais

Hot, envious, noise, proud, the scribbling fry
Burn, hiss and bounce, waste paper, stink, and die.
　　　　　　　　　　　—Edward Young

They who write ill, and they who ne'er durst wrote,
Turn critics out of mere revenge and spite.
　　　　　　　　　　　—John Dryden

Thou eunuch of language . . . thou pimp of gender . . . murderous accoucheur of infant learning . . . thou pickle-herring in the puppet show of nonsense.　　　　　　　　　—Robert Burns

A louse in the locks of literature.
　　　　　　　　　—Alfred, Lord Tennyson,
　　　　　　　　　　　on the critic Churton Collins

Critics are like horse-flies which prevent the horse from ploughing.
　　　　　　　　　　　—Anton Pavlovitch

Many critics are like woodpeckers, who, instead of enjoying the fruit and shadow of a tree, hop incessantly around the trunk pecking holes in the bark to discover some little worm or other.
　　　　　　　　　　　—Henry Wadsworth Longfellow

A young critic is like a boy with a gun; he fires at every living thing he sees. He thinks only of his own skill, not the pain he is giving.
　　　　　　　　　　　—Henry Wadsworth Longfellow

The critic's symbol should be the tumble-bug; he deposits his egg in somebody else's dung, otherwise he could not hatch it.
　　　　　　　　　　　—Mark Twain

A critic is a legless man who teaches running.
—Channing Pollock

Curse the blasted, jelly-boned swines, the slimy, the belly-wriggling invertebrates, the miserable sodding rotters, the flaming sods, the snivelling, dribbling, dithering, palsied, pulseless lot that make up England today. They're got white of egg in their veins, and their spunk is that watery it's a marvel they can breed. They can nothing but frog-spawn—the gibberers! God, how I hate them!
—D. H. Lawrence

I have just read your lousy review buried in the back pages. You sound like a frustrated old man who never made a success, an eight-ulcer man on a four-ulcer job, and all four ulcers working. I have never met you, but if I do you'll need a new nose and plenty of beefsteak and perhaps a supporter below.

—Harry S Truman (1884–1972),
to *Washington Post* music critic
Paul Hume, who had criticized
his daughter's singing voice

CLAQUE

*P*LAYWRIGHTS HAVE had an advantage over most authors in the past because they or their backers could hire a *claque*, a body of people to applaud their work. The French, who originated the system in 1820 or so, had it down to a science. *Claqueurs* were divided into:

Commissaires—memorized the play and pointed out its literary merits.
Rieurs—hired to laugh at the jokes.
Pleureurs—women hired to cry when appropriate.
Chatouilleurs—kept the audience in good spirits.
Bisseurs—hired to cry *bis!*, "encore!"

THE REVIEWED REVIEW REVIEWERS

*J*OHN MIDDLETON MURRY said, "Putting a valuation upon new books is perhaps the least valuable, as it is certainly the most dangerous, part of criticism." Henry James thought book reviewing "a practice in general that has nothing in common with the arts of criticism." Charles Dickens was far more bitter than either, calling reviewers "rotten creatures with men's faces and the souls of devils," "the lice of literature." Thomas Mann saw it this healthy way:

We all bear wounds; praise is a soothing if not necessarily healing balm for them. Nevertheless, if I may judge by my own experience, our receptivity for praise stands in no relationship to our vulnerability to mean disdain and spiteful abuse. No matter how stupid such abuse is, no matter how plainly impelled by private rancors, as an expression of hostility it occupies us far more deeply and lastingly than the opposite. Which is very foolish, since enemies are, of course, the necessary concomitant of any robust life, the very proof of its strength.

America's first book review newspaper supplement was *The New York Times Book Review*, which was initially issued on a Saturday instead of a Sunday. Edited by Francis Whiting Halsey, it consisted of eight pages and was first published October 10, 1896. Magazines, of course, had been devoted to book reviews long before this.

REPLY TO A CRITIC

I AM SITTING in the smallest room in my house. I have your review in front of me. Soon it will be behind me.

—Max Reger, German composer

THE "FINAL" WORD ON CRITICS

> *Bullfight critics ranked in rows*
> *Crowd the enormous Plaza full;*
> *But only one is there who knows—*
> *And he's the man who fights the bull.*
> > —Bullfighter Domingo Ortega,
> > translated by Robert Graves,
> > and a favorite quotation
> > of John F. Kennedy

"WHO READS AN AMERICAN BOOK?"

*B*RITISH AUTHOR Sydney Smith almost set off a full-scale literary war when he asked this famous sardonic rhetorical question in a book review he wrote for the *Edinburgh Review* in 1820. Smith, however, had been reviewing the *Statistical Annals of the United States* by Adam Seybert and was on his way toward making an ironic point that has little to do with literature, as the last paragraph of his essay shows:

In the four corners of the globe, who reads an American book? or goes to an American play? or looks at an American picture or statue? What does the world yet owe to American physicians or surgeons? What new substances have their chemists discovered? or what old ones have they analyzed? What new constellations have been discovered by the telescopes of Americans? What have they done in mathematics? Who drinks out of American glasses? or eats from American plates? or wears American coats or gowns? or sleeps in American blankets? Finally, under which of the tyrannical governments of Europe is every sixth man a slave, whom his fellow-creatures may buy, and sell, and torture?

LITERARY SQUABBLES

Ah, God! the petty fools of rhyme
  That shriek and sweat in pygmy wars
Before the stony face of Time,
  And looked at by the silent stars;—

That hate each other for a song,
  And do their little best to bite;
That pinch their brothers in the throng,
  And scratch the very dead for spite;—

And strive to make an inch of room
  For their sweet selves, and cannot hear
The sullen Lethe rolling doom
  On them and theirs, and all things here;—

When one small touch of Charity
   Could lift them nearer Godlike state
Than if the crowded Orb should cry
   Like those that cried Diana great.

And I too talk, and lose the touch
   I talk of, surely, after all
The noblest answer unto such
   Is kindly silence when they bawl.
            —Alcibiades*

A CRITIC LOSES IN COURT

ONE OF THE few people to bring a critic to court was artist and wit James Whistler, who claimed that author John Ruskin had libeled him by calling his pictures "unfinished" and charging that he "flung a pot of paint" on his canvases. Ruskin lost the case, largely because he was too nervous to appear in court, and kept his promise never to write criticisms again if he lost. He spent the rest of his life in seclusion. Whistler was awarded a mere farthing in damages and almost went bankrupt trying to pay his solicitors.

"I DISAPPROVE OF WHAT YOU SAY, BUT I WILL DEFEND TO THE DEATH YOUR RIGHT TO SAY IT"

VOLTAIRE DIDN'T say it. In her book *The Friends of Voltaire* (1906), E. Beatrice Hall, using the pen name S. G. Tallentyre, proposed this well-known quotation on freedom of speech as a paraphrase on a thought in Voltaire's *Essay on Tolerance*: "Think for yourself and let others enjoy the privilege to do so too." Possibly unknown to Miss Hall, Voltaire had written the following in a letter to an M. le Riche on February 6, 1770: "I detest what you say, but I would give my life to make it possible for you to continue to write."

THE UNSPEAKABLE CURLL

JOHN ARBUTHNOT remarked that English publisher Edmund Curll's inaccurate biographies were "one of the new terrors of death," but Curll was more notorious for the obscene books he published, these including *Venus in the*

---

*Although he never acknowledged it, this good advice is almost certainly from the pen of Alfred, Lord Tennyson, England's Poet Laureate, writing as "Alcibiades." The poem was the result of a literary quarrel provoked by Lord Lytton, Edward Bulwer-Lytton.

Cloister; *The Memories of John Ker of Kersland*; *The Nun in Her Smock*; a book on flagellation; and other inspirational works. Today "the unspeakable Curll" might be a rich man, but in his time he was fined, put in the pillory, and imprisoned for his efforts. His conviction on the grounds of obscenity in 1727 for *Venus in the Cloister* was the first such publishing conviction in the English-speaking world. Among the greats who lampooned him were Jonathan Swift, Daniel Defoe, and Alexander Pope, whose "Dunciad" described him as "a fly in amber." No one has identified the anonymous wit who coined the word *curlicism*, meaning literary indecency, from his name.

When Curll was exhibited in the pillory the crowd began to throw rotten eggs, vegetables, mud, and rocks at him, as they generally did in such cases, often killing the condemned. But Curll was rich enough not only to pay the hangman to wipe his face free of garbage so he wouldn't suffocate, but to buy off the crowd. "Filthiness drivels in the very tone of his voice," Defoe said of Curll. Pope tried to poison him by slipping ground glass into his drink, but the emetic only caused him a few unpleasant hours.

SELF-CRITICAL AUTHORS

*T*HERE WAS NEVER yet a true poet or orator that thought any one better than himself," Cicero said. This may be true, but a number of true poets have *said* there were better poets than themselves. Goethe and Heine, for example, deferred to Shakespeare; indeed, most authors wisely leave Shakespeare out of any such comparisons, though Robert Southey claimed that his work would be read when Shakespeare was forgotten (the scholar Richard Porson replied, "Yes, *but not till then*"), and Wordsworth pronounced that he could write like Shakespeare if he "had a mind to" (Charles Lamb retorted, "So, you see, it's the mind that's wanting"). Most authors, even Shakespeare ("Not marble nor the gilded monuments / Of princes shall outlive this lofty rhyme"), have thought highly of their own work. The examples of vanity are legion, those of modesty but a patrol in the wilderness of the id. Among American authors Hawthorne is noted for criticizing himself, but, as William Walsh pointed out over a century ago in *The Handy-Book of Literary Curiosities* (from which most of this information is drawn), James Russell Lowell's satire upon himself in his "Fable for Critics" is best known:

> *There is Lowell, who's striving Parnassus to climb*
> *With a whole bale of* isms *tied together with rhyme.*
> *He might get on alone, spite of brambles and boulders,*
> *But he can't with that bundle he has on his shoulders.*
> *The top of the hill he will ne'er come nigh reaching*
> *Till he learns the distinction 'twixt singing and preaching.*

His lyre has some chords that would ring pretty well,
But he'd rather by half make a drum of the shell,
And rattle away till he's old as Methusalem,
At the head of a march to the last New Jerusalem.

Wrote Lowell in an essay: "I am not, I think, specially thin-skinned as to other people's opinions of myself, having . . . later and fuller intelligence on that point than anybody else can give me."

Flaubert grew so weary of criticism and censure of *Madame Bovary* that he said he would buy up every copy if he had the money "and throw them all into the fire and never hear of the book again."

THE LITERARY WARRIORS

W HEN THE French Inspector General of Theaters censored passages in Victor Hugo's *Hernani* that were disrespectful of the monarchy, a literary war ensued in which romanticists supporting Hugo took sides against the classicists and there were pitched battles for weeks inside and out of the theater. Professional claques were hired by the classicists and Theophile Gautier led romanticist volunteers, urging them to take their stand "upon the rugged mount of Romanticism, and to valiantly defend its passes against the assault of the Classics." It was a costly victory for the romanticists, with many injured and at least one young man dead in a duel.

VICTOR HUGO

NOVEL READING AS "SELF-ABUSE"

N OVEL READING redoubles this nervous drain begun by excessive study. What is or can be as superlatively silly or ruinous to the nerves as that silly girl, snivelling and laughing by turns over a "love story"? Of course it awakens her Amativeness. In this consists its chief charm. Was there ever a novel without its hero. It would be *Hamlet* played without Hamlet. Yet how could depicting a beau so heroic, lovable and dead in love, fail to awaken this tender passion in enchanted readers. To *titillate Amativeness*, mainly, are novels written and read. For this they become "vade mecums," and are carried to table, ride, picnic, walk, everywhere. It is doubtful whether fiction writers are public benefactors, or their publishers philanthropists. The amount of nervous excitment, and consequent prostration, exhaustion, and disorder they cause is fearful. Girls already have ten times too much excitability for their strength. Yet every page of every novel redoubles both their nervousness and weakness. Only Amazons could endure it. Mark this reason. Amativeness, that is, love, and the nervous system, are in the most perfect mutual sympathy. Love-stories, therefore, in common with all other forms of amatory excitement, thrill. In this consists their chief fascination. Yet all amatory action with one's self induces sexual ailments. It should always be with the *opposite* sex only; yet novel reading girls exhaust their female magnetism without obtaining any compensating male magnetism, which of necessity deranges their entire sexual system. The whole world is challenged to invalidate either this premise or inference. Self-abuse is worse, because more animal; but those who really must have amatory excitement will find it "better to marry," and expend on real lovers those sexual feelings now worse than wasted on this its "solitary" form. Those perfectly happy in their affections never read novels, because *real* love is so much more fascinating than that described. —O. S. Fowler, *Sexual Science* (1875)

BANNED AMERICAN WRITERS

*T*HE TRADITION of censorship is longer but not stronger in older countries than in America. Here is a short list of famous writers who have been banned in one place or another for one foolish reason or another. It reads like a *Who's Who* of American literature. *Banned* here includes everything from the burning of books in Puritan or Nazi bonfires to the *New York Times* refusing to accept advertising for James T. Farrell's *A World I Never Made* in 1936, and most of these writers had more than one book banned:

Sherwood Anderson
James Baldwin
Joel Barlow
James Branch Cabell
Erskine Caldwell
Alex Comfort
Theodore Dresier
Will Durant
Mary Baker Eddy
James T. Farrell
Howard Fast
William Faulkner
Allen Ginsberg
Frank Harris

Nathaniel Hawthorne
Joseph Heller
Ernest Hemingway
Thomas Jefferson
James Joyce
Alfred Kinsey
Sinclair Lewis
Jack London
Norman Mailer
Arthur Miller
Henry Miller
John O'Hara
Eugene O'Neill
Thomas Paine

William Reich
Philip Roth
J. D. Salinger
Margaret Sanger
Upton Sinclair
Lillian Smith
John Steinbeck
Harriet Beecher Stowe
Mark Twain
Kurt Vonnegut, Jr.
Alice Walker
Walt Whitman
Tennessee Williams
Edmund Wilson

LUDICROUS MOMENTS IN THE HISTORY OF CENSORSHIP

W<small>E MIGHT</small> begin in 387 B.C. with Plato suggesting that Homer be banned for immature readers, or with Curll (see curlicism, *The Unspeakable Curll*) being pilloried centuries later, but these are the most ludicrous instances I could find:

• 1881. *Leaves of Grass* withdrawn from publication in Boston, where Wendell Phillips said, "Here be all sorts of leaves except fig leaves."

• 1885. Concord, Massachusetts, banned *Huckleberry Finn* as "trash and suitable only for the slums."

• 1900. Dreiser's *Sister Carrie* withdrawn from bookstores because the publisher's wife objected to it.

• 1917. Passages in David Graham Phillips's *Susan Lenox*, a novel about a prostitute, were removed because the deceased author's sister was offended by them.

• 1929. Soviet Union blacklisted Sherlock Holmes for his "disgraceful occultism and spiritualism."

• 1930. In the famed "Decency Debates" in the Senate with Utah Senator Reed Smoot, New Mexico Senator Bronson Cutting, in favor of modified censorship laws, enraged the Mormon senator with humorous insinuations that *Lady Chatterley's Lover* was one of his favorite books.

• 1931. China banned *Alice's Adventures in Wonderland* because "animals should not use human language and [it is] disastrous to put animals and human beings on the same level."

• 1932. One of Disney's Mickey Mouse syndicated comic strips suppressed because it depicted a cow in a pasture reading Elinor Glyn's then-controversial *Three Weeks*.

• 1933. Nazis imprison author Ernst Toller and force him to eat his own words—almost an entire volume of one of his anti-Nazi books.

• 1933. Mickey Mouse banned in Nazi Germany.

• 1936. Mickey Mouse banned in the Soviet Union.

• 1937. A Mickey Mouse comic strip banned in Yugoslavia because it depicted a revolution against a monarchy.

• 1938. Mickey Mouse banned in Fascist Italy.

• 1953. An Indiana State Textbook Commission member demanded that *Robin Hood* be removed from school texts on the grounds that he was a Communist—he took from the rich to give to the poor.

• 1954. Mickey Mouse banned in East Germany as an anti-Red rebel.

• 1959. *The Rabbits' Wedding* by Garth Williams banned in Alabama libraries because one rabbit was white, the other black.

• 1966. Samm Sinclair Baker's *The Permissible Lie, The Inside Truth about Advertising*, withdrawn from publication when the Reader's Digest Association purchased its publisher Funk & Wagnalls. Later, World Publishing Company took over Funk & Wagnalls, "and, while releasing the book, barred ads that called it 'the book that *Reader's Digest* suppressed.' "

• 1977. William Steig's *Sylvester and the Magic Pebble* (1969) denounced by the Illinois Police Association because its characters, all depicted as various animals, included police that are pigs, even though they were favorably portrayed.

• 1978. *The American Heritage Dictionary* (1969) banned in Elden, Missouri, library because it contained thirty-nine "objectionable" words.

INDEX LIBRORUM PROHIBITORUM

OF ALL THE censorship bodies in history perhaps best-known are the Catholic Church's list of forbidden books, the Inquisition, Savonarola's Bonfire of the Vanities, the Star Chamber, the Boston Watch and Ward Society, the Hays Office, Anthony Comstock, and Thomas Bowdler. But the Catholic *Index*, as the *Index Librorum Prohibitorum* is called, is practically a synonym for censorship. Established by the Holy Office in 1559, the *Index* mostly condemned books for doctrinal reasons, for seeming to criticize the Church, and for moral reasons. Pope Paul VI ended publication of the *Index* in 1966, making a paperback book that had once banned as many as 5,000 works no more than a "moral guide" without force of church law, though the Vatican can still issue warnings about books that might be "dangerous" to the faithful. No American novelist has ever been listed in the *Index*, although Harriet Beecher Stowe's *Uncle Tom's Cabin* got itself banned in the Papal States, just short of making the *Index*. Not one prominent American nonfiction writer has made the *Index*, either. Among the English it is a different story. They are well represented with Hobbes, Bacon, Milton, Addison, Steele, Locke, Defoe, Richardson, Hume, Gibbon, Sterne, Goldsmith, and Mill, among others. Among the thousands of well-known foreign writers represented were Descartes, Montaigne, Spinoza, Rousseau, Pascal, Kant, Stendhal, Hugo, Casanova, Balzac, Dumas, Flaubert, Zola, D'Annunzio, Gide, Sartre, and Moravia.

Chaucer, Shakespeare, Rabelais, de Sade, James Joyce, D. H. Lawrence, and many other authors one would think were on the *Index* never made it, mostly because their works weren't considered anti-Catholic—most of them, including Shakespeare, were banned in other places.

Several famous authors, Boccaccio and Galileo among them, had their names removed from the *Index* when they made changes in their works.

THE WRITER AND THE ASTERISK

A writer owned an Asterisk,
  and kept it in his den,
Where he wrote tales (which had large sales)
Of frail and erring men
And always, when he reached the point
  Where carping censors lurk,
He called upon the Asterisk
  To do his dirty work.

—Stoddard King (1913)

THE SATANIC SCHOOL OF WRITING

*I*MMORAL WRITERS . . . men of diseased hearts and depraved imaginations, who (forming a system of opinions to suit their own unhappy course of conduct) have rebelled against the holiest ordinances of human society, and hating revelation which they try in vain to disbelieve, labour to make others as miserable as themselves by infecting them with a moral virus that eats into their soul. The school which they have set up may properly be called 'The Satanic School.' "

Robert Southey wrote the above in the preface to his long poem "A Vision of Judgment" (1821). Southey violently attacked Byron, Shelley, Keats in the poem, not only for what he considered their impious work, which often scorned Christian dogma, but for their "immoral lives." Byron later replied with his satirical parody "The Vision of Judgment" (1822), but the name "Satanic School" stuck, counting among its proud members Hugo, George Sand, Rousseau, and Bulwer-Lytton, to name but a few.

BOG CAPITALIZED

*B*og is the Russian word for God. In 1930 one million copies of a school textbook containing a poem by Nekrasov with the word *Bog* in it were printed by the Soviet government. Then someone discovered, to the horror of the Kremlin, that *Bog* was spelled with a capital letter throughout the poem. Reducing *Bog* to *bog* required resetting type in sixteen pages of each of the million books printed, but the change was made, despite the expense, so that "the books reached the Soviet children uncontaminated."

Despite the past efforts of Soviet censors, the Russian language remains rich in references to God, such expressions as "God knows," "God save us," "Oh, my God," and "Praise God" being quite common. "Communism is gone," one anonymous wit said recently, "but God remains."

BANNING THE BARD

S<small>HAKESPEARE</small> never made the *Index*, but several of his plays were censored or banned in other places. Queen Elizabeth disliked the scene where the king is deposed in *Richard II* and had it deleted from all copies of the play. From 1788 to 1820 *King Lear* was forbidden on the English stage, due to George III's insanity. Thomas Bowdler (see *Bowdler the Bloodletter*) expurgated Shakespeare, as Coleridge had suggested before him, and in recent times *The Merchant of Venice* has been banned on the grounds that Shylock is a vicious characterization of a Jew.

ALEXANDER WAS HERE

A<small>LEXANDER</small> C<small>RUDEN</small> (1701–1770) would be included under the entry for mad poets if it weren't that he was a bookseller more than a writer. He believed himself divinely appointed to reform England, suffered periodic attacks of insanity, and was confined in lunatic asylums several times. Cruden compiled a highly regarded *Biblical Concordance*, but would be more valued today for his highly peculiar form of censorship. He was called "Alexander the Corrector" because he had a penchant for going about London with a sponge and erasing all the "licentious, coarse and profane" graffiti he saw.

BOWDLER THE BLOODLETTER

R<small>ECENT SCHOLARLY</small> research now makes it seem certain that Dr. Thomas Bowdler was not the first Bowdler to expurgate Shakespeare—his sister Harriet worked over the body of the Bard's work first. But Dr. Bowdler did more than enough gouging on his own to deserve to be known as the man behind the word *bowdlerize*. His inability to stand the sight of human blood and suffering had forced Dr. Thomas Bowdler to abandon his medical practice in London, but this weakness apparently did not apply where vendors of words were concerned. Bowdler so thoroughly purged both Shakespeare and Gibbon that they would have screamed in pain from the bloodletting had they been alive.

Bowdler, the most renowned of self-appointed literary censors, was born at Ashley, near Bath, England, on July 11, 1754. After he retired from medical practice, a considerable inheritance enabled him to travel about Europe, writing accounts of the Grand Tour that seem to have neither offended nor pleased anyone. Though he came from a religious family, Bowdler never earned the Reverend Doctor title often applied to him and his early years are conspicuous for the lack of any real accomplishments, unless one counts membership in organizations such as the "Society for the Suppression of Vice." Only when he was middle-aged did he retire to the Isle of Wight and begin to sharpen his rusty scalpel on the Bard of Avon's bones.

In 1807 Bowdler's sister had published an expurgated edition of Shakespeare's work called *The Family Shakespeare* without signing her name to it as editor—probably because people would have wondered how a spinster knew what to look for to expurgate. Dr. Bowdler, however, had no such fears about signing his name. He was proud of the revised and enlarged *Family Shakespeare* that he published in 1818. In justifying this ten-volume edition, Bowdler explained on the title page that "nothing is added to the text; but those expressions are omitted which cannot with propriety be read aloud in a family," adding later that he had also expunged "whatever is unfit to be read by a gentleman in a company of ladies." What this really meant was that Bowdler (and his sister before him) had completely altered the characters of Hamlet, Macbeth, Falstaff, and others, and totally eliminated "objectionable" characters like Doll Tearsheet. Strangely enough, the poet Swinburne, who saw his own works bowdlerized by others, applauded the doctor many years later, writing that "no man ever did better service to Shakespeare than the man who made it possible to put him into the hands of intelligent and imaginative children."

Few writers then or now would agree with Swinburne, though *The Family Shakespeare* was a best-seller and won some critical acclaim. Bowdler went on to expurgate Edward Gibbon's *The History of the Decline and Fall of the Roman Empire*, castrating that masterpiece by removing "all passages of an irreligious or immoral tendency." He firmly believed that both Shakespeare and Gibbon would have "desired nothing more ardently" than his literary vandalism and would probably have turned his scalpel to other great authors if death had not excised him in 1825. About ten years later Bowdler's name was first used as a verb, the official definition then "to expurgate by omitting or modifying words or passages considered indelicate or offensive." Today the word more often means prudish, arbitrary, ridiculous censorship. Bowdler himself has been described as "the quivering moralist who is certain in his soul that others will be contaminated by what he himself reads with impunity."

Conspicuous among many bowdlerized works in history are Tate's rewrite giving *King Lear* a happy ending; the Honorable James Howard, Dryden's brother-in-law, rewriting *Romeo and Juliet* so that the young lovers are happily married; and poet laureate Sir William Davenant's jolly production of *Macbeth*, complete with dancing and singing.

"BANNED IN BOSTON"

*I*N ITS HEYDAY during the 1920s the phrase "banned in Boston" made a number of books best-sellers throughout the rest of the country. Books were frequently banned in Boston for foolish reasons at the time because the local ultraconservative Watch and Ward Society wielded great power over the city censor, often an ignorant and unreasonable man. The Boston censor who banned Eugene O'Neill's plays, for example, was the mayor's cousin, appointed because he had lost an arm and was fired from his job as drummer in a burlesque show band.

PORNOGRAPHER STRIKES BACK

*W*hitehouse International had to have the most interesting name of any English or American magazine. It seems that "Britain's Only Quality Glamour

Magazine—Complete Adult Entertainment," which featured soft-core pornography, was named for Mrs. Mary Whitehouse, who headed the puritanical Viewers and Listeners Association, which monitored the British media for what it considered smut. Mrs. Whitehouse loathed the magazine's publishers and to show what they thought of *her* they named their new publication *Whitehouse International. Whitehouse International* featured not only all that the real Mary Whitehouse detested but also an editor who legally changed her name to Mary Whitehouse and wrote a monthly column about her sexual adventures.

MARK TWAIN, CENSOR

*I*N A STRANGE case of censorship, Mark Twain *agreed* with the Brooklyn, New York, Public Library when in 1905 it banned *Huckleberry Finn* from the Children's Room as a bad example for youth. "I wrote Tom Sawyer and Huck Finn for adults exclusively," Twain said, "and it always distresses me when I find that boys and girls have been allowed access to them. The mind that becomes soiled in youth can never again be washed clean." It is worth noting that Twain's wife had censored *Huckleberry Finn* before it was published, removing all profanity.

THE WORLD'S MOST HELPFUL CENSORS

*E*VERY SOUTH AFRICAN cannot go out and buy every new book and read it to decide if he will like it," explained Judge J. H. Snyman, South Africa's chief censor, late in 1978. "Now we have a body that can do it for him. We study the book and tell him if he will like it or not."

BOOK BURNER

*T*HE TERM *book burner*, meaning "self-appointed censor" and worse, didn't arrive until 1933 when thousands of pro-Nazi students ended a torchlight parade at the University of Berlin by burning a pile of 20,000 books while Nazi Propaganda Minister Joseph Goebbels proclaimed: "The soul of the German people can express itself. These flames . . . illuminate the . . . end of an old era and light up the new."

But the first mass book burners in American history were, oddly enough, the anti–mail-order small merchants at the turn of the century who burned mail-order catalogs to censor not the free expression of ideas, but free enterprise. Local merchants persuaded or arm-twisted people into tossing their catalogs into a bonfire in the public square every Saturday night. Prizes of up to $50 were offered to those who brought in the greatest number of catalogs to be burned. This practice seemingly descended to its nadir in a small Montana town where a movie theater gave free admission or 10 cents to any child who turned over a catalog to town authorities for public burning. Yet the Montana orgy of destruction was repeated in other states, all in the name of ensuring a continuance of "freedom of opportunity in America."

BURNED BOOKS—AND AUTHORS

as good almost kill a man as kill a good Booke . . .
who destroys a good Booke, kills Reason itselfe, kills the
Image of God as it were in the eye.
       —John Milton, *Areopagitica*

No one would agree with Montaigne, who said he would rather see his children burned than his books, but book burning is anathema to most authors. Though generally associated with the Nazis, book burning has far more ancient dishonorable origins. Here are some of the most infamous book burnings in history, including two authors burned along with their works.

• c.240 B.C. *The Analects* of Confucius burned and hundreds of his disciples buried alive.
• 213 B.C. *The Analects* of Confucius burned along with all the books in China except those in the Royal Library.
• 401. Plato burned all his own poems on deciding to follow Socrates.
• 1415. Jan Hus, author of *De Ecclesia*, burned at the stake in Switzerland with his book.
• 1497. The works of Ovid, Propertius, Boccaccio, Dante, and others burned by the monk Savonarola in Florence's great "Bonfire of the Vanities."
• 1521. All the works of Martin Luther ordered burned by Pope Leo X.
• 1553. Author Michael Servetus burned at the stake in France along with all of his books.
• 1554. *The Historie of Italie*, critical of Roman priests, burned by the common hangman, its author William Thomas hanged and quartered at the same time.

• 1579. John Stubbs's attack on Queen Elizabeth's proposed marriage, *The discoverie of a gaping gulf where into England is likely to be swallowed by another French marriage*, burned and the author's right hand hacked off with a meat cleaver. Stubbs is said to have raised his hat with his left hand immediately after and cried, "God save the Queen!"

• 1599. The works of Ovid burned in London.

• 1650. The first book burned in America—William Pynchon's *The Meritorious Price of Our Redemption*. Burned in the marketplace by the common executioner in Massachusetts Bay Colony (Boston).

• 1660. John Milton's *Pro Populo Anglicano Defensio* and *Eikonoklastes* burned by the common hangman.

• 1660. Blaise Pascal's *Lettres à un Provincial* burned by order of Louis XIV.

• 1703. Daniel Defoe's *The Shortest Way with the Dissenters* burned and the author pilloried.

• 1734. Voltaire's *Lettres Philosophiques sur les Anglais* and *Temple du Goût* burned; Voltaire holds the record for the author with the most books burned in the eighteenth century.

• 1795. All the works of Cagliostro burned; the author died in prison.

• 1881. An enraged John Greenleaf Whittier, who should have known better, considering his own persecutions as an abolitionist, threw his first edition of Walt Whitman's *Leaves of Grass* into the fire.

• 1890–1896. Lady Isabel Burton burned all the unpublished books and journals Sir Richard Burton left when he died.

• 1898. Havelock Ellis's *Studies in the Psychology of Sex* seized by U.S. customs and burned.

• 1932–1933. James Joyce's *Ulysses* burned in several countries throughout the world.

• 1933. All of Ernest Hemingway's works burned in Nazi bonfires, along with the works of Erich Maria Remarque and many other authors.

• 1933. All the works of Heine burned by the Nazis, but the poem *Die Lorelei*, so beloved by Germans, was listed as the work of Anonymous and spared.

• 1939. John Steinbeck's *The Grapes of Wrath* burned by the St. Louis, Missouri, Public Library.

• 1946. Kathleen Winsor's *Forever Amber* burned by British customs.

• 1965. Grove Press edition of John Cleland's *Fanny Hill* burned in Germany, England, and Japan.

Aristotle's works had to be buried in Asia Minor for almost a century to protect them from burning by the Pergamum kings. As a result many passages were lost.

WORLD'S WORST BOOK BURNER

CHINA'S FIRST EMPEROR, Shi Huang Ti (259–210 B.C.), probably takes the title. Shi, who buried alive 460 scholars in the process, burned all the books in his kingdom, except for one copy of each deposited in the royal library, which he planned to destroy before his death, reasoning that if all records were destroyed history would begin with him. For generations after, the Chinese expressed their hatred of Shi by "befouling his grave."

THE ULTIMATE CENSOR

THERE ARE many literary martyrs, but the following are authors through the centuries who were sentenced to death or suffered horribly because of their work.

• 399 B.C. Socrates (who left no known writings) was sentenced to death by drinking the draught of hemlock for introducing new deities and corrupting youth.

• Third century B.C. Greek poet Sotades, the inventor of palindromes, was sewn up in a sack and thrown in the sea by Ptolemy II, who considered his satires too scurrilous for him to live.

• A.D. 65. Lucan, Roman poet, was ordered to commit suicide by Nero, who was jealous of his poetry.

• A.D. 570. Persian poet Amra Taraja buried alive because he wrote a couplet critical of the King.

• 1603. The printer of Robert Parsons's *A Conference about the Next Succession to the Crowne of England* was hanged, drawn, and quartered.

• 1630. Alexander Leighton, English author of *An Appeal to the Parliament: or Sion's Plea against the Prelacie*, was manacled and thrown into a hole full of rats and mice. Later he was whipped, had his ears cut off, his nose split, and was branded with the letters *S.S.* ("Sower of Sedition") and imprisoned for life.

• 1633. English author William Prynne was branded and had his ears cut off for writing a criticism of plays and playgoing, which the Queen enjoyed. Archbishop William Laud prosecuted him and had his book burned publicly. Nine years later he was Laud's prosecutor when the archbishop was tried for high treason and beheaded.

• 1714. Hilkaiah Bedford, merely the messenger who delivered the manuscript of George Herbin's *Hereditary Right of the Crown of England* to the printer, was thrown in prison, where he died.

• 1795. Alessandro Cagliostro died in a Roman jail, where he was imprisoned for his heretical writings.

• 1797. François Émile Babeuf stabbed himself just before he was to be guillotined for writing *Le Tribun du Peuple*.

• 1794. André Marie de Chénier was guillotined for his writings against the French Reign of Terror.

• 1936. Although the evidence is not conclusive, it was charged in the Soviet treason trials of 1938 that author Maxim Gorky had been poisoned.

• 1956. Wilhelm Reich was sentenced to two years in prison for publishing books on his controversial therapy practices (*The Sexual Revolution*, etc.) and died in jail.

It should be added to these that John Milton narrowly escaped the scaffold in 1660 for writing against the divine right of kings, after some friends interceded for him. Many writers have had similar escapes, while others, such as Aleksandr Solzhenitsyn, suffered cruelties often worse than death. (See also *Burned Books—and Authors*.)

JOHN MILTON

GREAT WRITERS WHO WERE BANISHED FROM THEIR HOMELANDS

A NUMBER OF Russian writers, including Aleksandr I. Solzhenitsyn, were deported to the West under the former Communist regime. They are not alone in history, sharing their exile with

Euripides
Aristotle
Ovid
Dante
Villon
Voltaire
Victor Hugo

CHAPTER SEVEN

Of Books & Blurbs

BIBLIOBIBULI

This little-known word was coined by H. L. Mencken, who defined it thus: "There are people who read too much: the bibliobibuli. I know some who are constantly drunk on books, as other men are drunk on whiskey or religion. They wander through this most diverting and stimulating of worlds in a haze, seeing nothing and hearing nothing."

Other opinions from authors even more extreme than Mencken's include:

> We live too much in books and not enough in nature, and we are very much like that simpleton of a Pliny the Younger, who went on studying a Greek author while before his eyes Vesuvius was overwhelming five cities beneath the ashes.
>
> —Anatole France

I hate books; they only teach us to talk about things we know nothing about. —Rousseau

Books are fatal: they are the curse of the human race. Nine-tenths of existing books are nonsense, and the clever books are the refutation of that nonsense. The greatest misfortune that ever befell man was the invention of printing. —Benjamin Disraeli

It is my ambition to say in ten sentences what everyone else says in a whole book—what everyone else does not say in a whole book. —Friedrich Nietzsche

The multitude of books is a great evil. There is no measure or limit to this fever for writing; everyone must be an author; some out of vanity to acquire celebrity and raise up a name, others for the sake of lucre and gain. —Martin Luther

It is one of the misfortunes of life that one must read thousands of books only to discover that one need not have read them. —Thomas De Quincey

Never read a book, Johnnie, and you will be a rich man. —Sir Timothy Shelley to his poet-to-be son

Literature is the orchestration of platitudes. —Thornton Wilder

A great book, a great evil. —Callimachus (who said the best books were those that were the lightest to carry around)

BOOK

Here on my trunk's surviving frame,
Carved many a long-forgotten name . . .
As Love's own altar, honor me:
Spare woodman, spare the beechen tree.
        —Thomas Campbell,
        "Beech Tree's Petition" (1807)

SMOOTH-SKINNED beech trees, as the old poem above shows, have always been the favorite of lovers carving their names or initials inside a heart. The outer bark of the beech and slabs of its thin, inner bark were also the first writing materials used by Anglo-Saxon scribes. Saxons called the beech the *boc* and also applied this name to their bound writings made from slabs of beech, the word becoming *book* after many centuries of spelling changes.

Numerous terms for things related to writing come from the names of raw material. *Folio*, now a book of the largest size, is from the Latin word *folium*, a "tree leaf," which also gives us the word *foliage*. *Bible*, and words like *bibliography*, derive from the Greek *biblos*, "the inner bark of papyrus." *Volume* is from the Latin *volumen*, which meant a roll of papyrus manuscript; and *code*, a system of laws, is from the Latin *codex*, "the trunk of a tree," from which wooden tablets were made to write codes upon.

The beech tree lines quoted above are the real source of the familiar proverb "Woodman spare that tree," *not* the following more famous poem by George Pope Morris written in 1830, twenty-three years later:

> *Woodman, spare that tree!*
> *Touch not a single bough!*
> *In youth it sheltered me,*
> *And I'll protect it now.*

BOOKISH SAYINGS

*T*o KNOW like a book." Complete understanding is the meaning of this American expression, which dates from the time when there were few books in most homes. Those that were present, like the Bible, were often committed to memory, hence the familiar expression. "To know one's book," a British saying, means something different—to know one's best interest, to have made up one's mind. "To speak by the book," is to speak meticulously, and "to speak or talk like a book" is to speak with great precision, usually pedantically.

"To take a leaf out of one's book." These words are never used figuratively in America for plagiarism, to my knowledge. "To take a leaf out of someone's book" simply means to imitate another person. It is usually highly complimentary to the person aped, for it means he is a model for whatever you wish to do, that he succeeds at it so well that it is best to do it his way. The expression is first recorded in 1809, but the saying it appears to derive from, "to turn over a new leaf," to reform, goes all the way back to Holinshed's *Chronicles of England, Scotland and Ireland* (1577). In the earlier phrase the leaves of pages are from a book of lessons or precepts.

"Black book." None of the slang dictionaries seems to record it, but a "little black book" has for at least half a century been the name for any Casanova's address book filled with the names, addresses, and especially telephone numbers of desirable or compliant companions. But "black book" has far greater historical importance as the synonym for a book containing the names of people liable to censure or punishment, the term used most frequently in the phrase "I'm in his black book," in disfavor with someone. The first such black books were compiled by agents of Henry VIII, who listed English monasteries under the pretext that they were sinful but really in order to convince Parliament to dissolve them so that the crown could claim their lands—which Parliament did in 1536. Later, the British universities, the army, and the police began the practice of listing censured people in black books, which reinforced the meaning of the term.

"To throw the book at." I can find no record of a judge literally throwing a law book at a convicted criminal. But during Prohibition's "gangster era" many judges did figuratively throw the contents of law books at criminals when sentencing them, imposing every penalty found in books of law for their particular crimes. In underworld argot "the book" came to mean the maximum penalty that could be imposed for a crime, especially life imprisonment. Although its original meaning is still common, the metaphor has come to stand for penalties much less severe as well, sometimes nothing more serious than a parent's taking away the car keys from a child as a punishment for coming in too late.

"Witches weigh less than a Bible." When Jane Wenham was tried as a witch in 1712 she was set free because people at her trial insisted that she be weighed. A true witch always weighed less than a Bible, according to British superstition, and Jane weighed considerably more than the twelve-pound church Bible of the day.

INCUNABULA

THE WORD *incunabula* (the singular form is *incunabulum*) is used to signify books produced in the infancy of printing from movable type, usually those printed before 1500. Caxton's edition of *The Canterbury Tales*, printed in 1478, is a famous incunabulum. The Germans coined the name *incunabula* for these early books in the early nineteenth century, using the Latin word for swaddling clothes and cradle. Outside the bailiwick of rare book collectors incunabula means the earliest stages of anything. "Here they fancy that they can detect the incunabula of the revolutionary spirit," De Quincey wrote.

GUTENBERG BIBLE

THE FIRST printed Bible, long thought to be the first book to be printed from movable type in the Western world, is named for Johannes Gutenberg (c.1398–1468), the German printer generally believed to be the inventor of movable type. Few great men of relatively modern times have left such meager records of their lives as Gutenberg. No likeness exists of him and his life is veiled in obscurity. Gutenberg may have adopted his mother's maiden name, for his father's surname appears to have been Gensfleisch. It is known that the goldsmith Johann Fust loaned the printer money to establish his press at Mainz, which Gutenberg lost to him in 1455 when he failed to repay the loan. But no book extant bears Gutenberg's name as its printer and though he is still regarded as a likely candidate, he may not have invented printing in the West or even printed the *Gutenberg Bible* (1450). The Bible is certainly not the first book to be printed in Europe, Gutenberg himself printing several small books before it. As for movable type, it had been used in Korea before its uncertain European invention. Whoever printed the *Gutenberg Bible* produced a beautiful work complete with colored initials and illumination by hand. It is often called the *Mazarin Bible* because the first copy to come to attention was found in the library of Cardinal Mazarin in 1760.

GIDEON BIBLE

IN 1910 one very proper Bostonian sought an injunction to prevent the Gideon Society from distributing the Bible—"on the ground that it is an obscene and immoral publication." But not even crackpots have deterred the organization of traveling salesmen from their goal of placing a Gideon Bible in every hotel room and Pullman car in America. The Gideon Society, formally the Christian Commercial Young Men's Association of America, was founded in Boscobel,

Wisconsin, in 1899 and is now based in Chicago. Its name derives from that of the Biblical Gideon, a judge of Israel who became a warrior and ingeniously delivered Israel from the Midianites, giving his country forty years of peace (Judges 6:11–7:25).

OTHER BOOKS THAT ARE "BIBLES"

A CCORDING TO Hoyle" is the most famous of the many "according to" proverbs, and it honors English barrister Edmond Hoyle, who wrote *A Short Treatise on the Game of Whist* (1742) and *Hoyle's Standard Games*, which has been republished hundreds of times. Besides establishing firm rules for many games, Hoyle is responsible for popularizing the word *score* as a record of winning points in card games—a practice that was later carried over to sports. "When in doubt, win the trick," is Hoyle's most memorable phrase. He died in 1769 when about ninety-seven years old.

"According to Gunter" was once as popular in America as "according to Hoyle" is today. Edmund Gunter (1578–1623), the first eponym to be honored for his accuracy, was an English mathematician and astronomer who invented the forerunner of the modern slide rule and introduced the mathematical terms *cosine* and *cotangent*. The professor also invented *Gunter's chair*, a surveying instrument, the portable *Gunter's quadrant*, and *Gunter's scale*, commonly used by seamen to solve navigation problems.

Still heard today is "according to Fowler," which remembers Henry Watson Fowler (1858–1933), the noted classicist and lexicographer who wrote the standard reference work *A Dictionary of Modern English Usage* (1926). Even more popular is "according to Guinness," a tribute to the *Guinness Book of World Records*, the umpire of record performances that has been published annually since 1955 by the Dublin brewers Arthur Guinness, Son & Co., Ltd. "According to Emily Post" is still fairly common, too (although Emily Post died in 1960), and several professions have their own specialized "according to's" as well.

One has to be careful about citing authorities. "According to Cocker," for example, was used for 200 years and may have had poor Edward Cocker counting to ten in his grave. Edward Cocker (1631–1675), a London arithmetic teacher, reputedly wrote *Cocker's Arithmetick*, which went through 112 editions and gave rise to the proverb bearing his name. Two centuries later, however, a critic proved that the book was a forgery issued three years after Cocker died, a forgery so poorly done that it set back rather than advanced the cause of elementary arithmetic.

BAPTISM BY BOOK

THE ARCHAEOLOGIST Heinrich Schliemann, who rediscovered Troy, was "an old man mad about Homer" and baptized his children, named Andromache and Agamemnon, "by laying a copy of the *Iliad* upon their heads and reading a hundred hexameters aloud."

THE BOOK THAT HAS IT ALL

AFTER HEARING a dramatic sermon one Sunday, Mark Twain told the preacher it was a good one but that he had a book at home that contained every word of it. "Impossible," the preacher snorted. "I'd certainly like to see that book, if it exists." Within a week the preacher received a bulky package containing an unabridged dictionary.

DR. JOHNSON'S DICTIONARY

Dictionaries are like watches. The worst is better than none, and the best cannot be expected to go quite true.
—Dr. Samuel Johnson

DR. JOHNSON, as the great English writer and man of letters Samuel Johnson is usually called, remains most famous for his monumental *Dictionary* published in 1755 and the immortal *Life of Samuel Johnson* written by James

Boswell, generally considered the greatest English biography. A man of enormous energies who would have done even more were it not for the debilitating scrofula and often dire poverty that plagued him all his days, Johnson was revered as a moralist and a brilliant conversationalist. His *Dictionary* was the first to introduce examples of word usages by prominent authors. Along with his *Lives of the English Poets*, brilliant but essentially one-sided appraisals, it is still read today. Anecdotes about Johnson abound, but appropriate here in his reply to the lady who asked him why in his dictionary he defined *pastern* (part of a horse's foot) as the *knee* of a horse—"Sheer ignorance, Madam!" he explained. The two words that do Johnson honor reveal opposite sides of the Great Cham. *Johnsonian* refers to the good common sense reflected in his writings and conversation, while *Johnsonese* remembers the rambling polysyllabic style into which he would often slip—the very opposite of pithy *Johnsonian* phraseology. Partridge notes a third term honoring Johnson in his *Dictionary of Slang*: "*Doctor Johnson, the membrum virile*: literary: ca. 1790–1880. Perhaps because there was no one that Dr. Johnson was not prepared to stand up to." An observation worthy of London's influential Literary Club, which Dr. Johnson helped found in 1764. Johnson died in 1784, aged seventy-three. Boswell's biography gives us the essence of the Great Cham, but Macaulay's famous short essay is also excellent on the spirit of the man and the times.

WEBSTER'S

Noah Webster's name has become a synonym for a dictionary since he published his *Compendious Dictionary of the English Language* in 1806 and his larger *An American Dictionary of the English Language* twenty-two years later. But the "father of American lexicography" was a man of widespread interests, publishing many diverse books over his long career. These included his famous *Sketches of American Policy* (1785), on history and politics; *Dissertations on the English Language* (1789), advocating spelling reform; and *A Brief History of Epidemic and Pestilential Diseases* (1799). Webster also found time to edit *The American Magazine* and the newspaper *The Minerva*. Beginning in 1806, he lived on the income from his speller—which sold at the rate of over one million copies a year—while he took the twenty-two years needed to complete his monumental dictionary. Webster's, as it came to be called (it is now published as *Webster's Dictionary* by Merriam) introduced many "Americanisms," 12,000 new words that had never been included in any dictionary. Its annual sales of 300,000 helped standardize American pronunciation and simplify spelling. Webster's major fault seems to have been his prudery, the norm in those days. In 1833 he published a bowdlerized edition of the Bible, removing "offensive words" that might make young ladies "reluctant to attend Bible classes." "Breast" was substituted for "teat," "to nourish" for "to give suck," "peculiar members" for "stones" (testicles), and so on. This hardly fits in with the legend about his being caught kissing the chambermaid. "Why Noah, I'm *surprised*!" his wife is supposed to have said. "Madame," Webster replied, most correctly, "*you* are astonished; *I* am surprised."

ITALIC TYPE

Italic type, in which those two words are printed, was invented in about 1500 by the noted Italian printer Aldus Manutius, the Latin name of Teobaldo Mannucci. There is a tradition that the printer modeled his invention on the fine *Italian hand* of the poet Petrarch, but the *Italian hand*, a beautiful, cursive style, had been widely used for copying manuscripts since its development by scholars in the twelfth century. In fact, it was so well known that "a fine Italian hand" had already become a synonym for the scheming Machiavellian politics or assassination by stiletto for which Italian nobles were notorious. Manutius, also a classical scholar, had his type cast by Francesco Griffo of Bologna and in 1501 first used it to publish an edition of Virgil, dedicating the book to his native Italy. Because of that Aldine Press dedication, the new slanting style—the first type that wasn't upright—came to be known as *Italicus*, which means Italian or Italic. Today words are *italicized* in print mainly to give them emphasis, and to indicate titles and foreign language words. This is not the case in the King James or Authorized Version of the Bible, however, a fact which often creates confusion. Words *italicized* in the Bible should not be emphasized in reading, for they merely indicate that the original translators, who considered the text sacred, arbitrarily supplied a word not existing in the text in order to make its meaning clearer.

Aldus Manutius also established the custom of the publisher's colophon; his was a dolphin, symbolizing speed, and an anchor, symbolizing stability. A compulsive worker, he hung this inscription over the door of his study:

> Whoever thou art, Thou art earnestly requested by Aldus to state thy business briefly, and to take thy departure promptly . . . For this is a place of work.

RARA LIBRIS

*F*OR CENTURIES NOW, rare old books have sold for astronomical prices, though old books aren't necessarily rare and valuable books. The highest price yet paid for a book is the $5.39 million a Japanese bookseller paid for a Gutenberg Bible in 1987. Joyce's *Ulysses* brought $10,000 in 1977, while Hawthorne's *The Marble Faun*, inscribed, went for $6,250 in 1978, and Hemingway's high school yearbook, which contained his first published story, "Judgement of Manitou," sold for $1,000 in 1979. Several years ago the first *New York City Directory* brought $1,000, too. Leonardo da Vinci's notebook "Of the Nature, Weight and Movement of Water" sold for $5,126,000 in 1980, the highest price ever paid for a manuscript until the illustrated thirteenth-century *Northumberland Bestiary* sold for $11.4 million in 1990.

The highest price ever paid for a handmade book is the $12 million a German firm paid in 1983 for the illuminated book *The Gospel of Henry the Lion, Duke of Saxony* (c.1170).

BOOK PRICES BEFORE PRINTING

*I*N 1272 the price of a Bible, in nine handwritten volumes, was about £33, while the average laborer made about 20 pence a day. Figuring the money of those times to be only twenty times its present value, the same Bible would cost £660 today. In American money the Bible would sell for about $1,584 and the worker would earn about $4 a day with which to buy it.

BIBLIOTYPES

A *bibliopole* is simply a book dealer, while a *bibliotaph* is one who conceals or hoards books, keeping them under lock and key, and a *biblioclast* is somebody who destroys books for any reason, ideological or not. A *bibliophile* is someone who collects and treasures books either for their value or for what's in them, and a *bibliomaniac* is a *bibliophile* gone bonkers, one who loves books to the point of madness.

Legend has it that Don Vicente, a Spanish friar and scholar, murdered five or six collectors to steal a rare book, which makes him a *biblioklept* as well as a *bibliomaniac*. The story, according to William Walsh, *Handbook of Literary Curiosities* (1891), is as follows:

> Coming to Barcelona in 1834, Don Vicente established himself in a gloomy den in the book-selling quarter of the town. Here he set up as a dealer, but so fell in love with his accumulated purchases that only want tempted him to sell them. Once at an auction he was outbid for a copy of the *Ordinacions per los Gloriosos Reys de Arago*—a great rarity, perhaps a unique. Three days later the house of the successful rival was burned to the ground, and his blackened body, pipe in hand, was found in the ruins. He had set the house on fire with his pipe, that was the general verdict. A mysterious succession of murders followed. One bibliophile after another was found in the streets or the river, with a dagger in his heart. The shop of Don Vicente was searched. The *Ordinacions* was discovered. How had it escaped the flames that had burned down the purchaser's house? Then the Don confessed not only to that murder but others. Most of his victims were customers who had purchased from him books he could not bear to part with. At the trial, counsel for the defense tried to discredit the confession, and when it was objected that the *Ordinacions* was a unique copy, they proved there was another in the Louvre, that, therefore, there might be still more, and that the defendant's might have been honestly procured. At this, Don Vicente, hitherto callous and silent, uttered a low cry. "Aha!" said the Alcalde. "You are beginning to realize the enormity of your offence!" "Yes," sobbed the penitent thief, "the copy was not a unique, after all."

Another noted book thief was Innocent X, who, before he became Pope, was caught red-handed stealing *L'Histoire du Concile de Trente* from a painter's studio while visiting with a religious party. The future Pope was evicted bodily by the painter, and some historians believe that this action caused the ill feeling toward France that marked the pontifical reign of Innocent X.

The Inspector General of French Libraries under Louis Philippe was an infamous book thief who stole hundreds of thousands of dollars' worth of rare books from the libraries he inspected. Count Guglielmi "Libri" Carucci was sentenced to ten years in prison but fled to England. By 1890 he had sold back all of the stolen books to the French government.

Book theft in America today costs libraries so many millions of dollars that more and more are installing "electric eye" exit systems that set off an alarm if a special magnetic tape inside a book's spine isn't desensitized by the librarian when the book is checked out at the desk.

During the reign of Ptolemy III in Egypt (246–221 B.C.), book collecting became so widespread that confidence men dyed and spoiled new manuscripts in order to sell them as antiquities to bibliophiles.

BOOKWORM

*B*ookworms are literally the larvae of various insects, moths, and beetles that live in and feed upon the pages and bindings of books. No single species can properly be called the bookworm, but the little beetle *Anolium*, silverfishes (order Thysanura), and booklice (order Psocoptera) are widely known by the name. The *book scorpion* or *false scorpion* (order Pseudoscorpiones) somewhat resembles a tailless scorpion and takes its common name because it is sometimes found in old books.

A nineteenth-century journal called *The Bookworm* had this to say about bookworms:

> Bookworms are now almost exclusively known in the secondary and derivative meaning of the word as porers over dry books; but there was a time when the real worms were as ubiquitous as our cockroaches. They would start at the first or last page and tunnel circular holes through the volume, and were cursed by librarians as *bestia audax* and *pestes chartarum*. There were several kinds of these little plagues. One was a sort of death-watch, with dark-brown hard skin; another had a white body with little brown spots on its head. Those that had legs were the larvae of moths, and those without legs were grubs that turned to beetles. They were dignified, like other disagreeable things, with fine Latin names, which we spare our readers. All of them had strong jaws and very healthy appetites; but we are happy to find that their digestive powers, vigorous as they were, quail before the materials of our modern books. China clay, plaster of Paris, and other unwholesome ailments have conquered the *pestes chartarum*. They sigh and shrivel up. Peace to the memory, for it is now hardly more than a memory, of the *bestia audax*.

The human of the bookworm species also lives in and feeds upon the pages of books, but doesn't usually destroy them. Human bookworms have been scorned since before Ben Jonson wrote of a "whoreson book-worm." Authors especially are fools to be contemptuous of bookworms, but from Elizabethan times to Melville and his "pale consumptive usher," if I remember the phrase correctly, no scrivener has had anything good to say about them. The closest thing to praise is from Alexander Pope, who wrote in a letter: "I wanted but a black gown and a salary, to be as mere a bookworm as any there."

GROLIER BINDING

RICH ORNATE book bindings are called Grolier bindings after Jean Grolier, Vicomte D'Auigsy (1479–1565), who was not a bookbinder or printer, but a prominent French bibliophile. Grolier collected books and had them bound by the best artisans of his day, each book bearing the inscription *Groliere et Amicorum*. All the books in his library, sold in 1675, are world-famous collector's items.

The Grolier Club, which has published many books and catalogs of its exhibitions, was founded in New York City (1884) "for the study and promotion of the arts pertaining to the production of books."

ON BOOK JACKET PHOTOS

Reader, look
But not at his picture, but his book.
　　　　—Ben Jonson, on the portrait
　　　　of Shakespeare prefixed to
　　　　the first *Folio* (1623)

"KNOW A BOOK BY ITS COVER"

THE MISTRESS of French novelist Eugène Sue (1804–1857) directed in her will that a set of his books be bound with her skin. This was done and as recently as 1951 a special edition of Sue's *Vignettes: les Mystères de Paris*, its cover made from skin taken from the woman's shoulders, sold for twenty-nine dollars at Foyle's, the famous London bookstore.

Earlier in France a publisher with a weird sense of humor had produced an edition of Rousseau's *Social Contract* bound in the skins of aristocrats guillotined during the French Revolution.

Sold at auction in New York in early 1978 was a twenty-one-volume series about animals by French author Maurice Hammonneau. The author had hunted down each animal described and used the appropriate animal skin to bind each volume. Included was a book on human beings, no explanation being given about the source of the cover.

A Tegg's edition of Milton printed in 1852 is covered with the skin of one George Cudmore, who was executed for murder in England on March 25, 1830. "The skin," according to one description, "is dressed white, and looks something like pig-skin in grain and texture."

In a small volume at Bhutan's Taktsang monastery every other page is written in a white "ink" made from the bones of a great lama who had lived and died there.

Any of these books could be considered a macabre binding, but the *Macabre style* is, strictly speaking, that of book bindings made for France's Henry III after the Princess de Cleves died, a style that used tears, skulls, and bones tooled in silver to express the king's grief.

COLOPHON

ORIGINALLY, this word, derived from the Greek *kolophon*, meaning summit or finish, was the "finishing touch" at the end of a book, a bibliographical note on the last page giving the printer, date, place, and so on. Today the word has two meanings—the original one, which has been expanded to include design and typographic information, and a new one, referring to the publisher's trademark or emblem, which often appears on the title page of the book. Colophons are usually pictorial representations of publishing firms' names.

It is an interesting note that the American publisher Viking's colophon was in fact responsible for the name, rather than the other way round. When the company was founded in 1925, the founders wanted to call it Half-Moon Press, after Henry Hudson's ship, and they commissioned Rockwell Kent to design a suitable colophon. The artist did not care for the old English vessel, however, and, using artistic license, elected to draw a *drakkar*, a type of ship used by the Vikings. The design was so effective that the company changed its name, quickly providing themselves with a slogan to justify the switch.

TENNYSON BINDINGS

THE EXPRESSION *Tennyson bindings* is used to indicate affectation of culture. According to Willard Espy, or, rather, Timothy Dickinson, in *O Thou Improper, Thou Uncommon Noun*: "A *nouveau-riche* matron was showing a friend of similar stripe her library, which had been stocked by interior decorators.

'And here,' she said, 'is my Tennyson.' 'No no, darling,' corrected her friend. 'Those are green. Tennyson is *blue*.' " (See *How to Make a Library*.)

MISLEADING TITLES

W HEN the Marquis de Sade's *Justine, or the Misfortunes of Virtue* was published in 1791, it became popular for a time among mothers misled by the title who purchased it for their daughters to read "as an object lesson."

¹(FOOTNOTES)

U SED MOSTLY in scholarly works to list a source or make a minor or related comment on the main text of a work, footnotes are so called because they are usually placed at the bottom of a page.* Often called *bottom notes* in the early nineteenth century, when they were apparently used extensively for the first time, they are indicated in the text by superior numbers. Many readers agree with John Barrymore, who said: "A footnote is like running downstairs to answer the doorbell during the first night of marriage." Historian Sir John Neale published his excellent biography *Queen Elizabeth* without footnotes and an Oxford don told historian Eileen Power that this indicated he had "sold the pass"—that is, traded scholarship for popularity. "I don't know about selling the pass," Power rejoined, "but he has sold 20,000 copies."

TYPOS OR MISPRINTS

N EWSPAPERS and magazines regularly run features pointing out the best or worst typographical errors in other newspapers and magazines. For example, a Clive Barnes review in the *New York Times* of *A Midsummer Night's Dream* found "David Waller's virile bottom [instead of 'Bottom'] particularly splendid." Possibly the worst modern-day slip appeared in the *Washington Post* in 1915, where it was noted that President Wilson had taken his fiancée, Edith Galt, to the theater and rather than watching the play "spent most of his time entering [instead of 'entertaining'] Mrs. Galt." But one set of printers' errors caused an author's death. Italian writer Carlo Guidi "died of shock" when he translated a religious work into Latin, presented a copy to the Pope, and it was brought to his attention by the Pontiff that the Latin word *sine* (without) had been printed as *sin* throughout the book.

---

*Some authors arrange them by chapter at the end of the book.

Printers have made disastrous mistakes in various Bibles printed over the years. Following is a list of the seven most outrageous:

- *The Sin On Bible*—printed in 1716—John 5:14 contains the printer's error "sin on more," instead of "sin no more."
- *The Bug Bible*—1535—reads "Thou shalt not nede to be afrayed for eny bugges [instead of 'terror'] by night" in Psalm 91:5.
- *The Fool Bible*—printed in the reign of Charles I—reads "The fool hath said in his heart there is a God" in Psalm 14; for this mistake the printers were fined £3,000.
- *The Idle Bible*—1809—the "idole shepherd" (Zechariah 11:17) is printed "the idle shepherd."
- *The Large Family Bible*—1820—Isaiah 66:9 reads "Shall I bring to the birth and not cease [instead of 'cause'] to bring forth."
- *The Unrighteous Bible*—1653—I Corinthians 6:9 reads "Know ye not that the unrighteous shall inherit [for 'shall not inherit'] the Kingdom of God."
- *The Wicked Bible*—1632—the word *not* in the seventh commandment is omitted, making it read: "Thou shalt commit adultery."

PILCROW

Pilcrow is an old name for ¶ or , which are printing marks used to attract attention—a paragraph sign in the first case and a direction in the other. The word is apparently a corruption of the word *paragraph*. *Webster's* gives *pilcrow* as an obsolete name for a paragraph mark. But since there are no other names for the two signs above, *pilcrow* ought to be rehired.

STET

Stet is Latin for "let it stand," the printing term being used as a direction to the printer to leave uncorrected a word or words that had been deleted in a proof or manuscript. The term is a fairly recent one, first recorded in 1821. The only good story I know about *stet* is told by James Sutherland in *The Oxford Book of Literary Anecdotes*, which he edited. Relating a tale about an edition of Madame de Sévigné's letters, Sutherland writes:

> When the galley proofs began to reach the editor, he found that the proof-reader had his own idea of how to spell Madame de Sévigné's name, for he kept querying the accent on the first syllable. The editor meticulously wrote "stet" beside each query; but with the next batch of proofs the process of query and "stet" began all over again. When finally the page proofs arrived and the persistent proof-reader was still querying the accent, the editor lost his patience. Addressing himself to the proof-reader on the margin of the proof, he demanded that this futile exercise should stop. But now it was the printer's turn. When the editor at last received an advance copy of his book, he was horrified to find in the middle of one of Madame de Sévigné's letters the very words that he had written in anger on the final proof: "For God's sake, stop popping up between Madame de Sévigné and me!"

On one of Robert Benchley's manuscripts *New Yorker* editor Harold Ross, who had a "profound ignorance" according to Dorothy Parker, wrote "Who he?" in the margin opposite Andromache. Benchley wrote below: "You keep out of this."

[S I C]

*P*RONOUNCED *sik*, this little word is just the Latin for "thus, so." It is used in brackets by writers after a word or phrase to indicate that the word or phrase is being printed by the writer exactly as it is in the original, even though it is wrong in some way—either incorrect, absurd, or grotesque. *Sic* is also used outside brackets, as in: "The modern critic's taste is not really shaped by half the things he *sics* or otherwise castigates."

3 0

*F*OR OVER a century the symbol *30* has been used by reporters to mark the end of a typewritten newspaper story. It comes either from the old telegraphy symbol indicating the end of a day's transmission, a kind of "Good night, I'm closing up the office," or from old printers' jargon. The maximum line on

Linotype composing machines is 30 picas, about five inches, and when an operator reaches 30 picas, he can go no farther.

BOOKS LONG AND SHORT

HISTORY'S SHORTEST book would have to be Elbert Hubbard's *Essay on Silence*, which has no words (see *Books Without Characters, Words, or Pictures*). As for the longest modern novel written by one person, this is probably Jules Romains's (Louis Henri Jean Farigoule) twenty-seven-volume "novel cycle" *Men of Good Will* (1932–1946). The British *Parliamentary Papers* (1800–1900) in 1,112 volumes is the world's largest publication. One of the longest American books is the 38,000-page official manual of the Internal Revenue Service. Under the Ming emperor Yung Lo (1403–1425), an 11,095-volume encyclopedia was written, but it proved too expensive to be published. The Japanese author Bakin (1767–1848) probably holds the record for the longest novel of all time, with his 106-volume *Hakkenden* (*The Tale of Eight Dogs*).

Samuel Beckett's *Breath* (1970), which has no actors or dialogue, is, at thirty seconds long, the world's shortest dramatic work. The longest is *The Warp* by Ken Campbell, a ten-part play cycle presented in England on January 18–20, 1979, which ran for eighteen hours and five minutes not counting intermissions. Robert Wilson's play *Stalin*, which runs close to eight hours, is the longest American play yet produced.

BOOKS LARGE AND SMALL

TO SEE the world's largest book you'll have to journey to Beinn Ruadh Ardentinny, near Dunoon, Scotland, where *The Little Red Elf*, a children's story by William P. Wood, who also printed the book, is on display in a local cave, the book standing seven feet, two inches tall and ten feet across when open.

The world's smallest book printed with metal type consists of the Lord's Prayer in seven languages and measures 3.5 millimeters by 3.5 millimeters, or 0.13 of an inch square. It is on display at the Gutenberg Museum, Mainz, Germany.

In 1829 La Rochefoucauld's *Maximes* was published on pages one inch square, each page containing twenty-six lines and each line forty-four letters. The first miniature book printed in America, published in 1705 in Boston, contained ninety-two pages and measured 2 × 3½ inches. Written by William Secker, the book has a title that explains its subject nicely: *A Wedding Ring Fit for the Finger, or the Salve of Divinity on the Sore of Humanity With directions to those men that want wives, how to choose them; and to those women that have husbands, how to use them.*

Cicero wrote that Homer's *Iliad* was written in handwriting so small that all twenty-four books could be enclosed in a nutshell. This was proved possible by the Bishop of Avranches, who copied the *Iliad* so small that it would fit on a page two-thirds this size. The Bible and the Koran have also been copied in so small a hand as to fit in a walnut shell.

THE GREATEST "COOKBOOK"

Anthelme Brillat-Savarin's classic *Physiologie du Goût* (*Physiology of Taste*), still in print today, had to be published at the author's expense in 1825, after he had spent thirty years writing it. And when Brillat-Savarin's brother later sold the rights to a publisher, he got only $120—after throwing in a genuine Stradivarius as well! As for the great gourmet, appropriately enough born in the town of Belley, he frequently had to support his food-oriented life (he was admittedly something of an eccentric, often carrying around dead birds in his pocket until they became "high" enough for cooking) by scrounging from relatives and writing pornographic novels. *Brillat* was actually Anthelme's real name—he took on the hyphen and *Savarin* when his great-aunt left him her entire fortune on the condition that he add her name to his. Love of food seemed to run in the Brillat family. Anthelme's youngest sister, Pierrette, for instance, died at the dinner table. She was almost one hundred years old and her last words are among the most unusual in history: "And now, girl, bring me the dessert."

Fanny Farmer's *Boston Cooking School Cook Book* (1896), another classic cookbook, wasn't self-published, but the author had to pay Little, Brown and Company printing costs for the first 3,000 copies.

ATLAS

*I*N THE LATE sixteenth century French geographer Gerhard Mercator (1512–1594) published a book of maps whose frontispiece was a picture of Atlas holding the world on his back. Almost from then on any collection of maps has been called an *atlas*. A sixteenth-century Mercator atlas sold for $697,000 in 1979.

CHICKEN BOOKS

• Nineteenth-century poet Nancy Luce loved her chickens so much that they were the only things she wrote poems about. She kept busy on her Martha's Vineyard farm writing poems and inscribing them on eggs, along with the name of the chicken that laid each particular egg.

• A religious allegory of the seventeenth century had the title *Eggs of Charity, Layed by the Chickens of the Covenant and Boiled with the Water of the Divine: Take Ye and Eat.*

• A best-seller on chickens is *Chicken Doodle*, a book on how to run an automobile on chicken manure instead of gas.

• Betty MacDonald's book *The Egg and I* was a best-seller with a chicken-farming background; Sherwood Anderson published a famous collection of short stories entitled *The Triumph of the Egg*, though the stories depict maladjustment and frustration in American life; and the USDA pamphlets on chicken raising sell more copies each year than most books ever do.

THE LONGEST ONE-BOOK LITERARY CELEBRATIONS

*B*loomsday, sponsored by New York James Joyce-o-phile and bookstore owner Enrico Adelman, celebrates each year the June 16, 1904, day of Leopold Bloom's odyssey through Dublin in Joyce's *Ulysses*. A marathon public reading by actors is held at Mr. Adelman's New York bookstore Bloomsday and lasts from 8:00 A.M. until Molly Bloom says, "yes I said yes I will Yes" some forty hours later.

Longer than *Bloomsday* is the annual nonstop reading of Gertrude Stein's *The Making of Americans* held at the Paula Cooper Gallery and lasting fifty hours, from noon on December 31 to the afternoon of January 2.

A TREASURY OF ANTHOLOGIES

*T*reasury is just another word for *anthology*, which derives from the Greek word meaning "a collection of flowers"—the first recorded one, in fact, is the Greek *Garland of Meleager* (c.90 B.C.) Two of many historically famous ones include the *Anthologia Palatina*, called the *Greek Anthology* (c.925), and *Palgrave's Golden Treasury* (1861), the most noted of English anthologies. Tens of thousands of anthologies have been compiled since. Bennett Cerf told the story of a book called *The Ten Commandments* that was to be published for the armed services but was too long. "How about using only five of them," quipped editor Philip Van Doren Stern, "and calling it *A Treasury of the World's Best Commandments?*"

ALMANAC

Early to bed and early to rise
Makes a man healthy, wealthy and wise.

Never leave that till tomorrow which you can do today.

God helps them that helps themselves.

A little neglect may breed mischief:
for want of a nail the shoe was lost;
for want of a shoe the horse was lost;
for want of a horse the rider was lost.

Above is a sampling of the shrewd maxims and proverbs that Benjamin Franklin wrote or collected in his *Poor Richard's Almanack*. This was by no means the first almanac issued in America, that distinction belonging to *An Almanack for New England for the Year 1639* issued by William Peirce, a shipowner who hoped to attract more paying English passengers to the colonies and whose almanac was, except for a broadside, the first work of any kind printed in America. *Poor Richard's* was written and published by Franklin at Philadelphia from 1733 to 1758 and no doubt takes its name from the earlier English *Poor Robin's Almanac*, first published in 1663 by Robert ("Robin") and William Winstanley. Almanacs, which take their name from a medieval Latin word for a calendar with astronomical data, were issued as far back as 1150, before the invention of printing, and were compendia of information, jokes, and proverbs long before Franklin's day.

Among the most famous of English almanacs was *Old Moore's Almanac* (1699), published by Francis Moore in order to promote the sale of his pills. Moore would make weather predictions by guessing or writing down whatever came into his head. But he established a reputation for uncanny accuracy when his secretary woke him one afternoon to ask what prediction should be printed for June 3, Derby Day. "Cold and snow, damn it!" Moore replied irritably and went back to sleep. His prediction was recorded, however, and it *did* happen to snow that Derby Day. People never forgot and Moore was forgiven every mistake he made afterward because of that one lucky prediction.

Ben Franklin also owed a debt to his half-brother, James Franklin, who began publishing an almanac several years before him, and the pseudonym Richard Saunders with which he signed his prefaces was the same as that of the editor of another English almanac, though he gave Saunders the title *Philom* (from *philomath*, a combination of *philos*opher and *math*ematician). Franklin's rivalry with Titan Leeds, publisher of the earlier *The American Almanack*, resulted in one of America's first literary hoaxes. Franklin in his almanac of 1733 predicted that Leeds would die "on Oct. 17, 1733, 3 hr. 29 min., P.M." When Leeds vehemently denied this in a letter to *Poor Richard's* dated October 18, Franklin insisted that he *was* dead, declaring that "Mr. Leeds was too well bred" to write such an indecent, scurrilous letter. The hoax was patterned on Swift's similar "Bickerstaff Hoax" *(q.v.)*, but Franklin carried his version on right up to the day that Leeds actually died five years later.

Poor Richard's Almanack became *Poor Richard Improved* when Franklin sold it in 1748 and he contributed nothing to it thereafter. The only almanac to rival its fame is the still published *Farmer's Almanac* (1793), so accurate in its weather predictions that one town in India chose its editor as its guru. *Whitaker's Almanack* of England and America's *The World Almanac* are two old standbys today, and the new *People's Almanac* (1975) has inspired scores of offbeat almanacs.

Franklin also published the *Pennsylvania Gazette* (1729–1766) and *The General Magazine* (1741), the second monthly magazine issued in America. He in no way founded the *Saturday Evening Post*, despite the "Founded A.D. 1728 by Benjamin Franklin" that appeared on its cover. This has been known for years. The only connection between the *Saturday Evening Post* and Franklin is that the magazine was once printed in the same print shop where Franklin's newspaper the *Pennsylvania Gazette* was printed.

QUICKIES

All books are divisible into two classes, the books of the hour, and the books of all time.
　　　　　　　　　　　　　　　　　　　　　　　　—John Ruskin

QUICKIES," full-length paperback books that are based on fast-breaking news events and are written, edited, and printed within a matter of days, are increasingly common today, one firm, Bantam Books, having published scores of them. The practice originated in the early 1960s (pamphlets of course had been printed overnight long before this) and since then some of these works have literally been "books of the hour." *Miracle on Ice* (1980), the story of the 1980 U.S. Olympic hockey victory written by a team of *New York Times* reporters, "which was received, printed and on its way to distribution in 46 hours and 15 minutes." *The Pope's Journey to the United States* (1965) was written by fifty-one strikebound editors of the *New York Times* while the Pope traveled through America and published by Bantam 66½ hours after the completed manuscript was received. The world record is held by British publisher Scriptmate Editions, which produced Sir Frederick Mason's history *Ropely—Past and Present* in 12 hours, 26 minutes.

BIBLIA A-BIBLIA

I CAN READ anything which I call *a book*," wrote Charles Lamb. "There are things in that shape which I cannot allow for such. In this catalogue of books which are not *books*—*biblia a-biblia*—I reckon Court Calendars, Directories, Pocket Books, Draught Boards, bound and lettered on the back, Scientific Treatises, Almanacs, Statutes at Large; the works of Hume, Gibbon, Robertson, Beattie, Soame Jenyns, and generally, all those volumes which 'no gentleman's library should be without.'

"I confess that it moves my spleen to see these *things in book's clothing* perched upon shelves, like false saints, usurpers of true shrines, intruders into the sanctuary, thrusting out the legitimate occupants."

On the other hand, W. H. Auden wrote, "I enjoy reading railroad timetables, recipes, or, indeed, any kind of list," while Hemingway once said to Lincoln Steffens, "Cabelese. . . . Isn't it a great language!"

Lamb detested encyclopedias, considering them nonbooks too, but Aldous Huxley always took at least one volume of the *Encyclopaedia Britannica* with him whenever he traveled even a short distance and had the opportunity to read. When he went on a world cruise he had a special traveling case made so that he could take the whole set. According to James Thurber, *New Yorker* editor Harold Ross took the *E. B.* to the bathroom with him and "was up to the letter *H* when he died."

BOOKS WITHOUT CHARACTERS, WORDS, OR PICTURES

*T*HE MOST famous of blank books is probably American author Elbert Hubbard's masterful *Essay on Silence* (1898), which consisted of empty pages and was good practice for his message to Garcia. Hubbard never received just acclaim for his deep inscrutable Borgesean work, but in recent times a few nonbooks have won over the critics. Most notable of these was *The Nothing Book* (1970) subtitled *Wanna Make Something of It?* The *Cleveland Press* reviewed this with blank lines, and the *New York Times* said, "We have nothing to add," but the *Philadelphia Bulletin* called the book "a profound masterpiece of nothingness." The only bad news for the American publisher/author was the charge of plagiarism against *The Nothing Book* by the Belgian publisher of a blank book called *The Memoirs of an Amnesiac.* The American firm countered that blankness is in the public domain.

A religious allegory of seventeenth-century England entitled *A Wordless Book* consists of eight blank pages—two of which are black to represent evil, two red symbolizing redemption, two white for purity, and two gold for eternal bliss.

In 1738 Dutch physician Hermann Boerhaave died and left among his effects one copy of a self-published, sealed book entitled *The Onliest and Deepest Secrets of the Medical Art*. The book was sold for $20,000 at auction and when the buyer opened it, he found that all of the pages except the title page were blank. Written in hand on the title page was the advice: "Keep your head cool, your feet warm, and you'll make the best doctor poor."

Somewhere in between books with and without words are books with dots. The earliest example of the use of dots in literature that I can find is H. L. Mencken's editorial in the *Baltimore Sun* entitled "Object Lesson." It consisted of a million dots and a footnote explaining that each dot stood for a federal government jobholder. Not too long ago, however, a whole book of dots—one million of them—appeared. If I remember correctly, the number of dots on each page was related to an odd statistic (for instance, there are 8,000 Boy Scouts in Indonesia, or something like that many). The name comes back to me; it is *One Million*, by Hendrik Hertzberg, who became a speechwriter for former President Jimmy Carter.

A work consisting of just one letter repeated for several hundred pages is Juan Luis Castillejos untitled book full of *i*'s (1969), which is an assault on "the tyranny of words," according to the author. (See also *Lipograms: Books Without Certain Letters*.)

PAMPHLET

*P*amphilus, *seu de Amore* was the title of an erotic love poem of the twelfth century, but nothing is known about its author, Pamphilus, except his name in the title. No more than a few pages in length, the sheaf of Latin verses became very popular during the Middle Ages, the best-known love poem of its time. Just as the small book containing *Aesop's Fables* came to be familiarly called *Ésopet* in French, the little poem became known as *Pamphilet*, the English spelling this *Pamflet*, and eventually *Pamphlet*. By the fourteenth century any small booklet was called a pamphlet and within another 300 years the word had acquired its sense of "a small polemical brochure," the transition completed from sensuous love poem to political tract. Generally, a pamphlet is defined as a paperbound or unbound booklet of less than 100 pages. Pamphleteers employed them especially well during the eighteenth century, notable practitioners including Milton, Burke, Defoe, and Swift.

CATCHPENNY

*I*N 1824 London printer James Catnach sold at 1 penny each the "last speech by the condemned murderers of a merchant named Weare." When the sheet sold out in a day, Catnach decided to capitalize on the murder, headlining another penny paper WE ARE ALIVE AGAIN but running the first two words together so that the banner looked like WEARE ALIVE AGAIN. Gulled buyers of the Catnach penny paper punned on his name after discovering the cheap trick, referring to his paper as *catchpenny*, which soon came to mean any low-priced, fraudulent item.

A good story, one of the best and earliest examples of folk etymology. But the fault in this ingenious yarn lies in the fact that *catchpenny* was used in the same sense, "any flimflam that might catch a penny," sixty-five years before the Catnach ploy. I should add that James Catnach (1792–1841) was a real person, did a thriving business selling historically valuable "dying speeches of . . ." broadsides from his Seven Dials printing shop, and that his WEARE . . . paper did give the word *catchpenny* greater currency.

TABLOID, GOSSIP COLUMN

THE WORD *tabloid* was originally a trademark for a pill compressing several medicines into one tablet made by Great Britain's Burroughs, Wellcome and Company. The *Westminster Gazette* used the word for the title of a new newspaper it published in 1902 and won a court case in which the pharmaceutical company claimed that the word was private property. Though the first paper called a tabloid appeared in 1902, all of the journalistic practices associated with tabloids are much older. The gossip column, for example, is often credited to Dumas's friend Aurélier Scholl, who invented it when a cub reporter in Paris.

MAGAZINE

THIS Consideration has induced several Gentlemen to promote a Monthly collection to treasure up, as in a Magazine, the most remarkable Pieces on the Subjects abovemention'd," explained the editor of *Gentleman's Magazine* (1731), the first magazine to be called a magazine. The word *magazine* itself, however, is from the Arabic *makhzan*, "storehouse," and has been used in that sense in English since the sixteenth century. The highest price a magazine has paid an author is the $200,000 *Woman's Day* paid Rose Kennedy in 1974 for the first serial rights to her book about the Kennedys, *Times to Remember*.

ESSAYS

Montaigne's *Essais*, published in 1580, were the first in history to bear the name *essay* for a literary composition, while Bacon's *Essays Dedicated to Prince Henry* (1597) were the first in English to use the name. "To write treatises," Bacon explained, "requireth leisure in the writer and leisure in the reader . . . which is the cause which hath made me choose to write certain brief notes . . . which I have called essays. The word is late, but the thing is ancient."

There are three words for short essays, none of which, perhaps unfortunately, is used very much, if at all, anymore: *essaykin*, *essaylet*, and *essayette*.

LIBRARIES AND LIBRARIANS

Library derives from the Latin *liber*, "book," but the first library known with certainty to have existed was a collection of clay tablets in Babylonia in about the twenty-first century B.C. The first private library in ancient Greece was probably that of Aristotle in about 334 B.C. The dramatist Euripides was also said to have a large library, as did Plato and Samos, and later Mark Antony is supposed to have given the vast 200,000-volume library of the kings of Pergamum as a present to Cleopatra. Tradition ascribes the formation of the first public library at Athens to the beneficent tyrant Pisistratus in 540 B.C., but the earliest public library still existing today is the Vatican Library in Rome, founded in 1450. A public library was opened in Boston as early as 1653, and Benjamin Franklin proposed the Library Company of Philadelphia in 1731.

Among the most famous libraries in history was the Alexandria Library in Alexandria, Egypt, founded by Ptolemy I and containing 700,000 volumes at its peak. This vast library was gradually destroyed, beginning with Caesar's invasion in 47 B.C. and finally by the Arabs in 391. The Arabs burned the books to heat the city's 4,000 public baths, claiming that they were unnecessary, for all the knowledge needed by humanity was in the Koran.

England's Bodleian Library at Oxford, among the greatest in the world, honors its founder Sir Thomas Bodley (1545–1613), who devoted nearly twenty years of his life to developing the library. The Bodleian is entitled under the national Copyright Act to receive on demand a copy of every book published in the United Kingdom. Thomas Bodley, a Protestant exile who returned to England from Geneva when Elizabeth I ascended the throne, served in Parliament and as a diplomat in several European countries before retiring from public life in 1596. He began to restore the old Oxford library two years later and left most of his fortune to it as an endowment.

The purchase of Thomas Jefferson's library of 6,457 books formed the nucleus for the United States Library of Congress after the original holdings of the national library in Washington, D.C., were destroyed by fire in 1814. Created by Congress in 1800, the library is now the world's largest, with thirty-five acres of floor space containing 98 million items, including over 16 million books. By law the library on Capitol Hill must be given two copies of every book registered for copyright in the United States, and over 30,000 are published in America annually.

Other great libraries include:

• Lenin State Library—claims to have 24 million volumes, including periodicals.

• New York Public Library—founded in 1895 and the world's largest non-statutory public library.

• St. Mark's, Venice—founded with gifts from Petrarch in 1468.

• Sorbonne Library, Paris (1257).

• Bibliothèque Nationale, Paris (1350).

• Cambridge University Library (1475).

• Laurentian Library, Paris (1257).

• Mazarin Library, Paris (1661).

• British Museum Library (1823).

• Ambrosian Library, Milan (1609).

• Biblioteca Capitolare, Verona (A.D. 550).

• University libraries such as those of Harvard, Yale, Princeton, Chicago, Prague, Bologna, and Heidelberg.

The strangest of libraries belonged to Abdul Kassem Ismail (A.D. 938–995), the grand vizier of Persia. This consisted of 117,000 books arranged alphabetically on the backs of 400 camels, which walked in a fixed order wherever the grand vizier traveled.

Librarians in early times were thought to be uncultured people. Wrote Edward Young: "Unlearned men of books assume the care,/As eunuchs are the guardians of the fair." But this is far from the truth. Famous librarians include people as unlikely as Casanova, who worked as a librarian the last thirteen years of his life. Mao Tse-tung and J. Edgar Hoover also worked in libraries, and Pope Pius XI was in charge of the vast Vatican library before serving as Pope.

Among authors, Gottfried von Leibniz, David Hume, August Strindberg, and Archibald MacLeish were librarians. Perhaps the most widely known of American librarians is the father of American library science, Melvil Dewey (1851–1931), who first proposed his famous Dewey Decimal System in 1876 while serving as acting librarian at Amherst College. It is now used by the great majority of all libraries. The classification scheme, invented when he was in his early twenties, divides the entire field of knowledge into ten main classes (from 000 to 999), a second set of numbers following a decimal point indicating the special subject of a book within its main class. A man of fantastic energy and originality, Dewey later became chief librarian at Columbia College (1883–1888), where he founded, in 1887, the first American school of library science. As director of the New York State Library (1889–1906), he reorganized the state library, making it one of the most efficient in the nation, and originated the system of traveling libraries. Dewey also helped found the American Library Association, the New York State Library Association, and the *Library Journal*. He crusaded for simplified spelling and use of the metric system, among many other causes. (See also *Dedicated Readers*.)

COUNTRIES WITH THE MOST LIBRARY BOOKS

*T*HERE ARE some 4 billion volumes in all the world's public libraries, about one volume for each inhabitant of Planet Earth. Following are the countries with the most library books available for their people. The list, based on the latest (1974) UNESCO study, is limited to the top twelve, but the tiny country of San Marino ranks last in the world with one library containing 1,000 volumes.

COUNTRY	NUMBER OF BOOKS	NUMBER OF LIBRARIES
Former Soviet Union	1,507,836,000	130,653
United States	387,565,000	8,337
Poland	70,478,000	8,950
Rumania	52,882,000	6,575
Former West Germany	43,000,000	2,500
Japan	38,849,000	895
Former Czechoslovakia	38,764,000	10,861
Former East Germany	33,660,000	9,775
Denmark	32,713,000	251
Canada	31,282,000	780
Hungary	30,583,000	8,279
Sweden	30,534,000	416

HOW TO MAKE A LIBRARY

CHEWING GUM millionaire William Wrigley bought books by the yard. "Measure those bookshelves with a yardstick and buy enough books to fill 'em," he told his secretary while furnishing his Chicago apartment on Lake Shore Drive. "Get plenty of snappy red and green books with plenty of gilt lettering. I want a swell showing." At least more original is the advice *Lady Gough's Book of Etiquette* gave library owners in Victorian times: don't place books by married male authors next to those by female authors and vice versa. As far back as Roman times Seneca laughed at those who bought books for ostentatious display and never read them. (See *Tennyson Bindings*.)

THE WORLD'S ONLY LIBRARY BROTHEL

THERE MAY BE many figurative literary brothels or one kind or another, but the only actual one was the Reading Room in St. Louis, Missouri, a massage parlor where, until the place went out of business recently, a customer paid $12 or so for twenty minutes with a nude hostess who supposedly did nothing but read erotic or pornographic literature to him. The customer could supply his own reading matter if he desired, even things he had written himself. There is a precedent in Hortensia, "one of the favorite whores of Dr. Johnson," who would "walk up and down the park, repeating a book of Virgil."

THE BOOKKEEPERS

How hard, when those who do not wish
  To lend—that's lose—their books,
Are snared by anglers—folks that fish
  With literary hooks;

Who call and take some favorite tome,
  But never read it through;
They thus complete their set at home,
  By making one of you.

I, of my Spenser quite bereft,
  Last winter sore was shaken;
Of Lamb I'd be but a quarter left,
  Nor could I save my Bacon.

They picked my Locke, to me far more
  Than Bramah's patent worth;
And now my losses I deplore,
  Without a Home on earth.

Even Glover's works I cannot put
  My frozen hands upon;
Though ever since I lost my Foote,
  My Bunyan has been gone.

My life is wasting fast away;
  I suffer from these shocks;
And though I've fixed a lock on Gray,
  There's gray upon my locks.

They still have made me slight returns,
  And thus my grief divide;
For oh! they've cured me of my Burns,
  And eased my Akenside.

But all I think I shall not say,
  Nor let my anger burn;
For as they have not found me Gay,
  They have not left me Sterne.
                              —Anonymous

THE BOOK MUTILATORS

THE REVEREND James Granger (1723–1776) clipped over 14,000 engraved portraits from other books to use as possible illustrations for his *Biographical History of England*. Some of the books he pillaged were rare ones, and to make matters worse, he suggested in his preface that private collections like his might prove valuable someday. This resulted in a fad called *grangerizing*, or extra-illustration, thousands of people mutilating fine books and stuffing pictures and other material into Granger's. Editions following the 1769 *Biographical History . . . adapted to a Methodical Catalogue of Engraved British Heads* provided blank pages for the insertion of these extra illustrations, the book eventually expanding to six volumes from its original two. Sets of Granger illustrated with up to 3,000 engravings were compiled, and so many early English books were ravaged that "to grangerize" came to mean the mutilation that remains the bane of librarians today. Neither the author nor our discerning picture editors grangerized any books, rare or otherwise, for illustrations in this work.

DEDICATED READERS

THERE ARE some 100,000 libraries in America, with over 2 billion books in them. No library can charge a patron more than the cost of replacing a lost or overdue book, or its estimated fair market value, but the waived fine on America's longest overdue book—taken out from the University of Cincinnati library in 1823 and returned 145 years later in 1968 by the borrower's great-grandson—was calculated at $22,646. However, a fifty-eight-year-old New York attorney named Joseph Feldman—who didn't even have a library card—had over 15,000 books "overdue" from the New York Public Library. In 1973 firemen accidentally discovered the mountains of books in Feldman's apartment on an inspection tour after putting out a fire on the floor below. When asked why he had hoarded so many books, Feldman explained, "I like to read." He certainly outdid English author Dugald Stewart (1753–1828), who often forgot to return books he had borrowed. Stewart was so well known for this that when he confessed that he was deficient in arithmetic, a punster replied, "That might be true; but he certainly excells in bookkeeping." Another famous reader was British author John Campbell (1708–1775); Campbell once became engrossed in a book in a bookstore, purchased it, and didn't realize that he had written the book "until he had read it half through." A sad story is told about Sir Robert Walpole (1676–1745) after he retired from government. One day Walpole went into the library, "when, pulling down a book and holding it some minutes to his eyes, he suddenly and seemingly sullenly exchanged it for another. He held that about half as long, and looking at a third returned it instantly to its shelf and burst into tears. 'I have led a life of business so long,' said he, 'that I have lost my taste for reading, and now—what shall I do?' "

THE WORLD'S MOST CONSTANT READERS

JUDGING BY the number of volumes borrowed annually from public libraries per 1,000 inhabitants, the Danes are the world's most constant readers. Here are the top twelve nations, according to the latest (1974) UNESCO study. Not on the list but last is the Sudan.

COUNTRY	BOOKS BORROWED PER 1,000 INHABITANTS
Denmark	16,568.9
Finland	9,220.4
Sweden	8,712.5
Former Czechoslovakia	7,999.7
New Zealand	7,681.3
Iceland	7,296.2
Netherlands	6,975.4
Ireland	6,846.4
Hungary	5,389.3
Former East Germany	4,669.5
Poland	4,212.8
United States	4,150.4

MOST DIPLOMATIC READER

*D*ISRAELI HAD a standard reply unmatched for diplomatic ambiguity for people who sent him unsolicited manuscripts to read: "Many thanks; I shall lose no time in reading it."

READERS REWARDED

I HAVE sometimes dreamt that when the Day of Judgement dawns and the great conquerors and lawyers and statesmen come to receive their awards—their crowns, their laurels, their names carved indelibly upon imperishable marble—the Almighty will turn to Peter and will say, not without a certain envy when He sees us coming with our books under our arms, "Look, these need no reward. We have nothing to give them here. They have loved reading."
—Virginia Woolf

THE FIRST PUBLISHERS

*T*HE FIRST publishers may have been Egyptian undertakers, who put into each burial place a *Book of the Dead*, which was a guide to the afterlife.

MARK TWAIN ON PUBLISHERS

*I*N HIS *Memoirs of a Publisher*, F. N. Doubleday, dubbed Effendi by Kipling, relates Mark Twain's "perfect recipe" for making a modern publisher: "Take an idiot man from a lunatic asylum and marry him to an idiot woman, and the fourth generation of this connection should be a good publisher from the American point of view." Mark Twain, of course, later became a publisher himself.

PUBLISHERS PAST AND PRESENT

*A*BOUT 550 publishers in the United States bring out over 30,000 new titles every year, but a nonprofit publisher, the U.S. Government Printing Office, is the largest publisher in the country, and in the world for that matter, mailing out more than 150 million items every year and publishing 6,000 new titles annually. The largest nongovernment publisher in the world is Time Warner, with almost $3 billion in revenues annually, while McGraw-Hill's book division is the largest U.S. book-publishing company. The second largest nongovernment publisher in the world is Germany's Bertelsmann Group, with publishing revenues of $2 billion. Bertelsmann was built up from practically nothing by Rinehard Mohn, a POW in Kansas during World War II, by such original methods as exchanging new books for twice their weight in old books to obtain paper. It is still largely owned by Mohn.

As for printers, R. R. Donnelley and Sons Company, of Chicago, founded in 1864, is the world's largest, turning out over $200 million worth of work a year.

The first full-size book published in America was *The Whole Book of Psalms . . .* by Steeven Daye, which contained 296 pages and was published in July 1640 by the author's Cambridge Press in Cambridge, Massachusetts. Seventeen hundred copies selling at 20 pence each netted a profit of about £80. Daye, or Day, had published William Peirce's almanac before this. He had come to America under contract to a printer and when his employer died during the voyage, Daye set up the press at Cambridge, teaching himself typography.

CHANGING TIMES

GUIY PATIN, dean of Paris's Faculté de Médicine, writing in the sixteenth century: "As to our publishers—I can hope for nothing from them. They print nothing at their own expense but sex novels *(novela utrisque)*."

CHANGING TIMES II

TIMES HAVE changed since a certain author was executed for murdering his publisher. They say that when the author was on the scaffold he said goodbye to the minister and to the reporters, and then he saw some publishers sitting in the front row below, and to them he did not say goodbye. He said instead, "I'll see you again."
—James M. Barrie in a speech
at the Alpine Club (1896)

"NOW BARABBAS WAS A PUBLISHER"

THESE LINES are often attributed to Lord Byron but they may have their origin in words of English poet Thomas Campbell (1777–1844). Napoleon had had German publisher Johann Palm put to death for printing subversive pamphlets. Later, at an authors' dinner, Campbell proposed this toast: "To Napoleon. [Voices of protest] I agree with you that Napoleon is a tyrant, a monster, the sworn foe of our nation. But, gentlemen—he once shot a publisher!"

MORE KIND WORDS ABOUT PUBLISHERS

He was a very proud, confident, ill-natured, impudent, ignorant fellow, peevish and froward to his wife (whom he used to beat), a great sot, and a whoring prostituted wretch, and of no credit.
—Thomas Hearne
on his bookseller, Stephen Fletcher

A Petty Sneaking Knave, I knew
O Mr. Cromek, how do ye do?
—William Blake

These fellows hate us.
—Charles Lamb

What Authors lose, their Booksellers have won,
So Pimps grow rich, while Gallants are undone.
—Alexander Pope

As repressed sadists are supposed to become policemen or butchers so those with irrational fear of life become publishers.
—Cyril Connolly

It is with publishers as with wives: one always wants somebody else's.
—Norman Douglas

THE ANXIOUS PUBLISHER

ACCORDING TO the Russian journal *Sputnik*, Karl Marx received this letter while living in London and researching his seminal work in the British Museum:

Dear Herr Doctor:

You are already 18 months behind time with the manuscript of *Das Kapital* which you have agreed to write for us. If we do not receive the manuscript within six months, we shall be obliged to commission another author to do the work.

UNUSUAL PUBLISHING ARRANGEMENTS

So I began to write my first book. At once I found that writing was fun. I even forgot I hadn't seen Sherwood Anderson for three weeks until he walked in my door, the first time he ever came to see me, and said, "What's wrong? Are you mad at me?" I told him I was writing a book. He said, "My God," and walked out. When I finished the book—it was *Soldier's Pay*—I met Mrs. Anderson on the street. She asked how the book was going, and I said I'd finished it. She said, "Sherwood says that he will make a trade with you. If he doesn't have to read your manuscript he will tell his publisher to accept it." I said, "Done," and that's how I became a writer.　　　　　　　　　　　　　　　　—William Faulkner

ANDERSON WAS a very generous man to whom critics have never shown much generosity; the letters of introduction he gave Ernest Hemingway were largely responsible for Hemingway's getting a start in Paris, and he convinced his publisher, Boni and Liveright, to bring out Hemingway's first American book, an expanded edition of *In Our Time*. Hemingway repaid his kindness by satirizing him in *The Torrents of Spring*. There are those who say he couldn't forgive Anderson for teaching him, something Hemingway later said about Gertrude Stein's acid criticism of him. (He claimed he taught her how to write dialogue.) As Mark Twain said, so it goes.

"DON'T READ IT, JUST PRINT IT"

PUBLISHERS COMMONLY publish books they can't be expected to understand, Irish playwright Arthur Murphy (1727–1805) was told. "True," he replied, "some of 'em *do* deal in morality."

THE PUBLISHER'S RISK

PUBLISHERS OF Voltaire's complete works seem to have met with incredibly bad luck, at least in the eighteenth and nineteenth centuries, leading to a literary tradition holding that it was unlucky to publish his books. The first editor of his complete works, for example, lost a million francs in the stock market and died suddenly of a heart attack in 1798. Within the next seventy years at least eight publishers were ruined financially after publishing complete Voltaires, four of these becoming paupers and dying suddenly, one being killed by a woman he caught stealing a book, another going blind, and two forced to take jobs as workers in printing plants for the rest of their lives.

VOLTAIRE

THE CURSE OF THE WHITE GODDESS

ROBERT GRAVES'S *The White Goddess* was rejected by the first editor to whom he sent the book, and She promptly began working Her black magic, according to literary tradition. The editor died of a heart attack within a month. A second editor found the book of no consequence and he shortly after hanged himself from a tree, wearing a bra and panties. T. S. Eliot, the final editor to pass on the manuscript, insisted that *The White Goddess* must be published "at all costs," and he, of course, later won the Nobel Prize.

REJECTION SLIP RECORDS

> After being turned down by a number of publishers, he decided to write for posterity.   —George Ade

ENGLISH AUTHOR John Creasey (1908–1973), who wrote 564 books under thirteen pen names, received 743 rejection slips before a publisher accepted one of his mystery novels. However, many magazine writers have doubtless accumulated more rejection slips than this. Another English author, Gilbert Young (b. 1906), holds the official record for the most rejection slips for a single book-length manuscript—242 for his *World Government Crusade*. I know an author (quite successful now) who collected well over 100 rejection slips for a novel—he papered a wall with them—before abandoning the book.

Marianne Moore had a poem rejected thirty-five times, James Joyce's *Dubliners* was rejected twenty-two times, Pearl Buck's *The Good Earth* was rejected a dozen times, and J. P. Donleavy's *The Ginger Man* gathered thirty-six rejection slips. Short-story writer Frank O'Connor told how he submitted a story to a magazine, was advised by one editor that the magazine would take it, and was paid for it, only to have another editor send him a rejection letter when the manuscript accidentally wound up on his desk. There are a number of instances of hoaxed editors or first readers rejecting untitled typescripts of *War and Peace*, *Moby Dick*, *Gone with the Wind*, and other classics that came in "over the transom" into the "slush pile."

A REJECTION SLIP FROM A CHINESE EDITOR

*I*LLUSTRIOUS BROTHER of the sun and moon—Behold thy servant prostrate before thy feet. I kow-tow to thee and beg of thy graciousness thou mayest grant that I may speak and live. Thy honored manuscript has deigned to cast the light of its august countenance upon me. With raptures I have pursued it. By the bones of my ancestry, never have I encountered such wit, such pathos, such lofty thoughts. With fear and trembling I return the writing. Were I to publish the treasure you sent me, the Emperor would order that it should be made the standard, and that none be published except such as equaled it. Knowing literature as I do, and that it would be impossible in ten thousand years to equal what you have done, I send your writing back. Ten thousand times I crave your pardon. Behold my head is at your feet. Do what you will.

> Your servant's servant,
> The Editor

THE MOST LITERARY REJECTION SLIP

*G*ERTRUDE STEIN's editor, A. J. Fifield, sent her a rejection slip in a style she had no trouble appreciating, though the content might have bothered her:

I am only one, only one, only. Only one being, one at the same time. Not two, not three, only one. Only one life to live, only sixty minutes in one hour. Only one pair of eyes. Only one brain. Only one being. Being only one, having only one pair of eyes, having only one time, having only one life, I cannot read your MS three or four times. Not even one time. Only one look, only one look is enough. Hardly one copy would sell here. Hardly one. Hardly one.

VAMP

*T*HE NAME OF a bookseller in Samuel Foote's play *The Author* (1757) became synonymous for an avaricious publisher, because the character Vamp held that binding was more important than the contents of a book: "Books are like women; to strike they must be well-dressed. Fine feathers make fine birds. A good paper, and elegant type, a handsome motto, and a catching title, have driven many a dull treatise through three editions."

Vamp was later used as the name of a critic in Thomas Peacock's novel *Melincourt* (1817) and is supposed to be a caricature of the bitter author, editor, and critic William Gifford. Peacock also satirized Gifford, Coleridge (Mr. Mystic), Malthus (Mr. Fox), and Wordsworth (Mr. Paperstamp) in his book.

BLURB

*A*MERICAN HUMORIST Gelett Burgess (1866–1951) not only coined the words *blurb*, for a laudatory ad, *bromide*, for a boring or tiresome expression, and *goop*; he also wrote the immortal "Purple Cow" poem:

I never saw a Purple Cow
* I never hope to see one;*
But I can tell you anyhow,
* I'd rather see than be one!*

And the lesser known:

Ah, yes! I wrote the "Purple Cow"—
* I'm sorry now, I wrote it!*
But I can tell you anyhow,
* I'll kill you if you quote it!*

Burgess invented *blurb* with the publication of his *Are You a Bromide?* in 1907. His publisher, B. W. Huebsch, told the story:

It is the custom of publishers to present copies of a conspicuous current book to booksellers attending the annual dinner of their trade association, and as this little book was in its heyday when the meeting took place I gave it to 500 guests. These copies were differentiated from the regular edition by the addition of a comic bookplate drawn by the author and by a special jacket which he devised. It was the common

practice to print the picture of a damsel—languishing, heroic, or co-quettish . . . on the jacket of every novel so Burgess lifted from a Lydia Pinkham or tooth-powder adver-tisement the portrait of a sickly sweet young woman, painted in some gleaming teeth, and otherwise enhanced her pulchritude, and placed her in the center of the jacket.

His accompanying text was some nonsense about "Miss Belinda Blurb," and thus the term supplied a real need and became a fixture in our language.

THE BASHAW OF BLURBS

OVER A PERIOD of seventeen years New York City freelancer Lester Schul-man wrote some 6,000 blurbs for various publishers, making him, so far as is known, the Bashaw of Blurbs. Able to read almost any manuscript within an hour, he went to sleep after finishing a book, let his subconscious go to work and invariably woke up with an idea for a blurb that took a few hours to get down polished on paper.

COLPORTEUR

BOOK SALESMEN follow an honorable calling, one that dates back hundreds of years to when they carried Bibles and other books in a basket or pack hanging from their necks by a strap. For this reason they were, and sometimes still are, called *colporteurs*, from the French *col*, neck, and *porter*, to carry. Typical of these was Old Parson Weems, noted for his charming fabrication of George Washington's chopping down the cherry tree, not to mention his bold Homeric yarns about Ben Franklin and General Francis "The Swamp Fox" Marion. History often forgets that Weems, whose tales have become folklore, worked all his life as a book peddler; in fact, this vagabond colporteur died in harness on the Southern roads where he had begun hawking books in 1794. Fiddle at his side, he drove his Jersey wagon over bumpy rural roads for some thirty years, often playing gay tunes on his fiddle to stimulate his horses, dreaming up schemes for selling the books behind him, and implementing his plans with soaring spirits. Locks flying over his clerical coat, a quill pen stuck in his hat, and a small inkhorn hanging from a lapel, the vagabond bookhawker was a familiar, convincing figure wherever he went. One time while he was pitching Tom Paine's radical *Age of Reason* a conservative clergyman protested and Weems pulled out the Bishop of Llandaff's refutation of Tom Paine, advising that he sold the antidote as well as the poison. A pamphlet he wrote called *Hymen's Recruiting Sergeant; or, The New Matrimonial Tat-too for Old Bachelors* he advertised as "an attempt to wash out the leprous stains of old Bachelorism, and extinguish, if possible, the pestilence of celibacy." And, if he could make money out of it, this "Livy of the common people," who brought much culture to America, if he didn't help populate her, wasn't averse to pretending he was drunk in grog shops to push the sales of his own *Drunkard's Looking Glass.*

ENLIGHTENMENT

I THINK THAT I still have it in my heart someday to paint a bookshop with the front yellow and pink, in the evening, and the black passersby . . . like a light in the midst of darkness.   —Vincent van Gogh

SALES APPEAL

*T*HE YOUNGEST book salesman in publishing history may have been Roger Straus III, who started working part-time for Farrar, Straus when he was eight and became a book salesman in Manhattan when only twelve. "There was a certain shock appeal in being so young," he told an interviewer. "Buyers might have worried that if they didn't take my books I would cry."

BEST-SELLERS

*L*ISTED BELOW are the fifteen best-sellers of all time, as far as can be determined from largely inaccurate records. *Best-seller* is perhaps an inaccurate term here, for many of these books (especially those asterisked) were distributed free, at least in part. In fact, the number-one book, which should surprise most readers, had been distributed free for more than three-quarters of a century. Over 2½ billion copies of the Sears, Roebuck mail-order catalog have been distributed in the last ten years alone, and 7 billion may be a conservative estimate for its total distribution since 1896. To be fair, I must also include the Montgomery Ward catalog, which is even older, dating back to 1872, and is distributed free to 86 million people a year. Statistics for both the Sears and Ward "wish books" are the total of all the catalogs these companies issue in a year, supplements as well as their main catalogs. (Sears's main catalog alone used to go to 65 million people a year.) Sears's wish books took 175,000 tons of paper and 1 million gallons of ink to produce each year, which once made Sears, Roebuck the biggest publisher in the world next to the U.S. Government Printing Office.

Mail-order catalogs shouldn't be disparaged, either. In 1946 the distinguished Grolier Club, a New York society of book lovers, chose Montgomery Ward's catalog as one of the 100 books most influential on American life.

Certainly the mail-order catalog ranks with the railroad train, automobile, and airplane as one of the great unifying forces in American life. But people weren't thinking of that when they read their catalogs, ordered from them, reread them in place of literature on cold winter nights, used them in schools along with McGuffey readers, and—after the new catalog came—put them to good use in the outhouse (see *Bathroom Best-sellers*). Because they have been mentioned nowhere as best-sellers and are largely neglected in most respects, I have dwelt on them at some length here, even though Sears recently stopped issuing its catalog. In any event, they head this list of the books that the most Americans have read.

1. *Sears, Roebuck Catalog* (1896–1992)—5–6 billion copies*
2. *Montgomery Ward Catalog* (1872–   )—5–6 billion copies; today 86 million copies a year*
3. *The Bible* (all versions 1800–1975)—4 billion copies*
4. *Quotations from the Works of Mao Tse-tung* (booklet compulsory reading in China from 1966 to 1971)—900 million copies*

5. *McGuffey Reader* (all editions from 1836 to 1978)—125 million copies
6. *The Truth That Leads to Eternal Life* (Jehovah's Witness tract, 1968–1975)—100 million copies*
7. *Webster's American Spelling Book* (1783)—50–100 million copies
8. *A Message to Garcia* by Elbert Hubbard (pamphlet 1899–1970, distributed by many businesses to employees)—50–100 million copies*
9. *The World Almanac* (1868–   )—65 million copies
10. *Guinness Book of World Records* (1955–1992)—65 million copies
11. *The Common Sense Book of Baby and Child Care* by Dr. Benjamin Spock (1946–1992)—45 million copies
12. *In His Steps* by Charles Monroe Sheldon (1896–1978)—30 + million copies
13. *Valley of the Dolls* by Jacqueline Susann (1966–1992)—29 + million copies
14. *American Red Cross First Aid Book*—16 + million copies
15. *Infant Care*, U.S. Government pamphlet (1914)—15 + million copies

That would make the best-selling novel of all time Charles Monroe Sheldon's *In His Steps*. Sheldon, a minister in Topeka, Kansas, wrote what was essentially a Utopian fantasy of what the world might be like if people lived literally according to Christ's teachings, and tested the novel by reading it a chapter at a time to his Sunday evening congregation. Unfortunately for him, he sold the book for only $75 to the Chicago *Advance*, which printed it as a serial. Only part of the serial was sent to the Copyright Office, and thus the copyright was declared defective and Sheldon lost millions when numerous editions were released by various publishers. His novel was translated into twenty-three languages.

Early American best-sellers include the *New England Primer* and *The Day of Doom*, true chapbooks like Mary Rowlandson's *Captivity* (which sold 4 million copies), Thomas Paine's *Common Sense*, Parson Weems's *Life of Washington*, poems such as "Hiawatha," and many almanacs. Paine's book sold 500,000 copies, proportionate to over 45 million today in terms of total population, but he refused all royalties on the ground that payment would demean his patriotic worth. The first best-selling novel was *Charlotte, a Tale of Truth* by Susanna Haswell Rowson, which was printed in 1790 and went into 200 editions. Harriet Beecher Stowe's *Uncle Tom's Cabin* (1852) was the first novel to sell 1 million copies. Following are some more popular novels up to the time of *Gone with the Wind* (1936):

- 1821—*The Spy*, James Fenimore Cooper
- 1854—*The Lamplighter*, Maria Cummings
- 1867—*St. Elmo*, Augusta Jane Evans
- 1868—*Barriers Burned Away*, Edward P. Roe
- 1876—*Tom Sawyer*, Mark Twain
- 1880—*Ben Hur*, Lew Wallace
- 1888—*Looking Backward*, Edward Bellamy
- 1897—*Hugh Wynne*, S. W. Mitchell
- 1898—*David Harum*, Edward Noyes Westcott
- 1898—*When Knighthood Was in Flower*, Charles Major
- 1903—*The Call of the Wild*, Jack London
- 1903—*The Little Shepherd of Kingdom Come*, John Fox
- 1905—*The Clansman*, Thomas Dixon
- 1911—*The Winning of Barbara Worth*, Harold Bell Wright
- 1912—*Riders of the Purple Sage*, Zane Grey
- 1918—*Dere Mable!*, Edward Streeter
- 1925—*Gentlemen Prefer Blondes*, Anita Loos
- 1933—*Anthony Adverse*, Hervey Allen

Until the late 1940s best-sellers were rarely works of much literary significance, but with the publication of *The Naked and the Dead* by Norman Mailer in 1948 and James Jones's *From Here to Eternity*, in 1951, more books of lasting interest began to find large markets.

The only number-one best-selling American novel to hold that distinction two years in a row was Richard Bach's *Jonathan Livingston Seagull*, in 1972 and 1973.

In 1990 the top three best-selling fiction authors in the U.S. were Jean M. Auel, Stephen King, and Scott Turow.

ENDURING BEST-SELLERS

*B*EST-SELLERS aren't as ephemeral as we are often told. Of the following lists of twenty fiction and nonfiction best-sellers of 1953, only four (those without an asterisk) are out of print. The Bible is no longer included on best-seller lists, though it is still a best-seller, of course.

FICTION

*1. *The Robe*, Lloyd C. Douglas
*2. *The Silver Chalice*, Thomas B. Costain
*3. *Désirée*, Annemarie Selinko
*4. *Battle Cry*, Leon M. Uris
*5. *From Here to Eternity*, James Jones
*6. *The High and the Mighty*, Ernest K. Gann
 7. *Beyond This Place*, A. J. Cronin
 8. *Time and Time Again*, James Hilton
*9. *Lord Vanity*, Samuel Shellabarger
*10. *The Unconquered*, Ben Ames Williams

NONFICTION

*1. The Holy Bible (Revised Standard Version)
*2. *The Power of Positive Thinking*, Norman Vincent Peale
*3. *Sexual Behavior in the Human Female*, Alfred C. Kinsey, et al.
*4. *Angel Unaware*, Dale Evans Rogers
 5. *Life Is Worth Living*, Fulton J. Sheen
*6. *A Man Called Peter*, Catherine Marshall
 7. *This I Believe*, Edward P. Morgan
*8. *The Greatest Faith Ever Known*, Fulton Oursler and G. A. O. Armstrong
*9. *How to Play Your Best Golf*, Tommy Armour
*10. *A House Is Not a Home*, Polly Adler

The post–Civil War novel *St. Elmo*, by Augusta Jane Evans, is about as enduring a best-seller as a book can be. It was so popular that towns in at least thirteen states were named after it.

SLOOOOWEST-SELLING BOOK

PUBLISHED IN 1716 by the Oxford University Press, a translation of the New Testament from Coptic into Latin by David Wilkins sold 500 copies in the 191 years it remained in print (until 1907), for an average of about two copies a year.

BOOK CLUBS

AMERICA'S FIRST book club was the Book-of-the-Month Club, founded in April 1926 by Harry Scherman with Robert Haas as president. Its distinguished panel of judges were Dorothy Canfield, Heywood Broun, Henry Seidel Canby, William Allen White, and Christopher Morley, and they chose as the first Book-of-the-Month Sylvia Townsend Warner's *Lolly Willowes, or the Loving Huntsman* (Viking) to be distributed to 4,750 members. Within twenty years the club had revolutionalized the publishing industry and twenty-five similar clubs were distributing 75 million books, over one-sixth of all American book sales. Today U.S. book clubs are led in sales by the Literary Guild, founded in 1927. Customarily, members receive a free book or books upon joining a book club and a free book with every two or three books purchased. Book club editions are often, but not always, printed on cheaper paper. While the clubs have been criticized for inculcating a mediocrity of taste, they have offered many excellent books to their members and there is no doubt that they bring books to areas without bookstores.

Ancestors of the book clubs were the circulating libraries of the nineteenth century, which supplied popular novels to readers for a small subscription price. These libraries often forced publishers to conform to their puritanical standards and made good writing all the more difficult. George Gissing's *New Grub Street* (1891) treats the subject in detail.

"TO PENGUINIZE"

SINCE Penguin Books is a major worldwide publisher, a few words about the bird's name. Unfortunately, the name *penguin*, for the bird, is a misnomer. In the sixteenth century it was applied by Welsh sailors to the flightless great auk of the North Atlantic, which they probably named from the Welsh *pen* (head) and *gwyn* (white) for the white spots near its eyes. Later, sailors near the South Pole applied the same name to the flightless bird we call the penguin today, despite the fact that it has a black head. The publisher Penguin, which began business in Great Britain in 1935, merged with American publisher Viking in 1975. A leader in paperback publishing since its founding, the firm's name has become a synonym for a paperback book; the first of its books, published for sixpence, or 12½ cents, is now worth $100 to collectors.

In England *Penguinize* means "to publish or republish a book" in paperback. No doubt the company hopes that *Penguinize* or, better yet, *penguinize*, will have currency in America, too. *Pocket book* is a term for a paperback book in America, taking its name from the firm Pocket Books, Inc., founded in 1939. There seems to be no verb equivalent to *Penguinize* here; publishers speak of "bringing it out in paper" or "putting out a paperback edition," etc., but nobody *Pocketbookizes* a book. Here is one place where the English are clearly outdoing the American love of shortcuts in language. *Penguin* might yet fill this American language gap, unless someone at Bantam Books comes up with *Bantamize* first.

MUSIC PUBLISHING

THE ORIGINAL Tin Pan Alley was and is located between Forty-eighth and Fifty-second streets on Seventh Avenue in New York City, an area where many music publishers, recording studios, composers, and arrangers have offices. The place was probably named for the tinny sound of the cheap, much-abused pianos in music publishers' offices there, or for the constant noise emanating from the area, which sounded like the banging of tin pans to some. *Tin Pan Alley*, the term first recorded in 1914, means any place where popular music is published today, and it can stand for popular music itself.

"THE LOVE GAME I PLAYED ON MY BINGO NIGHT OUT": WRITING TRUE CONFESSIONS

CONFESSION MAGAZINES, which have been with us now for over sixty years, are an American invention th   were an outgrowth of long soul-searching letters sent to physical culture crusader Bernarr MacFadden's *Physical Culture* magazine in 1919. MacFadden's first confession book was *True Story*, the great-grandmother of the genre, which currently has a circulation of 5 million, but there are scores of other confessions on the newsstands today. The first stories dealt with sweet young things who did such terrible things as dare to elope against their parents' wishes, while contemporary tales have virtually no taboo themes, ranging from well-written confessions about incest to stories such as "My Bride Is a Man" (where Julie was Jules before her sex-change operation). The yarns, which earn 5 to 10 cents a word, aren't all written by readers. Professional writers turn out a large number, perhaps the majority of them, though some magazines do require an author to sign a release saying his or her story is based on a true experience.

PLACE MAT PUBLISHING

*T*HERE HAVE been attempts to link the place mat with the doily, which would make it an English invention, as an Englishman surnamed Doily, Doiley, Doyley, or Doyly probably invented the doily napkin that may have become the first place mat in the early eighteenth century. But no Britisher of the time would have considered writing prose or poetry on a place mat, and the first international place mat is a Yankee invention. Clearly someone who noticed how much we like to read newspapers, cereal boxes, soup cans, or whatever while we eat got the idea in the early 1950s. Bitter controversy exists about just who was responsible. Both Kurt Strauss, chairman of the board of Royal Paper Products, Coatsville, Pennsylvania, and John Harwood, president of Springprint Paper Products, Inc., Springfield, Ohio, claim the honor, Strauss citing a place mat listing the presidents of the United States and Harwood a place mat on the solar system. Since then there have been place mats published on everything from antique autos to zoos. Unfortunately, their authors earn flat fees with no royalties—"unfortunately" because informative place mats sell some 2 *billion* copies a year in America alone.

FORTUNE COOKIE PUBLISHING

*F*ORTUNE COOKIES may derive from an ancient Chinese game in which players were given a cookie containing a piece of paper with a proverb written on it and told to write a short essay about the message. But the first cookie with a fortune inside was invented in 1918 by David Jung, a recent Chinese immigrant who had established Los Angeles's Hong Kong Noodle Company. Jung got the idea after noting how bored customers got while waiting for their orders in Chinese restaurants. He employed a Presbyterian minister (the first fortune-cookie author!) to write condensations of Biblical messages and later hired Marie Raine, the wife of one of his salesmen, who became the Shakespeare of fortune cookies, writing thousands of classic fortunes such as "Your feet shall walk upon a plush carpet of contentment." The Hong Kong Noodle Company is still in business, as are hundreds of other fortune-cookie publishers. Notable ones include Misfortune Cookies of Los Angeles: "Look forward to love and marriage, but not with the same person"; Grass Valley, California's Ms. Fortune Cookies: "If you're good for nothing, for heaven's sake don't be bad for nothing"; New York City's Dr. Wing Tip Shoo's X-rated Fortune Cookies: "A Chinese voyeur is simply a Peking Tom," and many more.

Fortunes are inserted into each cookie as it comes off a large semiautomatic griddle machine, workers inserting the paper and folding the baked dough into a fortune-cookie shape before it hardens. Authors whose agents don't specialize in fortune cookies sometimes publish their own by taking one cup of flour, an egg, a quarter of a cup of sugar, a teaspoon of vanilla extract, and a cup of water. All ingredients are mixed in a large bowl and allowed to stand for ten minutes. A tablespoon of the mixture is then spooned onto a Scandinavian Krumkater Iron, heated for three to four minutes and turned and heated for another three minutes. The cookie is then removed from the iron, the poetic fortune (written beforehand, of course) inserted, and the cookie folded in half and then bent over again to make a fortune cookie.

THE CRUMBLING BOOK BUSINESS

*I*F PUBLISHERS used alkaline paper, some experts say, books would last 1,000 years or so at little additional cost. As it stands today, about 97 percent of all books published between 1900 and 1937 have useful lives of fifty years or so remaining. Half of the New York Public Library's 5 million books are so badly decayed that they are near disintegration—there are 3,000-year-old papyrus ledgers in better condition. But although paper is usually made as cheaply as possible today, some artisans persist in making a quality product. Japanese *gampi*, a lustrous, vellumlike paper made from the wild thyme shrub, is often called "the king of papers" and the genius at making it is Eishiro Abe, eighty-nine, who has been designated a Japanese national treasure for his art.

He and his assistants make over 176 different kinds of paper by hand, using a complicated process that includes pressing and drying for a night and a day.

LITERARY TRASH TAX

*U*NDER HUNGARY's old Communist government, the Ministry of Culture leveled a "trash tax" on popular works of fiction, nonfiction, drama, the cinema, painting, and music. The proceeds were put into a "Culture Fund" used to finance what the Ministry of Culture deemed works of artistic merit.

CHAPTER EIGHT

Art Imitates Life
(from Prototype to Linotype)
& Vice Versa

ROMAN À CLEF

*R*oman *à clef* translates from the French as "novel with a key" and is also known as a *livre à clef*, "book with a key," and in German, a *Schlüssel-roman*. In such novels thinly disguised portraits of actual well-known persons are presented under fictitious names. When the *roman à clef* originated in seventeenth-century France real "keys" to the real persons involved were often published after the books appeared. Notable instances of "key novels" in England include Thomas Love Peacock's *Nightmare Abbey* (1818), which caricatured Byron, Shelley, and Coleridge; Benjamin Disraeli's *Venetia* (1837); Aldous Huxley's *Point Counter Point* (1928), featuring a disguised D. H. Lawrence, among others; and Somerset Maugham's *Cakes and Ale*, among others of his novels, in which the characters were often hardly disguised at all. American *romans à clef* include Hawthorne's *The Blithedale Romance*, in which Herman Melville appears as Hollingsworth; Hemingway's *The Sun Also Rises*, in which several characters were based on the author's friends; and Robert Penn Warren's *All the King's Men*, in which the main character is based on Huey Long.

Many great authors have also used real unknown people as a basis for their fictional creations. Yeats, for example modeled the Crazy Jane in some of his poems on an eccentric woman called Cracked Mary who lived near his associate Lady Gregory. Melville was particularly prone to borrowing from reality for his fiction. *Israel Potter, Benito Cereno, Billy Budd*, and many of his stories are based on real people or events. Melville even patterned *Moby Dick* on the activities of a real whale called Mocha Dick and many of the incidents in *Moby Dick*, including the last scene, in which Ishmael is saved by clinging to a coffin, actually happened in real life. (See *The Search for Moby Dick*.)

Dickens modeled the parasitic sponger Skimpole in *Bleak House* on a newspaper editor, Leigh Hunt, while Poe's story "The Mystery of Marie Rogêt" is based on the case of Mary Rogers, a young New York City woman who was murdered in 1841, and James Barrie based *Peter Pan* on his best friend's children. Other real-life inspirations include Jane Clairmont, Lord Byron's mistress, who inspired Juliana Bordereau in Henry James's *The Aspern Papers*, and Chester Gillette, whose murder of his pregnant factory-girl lover in 1906 prompted Theodore Dreiser to write *An American Tragedy*.

THE ALICE OUTSIDE WONDERLAND

*F*OR OVER a century Lewis Carroll's *Alice in Wonderland* (1865) has been the most famous and possibly the most widely read children's book. That there is an *Alice* cult even among adults is witnessed by the numerous works of criticism devoted to the book, which has even been translated into Latin. The model for the fictional Alice was Alice Liddell, daughter of Dean Henry George Liddell, noted coauthor of *Liddell & Scott's Greek Lexicon*, still the standard Greek-English Dictionary. Carroll wrote *Alice* for his friend's daughter, who later became Mrs. Reginald Hargreaves. The author apparently made up the story while on a picnic with Alice and her sisters, actually improvising the classic tale as the group rowed about a lake. Incidentally, Carroll is regarded as the greatest nineteenth-century photographer of children and his best pictures were of Alice Liddell. An "Alice," in allusion to *Alice in Wonderland*, is sometimes used to refer to a person newly arrived in strange, fantastic surroundings.

D'ARTAGNAN

*M*EMOIRS ATTRIBUTED to Charles de Batz-Castelmore d'Artagnan (c. 1623–1673) were used by the novelist Alexandre Dumas *père* in his fictional series beginning with *The Three Musketeers*. In real life Gascon d'Artagnan did serve in the king's musketeers, but he wasn't a *comte*, as he called himself, claiming the title without right. About all that can be verified about the man is that he captained the contingent that arrested the powerful French Superinten-dent of Finances Nicolas Fouquet in 1661, became a brigadier general nine years later, and was fatally wounded at the siege of Maastricht. Yet d'Artagnan will always be remembered for the heroic adventures Dumas and his collaborator Maquet adapted or created from his story.

DR. JEKYLL AND MR. HYDE

*I*N Robert Louis Stevenson's novel *The Strange Case of Dr. Jekyll and Mr. Hyde* (1886), Dr. Jekyll, a physician, discovers a drug that creates in him a personality that absorbs all his evil instincts. This personality, which he calls Mr. Hyde, is repulsive in appearance and gradually gains control of him until he finally commits a horrible murder. Jekyll can rid himself of Hyde only by committing suicide. Stevenson, who wrote the novel in three days locked in his study after he had a dream about the story, based the main character on an Edinburgh cabinetmaker and deacon named William Brodie (1741–1788), who was a "double being," by day a respected businessman and by night the leader of a gang of burglars. Brodie was finally hanged for his crimes, but Stevenson, who was raised in Edinburgh, knew his story well and in fact wrote a play entitled *Deacon Brodie, or The Double Life* when he was only fifteen. This was the germ of the idea for the later work.

PETRARCH AND LAURA

It was the day when the sun's heavy rays
  Grew pale in the pity of his suffering Lord
When I fell captive, lady, to the gaze
  Of your fair eyes, fast bound in love's strong cord.

THE Laura of Petrarch's immortal love poems was no figment of the poet's imagination. According to tradition, the poet laureate of Rome wrote his poems for Laura, the daughter of Audibert de Noves and the wife of Count Hugues de Sade, an ancestor of the French nobleman who gave us *sadism*. Petrarch never revealed the real Laura's identity, guarding his secret jealously, but he wrote that he saw her for the first time in the church of St. Clara at Avignon on April 6, 1327, and that this first sight of her inspired him to become a poet. In the eighteenth century the Abbé de Sade identified her as the wife of Hugues de Sade, who bore the old man eleven children before dying of the plague in 1348, when she was only forty. But this identification is not certain. It is known only that Laura was a married woman who accepted Petrarch's devotion but refused all intimate relations. Their platonic love inspired the long series of poems that are among the most beautiful amorous verse in literature, the most famous the sonnet in praise of their first meeting quoted above. The Italians call this collection of lyrics the *Canzoniere* and it is titled *Rime in Vita e Morte di Madonna Laura*. Petrarch died long after his Laura (whoever she was), in 1374, in his seventieth year.

Lord Byron put the whole affair in a more humorous perspective when he wrote in *Don Juan*:

> *Think you, if Laura had been Petrarch's wife,*
> *He would have written sonnets all his life?*

ROMEO AND JULIET

NOT MUCH is known about Romeo and Juliet, but they were real lovers who lived in Verona, Italy, and died for each other in the year 1303. The Capulets and Montagues were among the inhabitants of the town at that time, and, as in Shakespeare's play, Romeo and Juliet were victims of their parents' senseless rivalry. Their story was told in many versions before the Bard of Avon wrote of his "star-crossed lovers." The tale can be traced to Masuccio's *Novelle* (1476) and even before that to *Ephesiaca* by the pseudonymous third- or fourth-century writer Xenophon of Ephesus. Shakespeare found the tale in Arthur Brooke's poem *The Tragicall Historye of Romeus and Juliet, containing a rare example of loves constancie . . .* (1562). *Romeo* alone means a male "lover" today and has a derisive ring, but *Romeo and Juliet* still means a pair of youthful, often helpless, lovers.

CAMILLE

IN HIS FAMOUS *La Dame aux Camélias* (1848), better known on the stage and screen as *Camille*, Alexandre Dumas *fils* wrote about Marguerite Gautier, one of the world's most endearing fictional creations, a courtesan who wore no flower other than the camellia—a white camellia for twenty-five days of the month and a red camellia the other five days. Marguerite was based on a real-life Parisian courtesan, or prostitute, Marie Duplessis, the mistress of many wealthy aristocrats and Dumas's lover for a time. Marie, who used the camellia as a trademark, died of tuberculosis at the age of only twenty-three and Dumas immortalized her in his book.

JENNY KISSED ME

A NOTHER STORY behind a poem. Leigh Hunt had been ill for several weeks during an influenza epidemic that had taken many lives, when he suddenly recovered and unexpectedly visited his friend Jane ("Jenny") Welsh Carlyle. Mrs. Carlyle impulsively jumped up and kissed him as he came in the door. This inspired Hunt's famous verse:

> *Jenny kissed me when we met,*
>   *Jumping from the chair she sat in;*
> *Time, you thief, who love to get*
>   *Sweets into your list, put that in:*
> *Say I'm weary, say I'm sad.*
>   *Say that health and wealth have missed me,*
> *Say I'm growing old, but add,*
>   *Jenny kissed me.*

James Henry Leigh Hunt (1784–1859) edited the well-known *Examiner* magazine and was imprisoned in 1813 for "libel," that is, for calling King George IV "a fat Adonis of 50." Hunt contributed greatly to the development of the light essay and through the *Examiner* introduced Shelley and Keats to the public. Another lasting line of his is "Abou Ben Adhem (may his tribe increase!)," which is from his poem "Abou Ben Adhem," wherein a man saw a vision of an angel writing the names of those who loved the Lord in a golden book. His own name wasn't included and he prayed that it would be written down as one who loved his fellow men. When the angel returned the following night, "Ben Adhem's name led all the rest."

SHERLOCK HOLMES

A. CONAN DOYLE probably named his detective after sage American author Oliver Wendell Holmes (1809–1894), who was also a professor of anatomy and physiology at Harvard. Sherlock Holmes, however, was modeled in large part on Dr. Joseph Bell (1837–1911), an eminent Edinburgh surgeon under whom Doyle studied medicine and who, like Holmes, often deduced the life and habits of a stranger just by looking at him. Doyle once admitted: "I used and amplified his methods when I tried to build up a scientific detective who solved cases on his own merits."

SIR ARTHUR
CONAN
DOYLE

It is said that Dr. John H. Watson, Holmes's Boswell, was intended as a parody of Doyle. In any event, working out of their rooms at 221B Baker Street, Holmes and Watson collaborated on some sixty cases, beginning with *A Study in Scarlet* (1887). In none of these stories did Holmes ever say "Elementary, my dear Watson," and although he was addicted to cocaine, the great detective never once cried, "Quick, Watson, the needle!"

"THE LAST OF THE MOHICANS"

THE MOHICANS live; contrary to James Fenimore Cooper's famous story, we have not seen the last of them. Cooper adopted the name of the Algonquian-speaking confederacy of tribes for the second of his "Leatherstocking Tales," and his title *The Last of the Mohicans* became an expression still used to indicate the last of any group with a certain identity or set of beliefs. But the Mohicans—at least mixed-blood remnants of the confederacy—still survive near Norwich, Connecticut, and in Stockbridge, Massachusetts, where they are part of the so-called Stockbridge Indians. The Mohicans, or Mahicans, were a powerful group in the past, occupying both banks of the upper Hudson in New York, while another branch, the Mohigans, lived in eastern Connecticut. War with the Mohawks and white settlements pushed them out of these areas—Dutch guns supplied to their enemies, hastening their dispersal—and they almost entirely lost their identity. Probably some 800 survive today.

THE REAL ROBINSON CRUSOE

DANIEL DEFOE's novel was based on the true adventures of Alexander Selkirk (1676–1721), a seaman who in 1704 asked to be put ashore on the tiny island of Más a Tierra off South America because he objected to conditions aboard ship. Selkirk spent more than four years alone on the island before being rescued and returning to England, where he became a celebrity. Defoe, a journalist, certainly heard of Selkirk's story and possibly interviewed him. In any case, he wrote the immensely successful *The Life and Strange Adventures of Robinson Crusoe* in 1719, embellishing Selkirk's account and presenting it as a true story. In truth it was the first book to reveal Defoe's genius for vivid fiction and it was written when the author was almost sixty. Selkirk never did go back to the Pacific island as Defoe had Crusoe do in two sequels, which appeared the same year. His experience had made him quite eccentric, however, and for a time he lived in a cave near his home in Largo, where it is said he taught alley cats how to do strange dances. According to another story, Selkirk lent the crudely written manuscript of his adventure to Defoe on the understanding that Defoe would "touch it up." Defoe

wrote *Robinson Crusoe*, Selkirk received not a penny from it, and the old sailor had to go back to sea for a living.

THE SEARCH FOR MOBY DICK

Mocha Dick, the stout gentleman of the latitudes, the prodigious terror whale of the Pacific, the redoubtable white sperm whale that fought and won a hundred sea battles against overwhelming odds—such was the reputation in the extravagant language of the time of the whale Herman Melville immortalized as *Moby Dick*.

There is no doubt about it—Mocha Dick was a real whale. Dick was probably first fought in 1819, the year Melville was born, and he was still terrorizing whalemen when the author was writing *Moby Dick* in 1850. So renowned was the leviathan that whenever whalers gammed, "Any news from Mocha Dick?" was a standard greeting. Boats and even ships were shattered by his immense flukes or ground to pieces in the crush of his powerful jaws. One report has him measuring out longer than a whaler—110 feet, his girth 57 feet, his jaw alone 25½ feet long. If we accept all contemporary accounts, he wrecked seven ships, destroyed some twenty boats, and killed at least thirty men. Truly a greater whale than Moby Dick in his physical prowess.

Melville probably first read about Mocha Dick in a piece by Jeremiah N. Reynolds in the May 1839 *Knickerbocker Magazine*; undoubtedly, though, he heard of him long before in the forecastles of ships in which he sailed. Reynolds told how Dick was sighted toward the coast of Chile, near the conical peak of Mocha Island, from which the white whale took his name, how, after two encounters, Dick was finally captured, his back encrusted with white shells and barnacles, and more than twenty harpoons rusted with age removed from him. But according to later accounts, Mocha Dick was fought again. Reynolds's story may have been correct except for the killing of the white whale, or it may be that other whales were later mistaken for him, but his name is mentioned in the logs of at least seven more ships, including an account of how he defeated not one but three whalers.

The last mention in history of Mocha Dick is dated August 1859, when off the Brazilian banks he is said to have been taken by a Swedish whaler. Measuring 110 feet in length, he weighed more than a ton for each foot. The whale that Melville and others believed caused the 1819 *Essex* sinking, which formed the basis for *Moby Dick*, was captured without much of a struggle. The Swedish whaler's log discloses that he was dying of old age, blind in his right eye, his head a mass of scars, eight teeth broken off, and the others all worn down. But no one would ever remember him this way. He had already become legend when

Herman Melville wrote *Moby Dick* in 1850—Melville changing his prenom to Moby probably to suggest his amazing *mobi*lity and to avoid association with the color mocha. Melville had made Dick something more than a whale. Mocha Dick, in the words of one writer, "had been absolved of mortality . . . readers of *Moby Dick* know that he swims the world unconquered, that he is ubiquitous in time and space."

THE ORIGINAL MICKEY MOUSE

*A*MONG OTHER THINGS, the expression *Mickey Mouse* means anything that is trite or commercially slick in character, such as "Mickey Mouse music." Probably the later Mickey Mouse cartoons and the use of Mickey in films with human actors suggested the term, for the early Mickey Mouse revitalized fantasy in our time and has an unassailable place in the pantheon of world folk heroes. From the time Walt Disney created him—on March 16, 1928, somewhere between Toluca, Illinois, and La Junta, Colorado, on a train carrying the cartoonist from New York to Hollywood—to the late thirties, Mickey Mouse won fame enough to satisfy the most ambitious human. In France he is called Michael Souris; in Italy, Topolino; in Japan, Miki Kuchi; in Spain, Miguel Ratoncito; in Latin America, El Ratón Miguelito; in Sweden, Muse Pigg; and in Russia, Mikki Maus. At the top of his career the mouse appeared in twenty foreign newspapers, was enshrined in Madame Tussaud's Wax Museum, and *Film Daily* estimated that over 100,000 people a day saw him on the screen. Disney patterned Mickey on a real mouse named Mortimer that he had trapped in a wastebasket and kept as a pet during his early days at the Newman Laugh O'Gram studio in Kansas City. When he proposed Mortimer as a name for his cartoon mouse, however, his wife disagreed and he came up with Mickey instead. Disney was always to be the squeaky voice of the mouse in sound films and he once told reporters that his "first born" was "the means by which I ultimately achieved all the other things I ever did—from Snow White to Disneyland." Mickey began to lose favor only when he was streamlined for later films, his tail cut off and his bare chest covered, among other "modernizations." He appeared as if he had come off an assembly line of drawing boards and this commercial slickness was reflected in phrases like "Mickey Mouse music."

In the armed forces during World War II and the Korean War (Conflict) *Mickey Mouse* meant anything childish, silly, or "chicken," such as white-glove inspections. "Mickey Mouse movie" was a humorous term GIs gave the frightening films servicemen were shown gruesomely detailing the effects of gonorrhea and syphilis, which caused many men to swear off sex for days.

MESDAMES BOVARY

GUSTAVE FLAUBERT and his publisher were charged with "immorality" when his novel *Madame Bovary* appeared in magazine form in 1856, but both were acquitted and the book was published a year later. The fictional Madame Bovary is based in part on Louise Colet (1810–1870), a French poet and novelist with whom Flaubert carried on an affair for some nine years, beginning in 1846. The real Madame Bovary lived in Paris with her husband, Hippolyte Colet, and her affair with Flaubert was the author's only serious liaison. It is hard to see where Flaubert could have gained his amazing insights into feminine psychology except by his intimate observations of this beautiful woman, who had obtained some notoriety by trying to stab a gossip columnist. However, the plot of *Madame Bovary*, and the heroine as well, to some extent, is based on the life of Delphine Delamare. This woman, well known by a close friend of Flaubert's, was the wife of a colorless country doctor. Dreaming of a more romantic life, she took many lovers, spent everything she and her husband had saved, and finally committed suicide in 1848, when only twenty-four years old.

A MASTERPIECE INSPIRED BY A COOKIE

MADELEINES, small, rich, shell-shaped cakes, are doubtless the most famous pastry in all literature. They are said to be named for their inventor, Madeleine Paulmier, a nineteenth-century pastry cook of Commercy, France, though André Simon and other gastronomes credit their invention to "one Avice, chief pastry cook to the Prince de Talleyrand." At any rate, Madeleine Paulmier and the anonymous Madeleine, for whom Avice may have named the cakes, both take their given names from Mary Magdalene. It was on a visit to his mother that Marcel Proust was served the scalloped *petite madeleine*, "so richly sensuous under its severe religious folds," whose taste brought back the flood of memories resulting in his eight-volume masterpiece, *À la Recherche du Temps Perdu*. One cynic has called Proust's work "the tale of a man who fell in love with a cookie." Proust's fragile *madeleine*, made with flour, butter, sugar, and eggs, "the same weight of each," flavored with lemon rind and baked in a small but deep scallop-shaped mold, is no relation to the English sponge bun bearing the same name.

THE REAL MAN WITHOUT A COUNTRY

CONTRARY TO what many people have believed since grade school, Edward Everett Hale's famous story "The Man Without a Country" is not a true tale. Only the name of the yarn's main character is real. In the story Lt. Philip Nolan cries out, "Damn the United States! I wish I may never hear of the United States again!," and is of course sentenced to sail the seas all his life on a Navy ship without ever hearing his country's name again. Nothing like this ever happened to the real Philip Nolan, an adventurer whose career Hale used as background. Hale later regretted using the man's name and wrote a book called *Philip Nolan's Friends* (1876), "to repair my fault, and to recall to memory a brave man," as he put it.

UNCLE TOM, SIMON LEGREE

AN AKRON WOMAN won $32,000 in damages from a Cleveland newspaper several years ago because it called her an *Uncle Tom*. The derogatory term, applied to toadying black men, mostly by other blacks, can also mean a black woman who kowtows to whites or puts up with the status quo, though *Aunt Thomasina* has been used instead. Everyone knows that *Uncle Tom* comes from the character in Harriet Beecher Stowe's *Uncle Tom's Cabin* (1852), the immensely popular American antislavery novel that caused President Lincoln to say on meeting Mrs. Stowe, "Is this the little woman whose book made such a great war?" Mrs. Stowe depicted Uncle Tom as simple, easygoing, and servile, willing to put up with anything, though it should be remembered that she intended him to be a noble, high-minded, devout Christian and that he is flogged to death by Simon Legree at the end of the book for bravely refusing to reveal the hiding place of Cassie and Emmaline, two female slaves.

Mrs. Stowe's model for Uncle Tom was a real-life slave named Josiah Henson, born in Maryland in 1789, who wrote a widely read autobiographical pamphlet. Henson was far from an *Uncle Tom* in the term's recent sense. Like many slaves, he served as the overseer, or manager, of a plantation before he escaped to Canada. Once free, he started a prosperous sawmill, founded a trade school for blacks, whites, and Indians, and helped over 100 slaves escape to Canada. When he journeyed to England on business, the Archbishop of Canterbury was so impressed with his speech and learning that he asked him what university he had studied at. "The University of Adversity," Henson replied.

Mrs. Stowe later told a visitor that she hadn't written her book: "God wrote it. I merely wrote his dictation." But she almost certainly got her idea for *Uncle Tom's Cabin* from Henson's seventy-six-page pamphlet. Her book also gives us the expression *Simon Legree*, which is still used humorously as a term for slave driver or a boss, and which comes from the name of the brutal, drunken planter—a renegade Northerner—to whom

Uncle Tom was sold. *Uncle Tom's Cabin* may be unpopular with blacks today, but in its time it was anathema to slaveowners. One piece of hate mail Mrs. Stowe received contained the ear of a slave.

UNCLE REMUS

JOEL CHANDLER HARRIS's Uncle Remus tales, collected in *Uncle Remus: His Songs and His Sayings* (1880) and many other books, were among the first and remain the greatest of black folk literature. In the books, old Uncle Remus, a former slave, entertains the young son of his employer with traditional "Negro tales" that in St. Augustine's words "spare the lowly and strike down the proud," including the "Tar-Baby" stories and other tales of Brer Rabbit (always the hero), Brer Fox, and Brer Wolf. Harris, born a "poor white" or "red-neck," a piney-woods "Georgia cracker," collected the authentic tales from numerous former slaves. One who helped him a great deal was an old gardener in Forsyth, Georgia, called Uncle Remus, and Harris named his narrator after him. The tales, however, probably go back to Africa, when they were born among people who spoke a Bantu language and of course no Uncle Remus is in them. Uncle Remus is considered "a servile, groveling 'Uncle Tom' " by some blacks today. Versions of the Brer Rabbit tales without him have been told by Arna Bontemps and Langston Hughes.

CYRANO DE BERGERAC

THE MOST FAMOUS proboscis in history. Anyone with a prodigious nose is likely to be called a *Cyrano de Bergerac* after the eponymous hero of Edmond Rostand's play of the same name (1897). Rostand's hero was based on the very real Savinien Cyrano de Bergerac (1619–1655), who had a nose as long as his fictional counterpart's and whose exploits were even more remarkable. The historical Cyrano was a brave soldier, great lover, and eloquent influential writer of comedies and tragedies. His works are said to have inspired Molière, as well as Swift's *Gulliver's Travels*. This swaggering swordsman fought countless duels with those foolish enough to insult or even mention his nose, and his single-handed duel against 100 enemies while serving as an officer in the Guards is a well-documented fact. Cyrano's exploits became legend long before Rostand fictionalized him. Surprisingly, he did not perish on the wrong end of a sword. Cyrano died as a result of a wound caused by a falling beam or stone while staying at the home of a friend.

SLAWKEN-BERGIUS AND OTHER
MORE PROMINENT PROBOSCISES:
LITERARY NOSES

Cyrano de Bergerac's is far from the only prominent nose in literary history. Besides *Pinocchio* the most famous nose-carrier is probably Hafen Slawken-Bergius, a German author in Sterne's *Tristram Shandy*, who not only has a long nose but is also a great authority on noses and has written a Latin treatise about them. Gogol's "The Nose" is probably the most famous story about a nose.

All "Nosey Parkers" may be named for Matthew Parker, who became Archbishop of Canterbury in 1559, and acquired a reputation for poking his nose into other people's business. Actually, he was an intelligent, if somewhat over-zealous, churchman of marked Protestant persuasion who introduced many administrative and ceremonial reforms into the Anglican Church. His reputation is largely undeserved, but Catholics and Puritans alike resented his good works, taking advantage of his rather long nose and dubbing him Nosey Parker, which has meant an unduly inquisitive person ever since. Parker had been chaplain to Anne Boleyn and Henry VIII before becoming archbishop. A scholar of some note, he died in 1575, aged seventy-one. All of this is at least the most popular folk etymology for Nosey Parker, but other candidates have been proposed. Richard Parker, leader of the Sheerness Mutiny in 1797, is one strong contender. This Parker poked his nose so deeply into what the military thought their exclusive bailiwick that he wound up hanged from the yardarm of H.M.S. *Sandwich* on July 30 of that year.

Another famous nose was that of the Danish astronomer and author Tycho Brahe (d. 1601), simply because it was gold. Brahe didn't cut off his nose to spite his face. He had lost his nose in a duel and kept the golden one attached to his face with cement.

Cleopatra's nose has been frequently mentioned in literature. "If the nose of Cleopatra had been shorter the whole face of the earth would have been changed," wrote the French philosopher Blaise Pascal (1623–1662) in his famous

Pensées. His proverbial observation refers to the effects of Cleopatra's charms on Caesar and Mark Antony, but a different queenly nose length, at least a moderately different one, would probably have made little difference to history. For Cleopatra's allure did not depend on her physical beauty; most sources, in fact, indicate that she wasn't a beautiful woman at all.

Keeping my nose to the grindstone, I find that Charles Darwin almost wasn't hired as the *Beagle*'s naturalist because he had a snub nose and Captain FitzRoy, a devotee of physiognomy, believed that this indicated a lack of energy and determination. And Dame Edith Sitwell was much ridiculed for her very prominent nose.

ANOTHER FAMOUS LITERARY NOSE

*I*N 1949 The House of Books Ltd. catalog offered for $75 a book described as damaged on page 95 by a spot caused by contact "with Mr. Eastman's nose when Mr. Hemingway struck him with it in a gesture of disapproval of the critical essay, 'Bull in the Afternoon.'" The book was Max Eastman's *Art and the Life of Action*, a collection of essays containing the piece Hemingway took exception to, and Hemingway had pushed it in Eastman's face to start their famous wrestling match in Max Perkins's office at Scribner's, a match both authors claimed to have won. Later Hemingway gave the book to *Esquire* publisher Arnold Gingrich. The nose smudge on page 95 was witnessed by Maxwell Perkins.

DORIAN GRAY, HERMIPPUS REVIVED, AND OTHER ETERNALLY YOUTHFUL CHARACTERS

*O*SCAR WILDE's well-known Dorian Gray (*The Picture of Dorian Gray*, 1891) has lots of company in literature among eternally youthful characters.

• Aeson, one of the Argonauts in Greek mythology, was restored to youth by Medea, who boiled him in a cauldron with magic herbs.
• According to Euripides, Iolaus, the son of Hercules, was miraculously restored to youth after his sister Maceria sacrificed herself to the gods.
• Aphrodite gave youth to the old boatman Phaon, the poet Sappho's beloved, when he ferried her (disguised as an old woman) across the sea and took no payment.

• Hebe, a daughter of Zeus and the handmaiden of the gods, for whom she poured out nectar, was not only eternally youthful, but had the power of restoring youth to whomever she chose.

• In medieval romance Ogier the Dane, 100 years old, was restored to youth by a magic ring given him by Morgan le Fay, the fairy sister of King Arthur, who then married him.

• *Hermippus Revived* (1743), a book by English author John Campbell, is the most curious work in the English language dealing with rejuvenation, if not the most curious work in literature. Wrote one critic: "Its . . . apparently serious object was to prove the possibility of prolonging of human life indefinitely by the inhalation of the breath of young girls; and great learning and ingenuity are expended upon the illustration of this thesis." Later, Elizabeth Buchan (Robert Burns lost his virginity to one of her disciples, Jean Gardner) proclaimed that she was the Third Person of the Trinity and that if she chose to breathe upon someone that person would thenceforth be immune to death.

• American author Edgar Rice Burroughs conferred immortality on his two most famous heroes, Tarzan and John Carter of Mars.

THE FIRST SADIST

*P*HYSICALLY, at least, Donatien Alphonse François, Comte de Sade (1740–1814) seems to have been one of the beautiful people, a handsome little man—five feet two, eyes of blue, but oh what those five feet could do, as a masochist might describe him. Actually, various descriptions of the miniature aristocrat exist. One writer gives him "blue eyes and blonde well kept hair," another "a delicate pale face from which two great black eyes glared," and a third tells us that he was "of such startling beauty that even in his early youth all the ladies that saw him stood stock still in rapt admiration." Unfortunately, there is no authentic portrait of de Sade, but one might expect the probable descendant of the Laura made famous in Petrarch's immortal love poems four centuries before to present a striking appearance.

In any case, this scion of the high nobility was reared by his grandmother and his uncle, a literary man who prepared him for the Collège Louis le Grand, which numbered among its other notable graduates that one-man Gestapo, Maximilien de Robespierre. School was followed by considerable active service in the army, beginning when he was only fourteen, and from there de Sade seems to have emerged a full-blown "fanatic of vice," the Philosopher of Vice and *professeur de crime* that Michelet and Taine called him.

When it happened, how it happened, would stymie a panel composed of Freud, Jung, Job, and the living Buddha. De Sade's upbringing was a factor, as were the licentious times in which he lived, his long years in prison, and perhaps there was even an organic problem. There is simply not enough reliable information available about de Sade—all his voluminous diaries were burned—and to try to make biography from a writer's fiction is fruitless. We know that de Sade married Renée-Pelagie de Montreuil for her money, trading his title for her half-million-dollar dowry.

The Count, who always encouraged people to call him Marquis, then embarked on a life of scandalous debauchery marked by habitual infidelity and sexual perversions. These included the notorious Rosa Keller affair, in which he whipped and tortured a Parisian prostitute, and what is sometimes called the Marseilles Scandal, an orgy in which he was accused of sodomy, torture, and poisoning participants with chocolate-covered bonbons containing powdered "Spanish fly." His mother-in-law, embittered about his treatment of her daughter, did her best to get him convicted on this last charge. De Sade had been in jail previously, but for the Marseilles Scandal—though the charges were ultimately proved untrue in great part—he was sentenced to death. He fled to Italy. On returning to Paris three years later, he found a none-too-comfortable jail cell waiting for him.

Though the authorities dropped the death penalty, de Sade from 1777 on would spend all but thirteen of his remaining thirty-seven years in prisons or in the lunatic asylum at Charenton. While imprisoned he began writing the novels and plays that give his name to the language. The *120 Days of Sodom* (1785), in which six hundred variations of the sex instinct are listed, *Justine, or Good Conduct Well Chastised* (1790), and *The Story of Juliette, or Vice Amply Rewarded* (1792) are among his works replete with myriad descriptions of sexual cruelty. Never able or willing to reform, de Sade died at the age of seventy-four, while still at Charenton, where he wrote and directed fashionable plays performed by the inmates, many of whom he corrupted in the process.

Sometimes his insights were deep and remarkable, but his was in the main the disordered, deranged mind reflected in his life and licentious work. *Sadism*, the derivation of satisfaction or pleasure from the infliction of pain on others, can be sexual in nature or stem from a variety of motives, including frustration or feelings of inferiority. De Sade's life indicates that many such causes molded his twisted personality. His final testament read in part: "The ground over my grave should be sprinkled with acorns so that all traces of my grave shall disappear so that, as I hope, this reminder of my existence may be wiped from the memory of mankind."

THE FIRST MASOCHIST

*I*N *masochism* the individual derives sexual pleasure through having pain inflicted on himself, but as with its opposite, *sadism*, the use of the term has broadened, now including pleasure derived from self-denial and from hardship and suffering in general. The word is taken from the name of Leopold von Sacher-Masoch (1835–1895), an Austrian novelist whose characters dwelt lovingly on the sexual pleasures of pain, just as he did.

Sacher-Masoch's early childhood was a terror of bloody, violent tales told him by both his wet nurse, Handscha, and his father, a police chief. His mother seems to have figured little in his formative years. At the windows of the elegant edifice that housed this well-to-do, sophisticated, and extremely intelligent man was always the trembling, baffled child who had been weaned on tales of cruel, dominating females like the Black Czarina and the concubine Esther; a child whose earliest memories were of brutal, half-savage Galician peasants. Outside, the house was surrounded by flowers, but they were mostly clumps of poisonous aconite and deadly nightshade, a Dr. Rappacini's garden, for the boy grew up in the midst of one of the bloodiest revolutionary periods in history.

Leopold received his doctorate in law when only nineteen, but had begun to act out his sexual fantasies even before this. He became the slave to a number of mistresses and two wives before he died, even signing one contract with a mistress that read in part: "Herr Leopold von Sacher-Masoch gives his word of honor to Frau Pistor to become her slave and to comply unreservedly . . . Frau Pistor, on her side, promises to wear furs . . . when she is in a cruel mood." Furs so fascinated him that they became prominent in his most widely read novel, *Venus in Furs*, and his first marriage was marked by a private ceremony in which he wore white tie and tails and his bride took her vows in a long fur coat. *Venus* not only described *masochism* fully but went far in explaining the pathetic life of a man who could be satisfied only by birches, studded whips, and the betrayals of the women he loved.

A prolific, talented novelist who had published several scholarly histories and had once been a professional actor, Sacher-Masoch became a leading literary figure of his time. But he finally suffered a complete breakdown before turning fifty, his second wife committing him to an asylum after he had tried to kill her on several occasions. In a fitting ending to his bizarre life, his wife officially announced that he had died, even mourning him, ten years before his actual death. The pre-Freudian neurologist Richard von Krafft-Ebing probably first used Sacher-Masoch's name to describe his ailment, and the word *masochism* was first recorded in 1893. (See also *Sadism*; *Tasteless Authors*.)

A QUIZ WITH CHARACTER(S)

Match each character with the book or play in which he or she appears:

1. Captain Ahab	A.	*Uncle Tom's Cabin*
2. Brett Ashley	B.	*The Hairy Ape*
3. Catherine Barkley	C.	*The Scarlet Letter*
4. Chingachgook	D.	*Gone with the Wind*
5. Henry Fleming	E.	*Of Mice and Men*
6. Eugene Gant	F.	*A Farewell to Arms*
7. Clyde Griffiths	G.	*The Caine Mutiny*
8. Tom Joad	H.	*Winterset*
9. Robert Jordan	I.	*Leatherstocking Tales*
10. Wolf Larsen	J.	*The Last of the Mohicans*
11. Simon Legree	K.	*Look Homeward, Angel*
12. Jeeter Lester	L.	*Ethan Frome*
13. Mio	M.	*Moby Dick*
14. Scarlett O'Hara	N.	*The Sea Wolf*
15. Hester Prynne	O.	*The Red Badge of Courage*
16. Lt. Comm. Queeg	P.	*The Grapes of Wrath*
17. Lennie Small	Q.	*The Sun Also Rises*
18. Uncas	R.	*Tobacco Road*
19. Yank	S.	*An American Tragedy*
20. Zeena	T.	*For Whom the Bell Tolls*

ANSWERS: 1. M, Herman Melville 2. Q, Ernest Hemingway 3. F, Ernest Hemingway 4. I, James Fenimore Cooper 5. O, Stephen Crane 6. K, Thomas Wolfe 7. S, Theodore Dreiser 8. P, John Steinbeck 9. T, Ernest Hemingway 10. N, Jack London 11. A, Harriet Beecher Stowe 12. R, Erskine Caldwell 13. H, Maxwell Anderson 14. D, Margaret Mitchell 15. C, Nathaniel Hawthorne 16. G, Herman Wouk 17. E, John Steinbeck 18. J, James Fenimore Cooper 19. B, Eugene O'Neill 20. L, Edith Wharton

FINNEGANS WAKE

*T*HIS IS the little-known American-Irish song "Finnegans Wake," which gave James Joyce the title for his novel *Finnegans Wake*. It was a song of Irish immigrant laborers in New York City and the lyrics go on to tell how Finnegan falls and is pronounced dead, only to revive when he gets hold of the whiskey bottle passed around at his wake. According to Padraic Colum, "James Joyce found in this song a comic statement of universal mythology—the Fall of Man, the Partaking of the Water of Life, the Renewal of Existence—and used it for the title of his last and enigmatic book."

Tim Finnegan liv'd in Walkin Street a gentleman Irish mighty odd. He had a tongue both rich and sweet, an' to rise in the world he carried a hod, Now Tim had a sort of a tipplin' way With the love of the liquor he was born, An' to help him on with his work each day, He'd a drop of the craythur ev'ry morn.

CHORUS
Whack fol the dah, dance to your partner Welt the flure yer trotters shake, Wasn't it the truth I told you, Lot's of fun at Finnegan's Wake.

THE FIRST ENGLISH PYGMALION

*T*HOMAS DAY, the eccentric or mad author of *Sanford and Merton* (1748–1789), wanted to "educate a wife" for himself, wanted his new wife to be as "simple as a mountain girl, in her dress, her diet, and her manners; fearless and intrepid as the Spartan wives and Roman heroines." Selecting two pretty eleven-year-old foundlings, he tested Sabrina and Lucretia, as he named them, by dropping melted sealing wax on their bare skin to see if they would scream, and by firing blank cartridges at them to see if they would jump. Fortunately for the young women, neither Sabrina nor Lucretia worked out for Day and he returned them to their respective foundling hospitals before they had completed his training program. Day himself died in 1789, aged forty-one, but there is no further mention of his "wives" in history.

RAISING THE DICKENS

NOVELIST Charles Dickens wasn't a boisterous man given to causing mischief or raising havoc. Neither were Micawber, Mr. Pickwick, David Copperfield, Steerforth, Oliver Twist, Scrooge, Tiny Tim, Sarah Gamp, Uriah Heep, Gradgrind, Fagin, Little Nell, the Artful Dodger, or any of Dickens's immortal characters responsible for the expression *raising the dickens*, as some people believe. *Dickens* in this case and in the phrase *go to the dickens* is, like *deuce*, just an old euphemism for *devil*, common in English since Shakespeare's time. Shakespeare, in fact, is the first to be credited with it, in *The Merry Wives of Windsor* (1598): "I cannot tell what the dickens his name is."

FICTION BECOMES REALITY

SCIENCE FICTION is usually cited as the literary genre where near-perfect examples of *promesia* ("memory of the future") are most often found. But it would be hard to find a better example of fiction's becoming reality than popular novelist Morgan Robertson's novel *Futility* (1898). Published fourteen years before the *Titanic* sank in history's most famous marine disaster, it told of a great "unsinkable" luxury liner named the *Titan* that sank on its maiden voyage after hitting an iceberg, with the loss of almost all passengers because there weren't enough lifeboats aboard. More similarities between the *Titan* and *Titanic* are shown in the chart below:

	TITAN	TITANIC
Ship length	800 feet	882.5 feet
Ship tonnage	75,000	66,000
Propellors	3	3
Speed at impact	25 knots	23 knots
Number of passengers	3,000	2,207
Number of lifeboats	24	20
Month of sinking	April	April

INVENTIVE FICTION

So accurate was Jules Verne's description of a periscope in *Twenty Thousand Leagues Under the Sea* that a few years later the actual inventor of the instrument was refused permission for an original patent on it.

SUICIDES CAUSED BY BOOKS

It's said that the philosopher Cleombrotus killed himself after reading Plato's *Phaedo* "so that he might enjoy the happiness of the future life so enchantingly described." The *Phaedo* is a dialogue narrating the discussion that took place between Socrates and his friends during the last hour of his life. This work also influenced the Roman Stoic philosopher Cato, Caesar's chief political rival, when he committed suicide by falling on his sword after realizing that his cause against the Caesarians was hopeless. Cato had spent all of the last night of his life reading Plato's *Phaedo*.

Eighteenth-century English poet Eustace Budgell was indirectly influenced by the *Phaedo* when he committed suicide by drowning himself, for he left behind a note reading: "What Cato did and Addison approved cannot be wrong."

Goethe's romance *The Sorrows of Young Werther* (1774), in which the hero Werther kills himself, probably influenced many suicides and it is known that one young lady, a Fräulein von Lassling, took her life immediately after reading it.

Similarly, the song "Black Sunday" is said to have inspired a number of deaths during the 1930s, and its author killed himself years later on a Sunday while listening to it.

Euthanasia: The Aesthetics of Suicide (1894) by James A. Harden-Hickey, self-styled King of Trinidad, no doubt influenced many people to kill themselves, describing as it does some ninety poisons and fifty instruments to use to commit suicide, and illustrating many methods with line drawings. Harden-Hickey killed himself by taking an overdose of morphine in 1898, aged forty-four.

KILLING WORDS

The celebrated but impoverished Greek poet Archilochus (seventh century B.C.) fell in love with a young woman who refused to marry him because her father detested him. The "scorpion-tongued" poet proceeded to write such biting satires of them that both father and daughter hanged themselves. Another

Greek poet who wielded killing words was Hippōnax of Ephesus (fl. c.540 B.C.). His physical ugliness was ridiculed by the artists Būpalas and Athēnis, who erected a mocking statue of him in the marketplace. The satirical poet lashed them with his bitter verses in retaliation and they hanged themselves in despair.

METICULOUS RESEARCH

WHILE WRITING *Roots* and trying to imagine how it felt to be a slave shipped to America aboard a slaver, the late Alex Haley, as reported in the press, boarded a freighter from Africa to the United States and got permission from the captain to spend every night stretched out naked on a plank in the cold black hold of the ship.

Frederick Forsyth's novel *The Dogs of War* (1974) tells of a band of mercenaries who overthrow an African government by killing its president. Four years after the book was published it was claimed that Forsyth and thirteen other men had in 1972 attempted to oust the government of Equatorial Guinea by kidnapping President Francisco Marcias Nguema. Unlike the plot in his book, Forsyth's plan failed, though it reportedly cost him $200,000.

The World of Words: From Letters to Language

INTERNATIONAL ABC'S

OF THE sixty-five alphabets now used around the world the Cambodian has the most letters, with seventy-two, and the Rotokas, spoken on Bougainville Island in the South Pacific, has the least, with eleven. Among others, the Russian alphabet has forty-one letters, the Armenian thirty-eight, the Persian thirty-two, the Latin twenty-five, the Greek twenty-four, the French twenty-three, the Hebrew twenty-two, the Italian twenty, and the Burmese nineteen. The German and Dutch alphabets, like the English, have twenty-six letters.

WORD POSSIBILITIES

*T*HE TWENTY-SIX letters of the English alphabet may be transposed 620,448,401,733,239,439,369,000 times. For all the inhabitants of the globe could not in a thousand million of years write out all the possible transpositions of the twenty-six letters, even supposing that each wrote forty pages daily, each page containing forty different transpositions of the letters.

—William Walsh (1892)

VOWEL VAGARIES

*T*HE MOST common vowel sound in English is the upside down *e* of the International Phonetic Alphabet, the *unaccented syllable* that is found in so many English words—as in the first syllable of *attend*, *observer*, and *alleviate*; in the last syllable of words like *custom* and *sofa*; and in most pronunciations of the indefinite article, such as *a man*. Alistair Cooke makes this point in discussing the lack of phonetic training in England and America, venturing that ninety-nine scholars in a hundred wouldn't know it.

Few would know, either, that *w* and *y* are also letters that can represent vowel sounds, of which there are as many as twenty-three in English.

Fewer still would know that the English word with the most consecutive vowel sounds is *queueing*, lining up, which has five.

The word with the most consonants in a row? Maybe the six in *latchstring*.

In order of frequency of use, the seven vowel sounds are *ə, a, i, o, u, w, y*.

When a certain Dr. Vowel died in the early nineteenth century, a certain Dr. Barton Warren commented to a friend: "Thank Heaven it was neither *you* nor *I*!"

THE STORY OF O

*O*F THE twenty-six letters in the alphabet, O has the most interesting and best-documented story. It began its life as a pictograph, common to many languages, describing the human eyeball within its protected socket, some drawings of it in ancient alphabets even giving it a dot in the center for a pupil. In time the socket and pupil were eliminated from the pictograph and we find it in North Semitic as a plain, full circle that was called "the eye." From there it passed into the Greek alphabet. Unlike the other letters, it has undergone no other major structural change in over 27,000 years.

In Anglo-Saxon, O's name was *oedel*, "home." It later became probably the only English letter to have a poem written about it by a philosopher (Dr. William Whewell):

A headless man had a letter (o) to write,
He who read it (naught) had lost his sight.
The dumb repeated it (naught) word for word,
And deaf was the man who listened and heard (naught).

O, the oldest of letters, is the only symbol on the famed Moabite stone that closely resembles a letter in any modern alphabet. This block of black basalt contains a thirty-four-line inscription giving an account of a war waged by the king of Moab, but is far more important as the earliest representation of the Phoenician alphabet, dating back to the ninth century B.C.; it helped to unlock many secrets of ancient writing. After the stone was discovered in 1868 by the Reverend F. A. Klein, a German missionary traveling in the area known today as Jordan, French and English scholars tried to claim it for history. But the Arabs had long considered the stone a fertility symbol and smashed it into pieces, which they distributed among their people rather than have the stone contaminated by foreigners. Luckily, the French had made impressions of the writing. They later managed to buy back almost all the pieces from the Arabs and restore the stone, which is now in the Louvre.

Giotto's O is another famous O. Tradition holds that the great Italian artist Giotto di Bondone was a shepherd boy when discovered by the Florentine painter Giovanni Cimabue. While serving his apprenticeship to Cimabue, he was approached by a papal messenger, who had been sent all over Italy to find artists to work on a new church. Giotto was asked to submit a drawing that could be shown to the Pope as evidence of his talent, and with a single flourish of his brush he drew a perfect circle on a panel, *Giotto's O* being proof enough for the Pope.

O is also the commonest single-letter surname, there being thirteen in the Brussels telephone directory alone. There is no evidence of an O living in the Japanese town of O. This O is one of the four shortest place names in the world, the others being the Norwegian village of A; U in the Pacific Caroline Islands; and Y, a village in France, whose residents are called *upsiloniens*. In America we once had a 6, West Virginia, but the best we can offer today are seven two-letter towns, including Ed, Kentucky, and a place in South Carolina called 96, which oldtime baseball fans may remember as the number Yankee pitcher Bill Voiselle wore on his uniform in honor of his hometown.

E

E IS THE most commonly used letter in English. It is followed in order of use by *t, a, i, s, o, n, h, r, d, l, u, c, m, f, w, y, p, g, b, v, k, j, q, x, z.*

The most common vowel in English is obviously *e* and the most common initial letter is *t*.

LIPOGRAMS: BOOKS
WITHOUT CERTAIN LETTERS

*I*F ANYONE has ever discovered the value of lipograms, except as exercises in verbal ingenuity, she or he ain't telling. A lipogram is "a written work composed of words chosen so as to avoid the use of specific alphabetic characters," and the first practitioner of lipography is said to have been the Greek lyric poet Lasus, born in Achaia in about 548 B.C. The next great poet to write a letterless poem was Lasus's pupil Pindar, who wrote *Ode minus Segma* late in the fifth century B.C. The Greek *Odyssey of Tryphiodorus*, however, outdoes both Lasus and Pindar. It consists of twenty-six books, with no *a* in the first book, no *b* in the second, no *c* in the third, and so on. Someone said of the work that it would have been better if the author left out the other letters, too.

Spanish playwright Lope Félix de Vega Carpio (1562–1635) wrote each of his five novels without using one of the vowels, but Lope de Vega is far better known for the 2,200 plays tradition says he completed (close to 500 survive). Another famous European lipogram is Ronden's *Pièce sans A* (1816). This was perhaps influenced by German poet Gottlob Burmann (1737–1805), who wrote some 130 poems without employing the letter *r* and for seventeen years omitted *r* from his daily conversation, never speaking his own name, which he hated anyway.

James Thurber wrote a story about a country where the letter *o* was illegal, but the best-known (probably because it is the only) American book without a certain letter is Ernest Vincent Wright's *Gadsby* (1939), which has no *e*'s in it. The author, a California musician, pried the *e* off his typewriter keyboard to restrain himself and typed a 267-page, 50,000-word epic using no word containing that most common of vowels. Sample paragraph (and try writing just a sentence without using an *e*): "Upon this basis I am going to show you how a bunch of bright young folks did find a champion; a man with boys and girls of his own; a man of so dominating and happy individuality that youth is drawn to him as is a fly to a sugar bowl. It is a story about a small town. It is not a gossipy yarn; nor is it a dry monotonous account. It is . . . a practical discarding of that worn-out notion that 'a child don't know anything.' "

Aside from his great lipogram, E. V. Wright is best known for his poem "When Father Carves the Duck":

> *We all look on with anxious eyes*
> *When father carves the duck,*
> *And mother almost always sighs*
> *When father carves the duck.*

This did considerably better than *Gadsby*, which sold about fifty copies. Since Wright's day the *e*-less novel *La Disparitim* (1969) has been published by

French author George Perec. (See also *Books Without Characters, Words, or Pictures.*)

i

WHEN E(dward) E(stlin) Cummings wrote his name, he wrote it e e cummings, refusing to capitalize it, as if to divorce himself from vanity and selfhood. He felt the same about the word *I*, not using the first person perpendicular, always writing it as *i*, even in the title of his book of poems *i* (1953). Cummings's poetry actually depended to a great degree on typographical distortion—unconventional punctuation, spacing, run-on words. While he was serving in France with an American ambulance corps during the First World War, one of his letters written in this special style aroused the suspicion of a censor and he was thrown into a French concentration camp for three months on an unfounded charge of treasonable correspondence, an experience that resulted in his book *The Enormous Room*. But Cummings's use of *i* for *I* wasn't original. Modest English author Benjamin Stillingfleet (1702–1771) did the same thing long before him. In fact, before the introduction of printing the nominative for the person speaking could be written as either a lowercase letter or as a capital. Printers standardized the capitalized form because a little *i* was easily dropped from lines in typesetting—that this was probably a matter of convenience, not egotism, can also be seen by the fact that *me* and *my* weren't capitalized.

Our word *I* is a shortening of the much older *ik*, the vowel in this word originally pronounced like the *i* in *his*, not *ai*. The letter *I* comes from the stylized drawing of the Phoenician alphabet and is thought to have been based on a picture of the human finger. People at first didn't have to remember to dot their *i*'s. The dot on the *i* wasn't added to the letter until the eleventh century, when scribes introduced it to distinguish two *i*'s coming together (as in *filii*) from the letter *u*. Up until the nineteenth century the written and printed *i* and *j* were interchangeable and dictionaries didn't treat them as separate letters.

H

THE REASON Dr. Johnson made his famous remark "I'd rather dine with Jack Ketch [the public hangman] than Jack Wilkes" is seldom told. John Wilkes had written a comic review of Johnson's *Dictionary* in which he addressed the great man's pronouncement that "The letter 'h' seldom, perhaps never, begins any but the first syllable." Wilkes wrote: "The author of this observation must be a man of quick appre-hension and of a most compre-hensive genius," going on in the same fashion for several paragraphs. Johnson never forgave him.

C IS FOR *OKBURN*

ONE OF THE strangest stories attached to any letter is told about *c*. It seems that an Admiral George Cockburn led the incendiaries who demolished the *National Intelligencer* when the British burned down Washington during the War of 1812. The gentlemanly incendiary had his men melt down all the *c*'s in the newspaper office "so that later they can't abuse my name."

R, THE DOG LETTER

THOSE WHO pronounce Harvard "Hahvad" won't find any precedent in the traditional pronunciation of the letter *r*. Since Roman times *r* has been thought of as the "dog's letter," or the "snarling letter," because its sound resembles the snarling of a dog—*r-r-r-r*. Ben Jonson, in his *English Grammar made for the Benefit of all Strangers* (1636), put it this way: "R is the dog's letter, and hurreth in the sound; the tongue striking the inner palate, with a trembling about the teeth." Shakespeare has Juliet's nurse in *Romeo and Juliet* call *r* the "dog-name," when she tells Romeo that his name and rosemary, an herb associated with weddings, both begin with an *r*. In parts of America, especially the Midwest, *r* is still pronounced as the "dog letter," while in other regions, particularly parts of New England and the South, it is sounded as "ah."

F f

PERSONAL NAMES beginning with a double *f* in English, such Ffoulkes or Ffrench, originated as mistakes when the medieval or Old English capital F, which in script appears to be two small entwined *f*'s, was transferred to print as two lowercase *f*'s. No word in English should really begin with two *f*'s.

X

ONE THEORY holds that the letter *x* stands for a kiss because it originally represented a highly stylized picture of two mouths touching. Furthermore, in early times illiterates often signed documents with a St. Andrew's cross or *x* and kissed that *x* to show their good faith (as they did with any cross or the Bible), which reinforced the association. But these explanations may be folk etymology, as may be the story that mathematically the *x* is a "multiplier"—in this case of love and delight.

Z

Z HAS BEEN CALLED *izzard*, *zed*, and *zee* in English. It has been considered useless by many writers, including Shakespeare, who wrote: "Thou whoreson Zed! Thou unnecessary letter!" It was the last letter in the Roman as well as the English alphabet.

ACROSTICS

From your bright sparkling Eyes I was undone;
Rays, you have; more transparent than the Sun,
Amidst its glory in the rising Day
None can you equal in your bright array;
Constant in your calm and unspotted mind,
Equal to all, but will to none Prove kind,
So knowing, seldome one so Young, you'll Find,
Ah! woe's me, that I should Love and conceal
Long have I wished, but never dared reveal,
Even though severely Love's Pains I feel;
Xerxes that great, wasn't free from Cupid's Dart,
And all the great Heroes, felt the smart.

The above is an acrostic poem by, of all people, George Washington, the first letters in each line of the poem spelling out his lover's name. But acrostics can be any composition (poems, puzzles, etc.) in which certain letters of the lines, taken in order, form a word, phrase, or sentence that is the subject of the composition. When the last letters of lines do this, the acrostic is sometimes called a *telestich* (from the Greek *tele*, "far," and *stichos*, "row").

Acrostic derives from the Greek *akros*, "extreme," and *stichos*, "row or line of verse." The term was first applied to the prophecies of the Greek Erythraean sibyl, which were written on separate pages, the initial letters forming a word when the pages were arranged in order. Another famous early acrostic was made from the Greek for "Jesus Christ, God's Son, Savior": *Iesus Christos, Theou, Uios, Soter*. The first letters of each word (and the first two letters of *Christos*) taken in order spell *ichthus*, Greek for "fish," which became a Christian symbol for Jesus. There are even earlier examples of acrostics in the Bible. In Hebrew, for instance, Psalm 119 is an acrostic in which the first letters of each of the twenty-two stanzas descend in alphabetical order. Such alphabetical acrostics are usually called *abecedarian hymns* or *abecedarius* and there are more complicated species of them in which each word in every line begins with the same letter:

> *An Austrian army, awfully array'd*
> *Boldly by battery besieged Belgrade*, etc.

The term *acrostic* is sometimes applied to words formed from the initial letters of other words, though such words are usually called acronyms *(q.v.).* The Greek *ichthus* above is an example of this, as is the English word *cabal.* *Cabal* really derives from an early Hebrew word, but its meaning was reinforced because the first letters of the surnames of five members of Charles II's ministry Clifford, Ashley, Buckingham, Arlington, and Lauderdale) spelled out *cabal* and the ministers were well-known for their political plots and secret intrigues.

Acrostic poems have never been highly regarded by literary critics. Samuel Butler wrote that a certain "small poet" made "the outside of his verses even, like a bricklayer, by a line of rhyme and acrostic, and [filled] the middle with rubbish." Addison didn't know which was worse, acrostics or their inventors. "I have seen some of them," he wrote, "where the verses have not only been edged by a name at each extremity, but have the same name running down like a seam through the middle of the poem."

The acrostic cited by Addison is called a triple acrostic. An example of a double acrostic can be seen in the puzzle below; the answer gives both the name of a famous writer and his pseudonym:

1. By Apollo was my first made
2. A shoemaker's tool
3. An Italian patriot
4. A tropical fruit

ANSWER:

1. L yr E
2. A w L
3. MazzinI
4. Banan A

(Charles Lamb, Elia)

CHARLES LAMB

I won't go into *quadruple* acrostics. (See also *Acronyms; In Praise of Palindromes; Anagrams.)*

LIVING WORDS

THE LIMITATIONS OF "picture writing," the precursor of the alphabet, can be seen in the old story about Darius the Great, king of Persia, who received a hieroglyphic message from his enemies the Scythians. The Scythians had sent him a live mouse, frog, bird, and arrows instead of pictures of these things. Darius interpreted this to mean they would surrender come morning—the arrows, he thought, meant they would give up their arms, mouse and frog represented surrender of the land and water, and the bird meant the Scythians would soon fly away from the field of battle. Accordingly, Darius went to bed without preparing his troops for attack and the Scythians raided his camp that night and overwhelmed his armies. They then explained *their* interpretation of the live hieroglyphics: the bird meant the Persians would never escape the Scythians unless they could literally fly, the mice and frog meant that the only other way they could escape would be to turn themselves into mice and burrow through the ground or into frogs and hide out in the swamps, and the arrows meant they would never escape the infallible Scythian weapons.

THE OLDEST ENGLISH WORDS

SCHOLARLY RESEARCH still unpublished contends that the following little words "of an Indo-European substrate" have the oldest lineage in English:

apple (apal)   *gold (gol)*   *bad (bad)*   *tin (tin)*

EGYPTIAN ENGLISH

ETYMOLOGISTS ARE at a loss to explain the many very similar words with identical meanings in Egyptian and English, languages that belong to completely different families. The two languages may have been related somehow long ago, but no one knows for sure. Some of these coincidences follow:

ENGLISH	EGYPTIAN
abode	abut
attack	atakh
nature	natr
twist	tust
youth	uth

UNIVERSAL ENGLISH

*E*NGLISH HAS borrowed words from practically every language. The following sentence, for example, contains words from twenty-one different tongues. Try to identify the italicized ones. Answers are below in order.

The *thug loafed* at a *damask*-covered *table* on the *café balcony Wednesday* eating *goulash* and drinking *chocolate* with a half-*caste* brunette in a *kimono*-sleeved *lemon frock* and a *crimson angora* wool *shawl*, while he deciphered a code notation from a *canny smuggler* of *tea cargoes* on the back of the *paper* menu.

ANSWERS:

1. *thug*—Hindustani
2. *loafed*—Danish
3. *damask*—Hebrew
4. *table*—Latin
5. *café*—French
6. *balcony*—Italian
7. *Wednesday*—Anglo-Saxon
8. *goulash*—Hungarian
9. *chocolate*—Nahuatl
10. *caste*—Portuguese
11. *kimono*—Japanese
12. *lemon*—Arabic
13. *frock*—Old High German
14. *crimson*—Sanskrit
15. *angora*—Turkish
16. *shawl*—Persian
17. *canny*—Scottish
18. *smuggler*—Dutch
19. *tea*—Chinese
20. *cargoes*—Spanish
21. *paper*—Greek

THE TWELVE MOST COMMONLY USED WRITTEN ENGLISH WORDS

1. the	4. to	7. that	10. it
2. of	5. a	8. is	11. for
3. and	6. in	9. I	12. as

*T*HE ABOVE LIST is based on a count made by the *World Almanac* (1950) of 240,000 words from books, magazines, and newspapers. It is seconded by a *Guinness Book of World Records* study, but the *American Heritage Word Frequency Book* (1971) doesn't agree, listing the twelve most commonly written words as: *the, of, and, a, to, in, is, you, that, it, he,* and *for*—in that order.

Stuart Berg Flexner, in *I Hear America Talking* (1976), says that the four most common *spoken* English words are *I, you* (these two account for 10 percent of all "informal conversation"), *the,* and *a.* The rest of the top fifty spoken words (in no special order) are: *he, she, it, we, they, me, him, her, them, what, an, on, to, of, in, for, with, out, from, over, and, about, now, just, not, that, this, is, get, was, will, have, don't, do, are, want, can, would, go, think, say, be, see, know, tell,* and *thing.* Flexner points out that ten basic words account for 25 percent of all English speech, fifty simple words account for about 60 percent, and just 1,500–2,000 words account for 99 percent of all we say. Seventy words make up 50 percent of our written language. Amazing statistics, considering that the English language contains about 800,000 words (including technical terms).

Shakespeare possessed a large vocabulary, having used 22,000 different words in his plays as compared to the 6,000 different words used in the entire Old Testament. Today the average American uses something like 2,000 words in everyday speech, while extremely learned persons use as many as 60,000 of the 800,000 or so words in English, which has the largest vocabulary of any language.

TO A THESAURUS

O precious codex, volume, tome,
  Book, writing, compilation, work,
Attend the while I pen a pome,
  A jest, a jape, a quip, a quirk.

For I would pen, engross, indite,
  Transcribe, set forth, compose, address,
Record, submit—yea, even write
  An ode, an elegy to bless—

To bless, set store by, celebrate,
  Approve, esteem, endow with soul,
Commend, acclaim, appreciate,
  Immortalize, laud, praise, extol

Thy merit, goodness, value, worth,
  Experience, utility—
O manna, honey, salt of earth,
  I sing, I chant, I worship thee!

How could I manage, live, exist,
  Obtain, produce, be real, prevail,
Be present in the flesh, subsist,
  Have place, become, breathe or inhale

Without thy help, recruit, support,
  Opitulation, furtherance,
Assistance, rescue, aid, resort,
  Favour, sustention and advance?

Alas! Alack! and well-a-day!
  My case would then be dour and sad,
Likewise distressing, dismal, grey,
  Pathetic, mournful, dreary, bad.

Though I could keep this up all day,
  This lyric, elegiac song,
Meseems hath come the time to say
  Farewell! Adieu! Good-bye! So long!
                    —Franklin P. Adams

BIBLICAL WORDS

THE ECCENTRIC British theologian Dr. Thomas Hartwell Horne (1780–1862) worked as a librarian in the British Museum days and dissected the King James Version of the Bible nights, his industry resulting in his truly amazing *Introduction to the Critical Study and Knowledge of the Holy Scriptures* (1818), probably the most painstakingly thorough statistical study of a book ever published. Here are some of the fruits of the Doctor of Divinity's labor:

	OLD TESTAMENT	NEW TESTAMENT	TOTAL
Books in the Bible	39	27	66
Chapters	929	260	1,189
Verses	23,214	7,959	31,173
Words	593,493	181,253	774,746
Letters	2,728,100	838,380	3,566,480

- The shortest book in the Bible is the Third Epistle of John, 294 words.
- The longest book is the Book of Psalms.
- The shortest chapter is Psalm 117, two verses.
- The longest chapter is Psalm 119, 176 verses.
- The shortest verse is John 11:35, "Jesus wept."
- The longest verse is verse 9 in Chapter 8 of the Book of Esther, a ninety-word description of the Persian Empire.
- The midpoint of the Bible, by word count, is Psalm 117, verse 2.
- The longest personal name in the Bible is Maher-shalal-hash-baz, symbolic name of Isaiah's second son (Isaiah 8:3).
- The word *Jehovah* occurs 6,855 times.
- The word *Lord* appears 1,855 times.
- Only in the Book of Esther is the name of God not mentioned.
- The word *and* occurs 46,277 times.
- All the letters in the English alphabet save *j* are contained in the twenty-first verse of the seventh chapter of Ezra.
- The thirty-seventh chapter of Isaiah and the nineteenth chapter of 2 Kings are identical; so are the last two verses of 2 Chronicles and the opening verses of Ezra; Ezra 2 and Nehemiah 7 are also identical.

Dr. Horne did the same job on the Apocrypha, in which he found 125,185 words and 1,063,876 letters. But three anonymous researchers, at least one of whom repeated his Herculean labors, later disputed some of his findings:

- One says that the Bible actually contains 773,692 words, but this may be because he used a different method to count hyphenated words.
- Another points out that longer by two letters than the personal name given by Horne is the title in the caption of Psalm 22 in Hebrew: Al-'Cyyeleth Hash-Shahar (twenty letters).
- The three researchers, working independently, put the Bible's total letters at 3,586,589; 3,586,489; and 3,567,180 respectively.

EARLY ENGLISH

Oᴎʟʏ ᴡᴏʀᴅs of Anglo-Saxon origin are found in Edna St. Vincent Millay's play *The King's Henchman* (1927), which is set in tenth-century England.

DID SHAKESPEARE WRITE THE BIBLE?

Aᴄᴄᴏʀᴅɪɴɢ ᴛᴏ some numerologists, yes—or at least he helped to write it. Their "evidence":

1. The King James Version of the Bible was published in 1610, when Shakespeare was forty-six.
2. *Shake* is the forty-sixth word of the Psalm 46.
3. *Spear* is the forty-sixth word from the end in the Psalm 46.

PLURALITY

We'll begin with a box and the plural is boxes,
But the plural of ox should be oxen, not oxes;
We speak of a brother and also of brethren,
But though we say mother, we never say methren.
Then the masculine pronouns are he, his and him,
But imagine the feminine she, shis and shim.
So English, I fancy you all will agree,
Is the silliest language you ever did see.

—Anonymous, nineteenth century

SHORTEST SENTENCE CONTAINING THE ENTIRE ALPHABET

*L*OGOLEPTS WOULD take issue with *The Guinness Book of World Records*, which says that the shortest English sentence containing all twenty-six letters of the alphabet is: "Jackdaws love my big sphinx of quartz." That's thirty-one letters. "Frowzy things plumb vex'd Jack Q." has only twenty-seven and there are certainly others just as short. Such a sentence is called a pangram.

ONE PICTURE IS WORTH A THOUSAND WORDS

*T*HE CHINESE PROVERB that inspired this cliché goes to greater extremes: "One picture is worth more than ten thousand words." Pictures certainly aren't always, or mostly, ten thousand or a thousand times more versatile than words. "If you're not convinced," author William Childress writes, "fall in a lake and start gulping water—and then, instead of screaming the word HELP, hold up a picture of yourself drowning. If someone pulls you out, I lose my argument."

FROZEN WORDS

AN OLD STORY from the Texas Panhandle tells of a winter so cold that spoken words froze in the air, fell entangled on the ground, and had to be fried up in a skillet before the letters would re-form and any sense could be made of them. The idea is an ancient one, used by Rabelais and familiar to the Greek dramatist Antiphanes, who is said to have used it in praising the work of Plato: "As the cold of certain cities is so intense that it freezes the very words we utter, which remain congealed till heat of summer thaws them, so the mind of youth is so thoughtless that the wisdom of Plato lies there frozen, as it were, till it is thawed by the refined judgement of mature age."

INVENTED WORDS

Men ever had, and ever will have, leave
To coin new words well suited to the age.
Words are like leaves, some wither ev'ry year,
And ev'ry year a younger race succeeds.
—Horace, *Ars Poetica*

B*raintrust.* Intellectual advisers, especially to politicians. *New York Times* reporter John Kieran coined the phrase in the 1930s as "brain's trust," in reference to President Roosevelt's unofficial advisers.

Bromide. A boring or tiresome person. Coined by humorist Gelett Burgess, coiner of *blurb (q.v.).*

Centrifugal. Coined by Sir Isaac Newton.

Centipetal. Another Newtonian coinage.

Cheesecake. Photographs of delectable female models. The old story is that in 1912 *New York Journal* photographer James Kane was developing a picture of an actress that included "more of herself than either he or she expected." As he looked at it, he searched for the greatest superlative he knew of to express his delight and exclaimed, "That's real cheesecake!"

Chortle. To chuckle gleefully—coined from *snort* and *chuckle* by English author Lewis Carroll in *Through the Looking Glass* (1871).

Copasetic. Excellent, the greatest. Possibly coined by the great black tap dancer Bill "Bojangles" Robinson.

Countdown. For a rocket launch. First used by director Fritz Lang in his early science-fiction film *The Lady in the Mirror.*

Debunk. To strip of false or exaggerated claims. Formed from the word *bunk* by American novelist William Woodward (1874–1950), who, indeed, wrote a lot of debunking books.

Diplomacy. Coined by English statesman Edmund Burke.

Electioneering. Also coined by Burke.

Entropy. Coined by German scientist Rudolf Clausius.

Equal or *= sign.* The sign of equality in mathematics, two parallel lines, was invented by English mathematician Robert Recorde.

Federalism. Coined by Edmund Burke.

Fifth column. Spies within. Coined during the Spanish Civil War by General Mola.

Folklore. Coined by British critic William John Thomas in 1846.

Gas. Coined by Dutch chemist Van Helmont in 1652.

Genocide. Acts intended to destroy national, ethnic, racial, or religious groups; based on the Greek *genos,* "race," and the Latin *cadere,* "to kill," the word was invented by Professor Raphael Lemkin of Duke University and used in the official indictment of Nazi criminals in 1945; in 1948 the United Nations made genocide a crime in international law.

Gerrymander. An arbitrary reshaping of voting districts to benefit a political party. Massachusetts *Centinel* editor Benjamin Russell coined the word in 1812.

Googol. A number that is equal to 1 followed by 100 zeroes. Coined by American mathematician Edward Kasner, whose nine-year-old nephew suggested the word.

Goop. Something messy and unpleasant to handle. Still another one coined by Gelett Burgess, this in his 1900 book *Goops and How to Be Them.*

Gotham. For New York City. Washington Irving first called New York this in his *Salmagundi* (1807), taking the designation from a mythical "town of wise fools" in England.

Heebie-jeebies. The jitters, the willies, a condition of extreme nervousness. Coined by American comic-strip artist William (Billy) DeBeck.

Hot dog. Frankfurter. Popular cartoonist T. A. Dorgan, who signed his work as Tad, coined the word at the turn of the century.

Hotsy-totsy. Perfect, as right as can be. Also coined by Billy DeBeck.

Infracaninophile. A person who favors the underdog. Coined by American author Christopher Morley to describe such a person, though the construction of the nonce word from Latin may be slightly wrong.

Intensify. Coined by English poet Samuel Taylor Coleridge.

Intensity. Coined by English scientist Robert Boyle.

International. Coined by English philosopher Jeremy Bentham, who also originated *maximize* and *minimize.*

Moron. A mentally deficient person, a fool. Coined by Dr. Henry Goddard in 1910 as an official designation for someone whose IQ is below 75, ranking above imbecile and idiot. Adopted by a convention of psychologists, it is the only word ever voted into the language.

Ms. Title for a married or unmarried woman (pronounced "miz"), coined by Kansas newspaperman Roy F. Bailey in 1950.

Municipality. Another word coined by Edmund Burke.

Nihilism. Total rejection of established laws and institutions, denied of all real existence. Coined from *nihil*, the Latin for "nothing," by Russian novelist Ivan Turgenev to name and describe the principles of a Russian revolutionary group in the later nineteenth century.

Nostalgia. Coined by Johannes Hofer in 1668 from the Greek *nostos*, "return home," and *algos*, "pain."

Pandemonium. Wild lawlessness, tumult, or chaos; coined by the English poet John Milton when he dubbed the capital of hell Pandaemonium.

Panjandrum. A self-important or pretentious official. Made up by English dramatist Samuel Foote.

Paraffin. Invented by the German physicist Karl von Reichenbach in 1830.

Pendulum. Coined by Robert Boyle.

Press notice. First used by Mark Twain, who rivals T. A. Dorgan (see *America's Greatest Word Inventor*) as a word coiner. Attributed to Mark Twain are *barbed wire, billiard parlor, cussword, dust storm, ex-convict, forty-niner, hayride, race prejudice*, and *Wild West*, among other words and phrases.

Propaganda. Deliberately spread rumors or information intended to harm or help a group or person. Pope Urban VIII organized a *congregatio de propaganda fide*, a congregation for propagating the Christian faith, and this became the basis for the word.

Quiz. Short test. The tale may be apocryphal, but it's said that in the late eighteenth century Dublin theater manager James Daly bet that he could invent and introduce a new meaningless word into the language almost overnight. He proceeded to pay Dublin urchins to chalk the word *quiz* on every wall in town. By morning almost all Dubliners had seen the word, and because no one knew what it meant, the meaningless *quiz* soon became the word for a test of knowledge.

Runcible spoon. A forklike utensil with two broad prongs and one sharp curved prong used for serving hors d'oeuvres. Coined in 1871 by English author Edward Lear; the spoon seems to have been invented after Lear described it thusly in "The Owl and The Pussycat":

> *They dined on mince and slices of quince,*
> *Which they ate with a runcible spoon.*

Scientist. Coined by British scholar William Whewell as late as 1840.

Self-help. An expression coined by English author Thomas Carlyle.

Serendipity. The faculty for making desirable discoveries by accident. English novelist Horace Walpole so named a faculty possessed by the three heroes of his story "The Three Princes of Serendip."

Shangri-La. A paradise on earth. The hidden paradise described by English novelist James Hilton in his novel *Lost Horizon.*

Slithy. A blend or portmanteau word concocted from *lithe* and *slimy* by author Lewis Carroll in *Through the Looking Glass.* Carroll also coined the word *portmanteau.* Other words in his "Jabberwocky" language included *galumph, guesstimation, mimsy, meniable,* and *flimsy;* his coinages *brunch, chortle,* and *squawk* have become part of standard English. " 'Twas brillig and the slithy toves did gyre and gimble in the wabe."

Smog. This word, meaning a blend of *smoke* and *fog,* was invented in London in 1905, by a newspaper editor.

Smoke-filled room. Associated Press reporter Kirke Simpson first employed the expression to describe the behind-the-scenes political manipulations used to secure Warren Harding's nomination for president in 1920. However, Harry Daugherty, a friend of Harding's, probably coined the phrase.

Spoof. A mocking imitation coined by British comedian Arthur Roberts, who invented a game called Spoof.

Squawk. A loud harsh cry. Blended by Lewis Carroll from *squeal* and *squall.*

Sundae. Ice-cream dessert. Wisconsin ice-cream-parlor owner George Giffy probably first called the concoction a *Sunday* because he regarded it as a special dish only to be sold on Sundays; no one knows why *Sunday* was changed to *sundae.* Giffy, however, did not invent the concoction itself.

Superman. Coined by the German philosopher Nietzsche, popularized by George Bernard Shaw.

Teetotal. Total abstinence from intoxicating drink. Coined by English abstainer Robert Turner in an 1833 speech urging everyone else to practice total abstinence, too.

United Nations. Suggested by Winston Churchill, who found the words in a poem of Byron's.

United States. Coined by Thomas Paine during the Revolution.

Whodunit. Two writers for the show-business paper *Variety* are usually proposed as the inventors of the word *whodunit* for a mystery story: Sime Silverman, in 1936, and Wolfe Kaufman in 1935. But the term wasn't coined by either of them. Donald Gordon used the word in the July 1930 *American News of Books* and probably invented it.

Yes-man. A sycophant. Cartoonist T. A. Dorgan first used the expression in a 1913 cartoon.

Shakespeare was the first to use over 1,700 words, including *aerial, auspicious, assassination, bump, critic, road,* and *livery.*

Other coined words are noted throughout the book. This list does not include any of the many words, such as *blatant* and *robot,* deriving from the names of fictional characters. (See also *America's Greatest Word Inventor.*)

Brobdignag Bonnet ⁓

SWIFT COINS A WORD FROM A HORSE'S WHINNY

Houyhnhnyms, of course, are the intelligent breed of horses Jonathan Swift created in *Gulliver's Travels* (1726). Swift said he coined their name from the characteristic whinny of a horse as it sounded to him. The talking horses, endowed with reason, ruled over the brutish *Yahoos,* another name coined by Swift in the book. *Gulliver's Travels* also gives us *brobdingnagian,* for any immense thing, after the giants Gulliver encounters in the country of Brobdingnag, and *lilliputian,* from Lilliput, a country of pygmies. Knowing that Houyhnhnyms is pronounced *whinims* makes it a little easier to recite Alexander Pope's poem "Mary Gulliver to Capt. Lemuel Gulliver" about the Houyhnhnyms:

> *Nay would kind Jove my organ so dispose*
> *To hymn harmonious Houyhnhnyms through the nose*
> *I'd call thee Houhnhnm, that high-sounding name;*
> *Thy children's noses should all twang the same.*

ECDYSIAST

STRIPTEASER Georgia Sothern, or her press agent, wrote H. L. Mencken in 1940 asking him to coin a "more palatable word" to describe her profession. The Sage of Baltimore, who had hatched other neologisms (for instance, *bootician* for a bootlegger), gallantly responded, suggesting that stripteasing be related "in some way or other to the zoological phenomenon of molting." Among his specific recommendations were *moltician* (too close to *mortician*); *gecko*, after a family of molting lizards called the Geckonidae (not very appetizing, either); and *ecdysiast*, which comes from *ecdysis*, the scientific term for molting. Miss Sothern adopted the last and it was publicized universally; born to the world was a new word and a new union called the Society of Ecdysiasts, Parade, and Specialty Dancers. But not every artfully unclad body was happy with Mencken's invention. Said the Queen of Strippers, Gypsy Rose Lee: " 'Ecdysiast,' he calls me! Why the man is an intellectual snob. He has been reading *books*. *Dictionaries*. We don't wear feathers and molt them off. . . . What does he know about stripping?" Most would agree that *stripteaser* is far more revealing.

O . K .

THE MOST shining and successful Americanism ever invented," as Mencken called it, is truly international in use today. Around the world, *O.K.* is used more often than *salud* in Spain, has displaced the English *righto*, is spelled *O-ke* in the Djabo dialect of Liberia. The most universally used of all words in any language since World War II, it is inscribed everywhere, from the town of Okay, Oklahoma, to the pieces of equipment marked with *O.K.*s that are doubtless on the moon. There are many explanations of the little word's origins, including:

• The Choctaw Indian word *okeh*, a theory none other than Woodrow Wilson championed.

• The Choctaw Indian word *hoke*.

• Old *Keokuk*, an Indian chief who approved treaties with his initials.

• Railroad freight agent Obadiah *Kelly*, who put his initials on bills of lading.

• Orrins-*Kendall* crackers, a favorite of troopers during the Civil War.

• The initials from *omnis korrectes*, which nineteenth-century teachers wrote on perfect examination papers.

• *Hoacky*, an English dialect word meaning the last of the harvest.

• The initials of the words *outer keel*, which shipbuilders sometimes carved on timbers.

• Initials for the illiterate "Orl Kerrect" that Andrew Jackson used on legal documents while a young court clerk (which he never was).

• Excellent rum from Aux Cayes, Haiti, which American sailors found so good that they made *Aux Cayes*, later *O.K.*, an expression of approval.

• The Finnish word *oikea*, "correct."

• About ten other words from various foreign languages.

But most etymologists believe that *O.K.* comes at least in part from the nickname of Martin Van Buren (1782–1862), who rose from being potboy in a tavern to become president of the United States. Columbia University Professor Allen Walker Read first traced the word to the president, who was O.K. in a *Saturday Review* article (July 19, 1941). Read explains that the expression *O.K.* was invented by Boston journalists and wits in late 1838 as part of a humorous fad of abbreviating phrases that they purposely misspelled—*O.K.* was the abbreviation of "oll korrect" (all correct), and *OW* of "oll wright" (all right). The earliest recorded use of these initials was in the *Boston Morning Post* of March 23, 1839, in a piece by its editor, Charles Gordon Green. Soon after, in early 1840, New York City politicians borrowed the word when they formed the Democratic O.K. Club. The mystifying initials, appealing to the human love of being on the inside of events, became a sort of rallying cry for the Democrats, one contemporary newspaper account reporting how "about 500 stout strapping men" of the O.K. Club marched to break up a rival Whig meeting where "they passed the word O.K. . . . from mouth to mouth, a cheer was given and they rushed into the hall like a torrent."

O.K. was reinforced as a rallying cry during the presidential campaign of 1840, in which Martin Van Buren carried the Democratic standard. "Old Kinderhook," a title bestowed upon the president from the name of his birthplace, Kinderhook, New York, sounded better to his supporters than "the Sage, Magician, or Wizard of Kinderhook." Prompted by the Democratic O.K. Club in New York, Democrats all over the country began to use the rallying cry *O.K.*, which came all the more to mean "all right, all correct" because "Old Kinder-hook" or "O.K." was all right to his supporters. Unfortunately for the Democrats, though, neither mystification, nor thugs who broke up rival meetings, nor new words did Van Buren any good; voters remembered the depression of 1837 and he was defeated in his bid for reelection.

In any case, *O.K.* was a fixture of the language after the election, became a verb by the 1880s, and now does English yeoman service. Surprisingly, the effort to give it an antonym (*nokay*) has failed, but the variants *oke, oke-doke,* and *okle-dokle*—plays on one of its forms, *okey*—are still commonly heard in everyday speech. The useful little word may become even smaller and more useful. It is already widely spelled without periods (*ok*). To this writer it sounds like *k* with more frequency every year and perhaps someday that will be the spelling.

APTRONYMS

*A*MERICAN COLUMNIST Franklin P. Adams (F.P.A.) coined the term *aptronym*, but writers have used aptronyms, "label names," that fit the nature or occupation of a character, at least since the time of Spenser's allegory *Faerie Queene* and Bunyan's *Pilgrim's Progress*. It is said that Plato's real name was Aristocles and that he was called Plato because of his broad shoulders. Mr. Gradgrind, Mr. Worldly Wiseman, Lord Easy (a careless husband), William Congreve's gossipy character Scandal, Sir Walter Scott's Dr. Dryasdust, and many of Charles Dickens's characters are famous fictional examples of aptronyms.

Susanna Centlivre used the same technique in her comedy *A Bold Stroke for a Wife* (1717), presenting a host of aptronyms. The most lasting proved to be one Simon Pure, a Pennsylvania Quaker who tries to win the heart of the heiress Ann Lovely. But Simon Pure's letter of introduction to her guardian Obadiah Prim is stolen by Colonel Feignwell, who pretends to be Simon Pure and convinces Ann Lovely's guardian to let her marry him. At the last minute Simon Pure shows up, proves that he is "the real Simon Pure," and provides a happy ending. As a result of the play, Simon Pure, an aptronym, became an eponym, his name becoming proverbial for anything authentic, true, the real and genuine article, "the real McCoy," as we say more often today. Mrs. Centlivre, married to Queen Anne's chef, turned to writing for a living when her husband died, and she became one of the few women of her time to earn her livelihood as a playwright. (See also *Malapropism*.)

Felis Tigris

THE GREATEST NAME CALLER OF ALL

"I have been given a species of eternity."
—British naturalist Peter Collinson
after Linnaeus named a species
of wild mint after him

LINNAEUS (1707–1778), the most famous of all naturalists, not only dubbed us *Homo sapiens* but chose the names for far more things than any other person in history, classifying literally thousands of plants, animals, and minerals. Carl von Linné—Carolus Linnaeus was the Latin form of his name—showed an early love of flowers that earned him the nickname the Little Botanist when he was only eight years old. The son of a Lutheran minister who cultivated his interest in nature, Linnaeus became an assistant professor of botany at Uppsala University, in Sweden, then studied medicine in Holland, where in 1735 he wrote his *Systema Naturae*. Linnaeus was only twenty-eight at the time, and his masterpiece was followed by the *Genera Plantarum*, published two years later. These books marked the beginning of a system of scientific nomenclature, or taxonomy, that would be elaborated in more than 180 works. The Linnaean system, developed by the naturalist, divided the kingdom of animals, vegetables, and minerals into classes, orders, genera, species, and varieties, according to various characteristics. It adopted binomial nomenclature, giving two Latin names—genus and species—to each organism. In this two-name system all closely related species bear the same genus name—for example, *Felis* (Latin for "cat") *leo* is the lion, and *Felis tigris* is the tiger.

An unusual eponymous word, the plant genus *Mahernia* is an anagram of *Hermannia*, another genus to which it is closely allied. Linnaeus must have been in a playful mood when he coined the word from *Hermannia*, which he had also originated. In any event, it is the only anagram that is an eponymous word—unless one includes *mho* (*Ohm* spelled backward) or *Voltairean* (Voltaire, the assumed name of the great French philosopher François Marie Arouet, is an imperfect anagram for Arouet, l.j., meaning Arouet the younger). Linnaeus named *Hermannia* for Paul Hermann (1646–1695), a professor of botany at the University of Leiden, who is surely the only man to be honored by two genera in this odd way.

Like *Mahernia*, the name of the plant genus *Quisqualis* is another joke played by Linnaeus. When he examined the plant, he did not know how to classify it or for whom he could name it. He therefore called the genus *Quisqualis*, which in Latin means, literally, "who or what for." *Quisqualis* (pronounced "kwis-kwal-is") clearly shows that the naming process is not always so serious a matter; it might even be called an anonymous eponymous word, or a word in want of an eponym.

AMERICA'S GREATEST WORD INVENTOR

SCATTERED THROUGHOUT these pages (and especially in the entry *Invented Words*) are references to T(homas) A(loysius) Dorgan (1877–1929), the great American cartoonist better known as Tad to millions of newspaper readers early in this century. Dorgan, born in a San Francisco tenement, taught himself to draw with his left hand when at the age of thirteen an accident deprived him of the use of his right hand. He worked for a time on San Francisco newspapers, but his great fame came when William Randolph Hearst hired him away to New York. "Judge Rummy," "Silk Hat Harry," and many of Tad's characters, all dogs in human dress, became household words in America, and Dorgan was recognized as the country's most prolific and original coiner of words and catch phrases. If there is a writer anywhere, excepting Lewis Carroll, who invented more lasting words and expressions than Dorgan, I've missed him. Just for the record, here are the most memorable ones, some of which are described at length in these pages. Many were listed by humorist S. J. Perelman, a student and early admirer of Tad, in a *New York Times Magazine* article:

ball-and-chain (for wife)
hot dog
hot dogs (feet)
dumbbell
dumbhead
Dumb Dora
nobody home upstairs (dumb)
applesauce (for insincere flattery)
drugstore cowboy
lounge lizard
chin music (pointless talk)

the once-over
the cat's meow
the cat's pajamas
23-skiddoo
flat tire
you said it
for crying out loud
Officer, call a cop
Yes, we have no bananas
The first hundred years are the hardest
  (sometimes attributed to Wilson Mizner)
hardboiled
See what the boys in the backroom will have
The only place you'll find sympathy is in the dictionary
Half the world are squirrels and the other half are nuts
as busy as a one-armed paperhanger with the hives (sometimes attributed
  to O. Henry, who in a 1908 story wrote: "Busy as a one-armed man with
  the nettle rash pasting on wall-paper.")

Other noted American word coiners whose creations are found in these
pages include Mark Twain, Thomas Haliburton (a Canadian who lived in the
U.S.), Phineas T. Barnum, Billy DeBeck, and Jack Conway. Aside from Lewis
Carroll, British adepts here include Gabriel Harvey, Ben Jonson, Shakespeare,
Burke, and Frederick Marryat.

INVENTING SLOGANS

Probably the most successful slogan ever written, or at least the most
profitable one, is the "Think Mink" button invented by Jack Gasnick (b. 1918),
which has sold 50 billion copies since 1950. Gasnick also invented the ubiquitous
"Cross at the Green . . . not in-between" slogan.

All slogans, whether they be catchy advertising phrases or the rallying cries
of political parties, are direct descendants of Gaelic battle cries, the word itself
deriving from the *sluagh-ghairm* (battle cry) of the Gaels. Gaelic soldiers repeated
these cries, usually the names of their clans or clan leaders, in unison as they
advanced against the enemy. The word over the years came to describe any
catchy phrase inducing people to support a cause (the "Liberty, Equality, Fraternity" of the French Revolution) or a commercial product (the "99.44% Pure"
of Ivory Soap). Sometimes *watchword* is used loosely for *slogan*.

We all have our favorite political campaign slogans, which have been with
us since the presidential election of 1840, when "Tippecanoe and Tyler, Too,"

swept William Henry Harrison and John Tyler into office. Like all slogans, good political slogans are usually short, simple, have rhyme or rhythm, and manage to say what the electorate feels but is unable to express. Yet some great ones have had few or none of these qualities. There are, for example, the negative scare slogans like "Rum, Romanism and Rebellion," which Herbert Hoover's backers used to defeat Al Smith in 1928, or the Democrat slogan used against Grover Cleveland's opponent in 1884: "James G. Blaine, James G. Blaine/Continental liar from the State of Maine!" Humorous slogans have also been effective, such as the Democrats' gem: "In Hoover we trusted, now we are busted." There is no space here for a complete accounting of political slogans, but below is a list of some famous ones that may or may not have succeeded:

"Fifty-four Forty or Fight"—James Polk (1844)
"Free Soil, Free Speech, Free Labor, Free Men"—Free-Soilers Party (1848)
"We Polked You in '44; We Shall Pierce You in '52!"—Franklin Pierce (1852)
"Forty Acres and a Cow"—Reconstruction Era, many parties
"Four More Years of the Full Dinner Pail"—William McKinley (1900)
"A Square Deal"—Theodore Roosevelt (1912)
"He Kept Us Out of War"—Woodrow Wilson (1916)
"Return to Normalcy"—Warren Harding (1920)
"Keep Cool with Coolidge"—Calvin Coolidge (1924)
"A Chicken in Every Pot"—Herbert Hoover (1928)
"A New Deal"—Franklin Roosevelt (1932)
"Happy Landin' with Landon"—Alfred M. Landon (1936)
"A Fair Deal"—Harry Truman (1948)
"I Like Ike"—Dwight Eisenhower (1956)

"He Kept Us Out of War"—Dwight Eisenhower (1956)
"The New Frontier"—John Kennedy (1960)
"All the Way with LBJ"—Lyndon Johnson (1964)
"AuH₂O = 1964"—Barry Goldwater (1964)
"In Your Heart You Know He's Right"—Barry Goldwater (1964)*
"Nixon's the One"—Richard Nixon (1968)†
"Let's Get America Going Again"—Richard Nixon (1968)
"We Can't Stand Pat"—Pat Paulsen (1972)

INVENTING UTOPIAS

Wᴵɴ ᴀɴ imaginary trip to your favorite utopia by matching these twelve authors with the fictional utopias they invented:

1. Thomas More	A. Oceana
2. Tommasso Campanella	B. Pala
3. James Harrington	C. Boston (in the year 2000)
4. Thomas Spence	D. Shangri-La
5. Edward Bellamy	E. Islandia
6. H. G. Wells	F. Walden II
7. Aldous Huxley	G. Triton
8. James Hilton	H. Utopia
9. B. F. Skinner	I. Spenconia
10. Ernest Callenbach	J. Ectopia
11. Austin Tappan Wright	K. Utopia
12. Samuel R. Delany	L. The City of the Sun

ANSWERS: 1. H or K 2. L 3. A 4. I 5. C 6. H or K 7. B 8. D
9. F 10. J 11. E 12. G

TRADEMARKS

Aspirin, *tabloid, shredded wheat, nylon, dry ice, hansom, windbreaker jacket, kerosene, milk of magnesia, calico, celluloid, linoleum, lanolin, mimeograph, raisin bran, cellophane, thermos, elevator, escalator, zipper,* and *cola* are

---

*Variations on this included "In Your Guts You Know He's Nuts"; "In Your Mind You Know He's Blind," etc.—all, of course, coined by the loyal opposition.

†The button with this slogan was sometimes worn by pregnant women—Democrats, of course.

all examples of trademarks that have become so popular and firmly entrenched in the language that they have fallen into the public domain and are regarded as generic names that do not belong to a single company anymore. Trademarks are marks, names, symbols, figures, letters, or words used to distinguish the goods of one manufacturer or merchant from those of another. Over a million of them have been registered since the protection of trademarks was initiated under United States federal law in 1870, but only about 40 percent of these enjoy protection today. Firms often lose their trademarks through carelessness as much as through inadequate laws, and valuable ones are constantly watched by their owners. *Xerox* spends about $100,000 a year for ads explaining that its name is not a synonym for making a photocopy but "a registered trademark for a special process involving only Xerox machines," while the Coca-Cola Company employs three attorneys just to watch out for its trademark, *Coke*. Owners of familiar trademarks such as *Jell-O*, *Frisbee*, and *Kleenex* constantly monitor newspapers, magazines, books, radio, and television, looking for any use of their trademarks that implies a wider, generic meaning (failure to capitalize trademarked names, for example). Offenders are usually warned first, then sued if they persist.

THE MOST BEAUTIFUL AND THE UGLIEST WORDS IN ENGLISH

Nᴏᴛ ᴍᴀɴʏ authors have nominated the most beautiful English word, probably because most realize that such a choice is so subjective as to mean nothing. Carl Sandburg, I believe, chose *Monongahela*, which rolls like a long river off the tongue, while James Joyce felt that *cuspidor* was the most euphonious word in the language. *M* words such as *melody* and *murmuring* are great favorites among many people, as are *lullaby*, *golden*, *silver moon*, *cellar door*, and *dawn*. As *his* favorite French word Baudelaire chose *hemorroïdes* (hemorrhoids).

A poll taken by the National Association of Teachers of Speech in 1946 gave the ten worst-sounding English words as *cacophony*, *crunch*, *flatulent*, *gripe*, *jazz*, *phlegmatic*, *plump*, *plutocrat*, *sap*, and *treachery*.

INTOXICATED AND OTHER WORDS FOR *DRUNK*

Tʜᴇʀᴇ ᴀʀᴇ more synonyms for *intoxicated* in the *Webster's Collegiate Thesaurus* than for any other entry in the book, sixty-six of them in all. *Intoxicate*, ironically enough, comes from a Greek word meaning poison—*toxikon*, the poison into which war arrows were dipped. Then, in the Middle Ages, the

Latin *toxicum* became a general term for any poison. This resulted in the English *toxic*, "poisonous," our *intoxicate* meaning "to poison" long before its use was limited to the temporarily poisonous effects of too much liquor. Which is something to remember the next time someone quips, "Name your own poison."

Synonyms for drunk include *loaded, pickled, plastered, blind, stewed, boiled, fried, juiced, oiled, jagged, polluted, smashed, stinking, stinko, sozzled, swazzled, tanked, knee-walking drunk,* and *zonked.* Politer words are *tipsy, tiddly, lit, squiffed, tight,* and odd ones include *capernoited, deleerit,* and *pifflicated.* Then there are idioms like "full as a tick," "three sheets to the wind," "half seas over," and "back teeth afloat." *The Dictionary of American Slang* alone lists close to 400 words or expressions for *drunk,* and Benjamin Franklin once compiled 228 such terms, including *cherry merry, top heavy, nimptopsical, seafaring in the suds,* and *gold headed.* A list of colorful ones from several sources follows:

alkied	blotto	cock-eyed
basted	blue around the gills	corked
battered	bombed	corned
bent	boozed up	crocked
bitten to the brain	bosko absoluto bosky	curved
bleary-eyed	canned	dead to the world
blind	cocked	decks awash

draped	loaded to the gills	squiffy
feel no pain	looped	stewed
fish-eyed	loose in the hilt	stiff
fractured	lordly	stifflicated
frazzled	lubricated	stinkarooed
gassed	lush	stinking
glazed	moon-eyed	stinko
glued	ossified	stoned
half-cocked	paralyzed	swacked
hang one on	petrified	tangle-footed
have a bun on	pickled	tee miny martoonies
have a can on	pigeon-eyed	tiddly
have a snoot full	pinked	tied one on
high	pissed	under the table
high as a kite	plastered	under the weather
illuminated	plowed	vulcanized
in one's cups	potted	wall-eyed
in the suds	pruned	weak-jointed
jammed	rocky	wet
jugged	sloshed	whipped
lappy	smashed	whooshed
lathered	snockered	wilted
limber	snoozemarooed	woofled
lit to the gills	snozzled	woozy
lit up like a Christmas	soused	zig-zag
tree		

Words that can mean drunk or stoned on drugs include:

blatso	freaked	shit-faced
blown away	fucked up (over)	twisted
bummed out	high	zapped
buzzed	off the wall	
flipped out	ripped	

Words for a drunkard are:

alcoholic	lush	souse
boozer	rummy	stew
booze hound	soak	tank
dipsomaniac or dipso	sot	wino

BUGGER

WHEN Dylan Thomas wrote his radio play *Under Milk Wood*, everyone who read the script assumed that the fictional village Llareggub therein was authentically Welsh—until someone spelled it backward, after the play was already aired, and realized the poet's bawdy joke. For *bugger* in British English never means a child, as it does in American expressions like "he's just a little bugger." A *bugger* in England is a sodomite and *to bugger* is to sodomize—in fact, use of the word in print was actionable in England for many years. *Bugger* in this sense, which is American slang as well, derives, down a tortuous path, from the Medieval Latin *Bulgarus*, meaning both a Bulgarian and a sodomite. The word first referred to a Bulgarian and then to the Bulgarian Albigenses or Bulgarian Heretics, an eleventh-century religious sect whose monks and nuns were believed, rightly or wrongly, to practice sodomy. Some historians claim that the charge of sodomy against these heretic dissenters was a libel invented with the approval of the Church to discredit them. They had already been banished from Bulgaria and were living in the south of France; the trumped-up story caused the French to oust or exterminate them, too.

PIG LATIN AND OTHER INVENTED LANGUAGES

I*xnay* (nix), *amscray* (scram), and several other slang words come to us directly from Pig Latin. First known as Dog Latin, the little language commonly used by schoolchildren can be traced back to at least mid-eighteenth-century England, when there was a Dog Greek as well as a Dog Latin. The *dog* in the terms means the same as it does in *doggerel*, something bad, spurious, bastard, mongrel. Dog Latin probably came to be called Pig Latin and Hog Latin because its sound resembles the grunting of hogs.

The lopped language was at first a combination of Latin and English. Today it is basically formed by taking the first letter of a word, putting it at the rear of the word and adding an *ay* to it. For example: "You can talk Pig Latin" is "Ouyay ankay alktay igpay Atinlay." One of the most interesting Pig Latin words is *ofay*, a derogatory black term for a white person, which is said to be Pig Latin for the word *foe*.

Pig Latin is much easier to decipher on paper than when the gibberish of words is heard in conversation, thus it has always been popular as a code or secret language. Other simple little languages similar to it are *Na*, *Gru*, and *Skimono jive*. In Na, the syllable *na* is added to every word: "Youna canna talkina itna" ("You can talk it"). In Gru the same is done with the syllable *gru*:

"Yougru cangru talkgru itgru." Skimono jive just adds *sk* before every spoken word. "Skiyou skican skitalk skit."

More complicated invented languages include *Ong, Pelf Latin,* and *Carnese,* the last a carnival argot that is also called *Goon Talk. Double talk* isn't an invented language at all, but a humorous device that doesn't attempt to convey meaning.

En la komenco Dio kreis la cielon kaj la teron. Kaj la tero estis senforma kaj dezerta, kaj mallumo estis super la abismo; kaj la spirito de Dio svelis super la akvo. Kaj Dio diris: Estee lumo; kaj farigis lumo.

The above rendition of Genesis 1:1–3 in *Esperanto* is supposed to demonstrate that anyone with at least one foreign language can make some sense out of the artificial language without ever having studied it. In fact, surveys have shown that Esperanto can be learned in one-tenth to one-twentieth the time it takes to learn a national language. Over the past seven centuries hundreds of artificial universal languages have been invented, including one that Sir Thomas Urquhart based on palindromes (see *In Praise of Palindromes*). The French philosopher Descartes devised an artificial language in 1629; there is another, called *Solresol,* based on the notes of the musical scale; and a third, *Timerio,* is written solely in numerals (for example, 1-80-17 means "I love you"). Esperanto is far better known than any such invention. It takes its name from the pseudonym chosen by its inventor, Lazarus Zamenhof, when he wrote his first book on the subject, *Linguo Internacia de la Doktoro Esperanto.* Dr. Lazarus Ludwig Zamenhof (1859–1917), the "Doctor Hopeful" of the title, was a Warsaw oculist who believed that a world language would promote peace and understanding. He launched his system in 1887 and today the movement has some 8 million supporters, from half a million to a million people capable of speaking Esperanto fluently. Advocates claim that the language—based primarily on words common to the major tongues, with a grammar like that of Latin—is much easier to learn than any other. Esperanto is now taught in over 750 schools in forty countries around the world, has textbooks for study in fifty-four languages, has been used in more than 30,000 books, and is the subject of some 145 periodicals.

Ido, Esperanto II, and *Nov-Esperanto* are all even simpler offshoots of Esperanto—indeed the word *ido* is the Esperanto word for "offspring." Since Descartes's time alone, some 700 artificial languages have been invented. Notable ones besides those already mentioned include *Basic English,* invented by linguists I. A. Richards and C. K. Ogden, which has a vocabulary of only 850 words but is rather unwieldly ("winged machine for flight" is the phrase for "airplane"); *Novial,* invented in 1928 by Danish philologist Otto Jespersen; *Latino Sine Flexions,* which derives from classical Latin; *Interlingua,* developed over a period of twenty-five years by the International Auxiliary Language Association; the

Gibson Code, another language that uses numbers instead of words; *Monling*, which employs only monosyllabic words; and *Lincos*, a truly universal language composed of scientific symbols that is translatable into the binary code and could be transmitted to any place in the universe! Still other artificial languages, should you want to find out more about them are *Mandolingo*; *Volapuk*; *Idiom Neutral* (simplified *Volapuk*); *Vertparl*; *Bopal*; *Dil*; *Balta*; *Ro*; *Neo*; *Loglan*; *Arulo*; *Suma*; *Latinesce*; *Gloro*; *Universal*; *Interglossa*; *Nordlinn*; *Lanque Bleue*, and *Romanal*.

PITMAN

In memori ov
MERI PITMAN,
    Weif of Mr. Eizak Pitman,
Fonetik Printer, ov this Site.
Deid 19 Agust 1857 edjed 64
'Preper tu mit thei God'
—EMOS 4,12.

S**O READS** the phonetic epitaph Sir Isaac Pitman, author and inventor of *Stenographic Soundhand*, wrote for his wife, Mary. Pitman devised his system in 1837, basing his simpler phonetic shorthand on an earlier method invented by Samuel Taylor. The former clerk and schoolteacher lived to see almost universal acceptance of his invention, which his brother Benn helped popularize in the United States when he immigrated here in 1852 and established the Phonographic Institute in Cincinnati. Isaac Pitman, a former Sunday School superintendent, devoted his life to spelling reform and improving his method for shorthand based on phonetics, issuing many works from his own publishing house. The phonographer died in 1897, aged eighty-four, but even at that time the simpler Gregg system was replacing Pitman, which had already become synonymous with shorthand. Gregg, based on ordinary, written script, did not require the intricate forms and shadings of distinctive sounds that made Pitman so difficult to master.

LABANOTATION

P**ERHAPS IN** some future 1984 a form of *labanotation* will be used by "Big Brother" and computer to chart tomorrow's movements for the omniverse—such would at least be the theme for a good science-fiction story. This little-

One symbol denotes by its placement on the staff the part of the body executing the movement; by its shape, the direction of the movement; by its shading, the level; and by its length, the duration of the movement.

known word—oddly, no major dictionary defines it—describes an important notation system that amounts to a graphic shorthand for dance, enabling a choreographer to delineate every possible movement of the human body individually or in ensemble. Introduced by its creator, Rudolf von Laban, in his book *Kinetographie Laban* (1928), labanotation was the first practical method capable of scoring the various complex movements and positions of an entire ballet or musical comedy. (There are now labanotation typewriters.)

Unlike the old numbered-footprint plans familiar to us all, the Laban system amounts to a complete break with tradition. It dispenses entirely with the musical five-line horizontal staff, using a three-line vertical staff that is divided in the center. Code symbols on each side of the line indicate foot and leg movements, while symbols in parallel columns outside the lines pertain to all other body gestures. Every slight movement from toe to head can be noted, as well as their direction, timing, and force; by grouping together the staffs for individual dancers an entire work can be "orchestrated."

Laban did for the dance what Guido d'Arezzo had done for musical notation almost a thousand years before. Prior to his system, dancers had to rely on their memories of performers who had appeared in classical ballets, but now almost exact revivals can be given and ballet composers can finally adequately copyright their creations. Born in Pressburg (Bratislava) on December 15, 1879, the German dance teacher and choreographer had a great influence on modern dance, with Mary Wigman and Kurt Jooss among his pupils. Rejecting nineteenth-century traditionalism, he tried to express industrialized urban life in his work, even experimenting with group improvisations, using masses of German factory workers after World War I. Laban wrote many books, including *Effort* (1947) with F. C. Lawrence, and *Principles of Dance and Movement Notation* (1956). He died in London on July 1, 1958.

ACRONYMS

ACCORDING TO THE *Guinness Book of World Records*, there is a Russian acronym of fifty-six letters: NIIOMTPIABQPARMBETZHELBETRABSBOMONIMON-KONOTDTEKHSTROMONT. *Guinness* also claims that the longest English acronym is the twenty-two-letter ADCOMSUBORDCOMPHIBSPAC, used in the U.S. Navy to denote the Administrative Command, Amphibious Forces, Pacific Fleet, Subordinate Command. But there is at least one longer English monster: the twenty-six-letter COMSUBCOMNELMCOMHEDSUPPACT, which stands for Commander, Subordinate Command, U.S. Naval Forces Eastern Atlantic and Mediterranean, Commander Headquarters Support Activities—itself abbreviated as CSCN/CHSA. Strictly speaking, these are both acronyms, new words formed from the initial letters or syllables of successive words in a phrase. But *acronym* has come to mean any such word that can be easily *pronounced* as a word, and not even Demosthenes could pronounce these abbreviations designed to appeal to the eye rather than the ear.

The term *acronym* derives from the Greek *akros* ("tip") and *onym* ("name"); it is a fairly new coinage, although scholars claim to have found early examples of acronyms in Hebrew writings dating back to Biblical times. Acronyms came into prominence during World War I with coinages like AWOL (Absent Without Leave), proliferated during the New Deal with all its "alphabet agencies," and got entirely out of hand during World War II, as can be seen by the two monsters above. The good ones appeal to the American preference for brevity and wit in speech. New acronyms are invented every day, especially by advertising copywriters, but relatively few stand the test of time. Below are some that have, including samples of acronyms like *motel* that combine the initial portion of a first word with the final part of a second. A number are apparently happy accidents, but in many cases the long form was invented so that the acronyms could be born. There is no good explanation for why common abbreviations like G.O.P., F.O.B., and O.P.A. haven't become acronyms except that they just don't sound right to most ears when pronounced as words. Unfortunately, there isn't room here for interesting place-name acronyms such as Pawn, Oregon, which wasn't named for a pawnshop but comes from the initials of four early residents named *Poole, Aberley, Worthington,* and *Nolen.*

ASAP (ay-sap)—**A**s **S**oon **A**s **P**ossible.

AWOL (ay-wall)—**A**bsent **W**ithout **O**fficial **L**eave (military, World War I).

BASIC ENGLISH (an invented language)—**B**ritish-**A**merican **S**cientific **I**nternational **C**ommercial **English**.

BOPEEP—**B**angor **O**range **P**osition **E**stimating **E**quipment for **P**astures. (An electronic beeper attached to sheep that shepherds in Bangor, Wales, use to keep track of their charges.)

CARE—Cooperative for American Remittances to Europe.

CINCUS (sink-us)—for the World War II Commander-in-Chief of the United States Navy. It was changed after Pearl Harbor.

CORE—Congress of Racial Equality.

CREEP—Committee for the Re-election of the President (Watergate).

FIB—Fisherman's Information Bureau (Chicago).

FLAK—From the German *Fliegerabwehrkanone*, for "antiaircraft cannon."

LASER—Light Amplification through Simulated Emission of Radiation.

MASER—Microwave Amplification through Simulated Emission of Radiation.

MOUSE—Minimum Orbital Unmanned Satellite of the Earth.

NASA—National Aeronautics and Space Administration.

NAZI—*Nationalsozialistische* (German political party).

RADAR—Radio Detection and Ranging.

SCUBA—Self-Contained Underwater Breathing Apparatus.

SEABEES—the initials C.B., for "construction battalion," spelled out.

SNAFU—Situation Normal—All Fouled (Fucked) Up (World War II). Variations include TARFU (Things Are Really Fucked Up); JANFU (Joint Army-Navy Fuck Up); and FUBB (Fucked Up Beyond Belief).

SONAR—Sound Navigation Ranging.

SPAM—Spiced Ham.

SPAR—*Semper Paratus*—"Always Ready," the Coast Guard motto and its translation, yields this ingenious acronym for the Woman's Reserve of the U.S. Coast Guard Reserve (World War II).

VEEP—Vice President (the initials V.P. spelled phonetically).

WAC—Women's Army Corps (World War II).

WASP—White Anglo-Saxon Protestant; also Women's Air Force Service Pilots (World War II).

WAVES—Women Accepted for Voluntary Emergency Service (U.S. Navy, World War II).

WRENS—Women's Royal Naval Service (Great Britain, World War I).

ZIP (code)—Zone Improvement Program for the United States Post Office.

Among the most interesting of acronyms is the eponymous one *jix*, a word coined from the letters of a person's name. *Jix* was a synonym for "prudish interference" popular in England during the late twenties and early thirties. Journalists nicknamed British Home Secretary Sir William Joynson-Hicks "Jix" by fusing Joynson and Hicks (the letters *cks* made into an *x*). The nickname became a word when Joynson-Hicks's actions suggested it and only passed out of use with his death in 1932.

AAA AND MORE ALPHABET SOUP

UNLIKE ACRONYMS, abbreviations aren't usually pronounced as words, but they do serve the same purpose as time- and space-savers. They have been popular since the earliest times, a good example being SPQR, the abbreviation for *Senatus Populusque Romanus*, the famous insignia of Rome. Most abbreviations merely suggest the whole word they represent to the reader (as *Dr.*), but many have become almost words themselves: the letters spoken, as in *IQ* for intelligence quotient. A few are even spoken as words, such as *vet* for veterinarian or armed service veteran, *ad* for advertisement, and *ad lib*. There are entire dictionaries devoted to the tens of thousands of abbreviations we use and a complete list of abbreviations of government agencies can be found in the *United States Government Organization Manual*. But below are some interesting and humorous ones from slang and standard English that illustrate the diverse and complex ways abbreviations are formed. Included are *eusystolisms*, "initials used in the interest of delicacy," such as *S.O.B.*

A.A.A.—American Automobile Association (1900), distinguished from the Agricultural Adjustment Administration, AAA (1933), by the use of periods.

A.A.A.S.—American Association for the Advancement of Science.

A.A.—Alcoholics Anonymous.

A.A.F.—American Airforce (World War II).

ACE—Adrenal cortex extract.

A.D.—from the Latin *anno domini*: in the year of our Lord; since Christ was born.

ad lib—from the Latin *ad libitum*, at one's pleasure; was first a musical term.

A.F.L.-C.I.O.—American Federation of Labor and Congress of Industrial Organizations.

A.K.—slang for **ass kisser**; a eusystolism mostly confined to schoolchildren.

A.M.—abbreviation of the Latin *ante meridiem*, before noon, not *ante meridian*, even though *meridian* also means noon.

atty.—attorney; an abbreviation formed by contraction, as is blvd., boulevard, and tsp., teaspoon.

B.C.—Before Christ, before the Christian era.

BCU—television talk for a **big close up** of an actor, showing only his or her face; an **mcu**, a medium close up, shows some background.

B.I.D.—the abbreviation, often found on prescription drug labels, is from the Latin *bis in die* (twice a day).

B.L.T.—bacon, lettuce, and tomato sandwich.

B.T.O.—big time operator.

c.—a lowercase *c.* with a period signifies at least thirty things, including "carat," "cent," "centimeter," and "about" (for example, c.1775), deriving in the last case from the Latin *circa*, "about."

C.—C. can abbreviate at least ten things when capitalized and followed with a period, including "Centigrade," "Catholic," and "College."

C. (after the clef sign on sheet music)—the C is not an initial standing for "common" 4/4 time, but stands for an incomplete circle, is a symbol representing what was once considered "imperfect time." A circle, symbolizing the Trinity, was used in the early days of music to indicate "perfect time," three beats to the bar.

C.A.B.—Civil Aeronautics Board.

CAPT.—**capt**ain; an abbreviation formed by shortening, like so many others.

CCCP—There isn't a "Communist" behind any of these *c*'s. The abbreviation stood for *Soiuz Sovetskihh Sotsialisticheskikh Respublik*, the Union of Soviet Socialist Republics, written as CCCP in English because in the Russian alphabet *c* is equivalent to our *s* and *p* to our *r*.

C-NOTE—century note, $100.

C.O.—Both commanding officer and conscientious objector.

C.O.D.—collect on delivery; has been traced back to 1859.

D-DAY—the first *D* in the word also stands for "day," the term, of course, a code designation for June 6, 1944, when the Allied forces first invaded Western Europe in World War II.

DDT—dichlorodiphenyltrichloroethane.

D.O.A.—dead on arrival.

DP— displaced person.

D.T.S.—delirium tremens.

E.G.—see I.E.

E.T.A.—estimated time of arrival.

ET AL.—from the Latin *et alia*, "and others."

ETC.—abbreviation of *etcetera*, which is from the Latin *et cetera*, "and other," "and so forth," "and so on." . . .

F.A.A.—Federal Aviation Agency.

F.B.I.—Federal Bureau of Investigation.

F.C.C.—Federal Communications Commission.

F.C.I.C.—Federal Crop Insurance Corporation.

F.D.I.C.—Federal Deposit Insurance Corporation.

F.F.V.—first families of Virginia; a snobbish term first used about 1847.

F.O.B.—free on board; meaning that the ship is free from all risk after an item is shipped.

F.T.C.—Federal Trade Commission.

F.Y.I.—For Your Information; ubiquitous on office memos.

G.P.O.—Government Printing Office.

G.A.R.—Grand Army of the Republic, the Civil War veterans organization.

G.D.—God damned; another eusystolism.

G.I.—government issue, originally; has come to mean a soldier in the ranks, who in a way is government issue.

G-MAN—government man; once commonly used for an F.B.I. agent.

G.O.P.—Grand Old Party, official nickname of the Republicans; used since 1887 when it also meant "get out and push" (your horse or car), and was probably suggested by G.O.M., which the English called their Grand Old Man, Prime Minister Gladstone.

G.P.—general practitioner (or grateful patient).

G.Y.N.—gynecology.

H.M.S.—Her (or His) Majesty's Ship; appears only on ships in the British service. O.H.M.S. means On Her/His Majesty's Service.

IBID.—from the Latin *ibidem*, "in the same place."

ID.—abbreviation of the Latin *idem*, "the same."

I.E., E.G.—i.e. is from the Latin *id est*, "that is," and the term introduces a definition; while e.g. (from the Latin *exempli gratia*, "for example") introduces an example.

IHS—the abbreviation is simply the first two letters and last letter of the Greek word for Jesus, capitalized and Romanized. It does not stand for *in hoc signo* ("in this sign") or any other phrase.

I.O.U—for "I owe you"; an unusual abbreviation that is based on sound, not sight.

IQ—intelligence quotient.

IWW—the initials of the "Wobblies" stand not for International Workers of the World, as is commonly believed, but for Industrial Workers of the World.

K.O.—knockout.

LB.—this abbreviation for "pound" comes from the Latin *libra ponda*, "a pound in weight."

L.P.—long-playing record.

LSD and L.S.D.—LSD is the abbreviation for both the amphibious vessel (formed from landing ship deck) and lysergic acid diethylamide, which is more properly abbreviated LSD-25. L.S.D., with periods, stands for shillings, pounds, and pence, deriving from the Latin *librae, solidi, denarii.*

L.S.T.—landing ship tank.

LTD.—stands for "limited" and is used in England simply to indicate that any partner in a firm has limited financial liability, never more than his investment in the concern.

M.C.—**m**aster of **c**eremonies; often spelled *emcee*, making it a full-fledged word.

MIG—standing for a Russian jet fighter, from the initials of the designers of a series of Russian fighters.

MRS., MR.—originally Mrs. stood for "mistress," when "mistress" meant a married woman; but since a mistress today is something entirely different, Mrs. cannot be considered a true abbreviation anymore—unlike Mr. (mister) there is no full form for the word.

MS.—"manuscript"; also a title for a married or unmarried woman.

N.G.—for "**n**o **g**ood"; goes back to 1839.

O.C.S.—Officers Candidate School.

P.J.s—**p**a**j**amas.

P.O.ed—**p**issed **o**ff, mad.

P.R.—**p**ublic **r**elations.

P.D.Q.—stands for "pretty damn quick," e.g., "You'd better get started P.D.Q." Its origin hasn't been established beyond doubt, though it has been attributed to Dan Maguinnis, a Boston comedian appearing about 1867–1889.

P.O.W.—**p**risoner **o**f **w**ar.

P.M.—abbreviation of the Latin *post meridiem*, "after noon."

P.S.—from the Latin *post-scriptum*, "written afterward."

PTA—**P**arent-**T**eacher **A**ssociation; has become simply **PA, Parents Association**, in many communities.

Q.E.D.—from the Latin *quod erat demonstrandum*, "which was to be demonstrated"; always capitalized.

Q.T.—an abbreviation for "quiet"; "on the q.t." means stealthily, secretly, e.g., "to meet someone on the q.t." Origin unknown.

Q.V.—from the Latin *quod vide*, "which see."

℞—the Latin *recipere* (take this) provides the R in the symbol ℞ used by pharmacists for centuries, while the slant across the R's leg is the sign of the god Jupiter, the Roman patron of medicine. The symbol looks like R_X and is pronounced that way.

R&D—**r**esearch and **d**evelopment program.

R&R—**r**est and **r**ecuperation leave, armed forces.

RE—often used as an abbreviation for "in regard to," this is actually the ablative of the Latin *res*, "thing" or "matter."

R.F.D.—**r**ural **f**ree **d**elivery (U.S. Post Office).

R.I.P.—from the Latin *requiescat in pace*, "rest in peace."

R.P.M.—revolutions per minute.

R.S.V.P.—stands for the French *répondez s'il vous plaît*, "please reply," "the favor of a reply is requested."

S.E.C.—Securities and Exchange Commission.

S.O.B.—son of a bitch; first appeared widely in written form when Harry Truman criticized the music critic who criticized his daughter.

S.O.L.—slang for "strictly out of luck."

S.O.P.—standard operating procedure.

S.R.O.—standing room only.

S.S.—steamship; used for ships of all nationalities.

SS CORPS—the dreaded *Schutzstaffel*, black-uniformed Nazi elite corps.

SWALK—sealed with a loving kiss (initialed on back of envelopes).

T.I.D.—abbreviations of the Latin *tres in die* ("three times a day"), often printed on prescription drug labels.

T.K.O.—technical knockout, boxing.

T.L.—a compliment returned to one who has given a compliment; from the archaic "trade last."

T.S.—tough shit; still another example of a eusystolism. "Tough stuff" is its euphemism.

T.V.A.—Tennessee Valley Authority.

U AND NON-U—the *U* in the abbreviations stands for "upper class."

UFO—unidentified flying object, the term coined in recent times, though the first sightings of such objects were reported as far back as 1896!

U-BOAT—this term for a German submarine is an abbreviation of the German *Unterseeboot* (underwater vessel).

U.S.S.—United States Ship, used only on U.S. Navy ships.

V.A.—Veterans Administration.

V.D.—venereal disease.

V.I.P.—very important person.

VIZ—represents the Latin word *videlicet*, "namely," and needs no period.

VS.—abbreviation of the Latin *versus*, "against."

WC—water closet, British for "toilet."

W.P.A.—Works Progress Administration.

IN PRAISE OF PALINDROMES

So SCURRILOUS in his satires was Sotades, a Greek poet of the third century B.C., that Ptolemy II had him sewn up in a sack and thrown into the sea. But his coarse, vile verses must have been clever, for Sotades is reputed to have invented palindromes, which are sometimes called *Sotadics* in his honor. Palindromes take their more common name from the Greek *palin dromo*, "running back again," and they are simply anagrams (*q.v.*) that read the same backward as forward. Making words or sentences that read the same backward as they do forward has been a favorite word game at least since early Grecian times, but English, with the largest and most varied vocabulary of all languages (some 800,000 words), provides the most fertile ground for the palindromist. It's said that Sir Thomas Urquhart even invented a universal language based entirely on palindromes.

Probably the longest common English palindromic word is the nine-letter *redivider*, but the nine-letter *Malayalam*, the name given to the language of the Malayali people in southern India, equals it, and the rare *kinnikinnik*, a dried leaf and bark mixture smoked by the Cree Indians, tops it by two letters. *Detartrated*, a contrived chemical term, also has eleven letters.

The longest palindromic composition seems to be the 11,125-word opus constructed by New Zealander Jeff Grant in 1979, which begins: "No elate man I meet sees a bed . . ." But the longest halfway-sensible one was coined by an anonymous nineteenth-century English poet:

> *Dog as a devil deified*
> *Deified lived as a god.*

"Madam, I'm Adam," Adam might have said when he first met Eve, and she, pointing to herself, might have said, palindromically, "Eve." Obviously they didn't, though, not speaking English, just as Napoleon couldn't have moaned, "Able was I ere I saw Elba," when he was deported to that lonely isle. Actually, there are not many unintentional palindromes, though places like the *Yreka Bakery* in Yreka, California, may qualify. (The odd-named town takes its name from a misspelling of *Eureka*.) The sign "Redroot Put Up to Order" spotted by someone in an Alabama town might be unintentional, too, but the phrase has been known as a palindrome for at least a century.

Most palindromes have been invented, the best example being the tribute English author Leigh Mercer wrote for Ferdinand de Lesseps, the man who built the Panama Canal: *A Man, A Plan, A Canal: Panama!* The only palindrome considered to be anything approaching literature is the imperfect line written by English poet John Philips in 1706: "Lewd did I live & evil I did dwel," which uses an ampersand and an old spelling of dwell.

Palindromes are usually anonymous, though. Other old-time favorites include "Name no one man"; "Dennis and Edna sinned"; "Pa's a sap"; and "Niagara, O roar again!" These all make sense, as does any good palindrome. Examples such as "Lew, Otto has a hot towel" and "A dog! A panic in a pagoda" are questionable at best. One of the best conversational palindromes has been recorded by Martin Gardner, publisher of *Scientific American*. Two people are discussing the best cure for warts and one says: "Straw? No, too stupid a fad. I put soot on warts."

ANAGRAMS

AN *anagram* is the rearrangement of the letters of a word or group of words to make another word or group of words, the word *anagram* itself deriving from the Greek *ana graphein*, "to write over again." Popular as wordplay since the earliest times, anagrams were possibly invented by the ancient Jews, and the cabalists, constantly looking for "secret mysteries . . . woven in the numbers of letters," always favored them, as did the Greeks and Romans. A famous Latin anagram was an answer made out of the question Pontius Pilate asked in the trial of Jesus. *Quid est veritas?* ("What is truth?") was the question, the answer *Est vir qui adest* ("It is the man who is here").

Anagrams became so popular in medieval Europe, particularly in France, that one Thomas Billon was appointed "anagrammatist to the king," by Louis XIII. Some medieval astronomers even wrote their discoveries in anagrams to prevent others from taking credit for them before they could be verified.

Though poet John Dryden called anagrams the "torturing of one poor word ten thousand ways," the English are among the best and most accurate anagrammatists. Samuel Butler's novel *Erewhon* derives its title from the word *nowhere*, almost spelled backward, and a tribe in the book is called the Sumarongi, *ignoramus* spelled backward. Other noted English anagrams include the names of Horatio Nelson made into the Latin *Honor est a Nilo*; Florence Nightingale changed into "Flit on, cheering angel"; "Queen Victoria's Jubilee" made into "I require love in a subject"; Adolf Hitler into "hated for ill"; Sir Robert Peel into "terrible prose"; Robert Louis Stevenson into "our best novelist, señor"; Oliver Wendell Holmes into "He'll do in mellow verse"; William Shakespeare as "I ask me, has Will a peer?"; and Henry Wadsworth Longfellow as "Won half the New World's glory." Among the many interchangeable words which can form *anagrams* in English are *evil* and *live*, and *eros* and *rose*, but the longest are two sixteen-letter pairs: *conservationists* and *conversationists*; and *internationalism* and *interlaminations*. A recent apt anagram suggested by Martin Gardner is *moon starers*, an anagram for *astronomer*.

Authors' pseudonyms (see *Pseudonymous Authors*) have many perfect and imperfect anagrams among them. *Voltaire* is said to be an anagram of the French author's family name—that is, *Arouet, l.j.*, or Arouet the younger. Others include *Alcofribas Nasier*, a pseudonym François Rabelais made from his name; and *Fernán Caballero*, the pen name Spanish novelist Cecilia Böhl de Faber constructed from her name.

In the early seventeenth century Lady Eleanor Davies believed that she had supernatural prophetic powers similar to the Biblical Daniel's because her name made the imperfect anagram "Reveal O Daniel!" She only renounced such claims when a judge anagramized "Dame Eleanor Davies" into "Never so mad a ladie." (See also *In Praise of Palindromes* for another species of anagram.)

A HISTORICAL ANAGRAM

AT THE URGING of Thomas Jefferson's administration Congress passed the Embargo Act of 1807 in answer to British and French restrictions on American shipping. The act, the only one of its kind in American history, forbade all international trade to and from our ports, refusing entrance to foreign ships and confining American ships. It proved highly unpopular, especially in coastal areas where ships rotted at the wharves, and the Embargo Act was dubbed *O-Grab-Me*, which was *Embargo* spelled backward and one of the few anagrams in American political history. The act may have been named *O-Grab-Me* because all sorts of schemes were used to evade the law and New England sea captains facetiously said the government "would have to grab me first" before they obeyed it. In any case, the British and French stood firm, enough pressure could not be brought to bear, and the Embargo Act was abandoned, though not before it had tarnished Jefferson's prestige.

SENTENCES AND CIVILIZATION

I REALLY DO not know that anything has ever been more important than diagramming sentences.   —Gertrude Stein

PARTS OF SPEECH

Three little words you often see
Are ARTICLES, a, an *and* the.
A NOUN'*s the name of anything;*
As school *or* garden, hoop *or* swing.
ADJECTIVES *tell the kind of noun;*
As great, small, pretty, white, *or* brown.
Instead of nouns the PRONOUNS *stand;*
Her face, *his* face, *our* arms, *your* hand.
VERBS *tell of something being done;*
To read, count, sing, laugh, jump *or* run.
How things are done the ADVERBS *tell;*
As slowly, quickly, ill *or* well.
CONJUNCTIONS *join the words together;*
As men *and* women, wind *or* weather;
The PREPOSITION *stands before*
A noun, *as* in *or* through *a* door.
The INTERJECTION *shows surprise;*
As oh! *how pretty!* ah! *how wise!*
The whole are called nine parts of speech,
Which reading, writing, speaking teach.
                    —Anonymous

OF SIGNS AND SYMBOLS

All about ., or the period

*H*AS ANYONE written a book about periods, those at the end of sentences? I don't know, but one entire book is filled with dots, which might loosely be considered periods (see *Books Without Letters*). Periods are not always the last thing in a sentence; for example, a sentence ending with a quoted word must have its period inside the quotation marks. Marlowe wrote of all poetry distilled into "one poem's period," but the period's great lover in literary history was Russian author Isaac Babel, murdered by Soviet secret police in 1939, who wrote: "No iron can stab the heart with such force as a period put just at the right place."

The !

Like & (*q.v.*) *!* goes by a number of names. In America it's usually called an *exclamation mark* or *point*, but the British call it, more simply, an *exclamation*, and sometimes a *note* or *point of exclamation*. Anyone using the older rhetorical terms *ecphonesis* (the outcry) or *epiphonema* for the grammatical interjection rates an ! of surprise, which is called a *note of admiration*, or, depending on your taste, *a note of detestation*. Shakespeare used the phrase *note of admiration* (!) effectively in *A Winter's Tale*: "The charges I perceived in the King and Camillo were very Notes of admiration." But sometimes writers slashed pages with scores of them following words and phrases intended to be uttered with an intonation of exclamation or surprise, leading Swift to write that a reader should skip over sentences with *notes of admiration* at the end. For that matter the *exclamation* has had few friends throughout history. Dr. Johnson defined it as "a note by which a pathetical sentence is marked thus!"; while Spenser said, "The lowest form of language is the exclamation, by which an entire idea is vaguely conveyed through a single sound." But the powerful points do have their uses in small doses—showing strong emotions or emphasizing commands or warnings. They seem to have been invented by the Italians and came into English use about four centuries ago. Tradition says that the mark derives from the Latin *io* (exclamation of joy), written vertically as I̞, which became ! in time.

I see—I see— I know not what:
I see a dash above a dot,
Presenting to my contemplation
A perfect point of admiration

(?!.ö&)

—impromptu verse
by Dr. Johnson

The ?

The question mark, interrogation mark, or interrogation point, one tradition has it, was formed from the first and last letters of the Latin *quaestio* ("a seeking") which was first contracted to Q , and finally became ?. Some authorities claim, however, that it originated as the Greek semicolon—upside down. Another kind of question mark is a butterfly (*Polygonia interrogationis*) with two silver spots shaped like a question mark under each wing.

The Umlaut

The only English authors, and perhaps the only English family, with an umlaut in their name are the Brontë sisters—Charlotte, Emily, and Anne. Their father, Patrick Brunty, a poor Irishman trying to distinguish himself at Cambridge, changed the family name to Brontë soon after Lord Nelson was created Duke of Bronte, adding the German umlaut to give himself more éclat. In German the umlaut is used to indicate an internal vowel change in a word or to show that a letter is pronounced differently than it ordinarily would be. It is also called a diaeresis in English, when it is used above the second of two coupled vowels to show separate pronunciation, as in *coöperate*. Please advise of any other noted Englishman or American with an umlaut in his or her name.

(Parentheses)

A *parenthesis* is a word, phrase, or clause inserted in a sentence that is grammatically complete without the insertion. The device goes back to at least the sixteenth century, when the *parentheses* or "upright curves" themselves (the marks enclosing these words) were sometimes called "halfe circles" and "round brackets." Parenthetical remarks, however, can be made between dashes and commas as well as within parentheses. Mark Twain had the last word on parentheses. "Parentheses in literature and dentistry are in bad taste," he wrote, comparing *parenthetical expressions* "to dentists who grab a tooth and launch into a tedious anecdote before giving the painful jerk."

The History of ♀ and ♂

Perhaps you've wondered about the derivation of these standard scientific symbols for female and male. The female symbol is the representation of a hand mirror and is associated with Aphrodite, the Greek goddess of beauty; it also serves as the symbol of the planet Venus (the Roman name for Aphrodite). The male symbol represents the shield and spear of Mars, the Roman god of war; it serves also as the symbol of the planet Mars.

The Interrobang

Interrobang? Yes. It is the very newest of punctuation marks, devised by an American typecasting company. A combination question mark and exclamation point, it is used after an expression that could be both a question and exclamation, such as "Where's the fire?!" Resembling an exclamation point superimposed on a question mark (‽), it takes its name from the *inter* in *interrogation* and the printer's slang *bang* for an exclamation point.

And All About &

& is the oldest word symbol known & means the same in over a hundred languages. But first, a little about &'s history. & was invented by Marcus Tullius Tiro, who introduced it in about 63 B.C. as part of the first system of shorthand of which there is any record. A learned Roman freedman & amanuensis to Cicero, Tiro invented his *Tironian Notes* to take down his friend's fluent dictation, but he also used it to write works of his own, which included some of the great orator's speeches & even some of Cicero's letters to him! Tiro's shorthand system was based on the orthographic principle & made abundant use of initials, the & sign that was part of it being a contraction for the Latin *et* ("and").

Tiro's system was taught in Roman schools, used to record speeches in the senate, & saw wide used in Europe for almost a thousand years. That brings the history of & up to the Middle Ages, when it was still called the *Tironian sign*, in Tiro's honor. At this time & acquired the name *ampersand*. This happened when children learning the alphabet were taught to distinguish between the letter *a* & the word *a*—as in "a girl," "a boy," etc. A as a word was always recited "*A* per se *A*," meaning "*A* by itself (per se) *A*." The same was done to distinguish the letter *i* from the pronoun *I*—the pronoun was called "*I* per se *I*" (*I* by itself *I*) whenever the alphabet was recited. Finally, at the very end of the old alphabet books, the common symbol & was listed. It was always recited "*And* per se *and*"—& children's ears being less than accurate, soon came to be pronounced *ampersand*. & from then on *ampersand*, not *Tironian sign*, meant *and* or &.

PUNCTUATING NONSENSE

MAKE SENSE from nonsense by punctuating the following rhyme properly, using just one kind of punctuation:

I saw a peacock with a fiery tail
I saw a blazing comet pour down hail
I saw a cloud all wrapt with ivy round
I saw a lofty oak creep on the ground
I saw a beetle swallow up a whale
I saw a foaming sea brimful of ale
I saw a pewter cup sixteen feet deep
I saw a well full of men's tears that weep
I saw wet eyes in flames of living fire
I saw a house as high as the moon and higher
I saw the glorious sun at deep midnight
I saw the man who saw this wondrous sight.

Solution: A semicolon placed after the first noun in every line but the last makes the rhyme intelligible.

"YOU HAVE A POINT THERE"

THE WISEST point ever made about punctuation was made by John Benlow in the Oxford University Press style book: "If you take hyphens seriously, you will surely go mad." He should have applied it to all punctuation, about which no writer has ever made much sense. The best rule I can give for literary punctuation is the old or perhaps legendary practice of typesetters: "Set type as long as you can hold your breath without getting blue in the face, then put in a comma; when you yawn put in a semicolon; and when you want to sneeze, that's time for a paragraph."

Dumas *père* left all punctuation to his secretaries. Gertrude Stein hated commas and would have rid the world of them. Said she: "If you want to take a breath you ought to know yourself that you want to take a breath."

But the wrong punctuation can be costly. In the 1890s a congressional clerk was supposed to write: "All foreign fruit-plants are free from duty" in transcribing a recently passed bill, but changed the hyphen to a comma and wrote: "All foreign fruit, plants are free from duty." Before Congress could correct his error with a new law the government lost over $2 million in taxes. There have been several similar cases concerning wills.

In another instance a district attorney introduced an unpunctuated confession taken down by a police officer that read: "Mangan said he never robbed but twice said it was Crawford." The prosecution contended this should have been punctuated: "Mangan said he never robbed but twice. Said it was Crawford." The defense said the sentence should read: "Mangan said he never robbed; but twice said it was Crawford." The last introduced a reasonable doubt and the accused went free.

Before the word *comma* took on its present meaning as a punctuation mark, it meant "a short phrase"; similarly a *colon* was a long phrase, and a *period* was two or more phrases.

In a late-nineteenth-century book called *The Queen's English* the author writes: "I have some satisfaction in reflecting, that in the course of editing the Greek text, I believe I have destroyed more than a thousand commas, which prevented the text from being properly understood." The sentence contains a superfluous comma after *reflecting* and, more important, another redundant comma after *commas* which ironically prevents his own text from being properly understood.

A German burgomaster said that he cared nothing for such trifles as commas and the village schoolteacher had a pupil write on the blackboard: "The burgomaster of R———, says, the teacher is an ass."

He then told the boy to reposition the commas so that the sentence read: "The burgomaster of R———, says the teacher, is an ass."

PUNCTUATION POSERS

MATCH the following diacritical marks and other typographical signs with their names.

1.	reëstablish	A.	exclamation mark
2.	señor	B.	asterisk
3.	&	C.	circumflex
4.	*	D.	grave accent mark
5.	être	E.	ampersand or Tironian sign
6.	père	F.	parentheses
7.	[ ]	G.	diaeresis, or umlaut
8.	( )	H.	cedilla
9.	!	I.	tilde
10.	façade	J.	brackets
11.	pensée	K.	apostrophe
12.	don't	L.	acute accent mark

ANSWERS: 1.G 2.I 3.E 4.B 5.C 6.D 7.J 8.F 9.A 10.H 11.L 12.K

The Worst of All Possible Words

NAUGHTY WORDS

Dr. Johnson silenced two spinsters who complimented him for the omission of "naughty words" in his great dictionary with the comment: "What! my dears! then you have been looking for them."

BLARNEY

Blarney Castle, built by Cormac McCarthy in 1446 and named for a little village nearby only a few miles north of Cork, Ireland, was put under siege by the British in 1602. But McCarthy Mor, the ancestor of its builder,

supposedly refused to surrender the fortress to Queen
Elizabeth's Lord President of Munster, Sir George
Carew. All poor Carew got from McCarthy day after
day for months were promises that he would eventually
surrender, followed by polite but fanciful excuses for
his delays in fulfilling the promises. His smooth talk
and empty vows became a joking matter, making
Carew the laughingstock of Elizabeth's ministers and
blarney a byword for cajolery, flattering, or wheedling
talk. One storyteller even claims that Queen Elizabeth

herself coined the word when she received an evasive letter from McCarthy and
said, "This is more of the same Blarney." Legends about Blarney Castle are
legion, but there is a stone about twenty feet from the top of the castle wall
inscribed "Cormac McCarthy *fortis me fieri fecit*, A.D. 1446," which may have
been set there to commemorate the verbal defeat of the English by the Irish. The
triangular stone is difficult to reach and a legend grew up in the seventeenth
century that if one could scale the wall and kiss the Blarney stone one would
be blessed with all the eloquent persuasive powers of McCarthy Mor, that is,
be able to lie with a straight face. The Blarney stone that people kiss today is a
substitute provided to make things easier for tourists.

MUMBO JUMBO

THE SCOTTISH EXPLORER Mungo Park wrote in his *Travels in the Interior
of Africa* (1779) that Mama Dyumbo was the spirit or god protecting the villages
of the Khassonke, a Mandingo African tribe on the Senegal River. The spirit's
name literally means "ancestor with a pompom," or one wearing a tuft on his
hat. Mama Dyumbo was also a ploy by crafty husbands to silence their noisy
wives. He was called upon when a man thought that one of his wives talked
too much, causing dissension in his house. The husband or a confederate would
disguise himself as Mama Dyumbo and seize the troublemaker, frightening her
with his mask, tufted headdress, and hideous noises. He would then tie the
offender to a tree and whip her until she was silent, amid the jeers of onlookers.
Mungo Park dubbed the bogey employed in this ritual Mandingo, but he became
known as Mumbo Jumbo, a corruption of *Mama Dyumbo*. Because the god
bewildered offending women, *mumbo jumbo* came to mean confusing talk,
nonsense, and meaningless ceremony, or even technical jargon that could just
as well be put into plain English.

GIBBERISH

GEBER, or more properly, Jabir ibn Hazyan (*Jabir* is the Arabic for *Geber*) was an eighth-century Arab alchemist who wrote his formulas in seemingly unintelligible jargon and anagrams in order to avoid the death penalty for sorcery. For this reason Dr. Johnson, the eighteenth-century English antiquary Francis Grose, and other prominent word detectives believed that the word *gibberish* (nonsense or words without meaning) derives from Geber's name. Geber could not have written all the 200 books attributed to him, but he was a prolific writer, sufficiently respected for many medieval scientists to cite him as an authority and for one fourteenth-century Spanish alchemist to go so far as to adopt his name. Today many authorities speculate that *gibberish* is imitative of the sound of nonsense, an onomatopoetic word like *jabber*, *gabble*, *giggle*, and *gurgle*, and at most was only influenced by Geber's name. *Gibberish* does not derive from the verb *gibber*, which it preceded in use.

BUNK

THE MISSOURI COMPROMISE was being hotly debated that morning of February 25, 1820, when long-winded Congressman Felix Walker of Buncombe County, North Carolina, rose on the floor of the House of Representatives and insisted that he be heard before a vote was taken. "Old Oil Jug" (as his fellow congressmen called him because of his well-lubricated vocal cords) did not address himself to the monumental question of the extension of slavery; his interminable oration actually had little to do with anything, and important members began interrupting him with cries of "Question, Question!" On being asked what purpose his speech served, Walker calmly remarked, "You're not hurting my feelings, gentlemen. I am not speaking for your ears. I am only talking for Buncombe." Old Oil Jug apparently had written his speech some time before and believed he would ingratiate himself with the voters back home if he delivered it in the midst of a great debate, but the strategy didn't work, judging by the fact that he lost the next election. Yet his reply *I am only talking for Buncombe* was widely published in newspapers covering the debate and became a synonym for speaking nonsense. Eventually, *Buncombe* became *bunkum*, and it finally (in the 1850s) took the shortened form *bunk*, meaning not only bombastic political talk but any empty, inflated speech obviously meant to fool people.

COCK-AND-BULL STORIES

*T*HESE LONG, rambling, unlikely yarns, like the similar *canard*, take their name from the barnyard. The phrase first appeared in about 1600 and has been constantly used ever since; even in such classics as Laurence Sterne's *Tristram Shandy* (1767), where the words end the book: " 'L—d' said my mother, 'what is this story all about.' '—A COCK and a BULL,' said Yorick—'and one of the best of its kind, I ever heard.' "

The expression *cock-and-bull story* hasn't been traced to the specific fable where it originated, but it arose, in all probability, from a fantastic tale about a cock and a bull that talked to each other in human language. Since people knew that such a conversation was impossible, they most likely labeled any incredible yarns *cock-and-bull stories*. There is another slim possibility that the original tale told of a cock and a bull that were changed into one animal having the characteristics of both. But the expression arose quite some time before that story was recorded anywhere.

Stories of talking animals have been common since the fables of Aesop and in medieval times were collected in volumes called bestiaries, where the behavior of the animals points a moral. Notable ones include Chaucer's Chanticleer story in the "Nun's Priest's Tale" and Goethe's "Reineke Fuchs." Modern developments of the form can be found in George Orwell's political satire *Animal Farm* and in Richard Adams's *Watership Down*, among many others. The French have used the expression *coq-à-l'âne*—literally, "cock to the donkey"—in the same sense as *cock-and-bull* for almost four centuries, too. But it is also the term for a satirical verse genre that ridicules the follies and vices of society, deriving in this sense from the old French proverbial expression *sauter du coq à-l'âne*, which signifies incoherent speech or writing.

CANARD

*S*OMETHING ONE *canardly* believe, as a punster put it. In French, *canard* means "duck," and the word *canard* for a ridiculously false story comes from the French expression *vendre un canard à moitié*—literally, "to half-sell a duck." As a duck, or anything else, can't be half-sold, the expression figuratively means to make a fool out of a buyer, or anyone else, with a false story. Tellers of "half-ducks," or *canards*, were known in France three centuries ago, and the word probably gained a firmer foothold with a hoax played by a Frenchman named Cornelessin. Cornelessin, testing the gullibility of the public, published a story that he had thirty ducks, one of which he killed and threw to the other twenty-nine, which ate it. Then he cut up a second, then a third, until the twenty-ninth duck was eaten by the survivor—an excellent bull, duck, or *canard* story.

GASCONADE

*T*HE INHABITANTS of Gascony, France, a region and former province near the Spanish border, have traditionally been regarded by other Frenchmen as flamboyantly boastful, a poor people except in their bravery and bragging. This tradition can be seen in Dumas *père's The Three Musketeers*, in which brave, boastful D'Artagnan is the very model of a Gascon.
Many old French *contes* illustrated Gascon braggadocio. One tells of a Gascon's being asked how he liked the great Louvre in Paris. "Pretty well," the braggart replies, "it reminds me of the back part of my father's stables." Such stories, and the sentiments that inspired them, led to the coining of *gasconade*—extravagant boasting or swashbuckling braggadocio—a word that became universal because it described so many people other than Gascons.

GHOST WORDS

*G*host *words* are words that never existed until someone mistook an error for a word or invented a word for a special occasion. An example of the latter, also called a *nonce word*, is Lewis Carroll's *jabberwocky*, invented for the nonce (for a single use in his book *Through the Looking Glass*). Many nonce words have become full members of the language (see *Invented Words*). Ghost words—the term was invented by etymologist Walter William Skeat—are usually spurious terms, the result of errors made by authors, typists, editors, and printers, and they hardly ever become part of the language. An example of a lasting ghost word is *dord* (meaning density) which can be found in the 1934 *Merriam-Webster Dictionary*, second edition. *Dord* began life as an error made in transcribing a card that read: "*D or d*, meaning a capital D or small d—for 'density.' " Eliminated from future Merriam-Webster dictionaries, the ghost word lives on in the 1934 edition.

HEDGE WORDS

*M*Y FAVORITE STORY about these common journalistic disclaimers of responsibility concerns Mark Twain and his first job as a reporter. Twain was told by his editor never to state as fact anything he couldn't verify by personal knowledge. After covering a gala social event, he turned in the following story: "A woman giving the name of Mrs. James Jones, who is reported to be one of the society leaders of the city, is said to have given what purported to be a party yesterday to a number of alleged ladies. The hostess claims to be the wife of a reputed attorney."

The use of such disclaimers does *not* automatically confer immunity from prosecution for libel, as the law punishes *publication* of a libel, which, legally, means "making public."

GOBBLEDYGOOK

No lost time injuries that do not result in a medical expense should not be reported to the OWCP.

*T*HE ABOVE "instructions" from the United States Department of Labor won a $10 prize for the worst phrase of the day in a *Washington Star* section called "Gobbledygook." Another sample, not reported by the *Star*, was received by a World War II veteran inquiring about a pension. Advised the Veterans Administration: "The noncompensable evaluation heretobefore assigned to you for your service-connected disability is confirmed and continued." (Translation: You don't get the pension.)

Gobbledygook (sometimes spelled *gobbledegook*) means obscure, verbose, bureaucratic language characterized by circumlocution and jargon, and usually refers to the meaningless officialese turned out by government agencies. The late Representative Maury Maverick, one of whose ancestors gave us the word *maverick*, coined *gobbledygook* in 1944, when he was chairman of the Smaller War Plant Committee in Congress. Maverick had just attended a meeting of the committee, at which phrases such as "cause an investigation to be made with a view to ascertaining" were rife. He wrote a memo condemning such officialese and labeled it *gobbledygook*, later explaining that he was thinking of the gobbling of turkeys while they strutted pompously. *Gobbledygook* is clearly better than *jargantuan*, *bafflegab*, *barnacular*, *pudder*, and *pentagonese*, all synonyms.

George Orwell's "translation" of a passage in Ecclesiastes is a good example of gobbledygook:

Ecclesiastes: I returned and saw under the sun, that the race is not to the swift, nor the battle to the strong, neither yet bread to the wise, nor yet riches to men of understanding, nor yet favor to men of skill; but time and chance happen to them all.

Translation into gobbledygook: Objective consideration of contemporary phenomena compels the conclusion that success or failure in competitive activities exhibits no tendency to be commensurate with innate capacity, but that a considerable element of the unpredictable must be taken into account.

So is Orwell's transformation of Lord Nelson's immortal phrase "England expects every man to do his duty":

England anticipates that, as regards the current emergency, personnel will face up to the issues, and exercise appropriately the functions allocated to their respective occupational groups.

There is an old story about a plumber who wrote Washington's Bureau of Standards saying that he had used hydrochloric acid for cleaning drains, and was it harmless? "The efficacy of hydrochloric acid is indisputable, but the chlorine residue is incompatible with metallic permanence," Washington replied. The plumber wrote back that he was glad the bureau agreed and the alarmed bureau answered: "We cannot assume responsibility for the production of toxic and noxious residues with hydrochloric acid, and suggest that you use an alternate procedure." Again the plumber was glad the bureau agreed with him. In fact, nothing would convince him that it didn't until Washington wired back: "Don't use hydrochloric acid; it eats the hell out of the pipes!"

According to the *Washington Post*, Philip Broughton, a veteran employee of the United States Public Health Service, has invented the "Systematic Buzz Phrase Projector," a surefire way to fashion gobbledygook should you want to use it for purposes of obfuscation. A writer just thinks of any three-digit number at random and selects the corresponding "buzzwords" from three columns of such words that Broughton provides. The number 257, for example, yields "systematized logistical projection," a phrase that can be used in almost any report. "No one will have the remotest idea of what you're talking about," says Broughton. "But the important thing is that they're not about to admit it." Author Gershon Legman has a similar four-column system of phrases called FARK (Folklore Article Reconstruction Kit) which he claims will enable any "Folklore Ph.D." to devise "40,000 new and meaningful, well-balanced, and grammatically acceptable sentences packed with Folklore terms." Choosing, for example, the numbers 7, 4, 8, and 2 from Legman's columns, the writer gets: "Based on my own fieldwork in Guatemala/initiation of basic charismatic subculture development/recognizes the importance of other disciplines, while taking into account/the anticipated epistemological repercussions."

"BEWARE OF AND ESCHEW POMPOUS PROLIXITY"

W HEN Charles A. Beardsley, then president of the American Bar Association, kidded his fellow lawyers with the above advice, he campaigned against what philosopher Jeremy Bentham called "literary garbage," legal talk that has nothing to do with communication. "Legalese" consists principally of long-windedness, stilted phrases such as "Know all men by these presents," redundancies including "separate and apart" or "aid and abet," such quaintisms as "herewith and heretofore," and foreign-language phrases that could easily be translated into plain English: e.g., *caveat emptor* ("let the buyer beware") or *amicus curiae* ("friend of the court"). Despite the efforts of Beardsley and many others, the situation has not improved much over the last millennium. Some, like Sir Thomas More, have believed that it never will. More, a lawyer himself, explained that lawyers are "people whose profession is to disguise matters."

AUTOMATIC WRITING

AUTOMATIC WRITING is writing performed without the will or control of the writer, sometimes without the writer's being conscious of the words written. The phenomenon first appeared in mid-nineteenth-century America as a tool of spiritualism, and the writer was sometimes (but not always) hypnotized or drugged and aided by instruments including a planchette, "a little heart-shaped board running on wheels," that was supplemented by a Ouija board containing the alphabet and other signs. Knowledge that had disappeared from conscious

memory, such as fragments of poetry or foreign poetry, often surfaced in automatic writing, and the writing frequently produced "anagrams, puns, nonsense verses, and occasional blasphemes and obscenities . . . markedly divergent from those of the normal consciousness." Books in "unknown tongues" written by automatists include Andrew J. Davis's *Great Harmonia* (1851), Charles Linton's *The Healing of Nations* (1854), and J. Murray Spear's *Messages from the Superior State* (1852). Thomas Flournoy reported a case of automatist's writing in Martian in his *Des Indées à la Planète Mars* (1900). Used by psychiatrists as well as spiritualists, automatic writing was also adopted as a tool by the illogical Dadaists and the nonlogical Surrealists who followed them, for it aided both schools in liberating their minds from logic and reason. William Butler Yeats, who had a great interest in spiritualism, experimented with automatic writing over a long period and it may have influenced his work.

HORATIO ALGER TALES

A HORATIO ALGER tale is a cliché-ridden rags-to-riches story, but ironically, none of the heroes the prolific Horatio Alger (1834–1899) created in his novels ever became rich. His poor but honest characters struggled to get ahead against overwhelming odds and always succeeded in improving their lot, even found fame and glory (at least one became a senator), but great monetary rewards never came to Ragged Dick and company. Alger's books, of little interest to anyone but historians and nostalgia buffs today, served a real need in his time. Dull and unimaginative and filled with preachments his pages were, but his philosophy of hard work and clean living influenced three generations of Americans. By far the most popular author of his day, Alger aspired to be the Great American Novelist, but according to Herbert R. Mayes in his biography: "Each book bound him closer to the mediocrity he chose to avoid. Each book made it less possible for him to accomplish the ambition of his life." An Alger biography even claims that this author of moralistic books for children was a pederast, obsessed with young boys. So much for shattered illusions, but here is a sample of the man's work, anyway. Thirteen-year-old Frank Whitney gives advice to Ragged Dick in Alger's book of the same name:

> "You began in the right way when you determined never to steal or do anything mean or dishonorable, however strongly tempted to do so. That will make people have confidence in you when they come to know you. But, in order to succeed well, you must manage to get as good an education as you can."
>
> "That is so," replied Dick, "I never thought how awful ignorant I was till now."
>
> "That can be remedied by perseverance," said Frank.

THE POETRY OF ERN MALLEY

Swamps, marshes, barrowpits and other
Areas of stagnant water serve
As breeding grounds.
—"Culture and Exhibit," Ern Malley

ACCORDING TO the editor of *Angry Penguins*, an Australian literary journal, Ern Malley, who had "recently died at the age of 25," was "one of the two
giants of contemporary Australian poetry." *Angry Penguins* published a large
selection of Malley's poems in 1944, including the lines above, his work supposedly submitted by his sister. Unfortunately, the journal had been hoaxed.
Ern Malley turned out to be two Australian servicemen, Lieutenant James
MacAuley and Corporal Harold Stewart, who had whiled away some time by
constructing "Malley's poems from lines pieced together from whatever books
they had on hand; the lines quoted above were taken verbatim from a United
States bulletin on mosquito control.

THE WORLD'S LONGEST LIST OF LONG WORDS

(Try making a paragraph out of these monsters if you have a few days):

1. According to the *Guinness Book of World Records* the longest of all
words is the systematic name for deoxyribonucleic acid (DNA), which "contains
16,569 nucleotide residues and is thus 207,000 letters long." Another scientific
word, describing Bovine NADP-specific glutamate dehydrogenase, has 3,600
letters.

2. *Mrs. Byrne's Dictionary of Unusual, Obscure and Preposterous Words*
includes a 1,913-letter word for an enzyme with 267 amino acids, called for
short Tryptophin synthetese A Protein.

3. A personal name belonging to Adolf . . . Wolfe . . . Senior, which contains
775 letters. Adolf . . . Wolfe . . . Senior has twenty-five given names following
Adolf and a family name that goes on for hundreds of letters. Born in Germany
in 1904, he shortened his surname to Wolfe 590, Senior, after moving to Phil-
adelphia. For the record his full name reads as follows: ADOLF BLAINE CHARLES
DAVID EARLY FREDERICK GERALD HUBERT IRVIN JOHN KENNETH LLOYD MARTIN
NERO OLIVER PAUL QUINCY RANDOLPH SHERMAN THOMAS UNCAS VICTOR WIL-
LIAM XERXES YANCY ZEUS WOLFESCHLEGELSTEINHAUSENBERGERDORFFVORAL-
TERNWARENGEWISSENHAFTSCHAFERSWESSENSCHAFEWARENWOHLGEPFLEGE-
UNDSORGFALTIGKEITBESCHUTZENVONANGREIFENDURCHIHRRAUBGIERIGFEIND-
EWELCHEVORALTERNWOLFTAUSENJAHRESVORANDIEERSCHEINENVANDERERSTEE-
RDEMENSCHDERRAUMSCHIFFGEBRAUCHLICHTALSSEINURSPRUNGVONKRAFTG-
ESTARTSEINLANGEFAHRTHINZWISCHENSTERNARTIGRAUMAUFDERSUCHENAC-
HDIESTERNWELCHEGEHABTBEWOHNBARPLANETENKREISEDREHENSICHUNDWO-
HNDERNEURASSEVONVERSTANDIGMENSCHLICHKEITKONNTEFORTPFLANZENUND-
SICHERFREUENANLEBENSLANGLICHFREUDEUUNDRUHEMITNICHTEINFURCH-

TVORANGEREIFENVONANDERERINTELLIGENTGESCHOPFSVONHINZWISCHENSTE-RNARTIGRAUM, SENIOR. In 1984 Mr. and Mrs. James Williams of Texas gave their newborn daughter first and middle names totaling 1,045 letters.

4. A Sanskrit word containing 152 syllables that is said to be "frightening to look at." There are at least two Sanskrit words of 36 letters.

5. A Greek word of 170 letters that occurs in Aristophanes' comedy *The Ecclesiazusae* and describes a fricassee or hash made of seventeen sweet-and-sour ingredients. The goulash transliterates into English as the 182-letter:

LOPADOTEMACHOSELACHOGALEOKRANIOLEIPSANODRIMHYPOTRIMMATOSIL-PHIOPARAOMELITOKATAKECHYMENOKICHLEPIKOSSYPHOPHATTOPERISTERALEK-TRYONOPTEKEPHALLIOKIGKLOPELEIOLAGOIOSIRAIOBAPHETRAGANOPTERYGON.

Translated it means "limpets, slices of salt fish, thorn-backs, whistle-fishes, cornelberries, a remoulade of leftover brains seasoned with silphium and cheese, thrushes basted with honey, blackbirds, ringdoves, squabs, chickens, fried mullets, wagtails, rock pigeons, and wings ground up in wine that has been boiled down."

6. A place name with 169 letters; the full name for Bangkok, the capital city of Thailand:

KRUNGTHEP MAHANAKHON BOVORN RATANAKOSIN MAHINTHARAYUTTHAYA MAHADILOKPOP NOPARATRATCHATHANI BURIROM UDOMRATCHANIVETMAHASA THAN AMORNPIMAN AVATARNSATHIT SAKKATHATTIYAVISNUKARMPRASIT.

7. The Hawaiian given name of Miss Dawne E. Lee of Honolulu, which is 102 letters long and means "the abundant, beautiful blossoms of the mountain begin to fill the air with their fragrance throughout the length and breadth of Hawaii":

NAPUA-MOHALA-ONAONA-A-ME-KA-WEHIWEHI-O-NA-KUAHIWI-A-ME-NA-AW-KE-HOOMAKA-KE-HOAALA-KE-EA-O-NA-AINA-NANI-AKEA-O-HAWAII-I-KA-WANAAO.

8. Ten "thunderwords" of 100 letters from James Joyce's *Finnegans Wake* rank seventh. First of these would be a word on the opening page meaning "a symbolic thunderclap that represents the fall of Adam and Eve":

BABABADALGHARAGHTAKAMMINARRONNKONNBRONNFONN-ERRONNTUONNTHUNNTROVARRHOUNAWNSKAWNTOOHOO-HOOROUDRNENTUHERNUK

9. The unofficial eighty-five-letter place name for a hill on North Island, New Zealand, which in Maori means "the place where Tameta, the man with the big knee who slid climbed and swallowed mountains, known as the Land-eater, played on his flute to his loved one":

TAUMATAWHAKATANGIHANGAKOAUAUOTAMATEATURIPUKAKAPIKIMAUNGAHOR-ONUKUPOKAIWHENUAKITANATAHU.

10. The seventy-one-letter word Bismarck coined to replace the word "apothecary," which he thought imprecise:
GESUNDHEITSWIEDERHERSTELLUNGSMITTELZUSAMMENMISCHUNGSVERHÄLTNIS-KUNDIGER.

11. A sixty-nine-letter German title of a North Bohemian official that translates as "Deputy-President of the Food-Rationing-Winding-up Commission":
LEBENSMITTELZUSCHUSSEINSTELLUNGSKOMMISSIONSVORSITZENDERSTELLVER-TRETER.

12. A town in Wales whose fifty-eight-letter Welsh name means "The Church of St. Mary in a hollow of white hazel, near to the rapid whirlpool, and to St. Tisilio church, near to a red cave." It is pronounced "Klan-fire-poothgwin-geth-go-gerith-kwin-drooble-klan-dissileo-gogo-gok":
LLANFAIRPWLLGWYNGYLLGOGERYCHWYRNDROBWLLLLANTYSILIOGOGOGOCH.

13. In the early eighteenth century, English medievalist Dr. Edward Strother coined this fifty-two-letter word describing the composition of the spa waters at Bristol:
AEQUEOSALINOCALCALINOCERACEOALUMINOSOCUPREOVITRIOLIC.

14. English novelist Thomas Love Peacock invented a fifty-one-letter term to describe the structure of the human body in his *Headlong Hall* (1816):
OSSEOCARNISANGUINEOVISCERCARTILAGININERVOMEDULLARY.

15. In Rabelais's *Gargantua*, a book on a library shelf has a ribald title whose first word alone is fifty letters:
ANTIPERICATAMETAANAPARCIRCUMVOLUTIORECTUMGUSTPOOPS OF THE COPRO-FIED.

16. A German word meaning "Association of Constantinople bagpipe makers" that is fifty letters long:
CONSTANTINOPOLITANISCHERDUDELSACKPFEIFENMACHERGESELLSCHAFT.

17. The longest place name in America, a forty-nine-letter lake in southern Massachusetts whose Indian name means "fishing place at the boundaries, neutral meeting grounds," but which has traditionally been translated freely as "you fish at your side, I'll fish at my side and no one fishes at the middle." Locals call the place Lake Chargogg:
CHARGOGGAGOGGMANCHAUGGAGOGGCHAUBUNAQWNAQUNGAMANGG.

18. Probably the longest word listed in a dictionary *(Webster's)* is a forty-five-letter giant meaning "a pneumoconiosis caused by the inhalation of very fine silicate or quartz dust, a miner's lung disease":
PNEUMONOULTRAMICROSCOPICSILICOVOLCANOCONIOSIS.

19. A late-nineteenth-century Flemish work of forty-one letters meaning "a carriage which is worked by means of petroleum, which travels fast, which has no horses, and which is not run on rails"—that is, an automobile:
SNELPAARDELOOSZONDERSPOORWEGPATROLRIJTUIG.

20. A forty-eight-letter word invented by lexicographer William Morris

meaning "the murder of a person who has a morbid fear of not being prevented from investing in convertible bonds":

ANTICONTRACONVERTIDEBENTURALARBITRAGINOPHOBICIDE.

21. A forty-four letter word for a chemical compound also known as salvarsan:

DIAMINODIHYDROCYARSENOBENZENEDIHYDROCHLORIDE.

22. A forty-letter medical term that means "the surgical formation of a passage between the gall bladder and hepatic duct, on the one hand, and between the intestine and the gall bladder on the other":

HEPATICOCHOLECYSTOSTCHOLECYSTENTEROSTOMY.

23. Chesterton invented this thirty-seven-letter word, which I can't find a definition for:

PLAKOPYTRIXOPHYLISPERAMBULANTIOBATRIX.

24. In his novel *Untimely Ripped* (1963) Mark McShane invented the longest regularly formed English word, a thirty-seven-letter term that means "the act of surpassing the act of transsubstantiation," that is, surpassing the transformation of bread and wine into the body and blood of Christ:

PRAETERTRANSSUBSTANTIATIONALISTICALLY.

25. A thirty-four-letter word meaning "superb" from the film *Mary Poppins:*

SUPERCALIFRAGILISTICEXPIALIDOCIOUS.

26. James Joyce's thirty-four-letter word from *Finnegans Wake*, for which I am at a loss to provide a good definition:

SEMPEREXCOMMUNICAMBIAMBIAMBISUMERS.

27. A thirty-four-letter word invented by Rabelais meaning "bruised blue and contused":

ESPERRUQUANCHURELUBELOUZERIRELICED.

28. Edward Lear's thirty-one-letter word:

SPLENDIDOPHOROPHEROSTIPHONGIOUS.

29. The thirty-letter:

HIERARCHITECTITIPTITOPLOFTICAL.

30. The longest word in the Oxford English Dictionary, a twenty-nine-letter term meaning "the action of estimating as useless" that was coined in 1741 and was later used by Sir Walter Scott:

FLOCCINAUCINIHILIPILIFICATION.

31. The old favorite of twenty-eight letters that was used by Prime Minister Gladstone and means "a doctrine of opposition to disestablishment (withdrawal of state patronage, support or exclusive recognition from a church)":

ANTIDISESTABLISHMENTARIANISM.

32. The twenty-eight-letter:

INCORNIFISTIGROPILIBUSTULATE.

33. A long word (twenty-seven letters) from Shakespeare's *Love's Labour's*

Lost that means "with honorableness," if it means anything. It has also been taken to be a rearrangement of the Latin sentence *Hi ludi F. Baconis nati tuti orbi* ("These plays, F. Bacon's offspring, are preserved for the world") and thus "proof" that Francis Bacon wrote Shakespeare's plays:

HONORIFICABILITUDINITATIBUS.

34. The twenty-seven-letter term for "one who doubts that consecrated blood and wine actually change into the body and blood of Christ":

ANTITRANSSUBSTANTIATIONALIST.

35. A twenty-five-letter beast I urge good readers to define and let me know the results:

PHILOSOPHICOPSYCHOLOGICAL.

36. Others may command this position before it, but the longest of long words in fairly common use is the twenty-one-letter:

DISPROPORTIONABLENESS.

These tapeworms could also be called *sesquipedalium words*, from Horace's *sesquipedalia verbs*, words a foot and a half long. The Greeks, too, had a word for mile-long words: *amaxiaia remata*, "words large enough for a wagon."

Smile, as the old riddle says, is longer by far than any other word, with "a mile between the first and last letter."

The practice of using long words is called HIPPOPO-TOMONSTROUSQUIPEDALIANISM, thirty-four letters.

LONGEST SENTENCE IN ENGLISH

A BOOK CALLED *Gates of Paradise* by George Andrzeyevski (Panther, 1957) has no punctuation and technically might be said to be one long sentence. And the 1942–1943 Report of the President of Columbia University contained a sentence of 4,284 words. But Sylvester Hassell's *History of the Church of God* (c.1884) has a sentence of 3,153 words (with 360 commas and eighty-six semicolons) that is regarded as the longest legitimate sentence in a book. James Joyce, William Faulkner, and many other writers have of course written long "sentences" with no punctuation, but the longest legitimate sentence in a highly regarded literary work is a 958-word monster in Marcel Proust's *Cities of the Plain*.

One Timothy Dexter (d. 1806), a rich English eccentric, wrote his autobiography, *A Pickle for the Knowing Ones*, without using any punctuation, but he included in the pamphlet a full page of commas, semicolons, colons, question marks, and periods for anyone who might want to insert them!

Among modern authors, Apollinaire's first book of poems contained no punctuation, Gertrude Stein used little punctuation besides the period, and e. e. cummings used punctuation erratically, if at all.

George Bernard Shaw reviewed Henry Arthur Jones's *My Dear Wells* (1921) and, despite the fact that Jones was vehemently critical of him, recommended that all read a long sentence in it: "It contains more than 800 words, and stops only because the printer, in desperation, bunged in a full-point. I read that sentence to my wife, and at the end we found ourselves cheering with excitement."

THE LONGEST WORDS
EVER DELIVERED ON STAGE

ALDIBORONTIPHOSCOPHORNIO! Where left you Chrononhotontho-logos?" begins Henry Carey's farce *Chrononhotonthologos, the Most Tragical Tragedy That Ever Was Tragedized by Any Company of Tragedians* (1734). Chrononhotonthologos was the King of Queerummania, and his name is now used for any bombastic person delivering an inflated address. Aldiborontiphos-cophornio was a courier in the play. Carey, who wrote the popular song "Sally in My Alley," may have written the words and music to the British anthem "God Save the King."

THE CLICHÉ CODE

O. HENRY WROTE in his story "Calloway's Code" (1910) that words are "oft associated, until not even obituary notices [by cliché hunters] do them part." He had demonstrated this in the story with a cablegram cliché code that his reporter-hero, H. B. Calloway, invented to enable him to send his stories back to New York without censorship while covering the Russo-Japanese War. Below is the code, which the New York office solved. Perhaps more revealing is the fact that the capitalized code words and their italicized meanings, which together make clichés, would be almost as easily linked together by Americans today as they were over eighty years ago:

Witching: *hour of midnight*	Existing: *conditions*
Foregone: *conclusion*	Great: *White Way*
Preconcerted: *arrangement*	Hotly: *contested*
Rash: *act*	Brute: *force*
Goes: *without saying*	Select: *few*
Muffled: *report*	Mooted: *question*
Rumour: *hath it*	Parlous: *times*
Dark: *horse*	Beggars: *description*
Silent: *majority*	Incontrovertible: *fact*

SLANG

*H*ERE ARE SOME of the more amusing sources suggested for the word
slang, which is of uncertain origin:

- Dutch General Slangenberg, "noted for his abusive and exaggerated epithets when he reproved the men under his command."
- The Italian *s-lingua*—*s*, the negative, and *lingua*, "language" equal *slingua* (slang), or "bad language."
- The French *esclandre*, "an event which gives rise to slander."
- The Greek *skandalon*, "an offense or scandal."
- The English *slangs*, "fetters for malefactors."

Though no one is sure, *slang* may come from the Norwegian *slengja-kef-ten*, "to sling the jaw," "to abuse." Ernest Weekley and other prominent
etymologists thought so, but the Oxford English Dictionary doesn't even hazard a guess.

VIOLENCE BEGINS IN THE NURSERY: JACK AND JILL VERSUS THE INCREDIBLE HULK

*I*N THE RUSH to condemn contemporary blood and horrors (especially comic
books) we tend to forget that violence is a tradition found in the very cradle of
literature. One respected critic of the day called Hans Christian Andersen's tales
"quite unsuitable for children." A biography of nursery rhyme literature published in 1952 by Geoffrey Handley-Taylor of Manchester, England, claims that
the following 199 "unsavoury incidents" occurred in the "average collection"
of 200 traditional nursery rhymes:

8 allusions to murder (unclassified)
2 cases of choking to death
1 case of death by devouring
1 case of cutting a human being in half
1 case of decapitation
1 case of death by squeezing
1 case of death by shriveling
1 case of death by starvation
1 case of boiling to death
1 case of death by hanging
1 case of death by drowning

4 cases of killing domestic animals
1 case of body snatching
21 cases of death (unclassified)
7 cases relating to the severing of limbs
1 case of the desire to have a limb severed
2 cases of self-inflicted injury
4 cases relating to the breaking of limbs
1 allusion to a bleeding heart
1 case of devouring human flesh
5 threats of death
1 case of kidnapping
12 cases of torment and cruelty to human beings and animals
8 cases of whipping and lashing
3 allusions to blood
14 cases of stealing and general dishonesty
15 allusions to maimed human beings and animals
1 allusion to undertakers
2 allusions to graves
23 cases of physical violence (unclassified)
1 case of lunacy
16 allusions to misery and sorrow
1 case of drunkenness
4 cases of cursing
1 allusion to marriage as a form of death
1 case of scorning the blind
1 case of scorning prayer
9 cases of children being lost or abandoned
2 cases of house burning
9 allusions to poverty and want
5 allusions to quarreling
2 cases of unlawful imprisonment
2 cases of racial discrimination

CROSSWORD PUZZLE WORDS:
AND THEN CAME THE INEE,
THE SNEE, AND THE STOAK, AND...

In [the former West] Germany a crossword puzzle addict kept waking her husband through the night for assistance with a difficult puzzle. Her husband became enraged the fourth time she woke him from a sound sleep and he strangled her. A court acquitted him of murder on grounds of temporary insanity.   —News item

A RECENT STUDY made in Hong Kong reveals that crossword puzzles cause horrible nightmares. Not ordinary horrible nightmares, either. Nightmares where you are stranded on an *ait* caught inside a giant puzzle, an *asp* coiled tight around your neck, where *gnus* are stampeding while *Ra* hurls down thunderbolts and *ais* scream.

The real trouble with these recurring nightmares is that they recur when you're awake. Almost all crossword addicts, including myself, have these problems, problems like *Ra* and *gnu*, and *ai*, and *stoak*, and *snood*.

All of us suffer. Take Ra, for example. Ra was an Egyptian god (although crafty constructors sometimes disguise him as "the sound made when cheering"). *Ra* is also called *Mantu* and *Atmu*. His children were *Athor Moat*, *Mu*, and *Shu*. He is often defined as "father-figure to Mu and Shu," or "Moat's sire." A poem by Keith Preston mentions Ra: "The great god Ra whose shrine once covered acres/Is filler now for crossword puzzle makers."

Too bad about Ra. What happened to him shouldn't even happen to a gnu.

Before crosswords came on the scene, the naturalist Mungo Park was about the only person alive who knew that the *gnu* existed. The four-foot-high wildebeest was harmless enough traveling in great herds in Africa (where he should have stayed), but now he slinks around all over the omniverse endangering the mental health of millions.

Then there is the *ai*, a very familiar poser which is not the battle cry of a vengeful puzzle plotter, as you might expect. With the ai, as with other crosswords, simplicity has nothing to do with length. The ai is really a hairy, disoriented, two-letter, three-toed sloth that hangs by its tail and legs from tree limbs all its natural life, chomping on leaves. "Ai!" the ai sometimes cries plaintively, which is why it is called the ai. *Aal*, a red dye, invariably drips down off the first letter.

Next most familiar of the crosswordian arcana is *em*. *Em* was Isaac Funk's greatest fear—because of *en*. It is impossible to be brief about em, which is a printer's measure, the square of pica *m*. Pica is a measure of type of about six lines to the inch, equal to twelve points. It should never be confused with *pics*, which are Turkish measures of length varying from eighteen to twenty-eight inches. *Em* should never be confused with its stunted fraternal twin, en. En is also a printer's measure, and that's how they always define it.

It has often been said that one doesn't learn anything at all from crossword puzzles, except how to do more crossword puzzles. The other day, for example, I found that if you ever get a chapped chilblain you can call it a *kibe*. In all fairness, though, it must be pointed out that crossword champions claim that puzzles do serve a definite purpose—by making once-dormant words useful again because of their frequent appearance. Among the once-dormant words they cite are *neb*, *coot*, and *eft*.

Now the *eft* is a real winner. The eft gets my vote for the pluperfect example of crosswordian utility. The eft is always defined as a newt in its land stage. A newt, on the other hand, is always defined as an eft in its aquatic stage. You sure learn a lot.

There is really no other crossword that rates a paragraph. Most don't even rate a lusty curse, not in my book—or even Wagnalls's. Just name your own poison, such as the *inee* spiteful Indians used to rub on their arrows. Or take the *emu*, an ostrich, or its variation, the *rhea*, which is a three-toed ostrich—both make me want to bury my head in the sand. Then there is *knub*, the innermost wrapping in a cocoon, and *stet*, which means "let it stand," and *knowt*, which is not in my Oxford English Dictionary.

The *snood*, a hairband, is another bitter vetch. Aside from the fact that James Joyce wrote a memorable early poem with a fine snood in it, snoods have no reference in the language. And don't forget that heartbreaker, the *stoak*, "the ermine when attired in brown summer fur," which shows you just how cruel constructors can be to us animals.

Aloes and *ait*, "a plant resembling the agave" and "a small island," are also two big little ones. As for *snee*, I have just encountered that intriguing little word and have postponed looking it up in order not to shatter my illusions. My illusions were too easily shattered when *wark* turned out to be nothing more than the obsolete word for *work*—just what it was to find the definition.

About the only benefit I can see derived from crosswords is that you can act *multo profundo* after your pen has gleaned the teeming squares. "Grey Wolf crouched down and popped a ceremonial *aal* into his mouth," you can explain to your much-impressed child at bedtime. "Then he took some *inee* from under his *snood* and rubbed it on his arrow. . . ."

"Inee, sire?" he'll ask.

You'll proudly answer, *"Stet, scion, inee poison,"* and he'll be even more impressed.

Your *scion* may, however, be wise enough to tell you that crosswords are for the *apteryx*, or *moas*, or birds; that you, in fact are withering on the *whin*. That is, if you ever have the time to help make any *scion*. Otherwise, I see only *snees*, at best, in every puzzler's future. Not to mention *oes* and *phats* and *titis* and *xylyls* and *skuas* and *luts* and *rotls* and *hoiks* and *blebs* . . .

MISINTERPRETED WORDS

I𝖥 THE Japanese word *mokusatsu* hadn't been misinterpreted, World War II might have ended sooner, atomic power might never have been used in warfare, and tens of thousands of lives might have been saved. *Mokusatsu* has two meanings: (1) to ignore, and (2) to refrain from comment. As historian Stuart Chase has written:

> The release of a press statement using the second meaning in July 1945 might have ended the war then. The Emperor was ready to end it, and had the power to do so. The cabinet was preparing to accede to the Potsdam ultimatum of the Allies—surrender or be crushed—but wanted a little more time to discuss the terms. A press release was prepared announcing a policy of *mokusatsu*, with the "no comment" implication. But it got on the foreign wires with the "ignore" implication through a mixup in translation: "The cabinet ignores the demand to surrender." To recall the release would have entailed an unthinkable loss of face. Had the intended meaning been publicized, the cabinet might have backed up the Emperor's decision to surrender.

Instead, there came Hiroshima and Nagasaki.

HENRY JAMES

BURN ONE CHOP!

HENRY JAMES, who constantly experimented with the English language and probably used more synonyms for words than any writer before or since, once gave the following order to a waiter in a restaurant:

> "Bring me . . . fetch me . . . carry me . . . supply me . . . in other words (I hope you are following me) serve—when it is cooked . . . scorched . . . grilled I should say—a large . . . considerable . . . meaty (as opposed to fatty) . . . chop."

AFFECTED AUTHORS

VOLTAIRE SAID that French author Pierre Marivaux spent his life weighing nothing in scales made of spiders' webs. Marivaux is only one of a number of writers whose names have become synonymous for literary affectation. Among the first was Spanish writer and moralist Antonio de Guevara (c.1480–1545), who is regarded as the father of *euphuism*, for which *guevarism* is the equivalent. But euphuism, an ornate, florid, artificial writing or speaking style characterized by alliteration, eloquence, and high-flown phrases, was coined more than a century after his death. Euphuism takes its name from *Euphues: the Anatomy of Wit* (1579), by John Lyly, who displayed such a style in his book while attempting to "soften" the English language, Euphues being the name of the main character in his romance. Lyly probably influenced Shakespeare and Sir Thomas Browne, among other authors, and Guevara may have been among his inspirations, for the Spanish writer's *The Golden Book of Marcus Aurelius* (1535) and other works were early translated into English. Below is a sample of euphuism from Lyly's work:

> For although the worm entereth almost into every wood, yet he eateth not the cedar tree; though the stone cylindrus at every thunder clap roll from the hill, yet the pure sleek stone mounteth at the noise; though the rust fret the hardest steel, yet doth it not eat into the emerald; though polypus change his hue, yet the salamander keepeth his colour; though Proteus transform himself into every shape, yet Pygmalion retaineth his old form; though Aeneas were too fickle to Dido, yet Troilus was too faithful to Cressida; though others seem counterfeit in their deeds, yet, Lucilla, persuade yourself that Euphues will be always current in his dealings.

Spanish author Luis de Góngora y Argote (1561–1627) will also be remembered forever for his literary affectations, but it's only fair to say that the arrows he made into "flying asps" and the birds he described as "feathered zithers" were part of a larger plan. Góngora wrote in a twisted, tortuous style in his later years, his syntax deliberately distorted in order to highlight words and create an unreal world. But he inspired many imitators, who inspired many critics, and unfortunately his name is now a synonym for a deliberately obscure, meaningless, and affected ornamental style. The Spanish poet after whom *gongorism* is named was essentially a lyric poet in his early years; his work was much admired by Cervantes, though no poem of his was published in his lifetime. Readers have discovered that his baroque gongorisms, a great influence on modern poetry, are far from meaningless, as difficult as long poems such as the *Soledades* are to read. Góngora, who adopted his mother's name, was a priest as well as a poet and dramatist. Toward the end of his life he turned back from cultivated obscurity to a simple, unaffected style.

Another poet whose overclothed visions inspired lasting ridicule was Il Cavalier Marino, as the pompous Neapolitan poet Gianbattista Marino (1569–1625) was called. Marino headed the *seicento* school of Italian literature, which became noted for its flamboyance and bad taste. Poems such as his 45,000-line *Adone* show brilliant mastery of technique but were intended to dazzle the reader at any cost, their extravagance causing *marinism* to become a word describing any florid, bombastic style, pages full of sound but signifying nothing. Marino, or Marini, had his troubles with censors, too. His satirical works were not appreciated by his satirized patrons and he was forced to leave Italy, taking refuge in Paris for eight years before he could return safely to his homeland.

Voltaire's object of derision, Pierre Carlet de Chamblain de Marivaux (1688–1763), actually made important advances in the development of the novel and is undeserving of his fate at the hands of the dictionaries. *Marivaudage*, however, means an affected, overstrained style, as exemplified by the witty bantering of lovers in his two unfinished novels and thirty plays. Marivaux's subtle, graceful works are mostly excellent studies of middle-class psychology and led a contemporary to remark that his characters tell each other and the reader not only everything they have thought but also everything they would like to persuade themselves that they had thought. Marivaudage has also been described as "the metaphysics of love making." The author was much admired in his own time, and it is said that Madame Pompadour secretly provided him with a large pension. Voltaire probably impaled him because he dared to criticize the master's work.

ILLEISTS AND OTHER WALKING PERSONAL PRONOUNS

*T*HE WORD FOR the habit of referring to oneself excessively in the third person singular is *illeism*. A nonce word modeled on the Latin *ille* ("he") and *egoism*, it was apparently invented by Coleridge, or at least he is the first author recorded to have used this coining for a consummate egotist (in about 1809). Using *he* does sound better than employing the royal *we*, and even a little better than constantly using *I*, for which Victor Hugo was called "a walking personal pronoun."

SOLECISM

*A*N ERROR IN grammar, or in the use of words, or a breach of etiquette is called a *solecism*. Soli, or Soloi, was an ancient Greek colony in the province of Cilicia, Asia Minor, far removed from Athens. Colonists who settled there developed a dialect of their own that Athenian purists considered barbarous and uncouth, leading them to coin the word *soloikos* as a slang term for ignorant speech. From *soloikos* came the Greek noun *soloikismos*, "speaking incorrectly," like an inhabitant of Soloi, which eventually, through the Latin *soloecismus*, made its entrance into English as *solecism*. In years to come, Yankee colonists would be criticized in much the same way by Englishmen, but the label *Americanism* has always been accepted with pride by Americans. Soli, located in what is now Turkey, was an important, prosperous port in the time of Alexander the Great. When Pompey rebuilt the city after it was destroyed by Tigranes in the

Mithridatic War, he named it Pompeiopolis. Few of Soli's ruins remain today, but *solecism*, originally slang itself, endures in all modern European languages as a remembrance of the way its citizens "ruined" Greek.

AMN'T I

*A*MONG OTHERS, James Joyce used it in *Dubliners*, which contains some of the most eloquent stories ever written; Rumer Godden employed it in *An Episode of Sparrows*; and Rebecca West used it in one of her novels ("I'm just awful, amn't I?"). So, as odd as it may sound to some ears, the locution is preferred to "Aren't I?" and "Ain't I?" by a number of good writers and is widely used. "Amn't *I*?" is especially popular in Ireland, dating back at least two centuries there.

WRITERS WHO HAVE SEEN FIT TO HAPPILY SPLIT INFINITIVES

*T*HE LATE Bergen Evans once compiled a list of writers who commonly split infinitives (that is, place a word between *to* and the simple form of a verb, as in "to quickly walk away") to show that it has been the practice of our best writers. Over a relatively short period he came up with Sir Philip Sidney, Sir Thomas Browne, Donne, Pepys, Defoe, Samuel Johnson, Burns, Wordsworth, Coleridge, Lamb, Byron, De Quincey, Macaulay, Holmes, Whittier, George Eliot, Carlyle, Browning, Arnold, Pater, Ruskin, Hardy, Meredith, Galsworthy, Conan Doyle, Kipling, Shaw, Benjamin Franklin, Abraham Lincoln, Theodore Roosevelt, Woodrow Wilson, Herbert Hoover, and even Henry James.

One theory intended to justify the split infinitive holds that in Latin the infinitive form of a verb is only one word and thereby unsplittable, whereas in English the two-word infinitive need not be governed by any such classical rule.

PREPOSITIONS AT THE END
OF A SENTENCE

ALTHOUGH etymologically the word *preposition* itself means "placed before," prepositions need not always be placed before their objects in a sentence. Most times they are, but in some instances a preposition must come *after* its object and in others the preposition can be placed either before or after the object. There are governing rules, but it is best to rely upon the ear in this matter. For example, "Where are you staying at?" sounds a lot better than "At where are you staying?" Though "Where are you staying?" sounds even better.

The record for the most prepositions strung together at the end of a sentence is the protest of a child against an Australian bedtime story book: "Mommy, what did you bring that book which I didn't want to be read to out of from about 'Down Under' up for?"

Angry at a critic who corrected one of his sentences on the basis of the old bromide that a preposition should not end a sentence, Winston Churchill wrote to him: "This is the kind of nonsense up with which I will not put."

British author Joseph Addison liked to end sentences with prepositions—at least he wrote a good many of them that way—and sentences ending with prepositions are therefore said to have "Addisonian terminations." Interestingly, Richard Hurd, the testy critic who invented "Addisonian termination," is heard of no more today, while Joseph Addison, dangling prepositions and all, remains a much-read author.

GHOTI

"A man haz az much rite tew spell a word az it iz pronounsed as he haz tew pronounse it the way it ain't spelt."
—Josh Billings

BACK AT THE beginning of the century, "simplified" phonetic spellings were all the rage. An example of just how simplified the method was is *ghoti*, which, as George Bernard Shaw pointed out, is the way *fish* would be written if spelled phonetically. The *f* in *fish* is represented as *gh*, as in *tough*; the *i* as *o*, as in *women*; and the *sh* as *ti*, as in *nation*. Shaw tried his best to introduce a more logical method of spelling, even leaving money in his will for this purpose, but all to no avail. Anyway, some of the greatest writers were poor spellers. Shakespeare, for instance, spelled his name two different ways in his will, and F. Scott Fitzgerald could hardly write a page without a spelling error. Following is an extract from a letter written by Daniel Boone in the last century:

Dear Sir:—This Instant I Start Down the River. My Two sunes Returned ameadetely from Philadelphia and Daniel Went Down With Sum goods in order to Take in gensgn at Lim Stone. I hope you Will Wright me By the Bear Mr. goe how you Com on with my horsis—I Here the Indians have killed Sum people Near Lim Stone and Stole a Number of horsis—

THE COPY EDITORS WEREN'T TO BLAME

W ORDS WERE often spelled incorrectly in early books because printers hadn't developed the technique of making printed lines equal by using spaces of different widths. To make lines balance, printers simply omitted or added letters to words arbitrarily, so that *we* might be spelled *wee*, and *hot* spelled *whot* or *hote*.

ANACHRONISMS

Cecil B. de Mille
Was feeling ill
Because he couldn't put Moses
In the Wars of the Roses

T HIS FAMOUS CLERIHEW by Nicholas Bentley, the son of the inventor of the clerihew, comments on filmmakers who often don't get ill about anachronisms in their epics. The word derives from the Greek *ana chronos*, "out of time," "to be late," or "back-timing," and means an error in chronology, putting a person, event, or thing in the wrong time period. Sometimes this is done intentionally by an author to achieve verisimilitude and timelessness, or for humorous purposes as in Mark Twain's *A Connecticut Yankee in King Arthur's Court*. Anachronisms have been common from Virgil to George Bernard Shaw. Some classic examples are Shakespeare's references to a striking clock in *Julius Caesar*, 1,400 years before such clocks were invented, his reference to billiards in *Antony and Cleopatra*, to cannon in *King John*, and to turkeys in *1 Henry IV*. Memorable American anachronisms include George Washington's throwing a silver dollar across the Potomac (there were no silver dollars at the time) and the flying of the Stars and Stripes in paintings of major Revolutionary war battles (the flag wasn't used until 1783). Sometimes the word *anachronism* is used to describe an institution or a person who lives in the past, such as Edwin Arlington Robinson's Miniver Cheevy, a human anachronism "born too late" and longing for earlier, happier times.

An anachronism that occurs at a date before the actual time period is sometimes called a *prochronism*, and one that occurs at a later date (Moses in the War of the Roses) can be called a *parachronism*, but *anachronism* adequately covers both categories. An *anachorism*, on the other hand, is the placing of a scene, action, or character in a place where it doesn't belong. This term derives from a Greek word meaning "something misplaced," and probably the most famous example is Shakespeare's line in *The Winter's Tale* when Antigonus says, "Our ship hath touched upon the deserts of Bohemia," Bohemia of course having no seacoast. Strictly speaking, any reference to "the battle of Waterloo" is anachorism, as the battle actually took place near another village four miles away.

SEACOASTS IN BOHEMIA, OR ERRORS BY AUTHORS

THERE ARE millions of these, some of them probably in this book, but here is a compilation of amusing errors by famous authors that shows how far from perfect even the greatest are:

• In the *Aeneid* Virgil mentions a harbor (Velinos) that didn't exist at the time, and kills off two characters (Chorinaeus and Numa) only to bring them back to life again later without any explanation.

• Chaucer in his tale of the siege of Troy has one of the characters refer to Robin Hood.

• In *Don Quixote* Cervantes has Sancho Panza sell his ass, and shortly afterward, inexplicably, has him riding the animal. Among other mistakes, Cervantes has Sancho lose his wallet and then use it again with no mention of his having found it; has Sancho lose his greatcoat with food in it and later says the food remained in Sancho's possession; makes the party at the Crescent Tavern eat two suppers in one night; and has Don Quixote's helmet broken to pieces, only to make it whole and sound again later in the book.

• As noted, in *The Winter's Tale* Shakespeare speaks of a vessel "driven by storm on the coast of Bohemia" when Bohemia has no seacoast. He also has Italian artist Giulio Romano alive some eight centuries before he was born.

• In Shakespeare's *Coriolanus* the city of Delphi is an island.

• The ghost in Shakespeare's *Hamlet* is apparently a Roman Catholic one, speaking of purgatory and absolution, at a time when the Danes were pagans.

• Shakespeare wrote of Elsinore's "beetling cliff" in *Hamlet*, though Elsinore has no cliffs at all.

• In *Robinson Crusoe* Defoe makes his hero swim naked to a wrecked ship and then put biscuits he finds into his pockets.

• In his fable "The Mouse and the Weasel" Pope has the weasel eat corn.

• Sir Walter Scott makes Malvoisin's first name Richard and later Phillip in *Ivanhoe*.

• Dr. Johnson defined *pastern* as the knee of a horse in his *Dictionary*. When asked why by a lady, he replied, "Ignorance, madam, sheer ignorance."

• Buffon in his important natural history book says that "all flowers in America are without perfume."

• Cowper calls the rose "the glory of April and May," when it blooms in June in England.

• Dickens has boys hoeing turnips in midwinter in *Nicholas Nickleby*.

• In *The Tale of Two Cities* Dickens calls the Biblical strongman Sanson instead of Samson.

• In *War and Peace* Tolstoy has Natasha seventeen years old in 1805 and twenty-four years old four years later. He also changes Prince Andrei's silver icon to gold.

• Among many errors in the Sherlock Holmes stories is the bullet wound Dr. Watson suffered at war. In one story (*A Story in Scarlet*) it is a shoulder wound; in another (*The Sign of Four*), it's a leg wound.

• In his play *Where the Cross Is Made* Eugene O'Neill gives stage directions describing a man with one arm who must sit at a table "resting his elbows, his chin in his hands."

THE WORST ANTICLIMAXES

DR. JOHNSON seems to have invented or at least been the first to record the word *anticlimax*, which he defines as "a sentence in which the last part expresses something lower than the first." Pope used the anticlimax humorously in his line "Men, monkeys, lap-dogs, parrots, perish all." Everyone has a favorite anticlimax, fine examples of which can be found in the anthology of bad verse by Wyndham Lewis and C. Lee, but one of the best is the last line of Tennyson's poem "Enoch Arden" (1864), in which Enoch Arden, thought dead at sea, returns home after some years to find his wife happily married, and resolves that she won't know of his return until his death. The poem ends this way:

So past the strong heroic soul away.
And when they buried him, the little port
Had seldom seen a costlier funeral.

BATHOS AND PATHOS

Pathos, which derives directly from the Greek word for "suffering," is the quality or power in any of the arts to evoke feelings of tender pity, compassion, or sadness, and gives us pathetic characters in literature such as Ophelia in *Hamlet* or even Dickens's Little Nell. *Bathos* means quite the opposite and was coined by Alexander Pope from the Greek word *bathos*, "depth" (not related to our English word *bath*), to indicate a descent from the sublime to the depths of the ridiculous. Pope and other writers of the early eighteenth century, including Swift, Gay, and Arbuthnot, made a sport of parodying contemporary writers. Out of this game of wits came Pope's satire "Bathos, the art of sinking in Poetry" (1727), in which he invented the word because no similar one existed in English to express the idea. "The taste of the Bathos is implanted by Nature itself in the soul of man," he wrote in his essay, and he proceeded to give an example of bathos at its worst:

> *And thou, Dalhousie, the great god of war,*
> *Lieutenant-general to the earl of Mar.*

Pope, however, had used bathos effectively before in his mock-heroic poem *The Rape of the Lock* (1712), which was based on a true incident, a feud that developed between two families when one Lord Petre snipped off a lock of hair belonging to a Miss Arabella:

> *Not louder shrieks to pitying heaven are cast,*
> *When husbands, or when lapdogs, breathe their last.*

Today *bathos* also means false pathos, an exaggerated, mawkish appeal to the emotions. But there are still abundant examples of it in the same sense that Pope used the word. A modern example is from Congressman H. C. Caufield's *Elegy on the Loss of U.S. Submarine S4*, which was entered in the *Congressional Record*:

> *Entrapt inside a submarine*
> *With death approaching on the scene,*
> *The crew composed their minds to dice,*
> *More for the pleasure than the vice.*

Which is really bathos in the depths.

A BOOK IN BREECHES

THE GREAT English historian Thomas Babington Macaulay was a walking library who had filled his head with learning ever since he began reading at age three. He was a "book in breeches," the Reverend Sydney Smith (1771–1845) said, but Smith had some reservations about his loquacity. "Yes, I agree, he is certainly more agreeable since his return from India," Smith said of the historian. "His enemies might perhaps have said before (though I never did so) that he talked rather too much; but now he has occasional flashes of silence that make his conversation perfectly delightful."

But then everyone had a bad word for Macaulay. "His conversation was a procession of one," said Florence Nightingale of him. "Macaulay is well for a while, but one wouldn't want to live under Niagara," said Carlyle. "I wish I was as cocksure of anything as Tom Macaulay is of everything," Viscount Melbourne said. Sydney Smith added that the historian "not only overflowed with learning, but stood in the slop."

BRINGING FORTH NOTHING, OR THE WORLD'S WORST LITERARY AFTER-DINNER SPEAKERS

I don't know whether Phoebus fled from the dinner table of Thyestes: at any rate, Ligurinus, we fell from yours. Splendid, indeed, it is, and magnificently supplied with good things, but when you recite you spoil it all. I don't want you to set before me a turbot or two-pound mullet: I don't want your mushrooms or oysters. I want you to keep your mouth shut!
　　　　　　　　　　　　　　　　　　　　　　　　　　　—Martial

AUTHORS ARE rarely public speakers, as Dickens and Mark Twain were. Many, in fact, manage to be in Patagonia or Peoria when their books are published in order to avoid speaking engagements, although more and more poor speakers are plugging their books on promotion tours each year. But some authors have been so much worse than others that they bear mentioning. Washington Irving, for instance, couldn't deliver a speech even when he wrote it out in full beforehand; worse yet, he could hardly utter a sentence in public without trembling. Irish poet Thomas Moore was a loss as a public speaker and English poet Thomas Campbell never did successfully deliver a speech. Probably the best anecdote on poor speech-making authors is told about Joseph Addison, founder of the *Spectator*. Addison once attempted a speech in the House of Commons, beginning: "Mr. Speaker, I conceive—I conceive, sir—sir, I conceive . . ." He was then interrupted by a member who quipped: "The right honorable secretary of state has conceived thrice, and brought forth nothing."

Poet Louis Untermeyer once returned his fee for giving a lecture to a small struggling group and asked that they put the money to good use. When Untermeyer later inquired just what good use they had chosen he was told the group was starting "a fund to get better speakers next year."

The classic description of good and bad literary talkers is Lord Macaulay's evaluation of Oliver Goldsmith:

> Minds differ as rivers differ. There are transparent and sparkling wines from which it is delightful to drink as they flow; to such rivers the minds of Burke and Johnson may be compared. But there are rivers of which the water when first drawn is turbid and noisome, but becomes pellucid as crystals and delicious to the taste if it be suffered to stand still till it has deposited a sediment; and such a river is a type of mind of Goldsmith. His first thoughts on every subject were confused even to absurdity, but they required only a little time to work themselves clear. When he wrote they had that time, and therefore his readers pronounced him a man of genius; but when he talked he talked nonsense and made himself the laughingstock of his hearers. He was painfully conscious of his inferiority in conversation; he felt every failure keenly; yet he had not sufficient judgement and self-command to hold his tongue. His animal spirits and vanity were always impelling him to try to do the one thing which he could not do. After every attempt he felt that he had exposed himself, and withered with shame and vexation; yet the next moment he began again.

Goldsmith for his part once echoed Talleyrand and Voltaire in writing: "The true use of speech is not so much to expose our wants as to conceal them."

Should anyone want to improve, recall that the great Greek orator Demosthenes overcame his stammering and inability to pronounce the letter *p* by practicing with pebbles in his mouth against the sound of the surf, or by declaiming as he ran uphill. (He also mastered language by copying Thucydides's direct and graphic *History of the Peloponnesian War* eight times.) As for Cicero, the eloquent Roman statesman who patterned himself on Demosthenes, he "never got over his nervous terror [of speaking publicly] until he warmed himself to the subject."

Dr. Johnson wrote of authors as speakers in *The Rambler:*

> A Transition from an Author's Books to his Conversation, is too often like an Entrance into a large City, after a distant Prospect. Remotely, we see nothing but Spires and Temples, and Turrets of Palaces, and imagine it the Residence of Splendour, Grandeur, and Magnificence; but, when we have passed the Gates, we find it perplexed with narrow Passages, disgraced with despicable Cottages, embarrassed with Obstructions, and clouded with Smoke.

PEACOCK

*E*NGLAND's George III, during one of his attacks of insanity, insisted on ending every sentence in all of his speeches with the word *peacock*. His ministers cured him of this by telling him that *peacock* was a beautiful word but a royal one that a king should whisper when speaking before his subjects so they couldn't hear it. As a result the speeches of George III were less absurd.

PERSON OVERBOARD!

*I*N HIS ARTICLE "Language Liberated" in *The University Bookman* (Spring 1976), Robert Beum considers some alternatives for sexist "man" terms in the language. Believing, as someone has said, that "the proper study of personkind is person," I've recorded a number of Mr. Beum's tongue-in-cheek suggestions below. Note his advice that "the key rule is that the root 'man,' even when it is derived etymologically from the Latin 'manus' (hand), bears the degrading connotations of sexist tradition and is to be dropped":

personners (manners)
personifest (manifest)
personslaughter (manslaughter)
persondate (mandate)
personhandle (manhandle)
personia (mania)
personnikin (mannikin)
personnuscript (manuscript)

And if these are *persona non grata* to you, how about: *Person overboard! Person the oars!* Several years ago a job-description list issued in Woonsocket, Rhode Island, did describe a manhole as a *personhole.* The word *person,* it should be made clear, derives from the Latin *persona,* which was the name of the mask actors in Greek and Roman dramas wore to portray a character. The word came to mean the part anyone played in this world, his or her individuality, coming into English as *person.*

MEANINGLESS WORDS: DINGBAT, DINGUS, DOODAD, DOOHICKEY, GISMO, HICKEYMADOODLE, JEESALAMSYLBORAX, THINGAMABOB, THINGAMAJIG, THINGAMADOODLE, WHATCHAMACALLIT, WHATSIT . . .

D*ingbat,* a favorite expression of Archie Bunker's, is American in origin, going back to at least 1861, when it meant "anything that can be thrown with force or dashed violently at another object," according to Farmer's *Americanisms* (1899). The word possibly derives from *bat,* "a piece of wood or metal," and *ding,* "to throw." But *dingbat* came to be used in describing anything of which the proper name is unknown or forgotten to a speaker, much as we more frequently use such meaningless words as *thingamabob* (an extension of the word *thing* that goes back to the late seventeenth century), *thingamajig, dingus, doohickey, whatsit,* and the other "infixes" above. A father describing how to assemble a complicated piece of equipment, such as a child's toy, might say: "You put this *thingamajig* into this *doohickey* and tighten this *doodad* and this *thingamabob;* then you take this *dingus* over here near this *gismo* and attach it to this *hickeymadoodle* so that it barely touches the *thingamadoodle* there near the *whatchamacallit*—then you have to grease it up with this *jeesalamsylborax* or the damn *dingbat* won't work!"

Dingbat has also served over the years as a slang term for a gadget, money, buns or biscuits, a woman, and a hobo or bum. But Archie Bunker's contemptuous use of the word for a "nut," an ineffectual, bumbling fool (that is, anyone he doesn't agree with), may come directly from the Australian expression *dingbats,* meaning eccentric or slightly mad, which dates back only to the first years of this century. The Australian word may derive from the American *dingbat*, or from the French *dingot*, "eccentric," or even from *the dingbats*, Australian slang for the D.T.s. On the other hand, it could just be a humorous independent coinage, possibly from the "bum" meaning in American.

NO SOAP! GREAT PANJANDRUM

*I*N 1755 young actor and author Samuel Foote (1720–1777) composed the following speech when pompous fellow actor Charles Macklin boasted that he could repeat anything after hearing it once: "So she went into the garden to cut a cabbage left to make an apple pie; and at the same time, a great she-bear coming up the street pops its head into the shop—What! no soap? So he died; and she very impudently married the barber; and there were present the picaninnies and the Jobilies, and the Garyulies, and the great Panjandrum himself, with the little round button at top."

"Old Macklin" (he lived to be a hundred) gave up in disgust, unable to memorize this nonsense, but the mnemonic exercise gave the language both the phrase *no soap*, for the failure of some mission or plea, and *great Panjandrum*, the big boss, or someone who imagines himself to be the big boss. *Great Panjandrum* was first used in this sense by Edward FitzGerald in his translation of the *Rubáiyát*, when he applied it to a self-important local official. Foote, disliked by Dr. Johnson, once announced that he was going to do an imitation of the Great Cham on the stage. Johnson sent word that he had ordered a new oak cudgel and would be present that evening to correct any faults in the impersonation with it. Foote canceled the show.

THAT WORD

For it be known that we may safely write
Or say "that that" that that man wrote was right;
Nay, e'en that that that, that "that THAT" has followed
Through six repeats, the grammar's rule has hallowed;
And that that that that that "that THAT" began
Repeated seven times is right, deny't who can.
—Anonymous

TONGUE TWISTERS

*P*ROBABLY the oldest or best known is "Sally (or "she") sells seashells at the seashore," etc. But experts hold that "the sixth sick sheik's sixth sheep's sick" is the worst tongue twister in English, especially if spoken rapidly. The seventy-two muscles we use in speaking one word seem to rebel against pronouncing all of these together.

Almost as famous as Sally and her seashells is:

Peter Piper picked a peck of pickled peppers
A peck of pickled peppers Peter Piper picked
If Peter Piper picked a peck of pickled peppers
How many pecks of pickled peppers did Peter Piper pick?

(Peter Piper picked a peck of pickled peppers, of course, and since pickled peppers are packed eighteen or twenty to the quart that would make 144 to 160 pickled peppers that Peter Piper picked.)

Try also: "The skunk sat on a stump; the skunk thunk the stump stunk, but the stump thunk the skunk stunk." Or say "Toy boat" fast five times.

More great old tongue twisters like "How much wood would a woodchuck chuck if a woodchuck could chuck wood?" can be found in *Peter Piper's Practical Principles of Plain and Perfect Pronunciation* (1834). In the meantime, try those seventy-two muscles on Carolyn Wells's:

A tutor who tutored the flute
Tried to tutor two tutors to toot
Said the two to the tutor,
"Is it harder to toot, or
To tutor two tutors to toot?"

and the vowelless Czech words for "stick a finger in the throat":

Strch prst skrz krk.

A TONGUE TEST

New Yorker critic Brendan Gill took the following "Announcer's Test" in pronunciation on his radio show "On the Town with Brendan Gill." Try your luck pronouncing the italicized words and checking your pronunciation against the dictionary—twenty out of twenty-five is excellent. I don't know Mr. Gill's score and won't tell mine:

> The old man with the *flaccid* face and *dour* expression *grimaced* when asked if he were *conversant* with *zoology*, *mineralogy*, or the *culinary* arts. "Not to be *secretive*," he said, "I may tell you that I'd given *precedence* to the study of *genealogy*. But since my father's *demise*, it has been my *vagary* to remain *incognito* because of an *inexplicable*,

lamentable, and *irreparable* family *schism*. It resulted from a *heinous* crime, committed at our *domicile* by an *impious* scoundrel. To *err* is human . . . but this affair was so *grievous* that only my *inherent acumen* and *consummate* tact saved me."

SPOONERISMS

*T*HE REVEREND William Archibald Spooner, dean and later warden of New College, Oxford, was a learned man, but not spell woken, or well spoken, that is. "We all know what it is to have a half-warmed fish inside us," he once told an audience, meaning to say, "half-formed wish." On another occasion he advised his congregation that the next hymn would be "Kinkering Congs Their Titles Take," instead of "Conquering Kings Their Titles Take," and he is said to have explained to listeners one time that "the Lord is a shoving leopard."

Spooner's slips occurred both in church, where he once remarked to a lady, "Mardon me Padom, this pie is occupied, allow me to sew you to another sheet," and where he told a nervous bridegroom that "it is kisstomery to cuss the bride," and in his classes, where he chided one student with, "You hissed my mystery lecture," and dismissed another with, "You have deliberately tasted two worms . . . and can leave Oxford by the town drain!" Other mistakes attributed to him are "The cat popped on its drawers," for "the cat dropped on its paws"; "one swell foop," for "one fell swoop"; "sporn rim hectacles"; "a well-boiled icicle"; "selling smalts"; "tons of soil" (referring to farmers); "blushing crow"; "Is the bean dizzy?" for "Is the dean busy?"; and "the Assissination of Sassero," for a Roman history lecture.

Spooner lived eighty-six years, and committed many spoonerisms in public, too. "When the boys come back from France, we'll have the hags flung out!" the canon told a gathering of patriots during World War I, and Queen Victoria once became "our queer old dean." Nobody knows how many of these spoonerisms were really made by Spooner, but they were among the many attributed to him. Spooner was an albino, his metathetical troubles probably due to nervousness and poor eyesight resulting from his condition. The scientific name for his speech affliction is *metathesis*, the accidental transposition of letters or syllables in the words of a sentence. The process was known long before Spooner made it so popular that his slips of the tongue and eye were widely imitated. Some of the best spoonerisms therefore aren't really spoonerisms at all, being carefully devised and far from accidental.

MALAPROPISMS

Then, sir, she should have a supercilious knowledge in accounts;—and as she grew up, I would have her instructed in geometry, that she might know something of the contagious countries . . . and likewise that she might reprehend the true meaning of what she is saying. This, Sir Anthony, is what I would have a woman know;—and I don't think there is a superstitious article in it.

*T*HE ABOVE is a speech of Mrs. Malaprop in the first act of Richard Brinsley Sheridan's *The Rivals*. Mrs. Malaprop is the name of an affected, talkative woman in the play, the aunt of the heroine, Lydia Languish. Sheridan coined her name from the French *mal à propos*, "unsuitable, out of place," for he had her ludicrously misuse many "high-sounding" words out of her ignorance and vanity, just as Shakespeare had Dogberry do in *Much Ado About Nothing* and Mistress Quickly in *Henry IV, Parts One and Two*. Sheridan's *The Rivals* was produced in London in 1775, and Mrs. Malaprop's name soon became a syn-

Sir Tunbelly Clumfy, and Mifs Malaprop .

onym for the misuse of words, especially by those who are trying to sound important. Here are more of Mrs. Malaprop's malapropisms from the play, words she always delivered with great aplomb:

- "She's as headstrong as an allegory on the banks of the Nile."
- "I would by no means wish a daughter of mine to be a progeny of learning."
- "Don't attempt to extirpate yourself from the matter."
- "He is the very pineapple of politeness."

As one of the play's other characters says of Mrs. Malaprop, "She decks her dull chat with hard words she don't understand." Other fictitious English ladies noted for their malapropisms are Mrs. Winifred Jenkins in Smollett's *Humphry Clinker* (1771) and Mrs. Slipslop in Fielding's *Joseph Andrews* (1742). Malapropisms have been called *slipslops* after the latter lady, who utters a few words nobody has been able to translate yet, including "ragmaticellest mophrodites."

THE GRANDEST LIST OF GOLDWYNISMS

A MODERN-DAY Mr. "Malaprop" unrivaled for his fractured English was American film pioneer Samuel Goldwyn (1882–1974). Goldwyn, born in Warsaw, Poland, came to America when only thirteen, immigration officials giving him the name Goldfish as the closest equivalent to his Polish name. Later, he legally changed this to Goldwyn, from the Goldwyn Pictures Corporation, which had been named for himself and his partners, the Selwyn brothers. Of this coinage Judge Learned Hand said years later: "A self-made man may prefer a self-made name."

A self-made man Goldwyn was. Even before forming Goldwyn Pictures he had produced Hollywood's first full-length feature, *Squaw Man*. After Goldwyn Pictures became part of Metro-Goldwyn-Mayer in 1924, he struck out on his own as an independent producer, his eighty-odd movies including *Dodsworth*, *Wuthering Heights*, *The Little Foxes*, *Pride of the Yankees*, *The Best Years of Our Lives*, *Porgy and Bess*, *The Secret Life of Walter Mitty*, and *Guys and Dolls*. Goldwyn received the Medal of Freedom in 1971 for "proving that clean movies could be good box office."

No doubt many of the thousands of *Goldwynisms* attributed to Goldwyn—word manglings, mixed metaphors, malapropisms, grammatical blunders, and the like—were invented by press agents, friends, and enemies. But, genuine or not, they became part of the legend surrounding this man. Here is a sampling I've collected over the years, a good number probably apocryphal:

• "The trouble with directors is that they're always biting the hand that lays the golden egg."

• In a toast to Britain's Field Marshal Montgomery: "Here's to Marshall Field Montgomery Ward."

• "An oral contract isn't worth the paper it's written on."

• "Include me out."

• "We have passed a lot of water since this" (for "a lot of water has passed under the bridge").

• "In two words: im-possible!" (Goldwyn categorically denied this one.)

• "A man who goes to a psychiatrist should have his head examined." (Also said to be invented by Lillian Hellman.)

• "We have to get some fresh platitudes."

• "This new atom bomb is dynamite."

• "It's dog eat dog in this business and nobody's going to eat me."

• "I felt like we were on the brink of the abscess."

• After a director changed a night scene to a daytime shot: "Nobody can change night into day, or vice versa, without asking me first!"

• "I've got a great slogan for the company—'Goldwyn pictures griddle [for *girdle*] the earth!' "

• Of an actress he had ballyhooed who didn't pass muster with the public: "Well, she's colossal in a small way."

• On his deathbed: "I never thought I'd live to see the day." (Invented by Clifton Fadiman.)

• On being told that a film script was "too caustic": "Never mind the cost. If it's a good picture, we'll make it."

• "Our comedies are not to be laughed at."

• To rival producer Darryl F. Zanuck: "We're in terrible trouble. You've got an actor and I want him."

• To Garson Kanin: "Sidney Howard tells me you're a real clever genius."

• To a bridge partner who protested that she hadn't overbid, how could she know he had nothing: "Didn't you hear me keeping still?"

• "If you won't give me your word of honor, will you give me your promise?"

• "Where did you get this beautiful new Picasso?" "In Paris. Somewhere over there on the Left Wing."

• "Modern dance is so old-fashioned."

• "What's that?" "A sundial. It tells time by the sun." "My God, what'll they think of next?"

• "I've been laid up with intentional flu."

• "He worked his way up from nothing, that kid. In fact, he was born in an orphan asylum."

• "We can get all the Indians we need at the reservoir."

• "Goldwynisms! Don't talk to me about Goldwynisms, f'Chrissake. You want to hear some Goldwynisms go talk to Jesse Lasky!"

Goldwyn's major rival for the title of Mr. Malaprop in Hollywood was Terence "Slip" Mahoney (Leo Gorcey) of the Dead End Kids, who in his films uttered hundreds of ghostwritten malapropisms such as "That removes the last elephant [element] of doubt." (See also *Malapropisms*.)

INVENTED WORDS THAT DIDN'T MAKE IT

When vorianders seek to huzzlecoo,
    When jurpid splooch or vilpous drillig bores,
When cowcats kipe, or moobles wog, or you
    Machizzled are by yowfs or xenogores,

Remember Burgess Unabridged, and think,
    How quisty is his culpid yod and yab!
No fidgeltick, with goigsome iobink,
    No varmic orobaldity—his gab!

No more tintiddling slubs, like fidgelticks,
    Rizgidgeting your speech, shall lallify;
But your jujasm, like vorgid gollohix,
    Shall all your woxy meem golobrify!

WHEN Gelett Burgess published his *Burgess Unabridged: A New Dictionary of Words You Have Always Needed* (1914), he wrote the above poem using some of his new words in the preface. None of the words (I'll leave you to his book to define them) survive today and, in fact, the only two of the 100 he coined that we still use are *bromide* and *blurb*. Hundreds of new words are invented every year, but few last more than months. One good example to rest our case on is Mark Twain, who, besides a number of winners, coined these losers, none of which is widely used today: *disenthuse, humanbeingship, jumbulacious, mental telegraphy, perhapser, psychologizer, Shakesperiod, soda squester, type girl, uncledom,* and *vinegarishly.*

HUH; UH, OH; UH-HUH; UM; UH-UH; HUH?; I MEAN; Y' KNOW

HUMORIST H. Allen Smith thought *uh, oh* was the most terrifying phrase in English, "as when a doctor looks at your X-rays and says 'uh, oh.'" It is not to be confused with *uh-huh* and *um*, "yes"; *uh-uh*, "no"; or *huh?*, "what?" All of these expressions or grunts have been traced back to at least the 1830s. Stuart Berg Flexner in *I Hear America Talking* has described *huh?, uh-uh,* and *um* as "among the most common 'words' heard in America . . . truly native earmarks of an American," and points out that perceptive English author Captain Frederick Marryat properly identified them as Americanisms over a century ago. Others have called them *Neanderthalese.* Flexner doesn't mention it but *y' know* is replacing *uh* as a surrogate crutch today, *y' know; I mean, uh, y' know* is a form of "inarticulatese," that is, *uh,* endemic, *y' know* . . .

ODD ENDINGS FOR BOOKS
AND/OR AUTHORS

• Legend says Alexander the Great always carried a treasured edition of Homer corrected by Aristotle and that he put it under his pillow at night with his sword. When Alexander found a golden casket studded with gems in the tent of Darius after he defeated the Persian king, he placed his edition of Homer inside and kept it there whenever he wasn't reading it for the rest of his life, saying, "There is but one thing in life worthy of so precious a casket."

• The Roman author Lucan cut his wrists, committing suicide at the order of Nero, and died reciting a work he had just written opposing tyranny.

• Dante died little more than an hour after finishing *The Divine Comedy*.

• Petrarch was found dead leaning over a book he was finishing.

• During the Black Death, the great Italian historian Giovanni Villanni died while working on a book at his desk, in the midst of the unfinished sentence "in the midst of this pestilence there came to an end . . ."

• Standing in a plaza in Guayaquil, Ecuador, is a statue honoring José Olmedo, who, like most poets, struggled to survive all his life. Looking closely, however, you might notice a resemblance to someone else. You would be right. The statue really represents English poet Lord Byron and was purchased secondhand because the town wouldn't spend enough money to have an Olmedo statue commissioned, reasoning perhaps that one poet was the same as the next, anyway.

• *Publishers Weekly* reported that the *Dieter's Guide to Weight Loss During Sex*, *The Expert's Cross Word Puzzle Book*, *The Book of Lists*, and *The People's Almanac # 2* had been published on toilet paper by Bathroom Bestsellers. T. H. Watkins has a fine essay unraveling this mystery in the *New York Times* (September 29, 1979), entitled "As Bacon said: 'Some books are to be tasted, others to be swallowed, and some few to be chewed and digested.'"

• "It was a very, very hot summer. We'd had no rain for months, and I kept thinking, my God, when will it rain? And then about 6 in the morning—I'd been writing all night—I finished the book. And at that moment the rain began . . . swiss-sshhh . . . And I thought, if I had only known I could bring rain to my countrymen, I would have ended before! *Après moi le déluge!*"

—Françoise Sagan,
on ending her novel
The Unmade Bed

• The writer who researched *De Sade* in Hamburg's notorious red-light district submitted an expense account including such items as "a party for 69 prostitutes, $430 . . . a farewell dinner for 21 masochists and 21 sadists, $300 . . . and rest cure in Garmisch-Partenkirchen, $1850 . . ."

• "There ain't nothing more to write about and I'm rotten glad of it, because if I'd a knowd what a trouble it was to make a book, I wouldn't a tackled it."

—Mark Twain,
Huckleberry Finn

• "For those who have come this far: thank you for your unseen but ever felt companionship."

—Will Durant,
The Life of Greece

—and my sentiments as well.

Index